ECOLOGICAL AND ENVIRONMENTAL ECONOMICS

Ecological and Environmental Economics

Selected Issues and Policy Responses

Clem Tisdell

Professor of Economics, School of Economics, The University of Queensland, Australia

Edward Elgar

Cheltenham, UK • Northampton, MA, USA

Published by
Edward Elgar Publishing Limited
Glensanda House
Montpellier Parade
Cheltenham
Glos GL50 1UA
UK

Edward Elgar Publishing, Inc.
136 West Street
Suite 202
Northampton
Massachusetts 01060
USA

A catalogue record for this book
is available from the British Library

Printed and bound in Great Britain by MPG Books Ltd, Bodmin, Cornwall

ISBN 1 84376 021 5

Contents

Preface

The chapters in this book have been published in scattered outlets in the last decade or so. Consequently, most readers are unlikely to have been aware of them as a whole. This volume will increase their accessibility. Hopefully, it will also add further value by enabling readers more easily to appreciate the way in which the themes in the different chapters are interconnected. Chapter 1 provides background information on the origins of many of the following chapters in this book and an extensive overview of the book's contents. The latter should facilitate the appreciation of the interdependence of these essays. The whole should, therefore, be more valuable than its fragmented parts.

Ecological and environmental economics is an exciting and challenging subject. It deals with matters at the forefront of knowledge. It addresses extremely important issues for the welfare of humankind and for the future of the biosphere.

Ecological economics is a particularly fascinating subject because it is not bound in its inquiries by traditional paradigms nor by settled theory. As pointed out by Robert Costanza, it is eclectic in nature and requires pragmatism in the formulation of policies. It is also a pleasing subject because it is multidisciplinary or interdisciplinary in character. This can be a basis of continuing vitality for the subject and a source of renewable enthusiasm for those who research in this area or must apply ecological economics. I hope this book adequately conveys the importance of ecological and environmental economics and stimulates enthusiasm for its study.

Some of the chapters in this book are co-authored and I would like to thank the co-authors for their contributions and for enthusiastically sharing research efforts with me. Their efforts have added to the depth of coverage of the chapters concerned.

Nearly all of the articles in this book were written after I came to The University of Queensland. I thank The University of Queensland and in particular the School of Economics for the support it has provided for my research and writing efforts. Assistance from Alison Mohr and Genevieve Larsen and other office staff in processing materials for the manuscript for this book is much appreciated. Thanks too to Isoa Korovulavulu, a postgraduate student at The University of Queensland from Fiji, for pointing out a printer's error in the original version of a diagram used in Chapter 16.

I am also grateful to Edward Elgar and staff for supporting this endeavour. Furthermore, I thank my dear wife Mariel for her encouragement, and my whole family for their patience as I continued with my efforts to produce the manuscripts for this book.

Clem Tisdell
Brisbane

Acknowledgements

Most of the articles/contributions in this book have been previously published. Unless otherwise stated, I am the sole author. I am grateful to the appropriate editors and/or publishers for permission to reproduce articles or material as specified below.

Clem Tisdell

2. *Ecological or green economics: genuine contribution or fashionable fad?*, The University of Queensland Press, Australia, 1991. Reprinted with permission of The University of Queensland Press.
3. 'Ecological economics and the environmental future', in Nicholas Polunin and John Burnett (eds), *Surviving With The Biosphere*, Proceedings of the Fourth International Conference on Environmental Future (4th ICEF) held in Budapest, Hungary, 22–7 April 1990, Edinburgh University Press Ltd, UK, 1993, 363–76. Reprinted with permission of Edinburgh University Press Ltd.
4. 'The environment and economic welfare', in David L. McKee (ed.), *Energy, the Environment, and Public Policy*, Praeger, New York, 1991, 6–16. Reprinted with permission of Greenwood Publishing Group Inc.
5. 'The nature of sustainability and of sustainable development', *The Middle East Business and Economic Review*, **4** (1), January 1992, 21–5. Reprinted with permission of the Editor.
6. 'Sustainability and sustainable development: are these concepts a help or a hindrance to economics?', *Economic Analysis and Policy*, **24** (2), September 1994, 133–50. Reprinted with permission of the Editor.
7. Reprinted from *Ecological Economics*, **22** (3), Clem A. Tisdell, 'Capital/natural resource substitution: the debate of Georgescu-Roegen (through Daly) with Solow/Stiglitz', 289–91, Copyright (1997), with permission from Elsevier Science.
8. A.E. Hohl and C.A. Tisdell, 'Ethics in modern economic thought and their consequences for environmental conservation, land and resource-use', *Humanomics*, **13** (2), 1997, 1–37. Reprinted with permission of the Editor.
9. 'Local communities, conservation and sustainability: institutional change, altered governance and Kant's social philosophy', *International Journal of Social Economics*, **24** (12), 1997, 1361–75. Reprinted with permission of MCB University Press.
10. Luca Tacconi and C.A. Tisdell, 'Rural development projects in LDCs: appraisal, participation and sustainability', *Public Administration and Development*, **12**, 1992, 267–78. © John Wiley & Sons Limited. Reproduced with permission.
11. 'Integrated regional environmental studies: the role of environmental economics', in C. van Wel and J. Quiggin (eds), *Contemporary Issues in Australian Economics: Essays in Honour of Professor Percy Harris*, Central Queensland University, Rockhampton, Australia, 1998, 95–111. Reprinted with permission of CQU Press.

12. 'Population, economic change, and environmental security', in Nicholas Polunin (ed.), *Population and Global Security*, Cambridge University Press, Cambridge, UK, 93–116. © Cambridge University Press 1998. Reprinted with the permission of the Cambridge University Press.
13. Reprinted from *Ecological Economics*, **31** (3), Irmi Seidl and C.A. Tisdell, 'Carrying capacity reconsidered: from Malthus' population theory to cultural carrying capacity', 395–408, Copyright (1999), with permission from Elsevier Science.
14. C. Tisdell and K. Roy, 'Good governance, property rights and sustainable resource use: Indian Ocean rim examples', *The South African Journal of Economics*, **65** (1), March 1997, 28–43. Reprinted with permission of the Managing Editor.
15. C.A. Tisdell and S.R. Harrison, 'Compensation for taking of natural resource interests: principles and practices in recent Queensland cases', *Australian Journal of Environmental Management*, **6** (2), June 1999, 99–108. Reprinted with permission of the Editor.
16. 'Taxation versus tradable permits and alternative policies for environmental management', in D. Thampapillai (ed.), *Taxation and the Environment*, Australian Tax Research Foundation, Conference Series No. 14, Sydney, 1993, 95–105. Reprinted with permission of the Australian Tax Research Foundation.
17. 'Economic policy instruments and environmental sustainability: another look at environmental-use permits', *Sustainable Development*, **6** (1), March 1998, 18–22. © John Wiley & Sons Limited. Reproduced with permission.
18. 'Environmental taxation versus tradeable permits: public finance, accounting and related aspects', *Environmental Taxation and Accounting*, **2** (2), 1998, 55–60. Reprinted with permission of the Editor.
19. 'Coevolution, agricultural practices and sustainability: some major social and ecological issues', *International Journal of Agricultural Resources, Governance and Ecology*, **1** (1), 2000, 6–16. Copyright is of Inderscience Enterprises Ltd; the paper was first published in the *International Journal of Agricultural Resources, Governance and Ecology* and is available online at: www.inderscience.com.
20. 'The environment and sustainable development in the Asia–Pacific: views and policies', *Asian-Pacific Economic Literature*, **11** (1), May 1997, 39–55. Reprinted with permission of the Editor.
21. 'Australian environmental issues: an overview', *Asia Pacific Journal on Environment and Development*, **6** (1), June 1999, 1–16. Reprinted with permission of the Editor.
22. 'Economic growth in China: can China cope with its environmental constraints and problems?', *Asia Pacific Journal on Environment and Development*, **8** (1), June 2001, 15–35. Reprinted with permission of the Editor.
23. 'Protection of the environment in transitional economies', *Regional Development Dialogue*, **18** (1), Spring 1997, 32–49. Reprinted with permission of the Editor-in-Chief.
24. Zhiyong Hong, Keguang Bao and C.A. Tisdell, 'Cadmium exposure in Daye County, China: environmental assessment and management, health and economic effects', *Environmental Management and Health*, **2** (2), 1991, 20–25. Reprinted with permission of MCB University Press.

25. D. Wibowo and C. Tisdell, 'Health, safe water and sanitation: a cross-sectional health production function for Central Java, Indonesia', *Bulletin of the World Health Organization*, **71** (2), 1993, 237–45. Reprinted with permission of the World Health Organization.

PART I

AN OVERVIEW

[1]

The role of economics in analysing ecological and environmental problems and in related policy decisions: an overview

Introduction

Arguably, most of the world's significant ecological and environmental problems (as perceived by humankind) arise largely from economic influences or are exacerbated by economic factors. Therefore, their genesis can only be appreciated by taking into account economic considerations. At the same time, it needs also to be recognized that economic factors are only a part of the whole picture of environmental change, albeit an important part in the modern world. Consequently, environmental and ecological problems involving economic considerations can only be effectively analysed and addressed in a holistic manner. Solving such problems requires adequate account to be taken of social systems and natural systems, as well as their interactions.

As economic growth has occurred worldwide, and as increasing globalization (economic and otherwise) has been experienced, the influences of economic systems on natural systems, including biological systems (as well as the effect of economic subsystems on the non-economic portions of social systems), have magnified. Furthermore, the potential for economic activities to alter natural systems in undesired ways has increased. It is now widely recognized that economic production has the potential to bring about environmental changes having disastrous long-term consequences for humankind. Even if economic production does not have disastrous consequences, it can have negative effects on attainable economic welfare, reduce economic productivity in the long term and conflict with widely held conservation values unless it is ordered in an appropriate manner.

Appropriately ordering economic production, and economic activity generally, requires consideration of alternative policy possibilities and their consequences. In turn, policy prescriptions depend on values, social systems (including their economic portions) and on natural systems, and the interaction between these systems. Actual and potential effects of economic systems on natural systems, including ecological systems, are now quite large. In turn, consequential changes in natural systems feed back to influence the economic worth of natural systems and their contribution to human welfare and the sustainability characteristics of these. Such interdependence cannot be rationally ignored in economic policy formulation and the choice of economic systems. Furthermore, economics and natural environments can be interrelated in another way: economic instruments can be used to foster desired environmental changes or ameliorate undesired ones on natural systems. Therefore, ecological and environmental economics has policy relevance both from a broad systems perspective as well as from the point of view of devising economic instruments to address specific environmental problems some of which may be localized or 'one-offs'. Thus the policy applications of ecological and environmental economics range from the general to the particular, as is demonstrated in this book. These chapters show the relevance of economics for understanding general ecological and environmental problems and specific ones, and how economics can assist with devising policies to deal with these problems.

The chapters were published in the period 1991–2001 in a diversity of outlets, and are arranged in four sets. Those in Part II cover broad issues of widespread concern involving ecological and environmental economics. The chapters in Part III outline and examine various governance and policy measures that may be adopted to deal with specific ecological and environmental problems. Parts IV and V contain case studies but nevertheless each chapter raises general issues. The chapters in Part IV outline and analyse significant economic problems in Australia, in the Asia-Pacific region and in transitional economies. Environmental health is the focus of Part V and the chapters in it involve cases from China and Indonesia. A more detailed overview of the coverage of the chapters in this book follows.

General issues in ecological and environmental economics – an overview of Part II

Chapter 2, 'Ecological or green economics: genuine contribution or fashionable fad?' is the text of my inaugural lecture given at the University of Queensland in 1990. It is a useful backdrop to all the other essays in this collection because it provides my perspective on the importance of ecological economics and identifies central issues that can be addressed by using ecological economics. Reasons are given as to why ecological or green economics (although a relatively new discipline) is unlikely to be a passing fad, despite the fact that the degree of interest in it may vary from time to time. It outlines the nature of ecological economics and its relationship to the problem of resource scarcity, the major problem addressed by economics. Economics addresses the basic problem of resource shortages primarily by searching for improved social mechanisms (such as price mechanisms) for resource management. The need for a new perspective (an ecological one) in analysing the basic economic problem is stressed, and it is shown that there is growing social and global recognition of the need for this new perspective. This is so, even though many social 'blind spots' still remain, some of which could have disastrous consequences for future economic scarcity. Major development and other issues to which ecological economics is relevant, such as those involving the sustainability of economic development and conservation of biodiversity, are identified. The importance of values in dealing with economic problems is stressed and doubts are expressed about the desirability of economics confining itself to anthropocentric values, as it has traditionally done. Many of the issues raised in this chapter are given detailed consideration later in the book.

The paper comprising Chapter 3, 'Ecological economics and the environmental future' was given at the Fourth International Conference on the Environmental Future held in Budapest in 1990 not long after the withdrawal of troops of the former Soviet Union and the independence of Hungary. As it turned out, an environmental issue, a proposal for a dam on the Danube River above Budapest, became a rallying point for Hungarian opposition to control by the Soviet Union. The conference consisted of invited participants with a broad range of backgrounds and interests in the environment.

In this contribution, I outline the scope of ecological economics and briefly outline and discuss its modern origins. The importance is emphasized of combining economics and ecology in deciding on economic development policies and in formulating nature conservation programmes. However, it is also stressed that traditional economic theories are not sufficient for this. New paradigms are required with evolving 'new' economic and ecological situations. This is particularly so when economic activity and development can have uncertain and irreversible effects on the state of the natural environment. Furthermore, environmental effects can involve discrete, even 'large' jumps in dependent environmental variables. Hence, economic decisions that can impact significantly on natural environments call increasingly for a cautious approach, as highlighted by the precautionary principle (see, for example, Wills, 1997, s. 16.7).

The biosphere is a critical asset influencing the level of economic welfare and the potential for sustainable economic development. However, the consequences of economic policies and development for the future state of the biosphere are often uncertain. In such instances, special care is required in economic decision-making, especially when the risks and uncertainties involved are borne collectively, as is often the case. This aspect is discussed generally and loss of genetic diversity is considered as a particular case. The importance of ecological economics for the future of humankind is demonstrated and it is argued that the survival of humans and their economic welfare are inextricably linked to the conservation of the biosphere. The arguments in this chapter are elucidated in a commentary in Polunin and Burnett (1993, pp. 377–81) but that is not reproduced here.

While Chapter 4, 'The environment and economic welfare', continues the same basic theme, as indicated above, it does so from a somewhat different perspective and introduces new aspects. It is based on a seminar presentation given in 1989 at the Institute of Rural Development of the Chinese Academy of Social Sciences in Beijing. At that time, I was an Exchange Fellow of the Academy of Social Sciences in Australia visiting the Chinese Academy. It begins by pointing out how environmental economics developed from welfare economics as an application of the theory of externalities to become a major discipline in its own right dealing with a broad range of topics including the living environment. Microeconomic policy instruments for the control of pollution or environmental degradation are briefly outlined but significant analyses of such policies are reserved for Part III. Particular attention is given to global environmental problems and the responsibilities of developed and developing nations in that regard as well as the role that aid to developing countries can play in environmental protection. Several of these matters are illustrated by examples from China and other developing countries.

Chapters 5–7 are concerned with the sustainability of development. Chapter 5 provides a short outline of the nature of sustainability and identifies four important concepts of sustainable development. It contains an early criticism of Rawls's (1971) theory of justice as applied to the concept of sustainability and intergenerational equity. Chapter 6 is based upon an article written at the request of Professor Allan Layton for *Economic Analysis and Policy*. It provides further discussion of concepts of sustainability and sustainable development, and asks whether these concepts are a help or a hindrance to economics. Five concepts are considered in this chapter, one more than in the previous chapter.

After reviewing policy applications involving the goal of sustainable development, this chapter outlines reasons for being concerned about sustainable development, why sustainable development is desirable (or more precisely, in what sense it is desirable) and the need to qualify standard economic evaluations (such as inferences from national accounting data) in the light of sustainability considerations. Furthermore, the issue is debated of whether economic growth can be maintained in perpetuity in view of environmental considerations. Doubts are raised about this possibility. In view of the basic problem of entropy raised by Georgescu-Roegen (1971), sustainable economic development may be impossible in perpetuity. Social choice may be between paths exhibiting different degrees of environmental and economic sustainability rather than the choice of a path or paths ensuring complete sustainability. Nevertheless, the concepts of sustainability and sustainable development are useful to economics for the reasons outlined in this chapter.

Chapter 7 concentrates on the issue of substitution between capital and natural resources, and supports the view of Georgescu-Roegen that perpetual economic growth by continual and increasing conversion of natural resources into human-made capital is likely to be impossible. In that regard, it is critical of the neoclassical economic growth models of Solow (1956; 1974) and of Hartwick's (1977) rule for reinvestment as a means to avoid sustainability problems arising from such substitution. A more recent and extended discussion of my views on capital/natural resource substitution in relation to sustainable development can be found in Dragun and Tisdell (1999) together with extensions of my analyses of sustainability and sustainable development.

Chapters 8–10 focus on the choice of appropriate values to adopt in choices involving ecological and environmental economics, and the role that local communities might play in improving choices about such values and other components of policy-making. Matters considered include the extent to which communities can provide appropriate values for economic-environmental models and policy choices; the extent to which devolution of political power to local communities is liable to result in improved conservation decisions; and the scope for drawing (through an interactive process) on the knowledge of local communities in order to improve economic-ecological-environmental modelling and, ultimately, policy choices impacting on the environment. The local community or region forms the focus of these chapters.

Doubts are raised in Chapter 8, 'Ethics in modern economic thought and their consequences for environmental conservation: land and resource-use', about the adequacy of the value systems implicit in neoclassical economics to address fully conservation issues. This is because many members of the community do not subscribe to these values. Consequently, if economics is to retain its relevance in environmental debates, it needs to allow for additional sets of values. Some of these sets might be derived from interactions with local communities. A further benefit of such interaction is that it may make economists fully aware of changes in community values. As pointed out, the scope for applying economics does not depend solely on the adoption of value systems inherent in neoclassical economics.

These themes are extended further in Chapter 9, 'Local communities, conservation and sustainability: institutional change, altered governance and Kant's social philosophy'. This originally appeared in a collection of essays in honour of Immanuel Kant. One of its concerns is with how best to reconcile the rights and wishes of individuals with the values and requirements of the community and its governance. Communitarianism is explored as one possible approach to such reconciliation. Communitarianism is based on the view that individuals have an 'internally divided self' involving a tension between their own selfish interest and their felt obligations to their community or society (Elster, 1985; Etzioni, 1986; 1988; Margolis, 1982). More generally it views individuals as having two sets of preferences: selfish ones and meta-preferences. The relative importance and nature of the latter may vary from individual to individual, with the community in which the individual belongs, with the type and nature of education received by the individual and so on. In addition, the nature and influence of communal values on individual decisions can be expected to vary historically. Apart from discussing such matters, this chapter considers the relationships between communitarianism, Kant's social philosophy and utilitarianism.

The sustainability of community is sometimes considered to be a desirable goal. The achievement of it depends in part on economic conditions. The desirability of sustaining local communities is discussed in this chapter and their role in conserving natural resources is examined. The view is put that devolution of political power to local communities is sometimes favourable and at other times unfavourable to environmental conservation depending on the circumstances. Therefore, we should be wary of blanket claims that empowerment of local communities is favourable to environmental conservation and vice versa. In general, local communities have to cope with altering social and natural conditions, especially in a world becoming more independent. The problem of maintaining sustainability of community in such circumstances can be enormous. This is illustrated by the cases of some local communities in Northeast India and, more generally, by communal problems posed by processes of globalization.

In the light of the analysis undertaken in this chapter, it is argued that total economic valuations by individuals of environmental phenomena lack independent moral standing. If communal values have a major influence on total economic valuations, as seems possible, the moral worth of such evaluations will depend, to a large extent, on one's evaluation of the moral worth of the communal values that had an influence on evaluations by individuals. Furthermore, while it is suggested that Kant's criticism of utilitarianism as a guide to major social policies is well founded, Kant's guide to social action also has significant limitations. Both preferences derived from a utilitarian approach and meta-values of overarching influence in Kant's social philosophy are subject to path dependence. Furthermore, just as many are not prepared to accept social choices based solely on a utilitarian approach so, too, can strong disagreements exist about appropriate meta-values. Therefore, we must recognize limits to our ability to make ideal social choices. Recognition of the limits of our rationality might be a first step towards greater respect for the rights of individuals and local communities. It should foster social empathy in policy-making. In any case, recognizing limits to rationality can be an important step towards greater realism and care in policy implementation.

Chapter 10, 'Rural development projects in LDCs: appraisal, participation and sustainability', sympathetically explores the roles for local communities in rural project appraisal and implementation, and the consequences of this for the sustainability of such projects. Especially in the case of local projects driven by funding from sources external to the local community (that is, central government funding or foreign aid), the long-term benefits from and sustainability of such projects can be highly dependent on local participation in decisions about these projects and adequate involvement of the local community in their implementation.

One reason why outside donors sometimes support local projects is because of environmental spillovers desired by them. For example, this is true of support by the Central Government in China for tree-planting by local communities in the headwaters of the Yangtze River (Ren and Tisdell, 1997) and local projects intended to divert local communities in Xishuangbanna Protecture from exploiting resources in Xishuangbanna State Nature Reserve in Yunnan Province (Tisdell, 1999, ch. 11). Foreign aid donors do not always look for tangible environmental benefits for themselves but sometimes desire intangible ecological benefits such as existence, bequest and option values from wildlife conservation. The success of such projects in developing countries, in particular, is highly dependent on support from local communities. While problems exist in combining bottom-up and top-down approaches to project assessment and implementation, in principle, there is much to be said for a side-by-side approach (Tisdell, 1999, ch. 11).

Chapter 11 includes in its coverage a side-by-side approach to environmental policy. This approach draws on the knowledge of a local community to model a local environmental problem, namely, the eutrophication of a coastal lake, Lake Tuggerah, north of Sydney in New South Wales. However, this chapter also involves a general discussion of the role of environmental economics in integrated studies of regional environmental issues. Furthermore, limitations of regional approaches when interregional environmental interdependence is present are mentioned. This theme is once again explored in Chapter 23.

Human populations and their implications for environmental and economic security are the main consideration in the remaining two chapters of Part II. Chapter 12, 'Population, economic change and environmental security', followed a request by Dr Nicholas Polunin to me to contribute a volume to supplement proceedings of the United Nations' International Conference on Population and Development held in Cairo in 1994. This chapter considers population as a variable in economic development models, discusses the relevance of economic theories of family fertility and family size, and includes case studies, primarily of a regional nature, of relationships between population growth, conservation of the natural resource-base and the state of the environment. Family decision-making, especially in developing countries, can be of crucial importance for long-term economic and environmental security. The nature of family decisions and the occurrence of gender discrimination can be partly, but not entirely, explained by economic theories of the family (Tisdell et al., 2001). Access to human capital, including gender discrimination in access within the family, has important implications for the sustainability of development (Tisdell, 2001).

Chapter 13 examines the concept of carrying capacity and considers views that there are definite limits to Earth's carrying capacity for environmental reasons. It addresses fears that these limits will be reached or transgressed, possibly soon, because of population expansion and economic growth. The concept of carrying capacity has its origin in the work of the Reverend Thomas Malthus (1798) and this concept subsequently exerted considerable influence on population theories in biology and ecology. While support for the carrying capacity concept has been found in controlled laboratory biological experiments on populations of species, such as insects, its applications to the environmental impacts of human activity are much less straightforward. In relation to human activities, relevant carrying capacities depend on value-judgements and surrounding institutional arrangements, as is illustrated. As shown, the socially determined carrying capacity of the Earth as far as human population is concerned is likely to be different and much lower than its biological carrying capacity. In reality also there is likely to be disagreement about what constitutes a socially optimal level of human population and about the conditions under which human population levels and their characteristics (such as their geographical distribution) transgress socially acceptable norms. This suggests that in relation to the formulation of environmental policies, much more attention should be given to cultural values as an influence on human populations and the desirability of those demographic features that may evolve with economic development and change. While this concept of carrying capacity does have some useful environmental applications, we need to be aware that there are a variety of such concepts. Hence, in applied work, the concept to be applied must be clearly identified. Furthermore, one must be sure that the concept is appropriate or does not give a misleading impression of scientific precision in analysing the environmental situation under consideration.

Governance and policy instruments for environmental controls – an overview of Part III

Part III is concerned with the impact of governance, institutional arrangements and property rights on sustainable resources use as well as the relative merits of different economic mechanisms, such as taxes and tradable permits, for environmental control. It reinforces the view stated in Chapter 13 (and elsewhere in Part II) that institutional and cultural factors are of fundamental importance in influencing the sustainability of resource-use. Chapters 14, 15 and 19 concentrate on the consequences for the natural environment and sustainability of governance arrangements and property rights whereas Chapters 16–18 focus mainly on the usefulness of environmental taxes and tradable permits as a means for protecting natural environments.

Chapter 14, 'Good governance, property rights and sustainable resource-use', identifies three distinct views about desirable sets of property rights each of which follows from the attitudes of their proponents to the role of the state in society. Hobbes favoured the ultimate allocation of all property rights to the Crown or an absolute central authority; Rousseau thought it proper that property be under the control of local communities; whereas the liberal economic system, advocated by Adam Smith, favoured a system of private property rights with the governance of resource-use largely devolved to individuals. A close connection exists between types of government felt to be desirable by these social philosophers and their favoured systems of property rights.

In modern times, western governments have promoted private property and state property, and have given little recognition and support to the presence of communal property. In fact, western governments in their major colonial phase often made communal property either state or private property. They, thereby, dispossessed tribal communities or, in some cases, created de facto open access to natural resources. However, this practice was not confined to Western colonial governments. Many newly independent countries and modern states in the developing world also adopted this practice. Although in India, Gadgil and Iyer (1989) state that rights in natural resources were primarily an outcome of British colonialism, the primacy of state rights or of the sovereign in such resources has an ancient history in India and is in fact mentioned by Kautilya in his book on political economy written more than 2000 years ago (Jha and Jha, 1997; Shamasastry, 1929). As pointed out by Gadgil and Iyer (1989), appropriation of communal property by the state can have adverse consequences for sustainable resource-use.

This, however, raises the question, how virtuous is communalism as a means for natural resource conservation and use? While communalism can have beneficial consequences, these appear to be not as great as proposed by its strongest advocates and their views call for qualifications. In some circumstances, for instance, co-management of natural resources by local communities and state bodies can yield superior results.

An interesting cultural phenomenon mentioned in this chapter is stratification in society via the caste systems and tribal groupings. Gadgil and Iyer (1989) claim that such stratification promotes sustainable resource-use because different social groups rely on different ecological niches for their livelihood. This means that inter-group natural resource competition is absent and, within social groups, codes and customs regulate resource-use and competition in ways that promote sustainable resource-use. Thus, the traditional socio-economic system of India is supportive of sustainable resource-use (Gadgil and Iyer, 1989). This system is, however, continuing to undergo change as economic globalization becomes more pervasive and erodes traditional social obligations.

In market-based economic systems, such as those that predominate in the West, security of private property rights is highly valued. Nevertheless, the common good sometimes requires the state to take away those rights, for example, resume private land to construct a public road or widen an existing road. In other cases, the state may restrict or withdraw pre-existing rights of individuals or local communities to utilize natural resources. Such 'rights' may have been initially established by custom or past practice or by arrangements or agreements with the state.

When such 'rights' are uncertain, security of tenure is uncertain and this can have negative consequences for the conservation of natural resources and their productivity in the long term. Furthermore, the taking of such entitlements raises important questions involving justice and equity. Chapter 15, therefore, discusses principles and practices involved in the taking of natural resource interests by the state. In doing so, it illustrates the issues involved by three Queensland cases. These are the withdrawal of logging rights in north Queensland in order to establish the Wet Tropics World Heritage Area, cancellation of logging 'entitlements' on Fraser Island in order to establish another World Heritage Area and limitations on pre-existing fishing rights enjoyed by Queensland fishers in view of the establishment of Dugong Protection Areas along the Queensland coast, as discussed in Tisdell (2002, ch. 16).

In most cases, environmental regulation involves the withdrawal of curtailment of pre-existing natural resource interests or entitlements of private or communal resource interests. This includes regulation of use of natural environments for waste disposal (pollution control) and rights to alter habitat or take actions on private land that may endanger designated species of wildlife. Virtually all environmental regulations raise issues about limitations on natural resource rights of individuals or communities.

Chapters 16–18 provide assessments of a number of alternative economic instruments for environmental regulation. However, most attention is given to taxation of activities giving rise to environmental 'bads' and systems of tradable permits as alternatives. Particular attention is given to the implications of the alternative methods of economic regulation for sustainability of resource-use and to the ability of such alternative policies to respond to circumstances that alter with the passage of time. In addition, the importance of agency and transaction costs is stressed.

The significance of the type of economic analysis discussed in Chapters 16–18, for instance, to the control of greenhouse gas emissions and evaluation of the Kyoto Protocol is underlined by recent publications by McKibbin and others (McKibbin, 2001; McKibbin and Vines, 2000; McKibbin and Wilcoxen, 2000a; 2000b). Some of these publications highlight the cost of errors in relation to emission taxes versus tradable permits, and hybrid models are considered as alternatives. In this respect they extend the error analysis mentioned in Tisdell (1993), reproduced here as Chapter 16, and they also help address flexibility concerns raised in Tisdell (1998a; 1998b).

Chapter 19 is concerned with the increasing tendency in modern societies to weaken or completely subvert mechanisms for the co-evolution of socio-economic systems and ecological ones. Local communities and environments are being increasingly decoupled from economic development and environmental change by increasing economic globalization and the rise of industrial/commercial agriculture under the 'patronage' of expanding oligopolistic capitalism. In such circumstances, community feedback mechanisms about environmental and social change brought about by technological and other changes can become blunted or disappear. Consequently, emerging environmental problems may not be addressed in a timely fashion. Furthermore, this decoupling combined with acceptance of intellectual property rights in many new products, such as genetically modified organisms, may result in their premature release by companies that possess such rights. Hence, irreversible global economic damage may be done before environmental and health problems are observed. How to control such developments effectively in a global setting is a major modern challenge for governance.

Environmental issues in Australia, Asia and transitional economies – an overview of Part IV

All the chapters in Part IV examine environmental issues in the Asia-Pacific but most of these issues are not peculiar to the Asia-Pacific and Chapter 23 is relevant to all transitional economies. 'The environment and sustainable development in the Asia-Pacific', Chapter 20, reviews the relevant literature and policies in the Asia-Pacific affecting the environment. Written at the request of the late Professor Heinz Arndt, the main topics covered are the nature and environmental consequences of population change in the Asian-Pacific region as well as urbanization and the growth of urban industry; agriculture, aquaculture and the environment; mining, resource depletion and the environment; and energy supplies and air quality. Rapid economic growth in several Asian countries, particularly China, has generated some new and major environmental problems for this region.

However, in the Asia-Pacific region, all countries have environmental concerns to some extent, and Australia is no exception. Chapter 21 provides a broad overview of environmental concerns in Australia. It was written because of a request from a German radio reporter to me for an interview on this subject. It considers the clearing of native vegetation in Australia, its marine environmental and ecological problems as well as pollution and wastes arising from its human settlements. All these environmental problems are anthropocentric in origin and are largely side effects of economic activity.

Chapter 22 also has a German connection because it developed from a seminar given at the University of Duisburg in 1997. It poses the question of whether the high rate of economic growth that China has achieved will be constrained in the future by its deteriorating environmental conditions. In considering this matter, it reviews the state of China's environment, specifies the main environmental and natural resource constraints that may limit China's economic growth, examines China's Agenda 21 as an indicator of China's environmental desires or objectives, and investigates China's environmental policies to determine the extent to which China's environmental objectives are attained in practice. Particular attention is paid to China's environmental impacts on the outside world and to changes in its air quality in relation to its use of energy. For example, its intensity of energy use in relation to its gross domestic product (GDP) is found to be falling after having at first risen. This suggests that its emissions of air pollutants may roughly be following the pattern suggested by the environmental Kuznets curve. However, as pointed out in Chapter 23, that can be consistent with a growth in total emission of air pollutants.

Chapter 23, 'Protection of the environment in transitional economies', was written at the request of the United Nations Center for Regional Development. It examines both regional and general environmental issues that are likely to emerge as previously relatively centralized planned economies transform themselves into market economies with greater political power devolved to local or regional levels. It mostly, but not exclusively, illustrates the analysis by taking Chinese examples, but the applicability of the analysis is not confined to China. It contains some general observations about the need to be wary in drawing environmental inferences from the environmental Kuznets curve. Some of the points in this article are further developed in Tisdell (2000).

Environmental health in Part V

As it transpires, the environmental health case studies in this book are drawn from Asia but the issues illustrated are not Asian specific.

As China has continued with its economic reforms begun in 1978, it has increasingly tried to apply the polluter-pays principle. Where this principle is invoked and applied, it results in the actual costs experienced by an economic agent being brought more closely into line with the social costs of its activity. Even if the principle is only partially invoked, its application can bring about a significant social improvement.

This is illustrated in Chapter 24, by a case study of the control of airborne cadmium emissions from a smelter in Daye County in China. The relevant enterprise decided to install new equipment after the government decreed that the enterprise would have to pay for the medical expenses of persons in the locality who contracted cadmium-related illnesses. The new equipment had the effect of significantly reducing airborne cadmium emission, the main source of cadmium poisoning in the locality. Using an avoided-cost approach, substantial net social economic benefits are shown to arise from the enterprise's investment in a new plant to reduce levels of airborne cadmium emissions.

Both provision of safe water and improved sanitation are capable of reducing the incidence of water-borne diseases. The provision of access to these can be regarded as inputs into the production of the improved health of a human population, or as inputs to produce a reduced incidence of the occurrence of water-borne disease and diarrhoea. The next chapter is based upon an exploration of this possibility.

Chapter 25 uses cross-sectional data from central Java to estimate this type of production formation relationship. Such a production function can be a valuable aid to rational public decision-making about investment in the provision of safe water and sanitation for communities. Given limited resources for such investment, it is usually necessary to make a trade-off between the provision of safe water and the supply of sanitary facilities. This use of production function techniques enables the combination of expenditure on, or investment in, the provision of these facilities to be determined so as to maximize the reduction in water-borne disease for a given total expenditure. Alternatively, a related production function technique can determine the minimum expenditure required (taking into account the optimal combination of safe-water and sanitary facilities) needed to ensure a targeted incidence of water-borne diseases, for example, a reduction of their incidence to a targeted level.

The scope for applying economics to public health issues, most of which have environmental attributes, is enormous. The case studies given here merely scratch the surface. Environmental health problems may be of a natural environmental origin as in the case of malaria, or due to human-induced environmental change as in the case of bronchial diseases caused or exacerbated by particulate emissions from industry, or due to a combination of natural and anthropocentric environmental effects. There is a need for much more exploration of the economics of environmental health but that is beyond the scope of this book.

Concluding comments

The book begins by pointing out the relevance of ecological and environmental economics to major issues facing modern societies and the world as a whole. It emphasizes that an ethical response and choice of values are needed to address such issues and then enquires about the extent to which local communities can provide appropriate guidance in the selection of the required values and also assist with selection of policies to promote sustainable resource-use. Sustainable resource-use and sustainability also constitute an important part of the subject matter covered. Levels of human population are clearly an important influence on the state of the environment and have implications for environmental security. In this context and from the point of view of sustainability, the concept of carrying capacity has historical and practical significance but is shown not to be such a precise concept as may be initially believed.

Attention next moves to an analysis of the role of governance and influences of closely connected property rights regimes on the sustainability of resource-use and the state of the environment. In doing so, the importance of evolutionary and convolutionary aspects is highlighted. Specific economic policy instruments (such as taxes and tradable environmental rights) for environmental regulation are assessed taking particular account of dynamic considerations, that is, changes in surrounding conditions with the passage of time and, thus, the occurrence of learning and the consequential need for policy adjustments.

This coverage is then followed by consideration of some specific environmental concerns and issues in the Asia-Pacific region (including some attention to transitional economies generally) and extends to include environmental health matters. While application in this segment of the book mostly focuses on the Asia-Pacific region, the analyses are not specific to this region.

Thus, it ought to be apparent that the chapters in this book cover a broad spectrum of issues and policies involving ecological and environmental economics. The ecological and environmental issues addressed affect us all.

References

Dragun, A.K. and C.A. Tisdell (1999), *Sustainable Agriculture and the Environment: Globalisation and the Impact of Trade Liberalisation*, Cheltenham, UK and Northampton, MA: Edward Elgar.

Elster, J. (1985), *The Multiple Self*, Cambridge: Cambridge University Press.

Etzioni, A. (1986), 'The case for multiple utility conception', *Economics and Philosophy*, **2**, 159–83.

Etzioni, A. (1988), *The Moral Dimension: Toward a New Economics*, New York: Free Press.

Gadgil, M. and P. Iyer (1989), 'On the diversification of common property resource use by Indian society', in F. Barkes (ed.), *Common Property Resources: Ecology and Community-based Sustainable Development*, London: Belhaven, pp. 240–55.

Georgescu-Roegen, N. (1971), *The Entropy Law and the Economics Process*, Cambridge, MA: Harvard University Press.

Hartwick, J.M. (1977), 'Intergenerational equity and the investing of assets from exhaustible resources', *American Economics Review*, **66**, 972–4.

Jha, K.N. and L.K. Jha (1997), *Chanakya: The Pioneer Economist*, New Delhi: APH Publishing Corporation.

Malthus, T.R. (1798), *An Essay on the Principle of Population as It Affects the Future Improvement of Mankind*, London: J. Johnson.

Margolis, H. (1982), *Selfishness, Altruism and Rationality: A Theory of Social Choice*, Cambridge: Cambridge University Press.

McKibbin, W.J. (2001), 'Moving beyond Kyoto', *Energy and Environment*, **12** (1), 1–16.

McKibbin, W.J. and D. Vines (2000), 'Modelling reality: the need for both intertemporal optimisation and stickiness in models for policymaking', *Oxford Review of Economic Policy*, **16** (4), 106–37.

McKibbin, W.J. and P. Wilcoxen (2000a), 'Beyond the Kyoto Protocol', in F. Lo, H. Tokuda and N. Cooray (eds), *The Sustainable Future of the Global System III*, Tokyo: The United Nations University/Institute of Advanced Studies (UNU/IAS), pp. 101–8.

McKibbin, W.J. and P. Wilcoxen (2000b), 'The role of international permit trading in climate change policy', *Oxford Energy Forum*, **41**, May, 3–6.

Polunin, N. and J. Burnett (1993), *Surviving with the Biosphere*, Edinburgh, UK: Edinburgh University Press.

Rawls, J.R. (1971), *A Theory of Justice*, Cambridge, MA: Harvard University Press.

Ren, Z. and C. Tisdell (1997), 'Community-based Forestry in Yunnan: Dictates of Environment and Socio-Economics', in C.A. Tisdell and J.C.H. Chai (eds), *China's Economic Growth and Transition*, Commack, NY: Nova Science, pp. 333–54.

Shamasastry, R. (1929), *Kautilya's Arthasastra*, Mysore: Wesleyan Mission Press.

Solow, R. (1956), 'A contribution to the theory of economic growth', *Quarterly Journal of Economics*, **170**, 65–79.

Solow, R. (1974), 'The economics of resources or the resources of economics', *American Economic Review*, **64** (2), May, 1–14.

Tisdell, C.A. (1993), 'Taxation versus tradeable permits and alternative policies for environmental management', in D. Thampapillai (ed.), *Taxation and the Environment*, Australian Tax Research Foundation, Conference Series No. 14, Sydney, pp. 95–105.

Tisdell, C.A. (1998a), 'Economic policy instruments and environmental sustainability: another look at environmental-use permits', *Sustainable Development*, **6** (1), March, 18–22.

Tisdell, C.A. (1998b), 'Environmental taxation versus tradeable permits: public finance, accounting and related aspects', *Environmental Taxation and Accounting*, **2** (2), 55–60.

Tisdell, C.A. (1999), *Biodiversity, Conservation and Sustainable Development*, Cheltenham: Edward Elgar.

Tisdell, C.A. (2001), 'Sustainable development, gender inequality and human resource capital', *International Journal of Agricultural Resources, Governance and Ecology*, **1** (2), 178–92.

Tisdell, C.A. (2002), *Economics of Conserving Wildlife and Natural Areas*, Cheltenham: Edward Elgar.

Tisdell, C., K. Roy and G. Regmi (2001), 'Socio-economic determinants of the intrafamily status of wives in rural India: analysis and empirical evidence', *Gender Issues*, **19** (3), 41–60.

Wills, I. (1997), *Economics and the Environment*, St. Leonard's, NSW: Allen and Unwin.

PART II

GENERAL ISSUES IN ECOLOGICAL AND ENVIRONMENTAL ECONOMICS

[2]

Ecological or Green Economics: Genuine Contribution or Fashionable Fad?

Introduction

Economics studies the relationship between the social administration or management of resources and scarcity. Scarcity arises because available resources are insufficient to satisfy human wants. Consequently one of the main contributions of economics is to suggest institutional and other changes (such as variations in market or political mechanisms, or in some cases the introduction or withdrawal of social mechanisms) to improve the management of resources in order to reduce scarcity.

Economists have claimed that there are four main ways to reduce economic scarcity (see for example, Kohler, 1977; Tisdell, 1982). These are:

(1) *by improving the allocation of resources between alternative uses* so that the efficiency of the economic system in satisfying human wants is increased,

(2) *by ensuring full employment of all persons wanting to work* for the value of their addition to production (that is, by eliminating involuntary unemployment of labour),

(3) *by promoting economic growth,* and

(4) *as far as relative scarcity is concerned, by improving the distribution of income.*

Basically, pursuit of the first three goals increases the size of the economic cake, whereas the pursuit of the last goal leads to a more equitable sharing of the economic cake.

Now, however, we realise that at least one of the suggested means for reducing scarcity may add to the problem. Economic growth *may* add to the problem of scarcity because it may not be sustainable. While economic growth may reduce scarcity in the short or medium term, it could result in much greater economic scarcity in the long term due to depletion of non-renewable resources and to the irreversible environmental deterioration caused by it. Thus economic growth of the past, which has been seen by many as the surest way to economic salvation for the human race, is being questioned.

Economic growth may result in increased scarcity in the long term. It may not lead to a socially satisfying society in terms of interpersonal relationships and self-development. It may have unacceptable environmental consequences, for example, it may result in the extinction of an unacceptably large number of species of other living things. Such issues have been debated by those interested in ecological or green economics for at least two decades, but it is only recently that there has been widespread interest in such issues.

What is ecological or green economics?

Different individuals have different ideas about what ecological or green economics is or should be. For some, ecological economics is no more than an alternative name for environmental economics or even natural resource economics. In practice, studies in all of these areas overlap considerably in subject matter. But basically ecological economics places much more emphasis than these other subjects on the importance of living things as a means to sustaining economic activity, on the need to protect the biosphere and on the importance of conserving living things in order to achieve or retain a desirable world.

The conservation of living things, even those not presently utilised by humanity, is central to ecological or green economics. While ecological economics can be regarded as a part of environmental economics, it differs from environmental economics because of its greater emphasis on living things as being important for future economic development, for sustaining economic production, and/or for the creation or maintenance of a "good society". Since living things, especially humans, rely on the use of non-renewable resources to maintain their current state of existence, the depletion of non-renewable resources (such as fossil fuels) is also of concern to ecological economists. Indeed, some ecological economists see the conservation of energy as being the prime issue requiring attention by ecological economics. While the rate of use of energy resources is an important issue, I do not see it as the prime issue. The problem of maintaining biological diversity is a more important issue.

Since the United Nations Conference on the Human Environment was held in Helsinki in 1972, interest in the relationship between economic development and the environment has passed through two phases. The first in the 1970s was concerned principally with the imminent prospect of exhaustion of non-renewable resources, such as fossil fuels, and with increasing levels of pollution arising from economic activity. These fears were fanned by the oil crises of the period and the pessimistic global predictions of the Club of Rome (Cf. Forrester, 1971; Meadows et al 1972) that many non-renewable resources would be exhausted in as little as fifty years. The second phase of interest in conservation and economic development began in the 1980s and is continuing. It is characterised by much greater interest in the conservation of the living environment, in the protection of the biosphere and in the maintenance of biodiversity. The publication of the *World Conservation Strategy* document by the World Conservation Union (IUCN) in 1980 marks the beginning of this new phase. In this new phase, ecological economics has become central.

Some ecological economists claim that ecological economics should be distinguished from other branches of economics because of its methodology. It is not committed to traditional economic paradigms or existing economic methods. Most ecological economists accept that the world is complex and that the same problem often needs to be studied from several different points of view to obtain an adequate appreciation of it. In this respect Costanza (1989) has said: "there is probably not one *right* approach or paradigm, because like the blind man and the elephant, the subject is too big and complex to touch it all with one limited set of perception tools." Norgaard (1989, p.37) claims that "all aspects of complex systems can only be understood through multiple methodologies. Since ecological economics seeks to understand a larger system than either economics or ecology seeks to understand, a diversity of methodologies is appropriate and pressure to eliminate methodologies for the sake of conformity should be avoided." A similar view has also been recently expressed by Soderbaum (1990) in contrasting neoclassical and institutional approaches to environmental economics.

Most ecological economists believe that dominant existing paradigms with their roots in neoclassical, Keynesian or Marxian economics are inadequate for dealing with the environmental and economic development problems facing the world today. Keynesian economists did not raise environmental issues. They did not feature in Marxian economics even though Marx himself did point to the human trauma that can arise if industrialisation and urbanisation alienate humanity from nature. But in practice Marx and his followers such as Engels were anti-Malthusian and pro-economic growth.

They rejected the views of Thomas Robert Malthus (1798) that human population is liable to outstrip the means of subsistence. They argued that while the level of human population may increase in geometrical progression, as suggested by Malthus, scientific knowledge increases in faster geometrical progression and nothing is impossible for science (Engels, 1959, p.204). In their view, scientific advance and capital accumulation can be relied on to overcome any resource constraints that might be encountered as human populations increase. They were technological optimists. Indeed, commencing in the last half of the last century, the bulk of economists, no matter what their persuasion (neoclassical, Keynesian, Marxian or otherwise), have been technological optimists.

In the case of neoclassical economic thought (the predominant current school of economic thought in the West which usually extols the economic virtues of the market system), environmental impacts of economic activity were mainly treated as minor until at least the 1960s. Environmental spillovers from economic activity were seen as examples of economic externalities. Followers of the English economist Pigou (1932) suggested that the presence of externalities in a market economy calls for a limited degree of government intervention involving, for example, taxes on unfavourable externalities such as pollution. On the other hand, members of the Chicago School of Economics, opposed in general to government intervention, argued that the frequency and size of external effects from economic activity are often exaggerated and that in any case, they usually disappear if private property rights are clearly defined and extended to cover environmental resources (Cf. Coase, 1960). However, the Chicago School recognised that in some cases, the costs of establishing private property rights or of the government intervening might exceed the benefits of doing so. In such cases, Chicago economists suggested that it would be best from an economic view to manage with an existing imperfect economic system and without government intervention. Hence, from both points of view, the Chicago School sees little need for direct government intervention in the economy.

As for the use of non-renewable resources, neoclassical economists claim that, on the whole, the market mechanism leads to the optimal conservation of such resources, provided that property rights are "correctly" established. Thus, the general thrust of recent neoclassical economic thought is that if market forces are allowed to operate and the market system is extended as widely as possible, few serious environmental and resource problems will occur and little direct government intervention will be needed.

This basically laissez-faire point of view is questioned by the neo-Malthusians, those who believe that unless positive action is taken by governments and other economic agents, considerable economic scarcity will occur in the future due to resource depletion or to pollution brought about by overconsumption and overpopulation of the globe by humans. Neo-Malthusians include Paul and Ann Ehrlich (1977), Hermann Daly (1968), Georgescu-Roegen (1971), Mishan (1967) and the New Zealand economist, Perrings (1987).

Neo-Malthusians focus attention on resource and environmental problems which were largely ignored or dismissed by neoclassical economists and by most economists prior to the great environmental debate which began in the 1970s. Most economists did not see overconsumption as a problem from the point of view of scarcity. Indeed, it was considered desirable for the economic system to be geared towards greater consumption because individuals (humans) could then have more of what they wanted to satisfy their needs. Greater consumption by humans was seen as the sole end of economic activity, if not of all activity. This view can be traced back to Adam Smith (1776) who, in arguing against the Mercantalist system of economics, emphasised that consumption is the sole end of economic activity, that is, consumption by the *whole* population of the nation. Basically, the aim of Mercantalists was to suggest economic measures to enhance or maintain the power (and wealth) of the prince or the king rather than that of the whole community.

The need for a new perspective

At the time when Adam Smith wrote, life was short and probably brutish for most people. There was a constant struggle to satisfy even basic economic needs. Humanity was at nature's mercy then. Today the position seems broadly to be the other way around. At the time, it seemed appropriate to emphasise the importance of increasing the material economic welfare of all by increasing their consumption of desired commodites. But per capita consumption levels in developed countries today greatly exceed those of these earlier times. Consumption levels are much greater than is needed to satisfy basic needs and for most permit a measure of luxury. Indeed, the health and welfare of some individuals in developed countries suffers as a result of their "excessive" consumption of commodities and as a result of their restless and never-ending desire for greater income and levels of material consumption. Therefore, it is legitimate to question in the case of the more developed countries whether an even higher level of material consumption per head is an appropriate goal.

Furthermore economists know, for example, from empirical studies estimating Engel curves, that as the incomes of individuals rise, the type of commodities demanded by them alters. We know that as the incomes (and educational attainment) of individuals rise, they demand proportionately more environmentally provided commodites. As incomes rise, we expect individuals to demand a lower proportion of material goods and a higher proportion of services including non-consumptive goods such as those provided by natural environments. Often the services provided by natural environments can only be retained through government intervention.

There are also other reasons why we need a new perspective. Today we face the prospect on a global scale of irreversible environmental impacts from economic activity of which the greenhouse phenomenon is just one example. Not only this, we are uncertain about the occurrence of such impacts, their rate of onset and their likely consequences. We face the possibility of sudden and *irreversible* jumps in environmental conditions. Past trends and signs may provide little forewarning of approaching economic and environmental collapse due to resource depletion and environmental degradation. By the time signs of future collapse become apparent, it may already be too late to reverse the deteriorating situation and avoid catastrophe.

The great English economist Alfred Marshall (1890) was able to declare in the last century that "Nature does not proceed by leaps and bounds". In his framework of thought, marginal certain change is almost assured. But now we fear that nature may sometimes proceed by leaps and bounds and can do so in unpredictable ways and irreversibly.

Since the effects of environmental change can be widespread, even global, we all can be affected. Thus, we all have a stake in what is happening to the environment. Essentially the global environment is a shared resource so the use of it can never ben an entirely individualistic matter. Resolving our conflicts about the use of our shared environment is no easy matter since many of us have different attitudes to risk taking and uncertainty and we differ in the relative gains and losses that we individually are likely to make in taking risks with this environment. This has to be recognised in our decisions about resource use.

Human beings have come to dominate nature but we are still subject to its basic laws. There is no guarantee that we will be able to sustain and expand economic activity in the same way as in the past, despite all technological change and optimism. There is a possibility of unwanted economic and ecological impacts or possible disasters from economic growth. In such circumstances, it is rational to retain flexibility in resource and response systems. For example, options can be kept open through conservation, for instance, by maintaining biodiversity. Thus for this reason and the others given above, there is currently considerable emphasis on the desirability of attaining sustainable development (Cf. Pearce et al, 1989).

Social recognition of the need for a changed attitude

Social recognition of the need for a changed attitude towards the environment and the relationship between economic growth and the environment has come from several quarters in the last two decades. It has occurred at the local, regional, national and international level.

The World Commission on Environment and Development (1987), which was established by the United Nations under the chairmanship of Gro Brundtland, former prime minister of Norway, points out in its report, *Our Common Future*, that the world does not face a separate environmental crisis, separate energy crisis or a separate development crisis. They are all one. Broad areas of concern (environmental, economic and social) cannot be compartmentalised or confined to local areas. The Earth has become a global village in which economic, ecological and social problems are interlocked and this calls for a holistic approach by governments to policy making. The UN commission points out that "Ecology and economy are becoming ever more interwoven – locally, regionally, nationally, and globally – into a seamless net of causes and effects'' (World Commission on Environment and Development, 1987, p.5).

The Brundtland Report was amongst a number of official reports and documents of international bodies in the 1980s championing the objective of sustainable development. Possibly the *World Conservation Strategy* document, (IUCN, 1980) published by the World Conservation Union (but a joint effort of several international agencies) was the first official international document to promote sustainable development as an important objective and to stress the importance of biological conservation for sustainable development. The interdependent nature of biological conservation and socio-economic conditions was explicitly emphasised in the document. It was pointed out, for example, that individuals in poverty in less developed countries are unlikely to be interested in biological conservation unless it results in rather immediate and tangible material benefits to them.

At the national level, political gains by ''green'' parties and by parties incorporating ecological concerns in their agenda are signs of increased public concerns about these matters (Cf. O'Riordan, 1988). Established parties which previously had not incorporated ecological or green issues in their agenda have been forced to do this in order to retain their electoral support. Despite this, representatives of ''green'' parties are being elected to parliaments and in Tasmania, for example, have managed to hold the balance of power.

Conflicts between environmentalists and developers are by no means new, least of all to Queensland. Past conflicts in Australia include mining on the Great Barrier Reef (particularly the possibility of oil mining); mineral sands development versus conservation, for instance, on Fraser Island and in the Cooloola sands; the Franklin River proposed hydro-electricity works, and so on. But there were no settled institutional mechanisms to deal with such conflicts nor were ecological concerns well integrated with economic considerations.

Some institutional developments have recently occurred at the Australian Federal Government level designed, at least partially, to remedy this situation. Recently there has been the appointment of an environmental (economics) commissioner to the Industries Commission, a body which makes recommendations to the Australian government about assistance for industry, and the establishment of the

Resources Assessment Commission as a result of The Resources Assessment Commission Act, 1989. This commission investigates matters referred to it by the prime minister and reports its findings directly to him.

The Resources Assessment Commission is currently inquiring into the options for Australia's forest and timber resources and into the future use of the Kakadu Exploration Zone. The Australian goverment may soon request it to examine major coastal zone development issues. In its assessments, the commission has been asked to take account of the environmental, cultural, social, industrial, economic and other values involved in the use of resources. Section 7 of the act sets out the principles that the commission should take into account in resolving competing claims for the use of resources. One of these principles is that "resource use decisions should seek to optimise the net benefits to the community from the nation's resources, having regard to efficiency of resource use, environmental considerations, ecological integrity and sustainability, the sustainability of any development, and an equitable distribution of the return on resources". The influence of the commission will depend upon the extent to which matters are referred to it by the prime minister for inquiry and the willingness of the government to act on its recommendations. Currently each inquiry of the commission is being undertaken by two commissioners, one of whom is an economist and the other an ecologist.

Major issues for ecological or green economics

Sustainability, whether of economic systems, or of development, or of ecosystems, or of human society, is currently a focal point for much debate about issues in ecological or green economics. The presumption is that sustainability in some sense is desirable. But whether or not that is so depends upon what we desire to sustain and why we want to do it. Sometimes these objectives are unclear in the debate. Little progress can be made until they are clarified (see for example, Tisdell, 1990a).

Some writers have suggested that our aim should be to sustain biodiversity, that is, as wide a range of species and variety of species as possible.

Loss of genetic diversity is occurring on a massive scale. While extinction is the normal fate of virtually all species, processes of gradual natural extinction are now being dwarfed by the rate of human-generated extinctions of species and their varieties. Possibly 15-20 per cent of existing species, that is half to two million species, could disappear over the next two decades or so, primarily as a result of human activity (Barney, 1980, pp.37-38). While these estimates cover all biota, they include about one thousand animals and birds as likely candidates for man-induced extinction.

Some of the most important genetic losses may not be of species but of subspecies and varieties of biota used commercially or directly by humans, such as foodgrains. It has been estimated that four-fifths of the world's food supplies are derived from less than two dozen plants and animal species. "Wild and local domestic strains are needed for breeding resistance to pests and pathogens into the high-yield varieties now widely used. These varietal stocks are rapidly diminishing as marginal wild lands are brought into cultivation. Local domesticated varieties, often uniquely suited to local conditions, are also being lost as higher-yield varieties displace them" (Barney, 1980). Thus modern agriculture becomes more vulnerable as its genetic base is constantly and surreptitiously eroded.

The importance of maintaining biodiversity has been argued from two points of view, (1) an anthropocentric or human-centred point of view, and (2) a non-anthropocentric viewpoint.

The anthropocentric point of view claims that genetic diversity is of considerable economic value to humanity and may be essential in the long term for maintaining the level and desired variety of economic production. Several arguments have been put forward for maintaining biological diversity on economic grounds, not all of which can be noted here.

However, some are:

(1) Strains and varieties of living things used in commercial production usually have a limited life of about five years and depend upon three or four varieties for the bulk of production of major crops (Cf. IUCN, 1980). For example, major crop varieties fall periodically due to lack of resistance to new diseases and scientists can usually only breed new varieties with resistance if they have access to the wild relatives or primitive cultivars of the do-

mesticated varieties. If this wild, diverse gene pool or bank is no longer available, commercial production may become unsustainable.

(2) Non-renewable resources such as minerals are being depleted by economic activity. Once these are depleted the human race will be entirely dependent on biological resources and the energy from the sun. Thus, in the very long term, the stock of biological resources will be essential resources for the survival of future generations. Even before non-renewable resource depletion or entropy occurs eventually, if it does occur, the degree of dependence of humanity on biological resources will increase dramatically, so the stock will be a valuable asset even in the shorter run.

(3) The depletion of non-renewable resources can be expected to be uneven. Biological resources may be important (substitutive) backstop resources for non-renewable resources depleted early. Biological resources, for instance, are potential sources of liquid or gaseous fuels. Thus back-up or backstop biological resources may be needed earlier than had previously been realised.

(4) Biological diversity helps to keep economic options open for the future. This is valuable given uncertainty about the exact future economic use and worth of many biological resources, e.g. particular species or varieties of species.

(5) Individuals place an economic value on biological diversity for recreation and enjoyment as evidenced by their willingness to pay, for example, for tourism based on such diversity, e.g. in the case of visitors and tourists to national parks.

Non-anthropocentric reasons have also been put forward for preserving genetic diversity. These include the "land ethic" of Aldo Leopold (1933, 1966). His land ethic was developed in opposition to the view that nature should be manipulated or species exterminated purely to satisfy the narrow economic interests of Homo sapiens. To him, humanity is part of a holistic organic community, and has no right to exterminate parts of that community but should live in harmony with it. This suggests that species other than Homo sapiens have an independent right to existence. It is possible that this ethic, at least in modified form, will gain increasing community support. Even if it does, there would still be a role for economics.

The survival or extent of survival of other species is likely to depend on control of levels of human population, regulation of per capita levels of material consumption by humans, more control of discharges of pollutants and wastes from economic activity and greater recycling as well as better planning of the nature of resource use at local level. For example, at local level, land-use planning might incorporate Biosphere Reserves along the lines suggested by UNESCO in its Man and the Biosphere (MAB) Program, even though this is not the only model worth considering (see, for example, McNeely et al, 1990). These are all matters about which we have a choice.

But if global economic growth is to be limited to attain ecological sustainability, this raises several issues. How will the poorest, less developed countries increase the incomes of their residents? Will less developed countries also be expected to forgo economic growth? To what extent are the developed countries prepared to redistribute income to the less developed countries if they forgo economic growth, especially bearing in mind that a redistribution of income is likely to mean a redistribution of economic and military power? If the less developed countries commence economic growth or continue to have economic growth, this could be damaging economically, environmentally and ecologically to developed nations because of the global environmental impacts of the developing countries. This has, for example, been pointed out strikingly in relation to the greenhouse effect, given the capacity of China, India and Brazil to add to it by their burning of fossil fuels (see, for example, Burnett and Polunin, forthcoming). If we ignore such issues, they certainly will not disappear.

Given the strong desire for economic growth, especially in less developed countries, humanity-induced extinction of species is likely to continue even though the consequences of this for the long-term economic well-being of the human race are uncertain and could be quite disastrous. In these circumstances, we may however have a choice of which species to save and which to extinguish. How should we choose which species to save? This is a question for ecological economics and one which we all have a responsibility to consider. We are being forced to be latter-day Noahs.

Conclusion

Economic systems are not ends in themselves but means to ultimate ends. Primarily we need to decide on the type of society that we want and then consider economic systems that will help to bring about that type of society. It is illogical and involves putting the cart before the horse to decide on the economic system that we want and then merely accept the type of society that results. Economic systems help to determine the nature and structure of society and sociological and interpersonal relationships within them. For example, an efficient society in providing material goods and services may be a non-caring society in which individuals are subjected to considerable emotional stress and alienation. It may also be that such a society pays insufficient attention to the preservation of nature.

There is associated with the conservation movement a school of thought which argues in favour of sustainable communities. It appears to favour small, sustainable communities in charge of their own affairs and is favoured by some "alternative lifestyle" groups. Proponents argue that there should be full participation by all in the social-political systems of the community, a fair distribution of income and cooperation with nature rather than domination of it. According to this view, individuals should not be subject to the tyranny of technologies such as those involving large economies of scale. Technologies should be appropriate to the community and to the demands of nature. Social structures which take decisions away from local communities, such as those involving large companies or "big" centralised governments are seen as a threat to a sustainable and satisfactory social and economic order in harmony with nature. Such views have, for example, been expressed by Schumacher (1978) and by others (Douglass, 1984).

If these principles were put into effect they would alter the social and economic fabric of existing developed economies fundamentally. They would have a cost in terms of forgone levels of material production, at least in the short term. Whether the social and ecological benefits from the system would outweigh the material costs is partially a value judgment. But it might be noted that a country putting these principles wholeheartedly into effect might be unable to defend itself against external aggression because the type of industries vital to an effective war effort would suffer. Thus, this way of life may only be a secure way of life in a world which has effective global government. From this point of view, as well as from many other points of view, it can be seen that social, economic and ecological considerations are all intertwined.

In studying ecological economics, one cannot avoid considering the ultimate purpose or values of economic activity and human existence, the "rights" of future generations and of living things apart from humans. Is it desirable to continue maximising current consumption per head and economic growth? Do growing human populations pose a threat to economic and ecological sustainability? If economic growth is no longer to be the norm, how will less developed countries overcome poverty? What economic sacrifices should be made to save other species from extinction and, if we must choose, which species ought to be saved? How do economic, social and ecological systems influence one another? Should economic systems be modified to obtain more acceptable "social structures" and ecological effects? These partly philosophical and ethical issues are central to ecological economics and affect us all. (They are discussed in Tisdell, 1990b).

We can conclude that ecological or green economics is unlikely to be a passing fad. Rather, it will continue developing and making a genuine contribution to economic thought. The issues involved in ecological economics are fundamental consequences of our current predicament and there is no retreating from the difficulties which we face. Everything cannot be turned backwards. At the same time, the degree of interest in this subject is likely to vary over the years and it may not always be as fashionable as it appears to be now.

References

Barney, G.O. 1980. *The Global 2000 Report to the President of the U.S. – Entering the 21st Century*. Vol. 1. New York: Pergamon.

Burnett, J. and Polunin, N., eds, (forthcoming). *Surviving with the Biosphere*. Edinburgh: Edinburgh University Press.

Coase, R.H. 1960. "The problems of social cost". *The Journal of Law and Economics*, 3.

Costanza, R. 1989. "What is ecological economics?" *Ecological Economics* 1: 1-7.

Daly, H.E. 1968. "On economics as a life science". *Journal of Political Economy* 76: 392-406.

Douglass, G.K. 1984. "The meanings of agricultural sustainability". In *Agricultural Sustainability in a Changing World Order*, ed. G.K. Douglass. Boulder, Colorado: Westview Press.

Ehlrich, P.R., Ehlrich, A. and Holdren, J.P. 1977 *Ecoscience: Population, Resources and Development*. 3rd ed. San Francisco: Freeman.

Engels, F. 1959. "Outlines of a critique of political economy". In *Economic and Philosophic Manuscripts of 1844*, K. Marx. Moscow: Foreign Languages Publishing House.

Forrester, J.W. 1971. *World Dynamics*. Cambridge, Mass: Wright Allen Press.

Georgescu-Roegen, N. 1971. *The Entropy Law and the Economic Process*. Cambridge, Mass: Harvard University Press.

IUCN. 1980. *World Conservation Strategy: Living Resource Conservation for Sustainable Development*. Glands, Switzerland: International Union for the Conservation of Nature and Natural Resources (World Conservation Union).

Kohler, H. 1977. *Scarcity and Freedom: An Introduction to Economics*. Lexington, Mass: Heath.

Leopold, A. 1933. *Game Management*. New York: Scribner.

Leopold, A. 1966. *A Sand Country Almanac: With Other Essays from Round River*. New York: Oxford University Press.

Marshall, A. 1890. *Principles of Economics*. 1st ed. London: Macmillan.

Malthus, T.R. 1798. *An Essay on the Principle of Population, as it Affects the Future Improvement of Mankind*. London: J. Johnson.

McNeely, J.A., Miller, K.R., Reid, W.V., Mittermeier, R.A., and Werner, T.B. 1990. *Conserving the World's Biological Diversity*. Glands, Switzerland: IUCN, WRI, CI, WWF-US, and the World Bank Washington, D.C.

Meadows, D.H., Meadows, D.L., Randers, J. and Behrens, W. 1972. *The Limits to Growth: A Report for the Club of Rome's*

Project on the Predicament of Mankind. New York: Universe Books.

Mishan, E.J. 1967. *The Costs of Economic Growth.* London: Staples Press.

Norgaard, R.B. 1989. "The case for methodological pluralism". *Ecological Economics* 1: 37-57.

O'Riordan, T. 1988. "The politics of sustainability". In *Sustainable Environmental Management,* R.K. Turner. London: Belhaven Press.

Pearce, D., Markandya, A. and Barbier, E.B. 1989. *Blueprint for a Green Economy.* London: Earthscan Publications.

Perrings, C. 1987. *Economy and Environment: A Theoretical Essay on the Interdependence of Economic and Environmental Systems* Cambridge, U.K.: Cambridge University Press.

Pigou, A.C. 1932. *The Economics of Welfare.* 4th ed. London: Macmillan.

Schumacher, E.F. 1978. *Small is Beautiful: A Study in Economics as if People Mattered.* London: Abacus.

Smith, A. [1776] 1910. *Wealth of Nations.* London: Dent.

Soderbaum, P. 1990. "Neoclassical and institutional approaches to environmental economics". *Journal of Economic Issues* 24: 481-492.

Tisdell, C.A. 1982. *Microeconomics of Markets.* Brisbane: Wiley.

Tisdell, C.A. 1990a. "The nature of sustainability and of sustainable development". Forthcoming in *Moving Toward Global Sustainability: Policies and Implications for Australia,* ed. M. Commons. Proceedings of an Australian National University Workshop, Centre for Resource and Environmental Studies, Australian National University, Canberra.

Tisdell, C.A. 1990b. Forthcoming *Natural Resources, Growth and Development: Economics, Ecology and Resource-Scarcity.* New York: Praeger.

World Commission on Environment and Development. 1987. *Our Common Future.* Oxford: Oxford University Press.

[3]

Ecological Economics and the Environmental Future

Clement A. Tisdell

Professor and Head, Department of Economics, University of Queensland, St Lucia, Queensland 4067, Australia

Introduction

Feuds between natural scientists and economists (and within their ranks) about the scope for future economic growth, not to mention its desirability, have been common in the last 25 years or so and reached their maximum intensity in the 1970s (Perrings, 1987 p. 47). The ferocity and emotionalism involved in many of the interactions were intensified by misunderstanding and distortion of the views of opponents, and by the relative lack of (experimental and other) evidence in relation to the environmental hypotheses under debate. Some economists also felt that their 'traditional' academic discipline-based territory and established preferential position as advisers to governments and to the public on social issues were under challenge.

In the course of such debate, many economists have felt it their duty to warn the public and policymakers about the dangers of accepting the social policy-prescriptions of natural scientists – on the grounds that, although natural scientists were experts in their own fields, they were naïve and untrained in social issues. At the beginning of this debate, there was a feeling amongst most (but not all) economists that those trained in a particular discipline should keep to their own areas of expertise. Such a reductionist, partial, compartmentalized approach to knowledge rather than a holistic view accordingly tended to prevail.

However, since 1970 the small nucleus of economists involved in environmental and ecological issues has expanded, particularly in North America, university courses on environmental economics have become widely established, journals such as *Environmental Economics* and *Ecological Economics* have come into existence, and more and more economists are co-operating with natural scientists to support a holistic approach to policy formulation. Journals such as, particularly, *Environmental Conservation*, and organizations such as the Foundation for Environmental Conservation, have encouraged natural and social scientists, and also economists, to interact constructively in this process.

Here I want to outline the scope of ecological economics and briefly consider its modern origins. Recent global policy reports such as *Our Common Future* (World Commission on Environment and Development, 1987) emphasize the importance of combining economics and ecology in framing economic development policies. The current success of political parties favouring ecological conservation programmes, gives additional emphasis to the importance of combining economics and ecology in policy proposals.

Today it seems that we have to deal increasingly with environmental phenomena of a more pervasive type than in the past. Global uncertainty, and irreversible environmental effects from economic growth, are no longer rare. If the type of economic growth which has been common in the past persists, it will continue to damage The Biosphere irreversibly and will increasingly threaten the future economic welfare of Mankind. In these circumstances, alert account needs to be taken of *ecological economics*.

THE SCOPE OF ECOLOGICAL ECONOMICS

Robert Costanza (1989 p. 1) sees ecological economics as addressing 'the relationship between ecosystems and economic systems in the broadest sense. These relationships are the basis of many of the most pressing current problems (*i.e.* sustainability, acid rain, global warming, species extinction, wealth distribution) but they are not well covered by any existing discipline'. Environmental and natural resource economics, as currently practised, tend to concentrate on neoclassical and conventional economic approaches to the analysis of environmental and resource issues. In the past, writers on these subjects have given relatively more attention to the non-living environment than to ecobiomes, ecocomplexes, or their component ecosystems, but one would expect ecological economics to have the opposite emphasis. Costanza (*idem*) claims that, while some ecologists deal with human impacts on ecosystems, most keep to natural systems. However, for many policy purposes, ecology and economics need to be linked, and this requires co-operation between ecologists and economists and a more open approach than hitherto on the part of the economists to the often all-pervasive environmental issues.

Methodological and conceptual pluralism is needed in studying ecological economics. As Costanza (1989 p. 2) suggests, 'there is probably not one *right* approach or paradigm, because like the blind man and the elephant, the subject is too big and complex to touch it all with one limited set of perceptual tools'. Norgaard (1989 p. 37) also so argues and develops the view that 'all aspects of complex systems can only be understood through multiple methodologies. Since ecological economics seeks to understand a larger system than either economics or ecology seeks to understand, a diversity of methodologies is appropriate and [so] pressures to eliminate methodologies for the sake of conformity, should be avoided.'

Ecological Economics: Historical Aspects of Its Emergence

The emergence of ecological economics as a recognized area of study is very recent. Indeed, it might be dated from as late as 1989 with the formation of the International Society for Ecological Economics and the publication of its journal, *Ecological Economics*, even though many earlier contributions fall into this field (*see*, for example, Martinez-Alier, 1987; Proops, 1989).

One of the first Authors to propose seriously the term ecological economics was Kenneth E. Boulding (1950), who suggested, in his ecological introduction to *A Reconstruction of Economics*, that social and economic systems be analysed with the use of ecosystem modelling, thus following an idea advanced by Alfred Marshall (1920). But at that time Boulding did not consider the interdependence of economic activity and the state of the environment; nor did he seem to be aware of scarcity problems arising from natural limits to economic growth. However, in 1966 Boulding introduced these issues to economists with his celebrated 'Spaceship Earth' article, thereby foreshadowing the neo-Malthusian debate of the 1970s on limits to economic growth.

This debate was stimulated by the Club of Rome Report and by the publication of Meadows *et al.* (1972), *The Limits to Growth*, which followed up the 'doomsday' modelling of Forrester (1971). While some economists, such as Pigou (1932), had been concerned about the external environmental effects (externalities) of economic activity and their policy implications, so that renewed interest in and development of those theories occurred in the 1950s, *e.g.* by Meade (1952) and Scitovsky (1954), mainstream economic theory in the early 1970s did not link economic development with major environmental and ecological changes, even though there were some exceptions – such as Mishan (1967) and the British economist David Pearce.

While classical economists such as the Englishmen Thomas Robert Malthus and David Ricardo were well aware of natural limits to economic growth, those limitations played no role in neoclassical and mainstream economic theories which dominated economic thought at the beginning of the 1970s (Perrings, 1987; Tisdell, 1990*a*, 1990*b*). But classical economists had not foreseen major modern environmental problems, *e.g.* global pollution arising from economic growth. Yet the importance, indeed the necessity, of interrelating economic development and environmental change was becoming increasingly clear by the end of the 1960s. Boulding (1966) helped to start the process of integration.

Important contributions towards the integration of economics and environmental thought, taking into account the difficulties of attaining a sustainable society, were made by Daly (1968, 1973) and by Georgescu-Roegen (1971). In addition, in the 1970s, a number of economic models appeared which, apart from including production and consumption as a part of economic activity, included wastes as a by-product (Ayres & Kneese, 1969; D'Arge, 1972).

Prior to the above, wastes and their possible environmental consequences had been largely ignored by economists, who had viewed them as generally irrelevant from an economic viewpoint. Accordingly during the 1970s, academics and economists who were interested in global environmental issues, mainly concentrated on the depletion of non-living resources, such as fossil fuels, and on pollution stemming from their use. Concern for *living* resources, and for the global economic and environmental crisis that seemed likely to be caused by their disappearance or by the loss of their life-support systems, though present, was not emphasized directly. But nor was it by any means absent.

The first major economic work to take account of biological extinction problems was possibly that of Ciriacy-Wantrup (1968). It introduced the concept of safe minimum standard (SMS) as a guide to species preservation. But it was not until the late 1970s that species extinction became part of a mainstream debate by economists. Bishop (1978, 1979), arguing along the lines of Ciriacy-Wantrup, criticized the approach to environmental conservation of economists from Resources for the Future (Smith & Krutilla, 1979). The latter group favoured a rather traditional (neoclassical) approach to economic analysis, including the formulation of policies for deciding on the preservation of species and of wilderness. Using the SMS approach, Bishop argued that more conservation was justified than was supported by traditional economic approaches.

Nevertheless, using the traditional approach, economists came in the 1970s to the view that, taking into account the existence of environmental uncertainty and of irreversibility, it is rational to err on the side of conservation in order to keep options open, *i.e.* to retain flexibility (Krutilla, 1967; Arrow & Fisher, 1974; *see* also Chisholm, 1988). Thus neoclassical economists came to favour conservation more than had previously been the case – even though not to the extent of proponents of the 'safe minimum standard'. Acordingly, advances in economic thought relating to the environment were also being made but using traditional paradigms.

Thus it has come about that economic thought is responding gradually to the new challenges posed by environmental changes, albeit with a lag and sometimes not as radically as may be appropriate. At the same time, however, there are still a large number of economists who see environmental issues as peripheral to their concerns. Nevertheless, policy documents which appeared in the 1980s – such as the World Conservation Strategy document (IUCN, 1980) and the report of the World Commission on Environment and Development (1987), widely referred to as the 'Brundtland Report', have provided a stimulus to the development of ecological economics, and one expects that the 1990s will see significant development of this subject.

Perceived Policy Significance of Ecological Economics

The two international policy documents just mentioned strongly favour combining economics and ecology in the forming of policies affecting economic development. In exploring strategies for sustainable development, the World Conservation Strategy (WCS) document (IUCN, 1980 Sec. 1.12) states 'there is a close relationship between failure to achieve the objectives of conservation and failure to achieve the social and economic objectives of development – or, having achieved them, to sustain the achievement'. For example, it states that in developing countries conservation must be combined with measures to meet short-term economic needs.

Framers of the World Conservation Strategy (WCS) supported the view that improved international economic conditions are needed in order to achieve conservation goals. They recommended that the measures suggested for the International Development Strategy (of the 1980s) be adopted. These measures included trade liberalization, transfer of more finance and aid to less-developed countries, reform of the international monetary system, adoption of an international code of conduct for transnational companies, and more rapid progress on disarmament. In addition, proposers of the WCS recommend that 'economic and social growth be accelerated, especially in the poorest countries, ensuring that economic and social goods are mutually supporting, and emphasizing better health, better housing, and higher educational levels and skills' (IUCN, 1980 Sec. 20.3).

Proponents of WCS claim that equitable, sustainable development requires adoption of the above-mentioned 'economic' measures as well as those recommended in the WCS document. However, there is no discussion of the extent to which these measures are compatible with, or synergistic with, one another. There will certainly be cases where increasing aid to less-developed countries threatens conservation goals, and one cannot be sure that free-trade is always supportive of conservation goals or is always economically ideal! While economic and social systems undoubtedly impact on conservation, and *vice versa*, the interrelationship is often more complex than appears to be the case at first sight. It seems likely that neither the extreme of a completely free-market economic system nor that of a centralized command system of economic management is most conducive to the conservation goals espoused in the World Conservation Strategy.

The World Commission on Environment and Development (1987) places even more stress on the importance of connecting economics, development, and ecology. The Report sees the possibility for 'a new era of economic growth, one that must be based on policies that sustain and expand the environmental resource base. And we believe such growth to be absolutely essential to relieve the great poverty that is deepening in much of the developing world' (*idem* p. 1). It points out that it is 'impossible to separate *economic* development issues from environment issues', and that it is 'futile to attempt to deal with environmental problems without a broader perspective that encompasses the factors underlying world poverty and international inequality' (p. 5). It also emphasizes that the world is involved in interlocking 'crises' which cannot be compartmentalized by regions, sectors, or broad areas of concern (environmental, economic, or social). There is not a separate environmental crisis, a separate energy crisis, or a separate development crisis: they are all one.

The interdependence of economy and ecology are summed up in the Brundtland Report as follows:

> 'These related changes have locked the global economy and global ecology together in new ways. We have in the past been concerned about the impacts of economic growth upon the environment. We are now forced to concern ourselves with the impacts of ecological stress ... upon our economic prospects. We have in the more recent past been forced to face up to a sharp increase in economic interdependence among nations. We are now forced to accustom ourselves to accelerating ecological interdependence among nations. Ecology and economy are becoming even more interwoven – locally, regionally, nationally, and globally – into a seamless net of causes and effects' (World Commission on Environment and Development, 1987 p. 5).

As for specific economic and social measures to be taken to help promote sustainable development, the Brundtland Report is more guarded about international arrangements than is the World Conservation Strategy document, but provides more details. It seems possible that it is less free-trade-orientated than the WCS document. But this is not the place to discuss the socio-economic recommendations (international and national) of the Brundtland Report. Enough has been said, nevertheless, to make it clear that the Brundtland Report recommends that ecological economics play a central role in policy formulations. Thus it provides encouragement for development of this field.

New Paradigms for Our 'New' Economic and Ecological Situation

The basic mathematical structure of theories may well reflect prevailing views about the nature of the cosmos, in the sense of the ordered nature of relationships in the universe as a whole. Commencing in the nineteenth century, economic theories began to be cast principally in terms of the differential calculus – to stress the widespread existence of stable equilibrium in economic systems and, by making use of comparative statistics for policy purposes, assumed that it was rational to act on the basis that economic systems are in practice rarely far from equilibrium. Marginalism was the order of the day and Marshall (1920) was led to proclaim that 'Nature does not proceed by leaps and bounds'. A world of certainty was assumed in which, if evolution of systems should take place, it would lead to an improved situation.

In economic circles, those views did not take a 'battering' until the Great Depression of the 1930s. In his *General Theory*, Keynes (1936) pointed to rigidities in the economic system and to uncertainties and 'animal spirits' of investors, which could cause disequilibrium or lead to an undesirable equilibrium at a low level of economic activity. The conception of an economic world of certainty, *i.e.* in harmonious equilibrium, was beginning to disintegrate. But the problems were seen to be of managing demand – insufficient aggregate demand was seen as the root cause of the Great Depression. Supply-side problems, such as might come from environmental constraints, did not appear to economists in this period to be real constraints to economic activity.

Despite the views expressed by J. M. Keynes, and the contributions of economists such as Knight (1921) and Shackle (1952), economic theory was, at the end of the 1960s, 'dominated' by models which assumed certainty, reversibility of processes, continuity of change, and change by small gradations. Supply-side constraints, arising from environmental limits, were absent from mainstream theories of economic growth which were developed – but assuming a world of certainty, technological optimism, and a high degree of substitutability for all exhaustible resources (Perrings, 1987).

More appropriate economic growth and development models for our current situation, incorporating ecological relationships especially at the global level, may be those which allow for uncertainty, irreversibilities, and 'jumps' in relationships – such as those suggested by catastrophe theory (Zeeman, 1976), and for phenomena of a type suggested by non-linearities and by chaos theory (Gleick, 1987). At least where natural relationships are of this nature, they will need to be incorporated in ecological–economic models which rely on natural relationships as building-blocks. Such models of natural systems are quite different from those which prevailed at the beginning of this century, and which exerted so much influence on the development of economic theory.

The Environmental Future, Sustainability, and Ecological Economics

Our economic and environmental futures are widely intertwined, but some optimists still do not foresee environmental limits to our economic future or serious risk from continuingly rapid economic growth. One of the more optimistic examples is Julian Simon (1977), who suggested that rising population poses no risk to the maintenance (improvement) of human living standards because the larger number of people will have more ideas, and this will make technological progress more rapid. However, there is no guarantee that this will be the case, and that technological progress will be sufficient to overcome tightening environmental constraints. Growing evidence suggests that continuing economic growth of the past type is likely to result in environmental and economic collapse, given inevitable ultimate irreversibilities. Thus to adopt the development policies proposed by Julian Simon would, it seems, be at best a foolhardy gamble.

We cannot simply extrapolate past economic results into the future. Furthermore, the larger the human population is, and the higher its level of economic activity, the greater will be the penalty of failure to counteract environmental constraints *via* technological progress and other means. In addition, most of the increasing risk and uncertainty is faced *collectively*, namely in common. It is a characteristic of the modern, interdependent world that we face greater *common* risks and uncertainties than in the past, from both the ecological and the economic points of view. Hence, by following the population growth and economic growth policies suggested by Simon, we would be faced not merely with a personal gamble but with a gamble for all.

Many of our modern ecological/economic problems involve *collective* (overall) risks and uncertainties – in contrast to what appeared to be the case in earlier times. This makes policy making, including the establishment of economic policies for development, extremely difficult. In many cases, we face great uncertainty about the consequences of our actions, and can rarely be sure that we have considered all the possibilities. To this must be added the problem that individuals often have conflicting values, *e.g.* differing ethical precepts. But, in addition, there is a new element to consider, namely the different attitudes of individuals to the bearing of risk and uncertainty.

Thus we may distinguish three possible elements of social conflict involved in major economic policies impacting upon ecological systems and *vice versa*: (1) Conflict about the accuracy of specification of the possibilities; (2) Conflict about the objectives which it is valuable to pursue; and (3) Conflict about the degree of risk that it is appropriate to take, or about how to act under uncertainty. This conflict may be intense, given irreversibilities in the environmental system and the possibility that environmental 'jumps' may occur with little or no forewarning and be difficult or impossible to predict accurately. When 'leading indicators' suggest that a 'jump' – a sudden and irreversible decline in environmental quality – is imminent, it may already be too late to prevent the catastrophe. Thus myopic trial-and-error procedures in decision-making, in which reactions are based on feedback, can no longer be fully trusted in the present era. This is of course alarming, but important to bear in mind.

Game theory and decision theory help us to perceive elements of our situation but do not capture it fully (Tisdell, 1968; Perrings, 1987 Ch. 7). Even game theory assumes much more knowledge than we actually have. We have no *ready* answer for deciding an optimal social choice where views about what is possible differ, views about what is desirable differ, and attitudes to collective bearing of risk and uncertainty are in conflict – even though we can work through the logical implications of different actions based on different points of view.

This of course is not to say that we should not have our own position and pursue it – over a period of time one may change the values of others, obtain greater consensus about what is possible, and alter attitudes to the bearing of risk and uncertainty, so that greater agreement can be reached. There are indications now that those favouring ecologically sustainable development are obtaining greater political support than formerly. However, O'Riordan (1988 p. 30) warns that this may pose dangers and suggests that 'once the notions that underlie sustainability are politicised, the concept is effectively devalued'.

One of our greatest problems today, both ecologically and from the point of view of sustaining economic production in the long-term, is our continuing loss of genetic diversity, both in the wild and of primitive cultivars and landrace varieties. Even with significant advances in genetic manipulation, most of these losses (possibly all) are irreversible. As the genetic stock falls, the growing precariousness of production from cultivated crops and domesticated animals may not become obvious until their wild relatives and primitive cultivars and landrace varieties are virtually all irreversibly eliminated.

Today we obtain high yields from modern varieties because we increasingly isolate them from the natural environment, creating relatively uniform suitable artificial micro-environments, *e.g.* in the case of plants by the use of pesticides, irrigation, and artificial fertilizers. In so doing, we depend on the use to a considerable extent of non-renewable resources, and eliminate varieties which may be able to cope better with natural environments and *co-evolve* to adapt to their changes. Consequently in the long-term, when we are no longer able to protect crops as completely against the natural 'environments' as now because of the loss of resources – especially non-renewable resources – we may have eliminated varieties and species that would have been optimal to the new set of conditions (*cf.* Oldfield, 1989; Tisdell, 1990*a*). The economic system does not ensure the preservation of these environmentally well-adapted varieties even though it may be rational from a collective point of view to conserve them (Tisdell & Alauddin, 1989).

Apart from the above 'back-drop' value of genetic diversity, there are other ways in which it is likely to be of value. For example, new uses may be discovered for a particular species, or uses may be found that were not previously imagined for it (Oldfield, 1989). Economists, using the approaches of safe minimum standard (SMS) and benefit-cost analysis (BCA), have addressed some of the issues involved, and Randall (1986) suggests that a combination of these approaches is needed to determine what species or varieties to save. While these approaches may be too mechanical and structured to employ, they do contribute to the debate, albeit from a limited perspective (*cf.* Tisdell,1990*b*).

Randall (1986) states that some extreme 'ecologists' believe living species to be so interdependent that the removal of any one species will lead to the extinction of all in the long run. If this were so it would be a matter of choosing the optimal path to complete extinction of particular species or groups of species. While there are chains of biological interdependencies, most living things are not as critically and as pervasively linked as this. Nevertheless, interdependencies of species can be wide and take unexpected forms. Indeed, in *some* ecological situations a 'butterfly effect' could operate (Gleick, 1987 Ch. 1), *e.g.* the local extinction of species or a small reduction in its population may give rise to a chain of extinctions of other species. This adds to the uncertainty of the decision-making problem, and neither the market system nor the political system may take account of such possibilities (*cf.* Lecomber, 1979 Ch. 5; Perrings, 1987 Ch. 9).

Clark (1976), using standard economic analysis, points out that when the rate of growth in the value (productivity) of a species is less than the *rate of interest* (the going rate of return on capital as for example indicated by the prevailing rate of interest payable on Government bonds), it may be most economical to eliminate the species. To do so would maximize the net present value (profit) from the available biological resource, *i.e.* the stock or population of the species. But this ignores any spillover or external benefits from saving the species. Furthermore, some economists would argue that the market rate of interest is too high to be used for social discounting. A lower rate of interest – even a zero rate of discounting of the future – should be used, it is suggested, so as to provide greater benefit to future generations (for further discussion *see* Perrings, 1987 Ch. 8). What, then, of a species which gives a negative return on its existence, namely is a pest? Some might argue that it could become valuable in the future. But what if that is not the case? Then the arguments for preservation would not be economic ones but would involve different types of ethics, such as the 'land ethic' expounded by Leopold (1933, 1966; *cf.* Tisdell, 1989).

To a large extent the economic future of Mankind appears to be intertwined with the conservation of other species and the preservation of their life-support systems. As non-renewable resources are depleted, and as entropy of matter is speeded up by human economic activity, the economic welfare of Mankind will become more dependent upon the sustainable use of living renewable resources. Therefore, those who feel a special obligation to provide for distant generations, have a particular reason to want to bequeath a large genetic resource-base, ensuring considerable genetic diversity, to future generations. Without a large genetic resource-base, the available resource-base for distant generations may be meagre. While it is unnecessary to think so far ahead to make out a case for greater conservation effort on economic grounds, to do so adds further support to the importance of conserving living resources.

Concluding Comments and Recapitulation

It goes almost without saying that the economic welfare of Mankind is dependent on the *equable* survival of The Biosphere. In addition, our scope for sustaining or improving our standard of living is linked to our actions in conserving and utilizing The Biosphere, the resources of which are increasingly shared in common. Human economic activity seems to be the greatest single cause of change in the state of The Biosphere, and the major beneficiary from the use of its resources – as inputs to economic production processes, as receptors for the wastes from economic and other human activity, and for direct consumption and enjoyment.

There is a real danger that excessive and profligate human activity will irretrievably destroy the resources of The Biosphere on which human survival and economic welfare depend, unless suitable strategies are adopted globally. While living resources may not be totally destroyed, they may be destroyed and damaged to a much greater extent than is desirable, even given widely-differing values and ethics. Economic welfare will suffer in the near future, and especially so in the distant future, as non-renewable resources are dissipated. For this reason economics and ecology are inseparable in considering the current predicament of Mankind as a component of The Biosphere. The problem is a pressing one, as present economic, social, and political, systems appear at best to be coping with it quite imperfectly. But at least and at last *some* progress is now being made in recognizing the problem.

The challenge facing ecological economics is to understand the problems which we face in managing and interacting with living resources and their life-support systems, to make these problems far more widely known than at present, and to suggest socio-economic and political mechanisms which will enable us to respond to these issues effectively in the future. In doing this, less partial and less insular discipline-based approaches are needed, and new paradigms, in the sense of patterns of activity or scientific assumptions, must be explored for solutions.

This is not to say that no role exists for more traditional economic fields linking economics and living resource conservation and utilization – such as bioeconomics, natural resource economics, environmental economics, agricultural economics, marine resource economics, fisheries economics, forest economics, and so on. But it is to be hoped that ecological economics will provide a wider perspective for all of these fields of enquiry, and will also make a substantial contribution to development economics. While this remains to be seen, there can be little doubt that such an approach is overdue.

Ecological economics has only recently begun to develop as a distinct area of enquiry, and this development has been given impetus by the formation of the International Society for Ecological Economics which has commenced publishing the journal *Ecological Economics*. The development of this area has also received encouragement from the Foundation for Environmental Conservation and its journal *Environmental Conservation*. Mainstream economics has been slow to recognize the major connections between economic activity, industrial development, and the state of The Biosphere – and also, in turn, the consequences of changing ecological conditions for future economic activity and welfare – but there has been considerable expansion in economic thought on this subject since the end of the 1960s.

During the 1980s, the World Conservation Strategy and the report of the World Commission on Environment and Development, *Our Common Future*, pointed out the many ways in which global economy and global ecology are intertwined, and the consequent imperative need for both to be kept in mind when formulating development policies. These global policy documents have given extra stimulus to the development of ecological economics.

It is clear that ecological economics will need to incorporate 'new paradigms' – *e.g.* irreversibilities, discontinuities, 'jumps', and chaos – in order to model and analyse our economic and ecological prospects effectively. It can no longer be accepted that there are no limits to our global economic future, but the future is uncertain because of ecological constraints on Mankind's numbers, greed, and profligacy. We face very difficult social choices because of conflicts in opinions about what is environmentally and otherwise possible, about what our objectives should be, and about how we should react to uncertainty.

The relevant decisions cannot be made in isolation, because they affect all of us; moreover, because of discontinuities and irreversibilities, many decisions cannot be made safely any longer by using trial-and-error procedures. The problems are highlighted by the loss of genetic diversity, which must be regarded as a major threat to the maintenance of economic welfare. Mankind's survival and economic welfare are inextricably linked to the conservation of The Biosphere. It is a challenge for ecological economics to explore these interdependencies further, make them far more widely known than at present and suggest improved socio-economic and political responses to them.

Acknowledgements

I would like to thank the International Steering Committee of the 4th ICEF: Surviving With The Biosphere, and particularly Professor Nicholas Polunin, for inviting me to prepare this paper and helping me to travel to Budapest to deliver it, and Dr Darrel Doessel, University of Queensland, and an anonymous referee, for useful comments on the first draft of it.

References

Arrow, K. J. & Fisher, A. C. (1974). Environmental preservation, uncertainty and irreversibility. *Quarterly Journal of Economics*, 88, pp. 313–9, illustr.

Ayres, R. V. & Kneese, A. V. (1969). Production, consumption and externalities. *American Economic Review*, 59, pp. 282–97.

Bishop, R. C. (1978). Endangered species and uncertainty: The economics of the safe minimum standard. *American Journal of Agricultural Economics*, 60, pp. 10–8.

Bishop, R. C. (1979). Endangered species, irreversibility and uncertainty: A reply. *American Journal of Agricultural Economics*, 61, pp. 377–9.

Boulding, K. E. (1950). *A Reconstruction of Economics*. John Wiley, New York, NY, USA: x + 483 pp., illustr.

Boulding, K. E. (1966). The economics of coming Spaceship Earth. Pp. 3–14 in *Environmental Quality in a Growing Economy* (Ed. H. Jarrett). Johns Hopkins Press, Baltimore, Maryland, USA: xv + 173 pp.

Chisholm, A. (1988). Sustainable resource use and development: Uncertainty, irreversibility and natural choice. Pp. 188–216 in *Technological Change, Development and the Environment: Socio-economic Perspectives* (Eds C. Tisdell & P. Maitra). Routledge, London, England, UK: xv + 351 pp.

Ciriacy-Wantrup, S. V. (1968). *Resource Conservation: Economics and Policies*, 3rd

edn. Division of Agricultural Science, University of California, Berkeley, California, USA: ix + 342 pp.
Clark, C. W. (1976). *Mathematical Bioeconomics: The Optimal Management of Renewable Resources*. John Wiley & Sons, New York, NY, USA: xiv + 352 pp., illustr.
Costanza, R. (1989). What is ecological economics? *Ecological Economics*, 1, pp. 1–7.
Daly, H. E. (1968). On economics as a life science. *Journal of Political Economy*, 76, pp. 392–406.
Daly, H. E. (1973). The steady state economy: Toward a political economy of biophysical equilibrium and moral growth. Pp. 149–74 in *Toward a Steady State Economy* (Ed. H. Daly). W. H. Freeman, San Francisco, California, USA: x + 322 pp., illustr.
D'Arge, R. C. (1972). Economic growth and the natural environment. Pp. 11–34 in *Environmental Quality Analysis* (Eds, A. V. Kneese & B. T. Bower). Johns Hopkins Press, Baltimore, Maryland, USA: ix + 408 pp.
Forrester, J. W. (1971). *World Dynamics*. Wright Allen Press, Cambridge, Massachusetts, USA: xiii + 142 pp.
Georgescu-Roegen, N. (1971). *The Entropy Law and the Economic Process*. Harvard University Press, Cambridge, Massachusetts, USA: xv + 457 pp.
Gleick, J. (1987). *Chaos: Making a New Science*. Viking, New York, NY, USA: xiv + 354 pp., illustr.
IUCN (1980). *World Conservation Strategy: Living Resource Conservation for Sustainable Development*. International Union for Conservation of Nature and Natural Resources, 1196 Gland, Switzerland: pack of *c.* 50 unnumbered pp., illustr., in stiff paper folder.
Keynes, J. M. (1936). *The General Theory of Employment, Interest and Money*. Macmillan, London, England, UK: xii + 403 pp.
Knight, F. H. (1921). *Risk, Uncertainty and Profit*. Houghton Mifflin, Boston, Massachusetts, USA: xiv + 381 pp.
Krutilla, J. V. (1967). Conservation reconsidered. *American Economic Review*, 57, pp. 777–98.
Lecomber, R. (1979). *The Economics of Natural Resources*. Macmillan, London, England, UK: viii + 247 pp., illustr.
Leopold, A. (1933). *Game Management*. Scribner, New York, NY, USA: xxi + 481 pp., illustr.
Leopold, A. (1966). *A Sand County Almanac: with Other Essays from Round River*. Oxford University Press, New York, NY, USA: xv + 269 pp., illustr.
Marshall, A. (1920). *Principles of Economics*, 8th edn. Macmillan, London, England, UK: xxxii + 730 pp., illustr.
Martinez-Alier, J. (1987). *Ecological Economics: Energy, Environment and Society*. Blackwell, Oxford, UK: x + 288 pp.
Meade, J. E. (1952). External economies and diseconomies in a competitive situation. *Economic Journal*, 62, pp. 54–67.
Meadows, D. H., Meadows, D. L., Randers, J. & Behrens, W. (1972). *The Limits to Growth*. Universal Books, New York, NY, USA: ix + 207 pp.
Mishan, E. J. (1967). *The Costs of Economic Growth*. Staples Press, London, England, UK: xxi + 190 pp.
Norgaard, R. B. (1989). The case for methodological pluralism. *Ecological Economics*, 1, pp. 37–57.
Oldfield, M. L. (1989). *The Value of Conserving Genetic Resources*. Sinauer Associates, Sunderland, Massachusetts, USA: xviii + 379 pp., illustr.
O'Riordan, T. (1988). The politics of sustainability. Pp. 29–50 in *Sustainable Environmental Management* (Ed. R. K. Turner). Belhaven Press, London, England, UK: xii + 292 pp., illustr.
Perrings, C. (1987). *Economy and Environment: A Theoretical Essay on the Interdependence of Economic and Environmental Systems*. Cambridge University Press, Cambridge, England, UK: xvi + 179 pp.
Pigou, A. C. (1932). *The Economics of Welfare*, 4th edn. Macmillan, London, England, UK: xxxi + 876 pp., illustr.

Proops, J. L. R. (1989). Ecological economics: rationale and problem areas. *Ecological Economics*, 1, pp. 59–76.
Randall, A. (1986). Human preferences, economics and the preservation of species. Pp. 79–109 in *The Preservation of Species: The Value of Biological Diversity* (Ed. B. G. Norton). Princeton University Press, Princeton, NJ, USA: xii + 272 pp.
Scitovsky, T. (1954). Two concepts of external economics. *Journal of Political Economy*, 62, pp. 143–51.
Shackle, G. L. S. (1952). *Expectation in Economics*, 2nd edn. Cambridge University Press, Cambridge, England, UK: xvi + 144 pp., illustr.
Simon, J. (1977). *The Economics of Population Growth.* Princeton University Press, Princeton, NJ, USA: xxx + 555 pp., illustr.
Smith, V. K. & Krutilla, J. V. (1979). Endangered species, irreversibilities and uncertainty: a comment. *American Journal of Agricultural Economics*, 61, pp. 371–2.
Tisdell, C. A. (1968). *The Theory of Price Uncertainty, Production and Profit.* Princeton University Press, Princeton, NJ, USA: x + 197 pp., illustr.
Tisdell, C. A. (1988). Sustainable economic growth, production and development: An overview of concepts and changing views. *Indian Journal of Quantitative Economics*, 4(1), pp. 73–86.
Tisdell, C. A. (1989). Environmental conservation: economics, ecology, and ethics. *Environmental Conservation*, 16(2), pp. 107–12, 162.
Tisdell, C. A. (1990*a*). Economics and the debate about preservation of species, crop varieties and genetic diversity. *Ecological Economics*, 2, pp. 77–80.
Tisdell, C. A. (1990*b*). *Natural Resources, Growth and Development: Economics, Ecology and Resource-scarcity.* Praeger, New York, NY, USA: xvi + 187 pp.
Tisdell, C. A. & Alauddin, M. (1989). New crop varieties: impact on diversification and stability of yields. *Australian Economic Papers*, 28(52), pp. 123–40.
World Commission on Environment and Development (1987). *Our Common Future.* Oxford University Press, Oxford, England, UK: xvi + 400 pp.
Zeeman, E. C. (1976). Catastrophe theory. *Scientific American*, 234(4), pp. 65–83.

[4]

The Environment and Economic Welfare

CLEMENT A. TISDELL

Today economists have considerable interest in environmental and natural resource economics. But the upsurge of this interest is relatively recent and dates approximately from the beginning of the 1970s. Before that time interest in environmental economics was slight; to the extent that it was discussed, it was as a special aspect of welfare economics (Tisdell 1990a, chs. 2 and 3; Tisdell 1990b).

Economists recognized as an aspect of welfare economics that environmental externalities, spillovers, or side effects from economic activity could lead to market failure — that is, failure of a market economy (in which economic agents pursue their own self-interest) to promote maximum economic welfare. When an externality exists, the social cost of benefits of an activity differ from the private costs and benefits. For example, a company, which operates a factory polluting its neighborhood or contributing to acid rain and not compensating those adversely affected by its pollution, imposes a cost on others that is a part of the social cost of its operation. Ideally, from a social viewpoint, its spillover cost should be taken into account in determining its economic activity — that is, its level of production and the type of techniques that it uses, assuming that different techniques give rise to different degrees of pollution or environmental spillover. However, these spillover costs are *not* a part of the private costs of the company's operation.

If the company follows its own self-interest and, say, maximizes its profit, then it will not take into account the environmental costs

This is a revised and extended version of a seminar presentation given at the Institute of Rural Development, Chinese Academy of Social Sciences, Beijing, May 1989. I wish to thank Professor Cheng Fuhu for inviting me to present such a seminar.

(externalities) that it imposes on others. It will only take into account the actual costs borne by it. Thus, in this case, the market system or the "invisible hand" does not give rise to an economic social optimum.

Arthur C. Pigou (1932) was the first economist to give serious consideration to such issues. He argued that because the market mechanism will not lead to maximum economic welfare in such cases, government intervention is required. He suggested that when unfavorable environmental externalities occur, the offending economic activities should be taxed appropriately by the government so as to align private and social marginal costs. Once social and private marginal costs are equalized by such a policy, private self-interest will promote the social good.

In recent decades, the Pigovian approach to environmental policy has been subjected to much criticism, especially by followers of the "Chicago School." In general, they argue that Pigovian welfare economics is too ready to recommend state intervention in the market as a desirable policy response because Pigovians do not take sufficient account of the transaction costs involved in government intervention and the possibility that government personnel may act in their own self-interest rather than promote the public good. The latter aspect has led some critics to brand Pigovian welfare economics as nirvana economics. Also many Chicago economists suggest that rather than the state intervening (for example, by imposing taxes on pollution), greater headway with environmental problems could be made by extending the system of private property rights to encompass a greater range of environmental goods. While one should be aware of this debate, it cannot be assessed here.

Nevertheless it should be noted that the occurrence of environmental spillovers is not confined to the market system. They also occur under systems of state ownership of production, as in People's Republic of China and the Soviet Union, since individual production units often only have regard to their own unit's interest. For example, administrators in the province of Hebei complain of water pollution from industry in Beijing and Tianjin. This adds to the cost of water purification in Hebei but this is not treated as a cost by industry in Beijing and Tianjin.

Much development and refinement of the theory of externalities has occurred since Pigou's time. However, a growing group of economists finds that this takes a much too restricted view of environmental factors since it does not consider broad relationships between economic growth and the environment. The theory is concerned with ensuring an optimal balance or allocation between economic activities and pollution activities but ignores the total or global environmental and welfare consequences of increased aggregate economic activity (as, say, measured by GDP), population growth, and aggregate pollution. Thus it has been suggested that to act in accordance with the theory and be preoccupied by it could be to ensure optimal balance on the way to ultimate environmental disaster. It is not that the theory is necessarily wrong, but to concentrate on it alone is dangerous because one must also take account of where the earth is headed as a whole.

ECONOMIC GROWTH AND THE ENVIRONMENT

Beginning in the 1970s, there has been a vigorous debate about the relationship between economic growth, the state of the environment, and economic welfare. This debate was triggered and fueled to a large extent by natural scientists. For example, Meadows et al. (1972) in *The Limits to Growth,* extending the speculations of Forrester (1971), claimed that the world was heading for economic and environmental catastrophe possibly within 50 years if it did not curb its rate of economic growth. Global economic collapse was believed to be a threat due to the rapid exhaustion of nonrenewable resources and pollution on a widespread scale, which could "choke off" production and adversely affect human health.

These neo-Malthusians, given their perceived limits to economic growth, recommended that measures be adopted to curb population growth and to limit consumption per capita, at least in advanced countries. Zero population growth (SPG) was considered most desirable, and it was suggested that if this were combined with a minimum level of consumption per capita, a steady-state sustainable economy might be achieved. At least such policies were perceived as a major step toward attaining economic sustainability and survival of mankind in the long term.

All economists were not unsympathetic to the general neo-Malthusian view. Mishan (1967), for example, suggested that many economists had failed to take account of the costs of economic growth. In particular he emphasized that Gross Domestic Product (GDP) and GDP per capita can be poor measures of economic welfare. GDP and GDP per capita may rise and welfare decline, for example, because greater pollution and stress occur.

H. Daly (1980) argued in favor of a steady-state economy with ZPG. Georgescu-Roegen (1976) went further and argued that population should be reduced to a level that can be sustained using renewable resources alone. Such policies were considered necessary to ensure the survival of the human species for as long as possible.

At the same time a group of orthodox economists rejected these views on the basis that nonrenewable resources are much more plentiful and substitutable than claimed by the Club of Rome and neo-Malthusians generally; technological progress is likely to overcome most difficulties; and the price mechanism is likely to have beneficial conservation effects.

Given this debate, we might ask whether greater economic growth necessarily results in increased environmental pollution. This is a very difficult question to answer because environmental quality has many dimensions.

Historically, environmental quality has improved in many respects. In particular, environmental health has improved. The incidence of tuberculosis, typhoid, and many other environmentally related diseases has fallen and average life expectancy has risen.

On the other hand, the extent of the natural environment, especially the living environment, has suffered continual reduction with economic growth. There are many possible illustrations of this trend. For example, the number of living species and the extent of biological diversity is being reduced rapidly — to a large extent because of habitat destruction by humans as natural areas are used more intensively to provide inputs for economic growth and the areas of human habitation are extended. While loss of species occurs normally, the rate of loss that is currently being experienced is not natural but is largely human-induced. Apart from reducing natural diversity that may be valued in itself by human beings, this largely irreversible loss may make it impossible to sustain agricultural production in the long term because a diverse genetic bank would no longer be available for breeding resistance to diseases and pests that often evolve into new forms. To give another example, in Xian, China, a stone tablet (stele) from the Tang Dynasty illustrates and describes the best natural scenic spots of the Xian (Changan) area. Of the eight scenes listed, approximately 1,000 years later only two remain: Lishan Mountain and Huaqing Hot Springs; and Hushan Mountain. The remainder seem to have disappeared largely as a result of human activity.

We now face environmental problems with dimensions unknown in the past. We face global pollution problems. These include the greenhouse effect and the destruction of the ozone layer. Furthermore, environmental damage can spread over very wide areas, for example, by acid rain resulting from fossil fuel use and nuclear fallout resulting from nuclear power station accidents. Thus the whole earth is environmentally interdependent to an extent previously unknown.

This raises new policy challenges particularly because science is unlikely to be able to reverse much of this environmental damage once it is done. Furthermore, if we allow population and GDP to continue to increase, we become more and more dependent on scientific advance to sustain or maintain our standard of living. Thus, as the level of income and population rises, the costs of not being able to maintain technological progress rise substantially.

THE LIVING ENVIRONMENT

Of particular concern is the disappearance of the natural living environment. Economists have still not given this matter the attention that it deserves. Disappearance of species is now happening at a very rapid rate, primarily due to the economic activity of humans.

The *World Conservation Strategy,* IUCN (1989) advocates sustainable economic development. It argues that unless adequate attention is paid to the conservation of living resources and their life support systems, economic development may prove to be unsustainable. It also recommends limitations on population growth and restrictions on consumption, among other things.

Some of the particular problems noted in *World Conservation Strategy* are

The disappearance of genetic diversity, which means greater constraints for sustainable agricultural production in the future.

Loss of arable land and agricultural land due to such factors as urban encroachment and soil erosion.

Loss of forests, especially tropical rain forests, which results in reduced biological diversity, may add to erosion and soil degradation, and to the greenhouse effect.

Loss of fisheries production due to water pollution and land reclamation in estuarine areas.

Pollution of water resources generally and growing water shortages.

All are major problems and should be taken into account in planning economic development.

All these factors could limit or reduce the production of physical goods. But it should be recognized that the living environment also has value for nonmaterialistic economic ends. It can be important for tourism, which relies on natural resources. Furthermore, some individuals value the mere existence of particular species or natural attractions irrespective of whether they view or use them. In addition to existence value, there may be a desire to bequeath such natural resources to future generations — bequest value. In addition, a further value can sometimes be ascribed to the conservation of a natural attraction, namely *option* value, the value that individuals place on the possibility of enjoying the attraction in the future if they so desire. While the asset may not be used now, option value arises from the possibility that it may be of use in the future. To keep an option open can be valuable.

The Brundtland Report (World Commission on Environment and Development 1987), which was commissioned by the United Nations, places more emphasis than *World Conservation Strategy* does on global environmental problems, the need to take into account economic considerations, and the interconnectedness of problems. It states that there is not a separate environmental crisis, a separate energy crisis, or a separate economic development crisis. They are all one and they cannot be compartmentalized by regions, sectors, or broad areas of concern (environmental, economic, social). The report emphasizes that it is "impossible to separate *economic* development issues from environment issues," and that it is "futile to attempt to deal with environmental problems without a broader perspective that encompasses the factors underlying world poverty and international inequality" (World Commission on Environment and Development 1987).

Before discussing global environmental issues, particularly in relation to the Third World, it is worthwhile to outline alternative sets of economic policies for controlling pollution or environmental degradation as suggested in the recent economic literature. Most of these microeconomic policies have been discussed in a partial framework and independently of variations in macro-variables.

MICROECONOMIC POLICY INSTRUMENTS FOR THE CONTROL OF POLLUTION OR ENVIRONMENTAL DEGRADATION

Some individuals argue that it is futile to concentrate on "fine-tuning," or policies for optimal adjustment of existing pollution, while neglecting macro-variables or economic growth variables, such as growth of GDP and population. But the fact of the matter is that we need to consider both.

For example, in the case of China, population control policies may not only help to raise income per head but also have a favorable environmental impact. However, if China is to maximize the value of its production, it must also give much more attention to correction of environmental externalities from production. Let us consider some possible policy instruments that may be used for controlling pollution and environmental degradation.

Figure 2.1 illustrates some of the alternative policy approaches to pollution control or control of environmental damage. In this figure the curve *DBE* represents the marginal net private benefit, or profit from being able to release a pollutant to the environment, and curve *OBC* represents the marginal spillover, or externality costs (marginal environmental costs), of such emission. In the absence of government control, economic units pursuing their own self-interest will release x_2 units of the pollutant to the environment per period.

FIGURE 2.1 — Microeconomic Policy Measures for the Control of Pollution

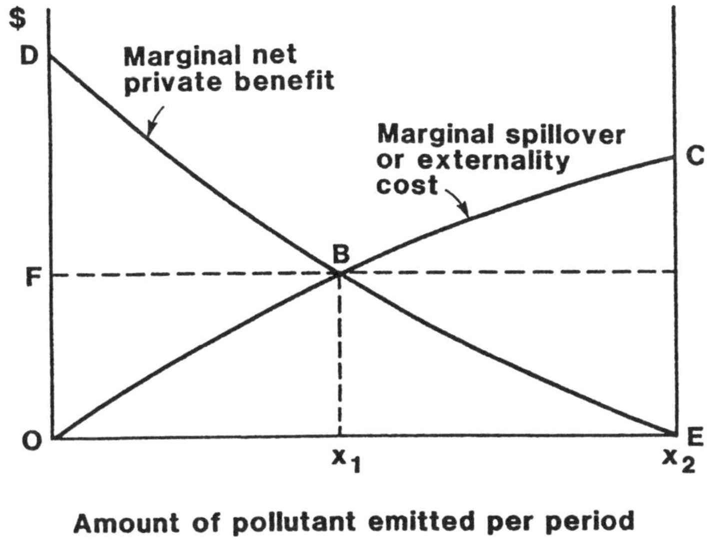

But from a social economic viewpoint, emissions of only x_1 per period are optimal.

Some of the alternative policies that can be adopted to ensure an optimal level of pollution emissions (for further discussion see, for example, Tisdell 1982) include the following:

A *tax* on the emission of the pollutant. A tax on each unit of pollutant emitted of *OF* would bring about the required result. In this case the polluter pays, or at least those benefiting from the emission of the pollutants pay.

A *subsidy* on reduction of pollution emission. In this case, a subsidy of *EG* for each unit reduction in pollution emission would bring about the required result.

Marketing of pollution rights. If the government issues pollution certificates for a total quantity of emission of x_1 and then auctions these in a competitive market, these should sell at an equilibrium price equal to *OF*.

Legal restrictions on emissions. The problem is that these rarely take account of the relative gains to different units of being allowed to pollute, whereas the other three measures mentioned above do allow units to adjust their response to the measures according to net benefits of them doing so. They are more likely to promote adjustment of control of pollution at minimum social cost.

Property rights clarification. Some economists see the creation of private property rights in environmental goods as creating a means to bring about optimal pollution control. For example, in the case just considered, the law may either give individuals the right to a pollution-free environment or give the right to polluters to pollute. In the former case, polluters would need to negotiate with those subjected to pollution and pay them compensation. In the latter case, those disadvantaged by pollution would need to pay or bribe polluters to reduce their pollution. Coase (1960) in particular argues that either approach can lead to an optimal level of pollution from an economic efficiency point of view. However, the efficiency of this approach depends on the transaction costs of negotiation being low and the costs of protecting property rights being low. Both of these conditions are often difficult to satisfy as far as environmental goods are concerned.

This, of course, is not to deny the importance of property rights issues in relation to the environment. For example, it is well known that common-property resources (those for which there is common access) are unlikely to be optimally conserved and/or husbanded. This, for example, applies to fish outside exclusive economic fishing zones, to underground water supplies that are being used by a large number of farmers for irrigation, and in general to living resources to which there is common access. Today the atmosphere is being used as a common-property sink for disposing of waste gases by all countries and this appears to be posing increasing global risks. Let us consider some of the issues raised by such global questions.

GLOBAL ENVIRONMENTAL PROBLEMS AND THE RESPONSIBILITY OF DEVELOPED AND DEVELOPING NATIONS

Today some types of environmental deterioration threaten the whole earth, and all countries contribute to this deterioration. One such case is the buildup of greenhouse gases in the atmosphere largely from carbon dioxide emissions as a result of the burning of fossil fuel. Others include destruction of the ozone layer by chlorofluorocarbons (CFCs). But even the loss of genetic diversity has similar dimensions.

Since each nation contributes to the damage, this raises the question of what responsibility each should have for moderating their contribution to such environmental danger. Should the burden (as some have suggested) be borne principally by developed nations? What are the prospects for global cooperation for dealing with these environmental issues?

Any solution to the problem is not straightforward because it involves income redistribution questions, and any agreed social solutions are highly unstable. The latter is so because although all nations collectively have an interest to limit such damage, each has an incentive to free-ride, that is, to continue to pollute globally irrespective of whether other nations limit their pollution emissions. This global environmental situation involves (near) pure public goods (or bads). It is akin to the prisoners' dilemma problem of game theory.

However, there can be little doubt that the issue of the relative responsibility of developed and developing nations for global pollution and for the promotion of environmental conservation will be a major issue in the decades ahead. In particular, the developed nations will not be able to ignore the issues involved. This is because the developing nations threaten to become the biggest single source of global pollution within the next 40 years. Already China, India, and Brazil are major contributors to global carbon dioxide emission. It is estimated that within 40 years developing countries will most likely be contributing more than half of global emissions of carbon dioxide. This is because of their large populations and modest industrialization and income expansion plans (Myers, Ehrlich, and Ehrlich 1990).

For example, China's energy use grew at about 5 percent per year during the 1980s, and it plans to increase this growth in the future. Already China has overtaken the United States as the world's number one coal burner. It now accounts for 10 percent of global carbon emissions even though its per capita carbon emissions are only one-tenth of those of the United States.

By the year 2000 China hopes to burn almost twice as much coal, and by the year 2030 it may be contributing 20 percent of global carbon emissions (Oppenheimer and Boyle 1990). This seems likely if its industrialization plans materialize and its population reaches the projected figure of 1.5 billion. It follows that even if the United States were to cease using coal altogether in the next decade and not replace it with other fossil fuels, China's planned expansion in coal use in the next decade would more than compensate for this. The situation is similar for India and Brazil. Because of the large populations involved, it is clear that even modest industrialization plans in such countries will have major global environmental consequences. Furthermore, several developing countries, including China, plan to increase their national stocks of refrigerators utilizing CFCs, which are a major source of global warming.

Naturally, developing countries are unenthusiastic about limiting their use of fossil fuels for global interests if this is likely to impede their quest to promote economic growth and raise per capita incomes. Their agreeing to such a strategy may relegate them to low income status for the indefinite future. At the very least, they are likely to demand income transfers from developed countries as compensation for adopting low energy use policies. The extent to which developed countries will be willing to make such transfers voluntarily remains to be seen. However, current signs are not encouraging in this regard. In recent years the developed countries have actually reduced the level of their aid to the Third World and there has been a net outflow of capital from the Third World to the developed world.

AID TO THE THIRD WORLD AND ENVIRONMENTAL PROTECTION

It is now widely argued that one cannot expect poor nations to be deeply concerned about environmental protection and that it is necessary to promote their economic development in order to achieve global environmental objectives. This, however, raises dilemmas about the extent to which economic development and growth of such countries is compatible with environmental protection. Even modest levels of economic growth in such countries can, as observed above, have major global environmental consequences because of their very large populations. If the global environmental effects of measures to raise per capita incomes of developing countries are to be minimal, a large reduction in their current levels of population seems to be necessary. While reducing per capita incomes in developed countries would help to reduce the environmental pollution load, it may not offset projected increases in emissions from the Third World. In addition, it might be observed that any change in relative incomes between major nations would change international balances of power. Therefore, nationalism may become a stumbling block. Because of this, some thinkers are calling for an end to nationalism and a move toward world government or at lest new forms of international governance.

Dr. M. Tolba, executive director of UNEP, recently called for the developed countries to provide more aid to less developed ones for assistance with their environmental progress. In his view only the developed countries can afford the luxury of environmental protection: "Developing countries — caught in the money squeeze and the vice-grip of poverty — cannot. The plight of the least developed countries continues to worsen, because of rising debt service payments, dropping export revenues, disappearing investment flows and accelerating resource destruction" (Tolba 1990b, 5). He goes on to suggest that developing countries need more foreign aid — some of which should be specifically for environmental protection — and that the source for diversion of funds could be the annual global military budget estimated to be nearly US$1 trillion.

It is true that developed countries in providing aid to developing countries now take more account of the environmental impact of projects, and institutions like the World Bank also take this into account. However, this has been a source of complaint from some quarters. It is argued that the need to build environmental protection measures into projects adds to their cost. This means that fewer projects can be undertaken for the same amount of aid, or developing countries are forced to borrow more funds to complete projects, which adds to their debt and interest burden. However, the fairness (or lack thereof) of imposing environmental protection conditions in relation to aid and loans to developing countries may need to be assessed in terms of who benefits. The position is likely to be viewed differently depending upon whether the environmental benefit (and often associated economic benefit) of such conditional aid or loans goes principally to developing countries or to developed countries.

CONCLUDING COMMENTS

The world faces environmental challenges of a global type that it has not faced before. While much progress has been made in devising policies to control pollution within national boundaries, the chief difficulty at present is to devise effective, workable, and acceptable means for the international governance of global pollution and environmental degradation. Given the income distribution questions involved and the possible changes in relative economic power of nations that may stem from income redistribution, a ready solution does not appear to be in sight. One view is that a solution will be particularly difficult to achieve until a world government is established that represents individuals rather than nations.

Selected Bibliography

Coase, R. H. (1960). "The Problem of Social Cost." *Journal of Law and Economics* 3 (October): 1–44.

Daly, H. (1980). *Economics, Ecology and Ethics.* San Francisco: Freeman.

Forrester, J. W. (1971). *World Dynamics.* Cambridge, MA: Wright-Allen.

Georgescu-Roegen, N. (1976). *Energy and Economic Myths: Institutional and Analytical Economic Essays.* New York: Pergamon.

IUCN (1980). *World Conservation Strategy.* Glands, Switzerland: International Union for the Conservation of Nature and Natural Resources.

Meadows, D. L., J. Randers, and W. Behrens (1972). *The Limits to Growth: A Report of the Club of Rome's Projection on the Predicament of Mankind.* New York: Universe Books.

Mishan, E. J. (1967). *The Costs of Economic Growth.* London: Staples Press.

Myers, N., P. R. Ehrlich, and A. H. Ehrlich (1990). "The Population Problem: As Explosive as Ever?" Paper delivered at the Fourth International Conference on Environmental Future, "Surviving with the Biosphere," Budapest, Hungary, April.

Oppenheimer, M., and Boyle, R. H. (1990). Dead Heat: *The Race Against the Greenhouse Effect.* New York: Basic Books.

Pigou, A. C. (1932). *Economics of Welfare,* 3d ed. London: Macmillan.

Tisdell, C. A. (1990a). *Natural Resources, Growth and Development: Economics, Ecology and Resource Scarcity.* New York: Praeger.

—— (1990b). "Ecological Economics and the Environmental Future." Paper presented at the Fourth International Conference on Environmental Future, "Surviving with the Biosphere," Budapest, Hungary, April.

Tolba, Mostafa K. (1990b). "Building Environmental Institutional Framework for the Future." Baer-Huxley Memorial Lecture, Fourth International Conference on Environmental Future, "Surviving the Biosphere," Budapest, Hungary, April.

World Commission on Environment (1987). *Our Common Future.* London: Oxford University Press.

The Middle East Business and Economic Review, Vol. 4, No. 1 (1992)

THE NATURE OF SUSTAINABILITY AND OF SUSTAINABLE DEVELOPMENT

CLEM TISDELL
University of Queensland

ABSTRACT
The rational pursuit of sustainability, global or otherwise, is only possible if we know what sustainability is, or, more exactly, if we know what we want to sustain and in what respect. This paper outlines and discusses a number of different concepts of sustainability. These include sustaining (1) intergenerational economic welfare, (2) the span of existence of the human species, (3) resilience in production and economic systems, and (4) sustaining community. This paper includes a number of criticisms of the applications of Rawl's theory of justice in the context of sustainability and intergenerational equity.

1. Introduction

The rational pursuit of sustainability, global or otherwise, is only possible if we know what sustainability is or, more exactly, if we know what we want to sustain and in what respect. Many individuals now claim that they favour sustainability, the attainment of a sustainable society or the achievement of sustaainable development. On closer examination, however, it is often found that they want to sustain different things. Some wish to promote and sustain close-knit caring (local) communities, some want to sustain the economic welfare of future generations, some want to ensure that the human species is sustained for the longest span of time possible and others wish primarily to sustain biodiversity. These are not exactly the same goals even though the means to achieve them may well run parallel up to a point.

A hallmark of most contemporary proponents of sustainable development is their emphasis on the need to conserve natural resources and natural environments as a means towards achieving their goals. Many take the view that existing institutions, including market mechanisms are likely, in the absence of pro-conservation directives, to conserve natural resources and environments inadequately, thereby making for non-sustainable development.

Let us consider some of the main concepts of sustainability which have been raised in the economic literature or closely associated literature.

2. Sustaining Intergenerational Economic Welfare

Teitenberg (1988, p.33) claims that "the sustainability criterion suggests, that at a minimum, future generations should be left no worse off than current generations". In broad terms, this amounts to saying that the actions of present generations in using resources should not reduce the standard of living of future generations below that of present generations. The ethical basis of this is often taken to be John Rawls'(1977) principle of justice. Given that every individual could have been born into the situation of any other, and that everyone in a hypothetical original position involving a 'veil of ignorance' would be uncertain of when and in what situation they would be born, they would, it is argued, opt for equality of 'income' unless inequality was to the advantage of all. Thus it would be fair or just to honour this hypothetical original contract.

However, once one adopts Rawls' principle one must not only apply it between generations but also within them for it also implies that a similar degree of equality is just between existing individuals. In particular it would seem to imply on a global scale that much larger income transfers should be made from developed to less developed nations than those taking place now or likely to take place in the foreseeable future. Indeed, we appear to have the irony at present that resource transfers from less developed nations exceed those in the opposite direction, and the developed nations are reducing their aid to the Third World.

Somewhat weaker equity rules between individuals now and in the future are also espoused. They are that the basic needs of all should be met because of the chance circumstances we all face or may face. In essence all should be assured a minimum standard of living, without standards of living being necessarily made equal.

The World Commission on Environment and Development (1987, p. 43) states that "sustainable development is development that meets the needs of the present without compromising the ability of future generation to meet their own needs". The interpretation, of course, all depends upon how one interprets the term 'needs' but if it implies basic needs then this is similar to the view just outlined.

The Commission goes on to say that overriding priority should be given to the concept of 'needs', in particular the essential needs of the world's poor and that full account should be taken of the influence of the state of the environment on the ability to meet present and future needs.

Pearce, Markandya and Barbier (1989, p. 2) express a similar point of view stating that "sustainable development places emphasis on providing for the needs of the least advantaged in society (intragenerational equity) and a fair treatment of future generations (intergenerational equity)". They suggest as a general principle that: "future generations should be compensated for reductions in the endowments of resources the endowments of resources brought about by the actions of present generations" (Pearce, Markandya and Barbier,1989, p.3).

Capital endowments by present generations are seen as one possible means of compensation and human capital endowment such as increases in scientific and technological knowledge are seen as particularly attractive bequests.

A number of critical observations can be make about the application of Rawls' theory of justice in this context. These include the following:

1. Should only human beings count (as is the case in the Rawlsian applications) in determining what is just? If we could have been born as any other individual could we not have been born as any other living thing, say an animal of some type? In other words, what is the appropriate universe of possibilities to consider? Could also, for example, an Australian have been born an Indian? What difference does it make to the application of Rawls' theory if one believes in reincarnation as do many Bhuddists and Hindus? Given these points, the Rawslian principle of justice is not unassailable in its strict form (Tisdell 1990b). If the possibility is accepted that a human being might have been born as any living thing this would seem to establish on the Rawslian approach some ethical responsibility for the caring for other living things.
2. The number of individuals who will be born in the future is uncertain but it is partially under the control of present generations. This of course raises a practical difficulty for determining the size of the appropriate bequest for future generations. It also means that we face the difficulty that future population sizes are not uncontrolled variables. If we are scrupulous about observing the logic of Rawls, we should ask what are the wishes or desires of those who could have been born but were not. If any of us could have also been in that position what would we have opted for? Would we have chosen to live if we were provided with at least bare subsistence? Optimal human population policy is not effectively addressed by the approach of Rawls and of those environmental economists following his line.
3. Rawls may overemphasize the role of chance rather than choice in our lives. Chance appears to be made dominant in his theory but arguably in our life we also have some choice, including in the amount of effort to expend on various goals. Thus his principle tends to de-emphasize reward for effort (Cf. Tisdell, 1982, pp. 416,417).

On a somewhat different point, the idea that capital can a suitable compensatory bequest for future generations is appealing to proponents of economic growth. But such capital formation may hasten environmental deterioration and may disappear itself long before the natural resources which produced it would have. Man-made physical capital is relatively impermanent whereas natural living resources such as forests and species have in normal circumstances much longer periods of longevity.

3. Maximising the Span of Existence of the Human Species

A rather different point of view of sustainability is that embraced by economists such as Hermann Daly (1980) and Georgescu-Roegen (1971, 1976). They suggest that our basic goal should be to ensure the survival of the human species for as long as is possible - in Daly's words, as long as is compatible with God's will. These are essentially man-centred approaches but differ from the above cases in relation to objectives. I have discussed these to some extent critically elsewhere (Tisdell, 1988). Daly suggests that our basic aim should be to ensure that the maximum number of people live in the maximum time-span for which it is possible for the human species to survive. He suggests in practice that this involves zero population growth, restrictions on the rate of use of non-renewable resources and restricting consumption per head to a minimum acceptable level. In his view, this will result in a sustainable society.

Georgescu-Roegen (1976), on the other hand, while favouring restricted per capita consumption, argues that human population should be reduced to that level which can be supported by the use of renewable resources alone. This, in his view, provides the best chance for the human species to survive for as long as is possible given the inexorable working of the Law of Entropy. This, I suppose, raises the question of whether Georgescu-Roegen has taken the concept of sustainability to extremes. In my view this is so. I cannot argue about these views here, but I have made some criticisms of these approaches elsewhere (Tisdell, 1988).

It might not be noted that neither of the above approaches make particular allowances for the "rights" of other species and in that respect they are similar to the previously mentioned economic approach. It is, however, true that Hermann Daly (1980) suggests that Christians have some duty to care for other living things, even if this is not a major duty. But these approaches, on the whole, avoid the open-endedness or fundamental indeterminacy of Rawlsian-based approaches. For example, Daly's approach is relatively clear on its population objective. Nevertheless, Daly's objective may not appeal to us all.

4. Resilience of Production and Economic Systems

Some thinkers such as Conway (1987) and Barbier (1987) have looked upon the sustainability of systems as their resilience, that is, their ability to recover when subjected to shocks. This is an interesting and useful concept which may have parallels with the concept of stability of equilibria (Tisdell, 1988). It is also discussed by Redclift (1987). As the amount of biodiversity is reduced, as variety of all types is reduced in the world and as the environment is degraded by economic processes, economic activity may become less resilient when subjected to environmental and other shocks. Thus desirable production and economic states may no longer be sustainable in the long-term given the possiblities of stresses on the system or shocks to it. System may become subject to jumps and irreversibilities (Tisdell, 1980a). The issues involved are worthy of continuing study and are of considerable relevance in modern times.

5. Non-Economic Concepts of Sustainability

There appear also to be a number of concepts of sustainablity which are not dominantly economic. Douglass (1984) suggests that sustainabilty of community is an important concept. It is a complex concept but it appears to be favoured in particular by some 'alternative "life-style" groups. It is a complex concept but it implies amongst other things full participation in the social-political systems of the community, a fair distribution of income and co-operation with nature rather than domination of it (Alauddin and Tisdell, 1988). Social structures which take power away from local communities, such as multinational corporations or large corporations with headquarters in distant places, are seen as being a threat to a sustainable economic order in harmony with nature (Tisdell, 1983, 1989).

A number of concepts of sustainability have also been established by a group of ecologists and conservationists who believe that Nature has a right to exist independently of the wishes of Mankind. Possibly Aldo Leopold is representative of this group which desire basically to sustain Nature in its diversity. Aldo Leopold (1933, 1966) sees Man as a part of holistic organic community in which Man has no right to exterminate a part of it. His "land ethic" was developed in opposition to the view that Nature should be manipulated or exterminated to satisfy the narrow economic interests of Man. It might be noted that prior to adopting this philosophy, Leopold was involved in USDA campaigns to control mammalian pests. Possibly this ethic will gain ground, at least in modified form. It is possible that humanity will come to accept increasing responsibility for Nature, and do so not merely for man-centred ends or purposes. Even within this framework, there would be a role for economics (Tisdell, in preparation).

This by no means exhausts the lists of possible non-economic concepts of sustainability. they are merely put forward to indicate that economists are not alone in the field in providing prescriptions for a "good society or for a good world".

6. Concluding Comments

Some of the early proponents of sustainability and of sustainable development have now become wary of the concepts because they feel that these concepts have become vague and debased in popular use, or because confusion has resulted from the multiplicity of concepts which have emerged. But to dismiss these concepts for these reasons would be premature. A multiplicity of concepts might even be regarded as a bonus provided they are defined and appropriately identified. Multiplicity of concepts provides scope for expanding knowledge in a number of different directions.

Already discussions of sustainability by economists have advanced our understanding of the world in several respects. Existing institutions mechanisms, including market mechanisms, for resource allocation have been found to be wanting from the point of view of economic sustainability (in one or more of its forms). The adequacy of traditional cost-benefit analysis has been questioned and modifications or alternatives to it have been suggested. Most recently Pearce, Markandya and Barbier (1989, pp. 127-129) suggested that "sustainability be integrated" into cost-benefit analysis by imposing a constraint (requirement) that for a group of projects "environmental damage (i.e. natural capital depreciation) should be zero or negative". One's mind "boggles" at how this damage will be measured but at least it is a positive suggestion for consideration. It might also be claimed that those who have argued for the application of a safe minimum standard in the preservation of species (Bishop, 1978, 1979) belong to the sustainability stream of thought. They reject conventional approaches adopted in cost-benefit analysis for taking account of risk and uncertainty (Chrishol, 1988; Tisdell 1990c). They argue that uncertainty rather than risk characterizes environmental decision-making. Proponents of sustainability concepts appear to believe that because of uncertainty less structured and mechanical approaches to choice than those traditionally employed in economics, especially neo-classical economics, are appropriate.

Another advance which is closely connected with the sustainability mode of thought is the development of environmental or natural resource accounting. This accounting involves the modification of national income accounts (which were developed principally with the needs of Keynesian economics in mind) so as to provide a measure of sustainable income (See for example, Pearce, Markandya and Barbier, 1989, Ch. 4), and/or to indicate national welfare more accurately, even if still crudely.

Thus in the last twenty years or so there have been a number of significant advances in economic thought which have been stimulated by sustainability concepts and debate. This stimulation is continuing and we can expect new worthwhile contributions in the years ahead.

REFERENCES

Alauddin, M. and Tisdell, C. (1988) "New Agricultural Technology Predicaments and Prospects", pp. 35-62 in C.A. Tisdell and P. Maitra (Eds.), *Technological Change, Development and the Environment: Socio-Economic Perspectives*, Routledge, London.

Barbier, E.B. (1987) "The Concept of Sustainable Economic Debelopment", *Environmental Conservation*, Vol. 14, No. 2, pp. 101-110.

Bishop, R.C. (1978) "Endangered Species and Uncertainty: The Economic of a Safe Minimum Standard", *American Journal of Agricultural Economics*, Vol. 60, pp. 10-18.

Bishop, R.C. (1979) "Endangered Species and Uncertainty: A Reply", *American Journal of Agricultural Economics*, Vol. 61, pp. 376-379.

Chisholm, A.H. (1988) "Sustainable Resource Use and Development: Uncertainity, Irreversibilty and Rational Choice", pp. 188 216 in C. Tisdell and P. Maitra (Eds.), *Technological Change, Development and the Environment Socio-Economic Perspectives*, Routledge, London.

Conway, G.R. (1987) "The Perspectives of Agroecosystems", *Agricultural Systems*, Vol. 24, pp. 95-117.

Daly, H. (1984) *Economics, Ecology and Ethics: Essays*

Towards a Steady-state Economy, Freeman, San Francisco.

Douglass, G.K. (1984) "The Meanings of Agricultural Sustainabiltiy", pp. 3-99 in G.K. Douglass (Ed.) *Agricultural Sustainability in a Changing World Order*, Westview Press, Boulder, Colorado.

Georgescu-Roegen, N. (1971) *The Entropy Law the Economic Process*, Harvard University Press, Cambridge, Mass.

Georgescu-Roegen, N. (1976) *Energy and Economic Myths: Institutional and Analyical Economic Essays*, Pergamon Press, New York.

Pearce, D., Markandya, A., and Barbier, E.B. (1989) *Blueprint for a Green Economy*, Earthscan Publications, London.

Rawls, J.R. (1971) *A Theory of Jusice*, Harvard University Press, Cambridge, Mass.

Redclift, M. (1987) *Sustainable Development: Exploring the Contradictions*, Methuen, London.

Tietenberg, T. (1980) *Environmental and Natural ResourceEconomic*,s 2nd Edition, Scott, Foresman and Company, Glenview, Illinois.

Tisdell, C.A. (1982) *Microeconomics of Markets*, Wiley, Brisbane.

Tisdell, C.A. (1983) Conserving Living Resources in Third World Countries", *International Journal of Environmental Studies*, Vol. 22, pp. 11-24.

Tisdell, C.A. (1988) "Sustainable Development: Differing Perspectives of Ecologists and Economists, and their Relevance to LDCs", *World Development*, Vol. 16, No. 3, pp. 373-384.

Tisdell, C.A. (1989) "Environmental Conservation: Economics, Ecology and Ethics", *Environmental Conservation*, Vol. 16, No. 2, pp. 107-112, 162.

Tisdell, C.A. (1990a) "Ecological Economics and the Environmental Future", *Discussion Paper in Economics No. 28*, Department of Economics, University of Queensland, Queensland 4072, April 1990. Revised version to be published in J. Burnett and N. Polunin (Eds.), *Surviving with the Biosphere*, Edinburgh University Press, forthcoming.

Tisdell, C.A. (1990b) *Natural Resources, Growth and Development: Economics, Ecology, and Resource-Scarcity*, Praeger, New York (in press).

Tisdell, C.A.(1990c) "Economics and the Debate about Preservation of Species, Crop Varieties and Genetic Diversity", *Ecological Economics*, Vol. 2, pp. 77 - 90.

Tisdell, C.A. (in Preparation) *Economics of Environmental Conservation*, Elsevier Science Publishers, Amsterdam.

World Commission on Environment and Development (1987) *Our Common Future*, Oxford University Press, Oxford.

Economic Analysis & Policy Vol.24 No.2, September 1994 **133**

SUSTAINABILITY AND SUSTAINABLE DEVELOPMENT: ARE THESE CONCEPTS A HELP OR A HINDRANCE TO ECONOMICS?

Clem Tisdell
Department of Economics
The University of Queensland
Qld 4074

The paper provides an overview of concepts of sustainability and sustainable development relevant to economics, discusses ways in which these have altered processes of economic evaluation and considers whether they have been a help or hindrance to economics. At least on the surface, there appears to be widespread support for the desirability of achieving sustainable development. This is reflected in international fora and policy decisions as well as within Australian, e.g., by the agreement of Australian governments in 1993 to a National Strategy for Ecologically Sustainable Development. Concern about sustainability has led to demands for new forms of social accounting, mainly demands to modify or supplement standard national income accounting by natural resource and environmental accounting. Furthermore, traditional methods of project evaluation and social choice have come under increased scrutiny. It has been suggested that traditional social cost-benefit analysis should be constrained by safe minimum standards and by restrictions to ensure maintenance of natural resource and environmental stocks. While a wide range of modern economic analysis has been influenced by such developments, neoclassical growth theories and their stemming new growth theories show no influence. Despite the optimism of the World Bank, it is still unclear whether continuing **global** economic growth (on scales which most countries would like to achieve) is compatible with improved environmental quality and a long-term reduction in economic scarcity. Sustainable development and **desired** levels of economic growth globally could be incompatible.

1. INTRODUCTION

The desirability of achieving sustainable development has now obtained widespread acceptance. Internationally the goal of achieving sustainable development was first given prominence by the United Nations Conference held in Stockholm in 1972 which marked the beginning of two decades of research and debate about this subject culminating in the United Nations Conference on Environment and Development (UNCED) held in Rio de Janiero in 1992. Throughout the whole debate, the main emphasis has been on the need to conserve natural resources and natural environments in order to achieve sustainable development.

However, emphasis in relation to the 'required' conservation of natural resources has changed. In the 1970s and early 1980s most attention was focussed on the need to conserve non-living natural resources such as minerals and fossil fuel deposits and to control pollution, e.g., acid rains, global warming, water pollution, that is the need to address the type of concerns raised by the Club of Rome (Meadows *et al.*, 1972). Beginning in the early 1980s and given momentum by the *World Conservation Strategy* (IUCN, 1980), focus shifted to the need to conserve living resources in order to obtain sustainable development. By the end of the 1980s this was the dominant theme in the literature on sustainable development and was signalled by the frequent addition of the world 'ecologically' to the cryptogram 'sustainable development'. Sustainable development in many quarters came to be identified with ecologically sustainable development (ESD) which amongst other things emphasised the need to conserve biological diversity in order to maintain economic development.

This new emphasis was not only apparent internationally but was also reflected in Australian policy considerations. In December, 1992, The Council of Australian Governments endorsed the *National Strategy for Ecologically Sustainable Development* (1992) (NSESD). The goal of this strategy is to achieve 'development that improves the total quality of life, both now and in the future, in a way that maintains the ecological processes on which life depends' (NSESD, 1992, p.8). Three core objectives are stated:

"• to enhance individual and community well-being and welfare by following a path of economic development that safeguards the welfare of future generations
• to provide for equity within and between generations
• to protect biological diversity and maintain essential ecological processes and life-support systems."

As will be discussed later, the first two objectives are incorporated into the objective most widely stated by economists for sustainable development. The third objective seems to be an ecocentric side-condition or constraint because it appears to favour protection of biological diversity up to a point as a worthy goal in itself. This is followed by a set of guiding principles for NSESD. In some cases however, there could be conflict between objectives and in the guiding principles. To deal with this issue NSESD (1992, p.9) states:

> "These guiding principles and core objectives need to be considered as a package. No objective or principle should predominate over the others. A balanced approach is required which takes into account all these objectives and principles to pursue the goal of ESD."

Although, this is not a very helpful statement from the viewpoint of determining appropriate degrees of trade-off, it does provide some political recognition of the desirability of maintaining biological diversity.

The NSESD was an outcome of nine ESD Working Groups which produced reports on sustainability covering agriculture, forest use, fisheries, manufacturing, mining, energy use, energy production, tourism and transport. In addition, two further reports were produced on intersectoral issues and the greenhouse phenomenon making eleven reports in all. Together with the NSESD, this led to a comprehensive

Economic Analysis & Policy Vol.24 No.2, September 1994 **135**

coverage of the issues. Both these reports and NSESD recognise the important role which economic instruments can play in achieving ESD. Despite this, since 1992, relative political emphasis seems to have shifted from ESD as far as Australian Governments are concerned to achieving greater aggregate employment and economic growth. There appears to be less willingness to forgo maintenance and generation of employment and economic growth for natural resource conservation. Political reconciliation of environmental conservation, employment and economic growth for reasons discussed by Tisdell (1994), remains difficult despite the allure of the phrase, 'sustainable development'.

2. WHY CONCERN ABOUT SUSTAINABLE DEVELOPMENT AND SUPPORT FOR IT?

A basic concern amongst those fostering the concept of sustainable development has been that existing socio-economic systems may lead to economic growth or production that is not sustainable and consequently future generations, could be impoverished rather than favoured economically by economic growth. Thus attempts to reduce economic scarcity by economic growth could create greater scarcity for future generations so making the economic problem for them a more serious one than otherwise. Hence, interest was motivated by concern for the future of humankind and its welfare. In addition, many nature-lovers were pleased to embrace the concept of ecologically sustainable development as a political rallying point because it favoured the preservation of biodiversity. The concept appeared to reconcile those embracing anthropocentric ethics with those espousing ecocentric ethics.

Many different reasons were put forward as to why existing socio-economic systems could fail to achieve sustainable development. They include the reasons listed below.

(i) Failure to control aggregate demands on natural resources due to expanding populations and levels of economic use and demand on these.

(ii) Failure of the socio-economic system to take adequate account of environmental externalities or spillovers.

(iii) The presence of open-access or common-property natural resources such as fish in the open sea or the use of the global atmosphere.

(iv) Short-sighted pursuit of the benefits of the present over future gains, for example, due to impatience amongst individuals or to political systems that require visible evidence of the short-term 'success' of governments to ensure their continuation in office.

(v) Deficiencies of socio-economic systems in making allowances for environmental risks and uncertainties particularly when they involve, as they often do, spillovers, especially global ones. Systems may fail to keep options open when it is optimal from a collective point of view to retain options.

(vi) Attitudes, policies and indicators appropriate to past economic problems may persist and block the development of new policies. For example, national income statistics were primarily developed to provide indicators of levels of production of goods and services and so likely employment generation. Those interested in sustainable development have severely criticised GDP as a welfare indicator because it ignores the question of sustainability. They argue that new methods of national accounting are needed such as natural resource accounting.

(vii) Socio-economic systems tend to be myopic, reacting to trends and localized conditions but there are considerable risks from an environmental viewpoint in extrapolating past trends. Furthermore, responses to localized conditions may not result in a global optimum or a satisfactory outcome.

Economists have differed about the extent to which that the above problems exist and on the extent to which specific policies are required to achieve sustainable development. Optimists have tended to dismiss the sustainability problem on the grounds that technological progress and capital accumulation will be able to offset or more than offset depletion of natural resources and environmental degradation and argue that rising incomes will limit population growth. Another group of economists, while in general agreement with this laissez-faire group, believe that although there are some failures in the economic systems, these failures can often be traced to the inadequate use of markets as allocative mechanisms. Their remedy is to extend the market system by ensuring clear definitions of private property rights in relation to the use of natural resources and the environment. Given this point of view, open-access property should be converted to private property (at least to the extent economical), rights to pollute or not to pollute should be clearly defined so obligations become certain and market-type mechanisms such as the use of tradeable pollution or natural resource-use rights should be implemented. This group of optimists basically believe that with the thorough-going adoption of market mechanisms, sustainability becomes a non-issue.

While it is true that greater use of market mechanisms can assist with the conservation of natural resources, they are not a panacea for achieving sustainable development. It is not always economic to establish markets, including private property rights. So there are limits to the economics of market-marking. Usually the most efficient socio-economic mechanisms are likely to involve a mixture of markets and hierarchies, because of the importance of market transaction costs (Pelikan, 1988). In practice, then this means that the debate needs to concentrate not on whether an all pervading market system should be established but on the spheres in which the establishment of markets is likely to be efficient.

Developments involving extension of property rights in recent years have included UNICLOS (The United Nations International Convention on the Law of the Sea). This enabled nations to extend their exclusive fishing and other natural resource rights for 200 nautical miles from their coastlines, thus giving national property rights and greatly reducing the amount of open-access resources on the high seas. In turn, this has enabled individual nations to adopt fishing policies to conserve and manage fishing stocks within their exclusive fishing zones. For example, some nations such as Australia and New Zealand have introduced individual transferable quota schemes for some types of fisheries, e.g., for southern

Economic Analysis & Policy Vol.24 No.2, September 1994 137

blue fin tuna in Australian waters. In parts of the United States, e.g, Southern California, transferable air pollution quotas (quotas for emissions of air pollutants) are being introduced. These all appear to be positive policies to use economics to help conserve the natural environment by establishing property rights and market systems. However, they do little to control rising aggregate demands on all natural resources. They are directed at the balance problem rather than problems involving the aggregate utilisation of natural resources (Tisdell, 1991, section 2.2).

While an extended market system can go far to promote conservation of the environment and sustainable development, it is not sufficient.

3. CONCEPTS OF SUSTAINABLE DEVELOPMENT AND SUSTAINABILITY

There are now several concepts of sustainable development and of sustainability of phenomenon of socio-economic relevance and new concepts are evolving. Therefore, to avoid confusion, it is useful to classify or codify these concepts, otherwise the concepts may fall into disrepute as a result of loose usage.

The following are some the conceptions of sustainable development identifiable in the literature and their sources.

(i) Development ensuring that future generations can meet their basic needs (WCED, 1986).

(ii) Development ensuring that the per capita incomes of future generations are no less than that of present generations (Pearce *et al.*, 1989).

(iii) Development or economic change designed to maximize the length of existence of the human race (Georgescu-Roegen, 1971; Daly, 1980).

(iv) Development that preserves 'community' that is, close sociological bonds and interrelationships within communities (Douglass, 1984).

(v) Development that maintains biological diversity and essential ecological processes and ecosystems (IUCN, 1980).

The first three concepts are associated with economists. The interpretation of the first depends upon how one defines basic needs. The second concept is the most widely accepted definition as far as economists are concerned of sustainable development and several economists suggest that its satisfaction is necessary for intergenerational equity, and argue this on the principles of justice developed by J.R. Rawls (1971). However, as Tisdell (1993, Ch. 9) argues, these principles are anthropocentric and problematic.

The third conception, sustaining the length of survival of the human race may be in conflict with the second conception. To maintain or increase per capita income, may hasten the disappearance of the human race due to growing natural resource depletion. In fact, Georgescu-Roegen has argued that maintaining current levels of per capita income, even with zero population growth, will lead to an earlier end to the human race than would be possible with falling levels of population and lower levels of per capita income. Thus, in his view the effect of achieving sustainable development in the second sense without population levels being reduced would be to hasten the end of the human race due to use or entropy of natural resources.

The last two concepts are sociological (social) and ecological concepts respectively. While some writers see these aspects as being of fundamental importance in themselves, others have seen the achievement of these types of sustainability as essential for economic sustainability.

Barbier (1987) suggests that sustainable development requires economic sustainability and social sustainability to be simultaneously satisfied. Be that as it may, what is not clear is whether all of these different requirements for sustainable development can be satisfied simultaneously in practice. It is unlikely that all can be simultaneously satisfied. If this is so, then one has to decide to what extent to forgo some (e.g., preservation of biodiversity to achieve) or more nearly achieve others (e.g., economic sustainability).

While the above are the best known concepts of sustainable development, sometimes other requirements are added as well such as political sustainability or the attainment of a host of objectives that are believed to be desirable. In the latter case, sustainability becomes little more than a list of normative requirements and often the sustainability characteristic is lost and buried under many objectives which appear to have little to do with sustainability and sometimes appear to be very much in the vein of wishful thinking. One also has to guard against the idea that sustainability in the abstract is desirable. It is not worth sustaining all the socio-political systems for example that exist in the world and we can be pleased that some of the more obnoxious dictatorial political systems of the past are less prevalent now.

A subsidiary but significant related theme to discussions of sustainable development has been consideration of the sustainability of production techniques or types of productive economic activity as well as the sustainability of returns from individual economic projects. This approach to sustainability involves a consideration of the choice of techniques or projects and has implications for cost-benefit analysis. This perspective has been given considerable attention in relation to agriculture.

In this respect at least two types of evaluation can be identified as far as sustainability is concerned:

(i) whether or not a technique, e.g. form of land management will have sustained use; and

(ii) whether or not the use of a technique will result in a significant characteristic such as level of incomes, rate of return or the potential of a natural resource, such as soil, to produce being maintained.

It is of course possible that the latter type of sustainability could influence the former but it does not necessarily determine the former. For example, the use of a particular agricultural technique may result in rates of return falling and the natural productivity of the soil being reduced but the technique may continue in use because there are no viable economic alternatives to it. Or, although the natural productivity of the soil is reduced, the price of the product may rise to compensate for increasing costs of supply and so the technique may continue in use, and so on.

An example of the first type of approach (the prospects for the sustained use of a technique or form of resource management) is the Framework for Evaluation of

Economic Analysis & Policy Vol.24 No.2, September 1994 **139**

Sustainable Land Management (FESLM) developed by the Food and Agriculture Organization of the United Nations in conjunction with a number of other major institutions of international significance. It specifies that a system of land managmenet to be sustainable would need to satisfy the following 'five pillars':

(1) maintain or enhance production/services (Productivity)
(2) reduce the level of production risk (Security)
(3) protect the potential of natural resources and prevent degradation of soil and water quality (Protection)
(4) be economically viable ([Economic] Viability)
(5) and socially acceptable (Acceptability)."

(quoted in Smyth, Dumanski *et al.*, 1993, p.7).

Given this point of view, (desirable) sustainable land managmenet practices are those that maintain or enhance productivity, increase security, protect the potential of natural resources and are economically viable and socially acceptable. It is not perfectly clear whether the framers of FESLM predict that such systems will be adopted or whether it is desirable that such systems be adopted or both. However, the framers of FESLM seem to believe that a system of land managmenet will not be sustained in use unless all the pillars are satisfied.

An example of the second approach is that of Gordon Conway (1985, 1987). He sets up a set of characteristics for judging the desirability of agricultural techniques of which sustainability of economic returns or productivity is just one. The four factors which he believes should be taken into account in judging the desirability of a technique are listed below.

(i) The **level** of yields, income or economic returns which it generates.
(ii) The **degree of variability** or instability of these.
(iii) The **sustainability** of these defined as their ability to recover after being subjected to an environmental shock. In other words, the resilience of the system when subjected to environmental stresses.
(iv) The **equitability** of the techniques in terms of their impact on the distribution of income.

Techniques which provide high levels of yield or economic returns, with a low degree of viability, a high degree of sustainability and result in relative equality of income are to be preferred in Conway's view to those that do not. In his view many modern agricultural techniques perform well in terms of the level of yields or economic returns generated but poorly in comparison to traditional techniques on the basis of the other attributes. While Conway does not tell us what trade-offs are desirable between the attributes, he believes decision-makers should take these all into account in reaching decisions about choice of techniques.

It should be noted that his concept of sustainability corresponds to stability in terms of dynamic models. An equilibrium is stable in terms of a dynamic model for some set of shocks if after the occurrence of these shocks the system tends to return to the equilibrium. Conway claims that the level of the yield/returns of traditional agricultural systems have a relatively stable equilibrium but those of modern agricultural system a relatively unstable one.

Conway's modelling relies on the impact of environmental shocks. These can result in returns not being sustained. However, even in the absence of environmental shocks some systems of economic production fail to sustain yields because 'a mining effect' is present. The technique or system of production used may regularly deplete a natural resource on which production depends and returns or yields may fall over time in a continuous fashion, unless compensatory action is possible. Some systems of land management, for instance, lead to regular reductions in the natural fertility of the soil and yields can be expected to fall continuously (even if slowly) unless this is compensated for, for example, by increasing applications of artificial fertilizer. However, in the end such means of compensation may no longer be efficacious, let along economical.

In an attempt to take account of this aspect of sustainability, Lynam and Herdt (1989) consider trends in economic returns from different techniques of production. In their view if the rate of change of the trend line of the economic value of output divided by the value of inputs for a technique is non-negative, the technique exhibits sustainability from an economic point of view. A problem, however, with many new agricultural techniques is that there has not been an opportunity to observe their performance over a long time period and, of course, one always has to be wary about extrapolating past trends.

A spin-off of the sustainability debate as far as agriculture is concerned is that a number of agricultural organizations are giving much more consideration in agricultural research to developing techniques resulting in greater sustainability of yields or economic returns. It has become apparent that 'green revolution' technologies lack this sustainability under some conditions (Alauddin and Tisdell, 1991) and their spread onto some marginal lands poses a serious risk in this regard, e.g., soils of low fertility irrigated from underground (unreliable) water supplies as in the Barind Track in Bangladesh. As discussed by Lynam and Herdt (1989) international agricultural research organizations are increasingly seeking to undertake research which promotes sustainability of output or yields.

4. SOME IMPLICATIONS OF SUSTAINABILITY CONCEPTS FOR STANDARD ECONOMIC EVALUATIONS

Consideration of sustainability as an important characteristic of economic and environmental systems has resulted in critiques of standard economic indicators of welfare and methods of project evaluation. In particular the use of GDP as an indicator of welfare has been seriously criticised and doubts have been raised about the value of the net present value criterion and cost-benefit analysis as decision-making devices. Let us consider those matters in turn.

GDP, or usually GDP per capita, is widely used as a crude measure of economic welfare and as a means of making international welfare comparisons. Nevertheless, it is a very deficient measure of economic welfare because it only takes account of commodities involving formal exchange. GDP does not take account of the value of services freely provided by nature, the value of leisure-time and the value of services provided by humans without formal exchange, e.g., within households. Furthermore, GDP may rise in value when economic welfare has definitely fallen. For example, increases in commercial production might lead to higher pollution

Economic Analysis & Policy Vol.24 No.2, September 1994 **141**

levels and greater transport delays the cost of which in terms of greater health bills, amenity loss, extra transport costs, etc. may very well exceed the value of extra commercial production. Nevertheless, GDP will rise not only on account of the extra commercial production but because costs such as extra medical bills, fuel costs and so on result in greater formal exchanges and will be added to GDP.

In addition, GDP measurement takes no account of its sustainability. In fact, it may rise substantially because natural resources are being unsustainably used. It has been argued that if sustainable development is the aim then new macroeconomic indicators are needed such as those suggested by natural resource accounting. Several suggestions have been made as to how to improve macroeconomic indicators of economic welfare. Young (1992) discusses adaptation and supplementation of national accounts from the perspective of sustainable development and welfare measurement. Doessel and Gounder (1991) review human welfare indices and their application.

Given the significance of sustainable development and the importance of the conservation of natural resources and environment for this, many policy-makers would like to have indicators of how their nation is faring in terms of sustainable development and conservation of natural resources and the environment. Standard systems of national accounts, such as the United Nations's System of National Accounts, are inadequate as indicators of human welfare and sustainable development.

This is not surprising because they were not designed for the above specific purposes. These accounts were originally to assist governments in market economies to achieve full employment and a desired degree of macroeconomic stabilisation. They are a direct outcome of the economic analysis of Lord Keynes (1936) which links the level of aggregate employment and economic activity in a nation in the short run to the level of aggregate effective demand (Tisdell, 1990, Ch. 2). Subsequently those accounts came to be used for analysis of economic growth and GDP, NNP, GNI and NNI, particularly expressed as per capita values, came to be used as indicators of economic welfare.

In order to deal with welfare/sustainability issues as far as national accounting and data collection are concerned, three basic approaches are being tried. They are listed below.

(1) **Adjustments to national income aggregates for changes in environmental/natural resource conditions**, e.g., adjustments to GDP or NNP to reflect sustainable welfare more accurately. This would provide an indicator in **value** terms.

(2) **Physical resource and environment accounting systems** such as those being used in Norway. These concentrate on measuring physical or real changes in the stock of natural resources and the state of the environment.

(3) **Integrated natural resource and economic accounts** involving both valuation and the measurement of physical entities. The United Nations Statistical Office (UNSO) has proposed a System of Integrated Environmental-Economic Accounting as has Peskin (1991).

Let us briefly consider each of these approaches without going into details.

Re 1): Two adjustments to national income aggregates such as GDP and NNP have been proposed to allow for environmental change and variations in natural resource stocks. These are: (a) deductions of expenditure providing protection against adverse environmental change and (b) deduction of a sum of money to allow for reductions in natural resource stocks, that is a sum of money to allow for the net depreciation or depletion of these stocks. However, the appropriate sum to deduct for defensive environmental expenditure, item (a), is not always clear. For example, to what extent is air conditioning installed to counteract outside air pollution or to moderate **natural** variations in temperature and weather conditions. It would be inappropriate to deduct expenditure in relation to the latter purpose. Furthermore, some non-defensive environmental costs should be considered for deduction such as lost earnings due to increased ill health because of pollution, the value of lost earnings and leisure-time due to increasing traffic congestion and reduced amenity value because of environmental deterioration.

It is generally argued in relation to systems of national accounting that NDP is a better indicator of welfare than GDP because it allows for the depreciation of man-made capital. However, national accounting systems make no allowance for the depreciation or depletion of natural stocks, that is capital-like assets provided by nature, even though the income or production obtained from their use is included. Thus the treatment of man-made capital and natural resource stocks (natural capital) in the existing natural accounts is asymmetric. Consistency requires, it is argued, this asymmetry to be removed. Two different methods have been proposed for depreciating natural capital: (1) the 'user-cost' method (Serafy, 1989) and (2) the 'net price' approach (Repetto *et al.*, 1989). These are discussed in detail by Bartelmus *et al.*, (1993).

The application of both of these methods is restricted to natural resources which produce commercial products, e.g., mineral resources and forests harvested for saleable timber. In general no allowance is made for non-consumptive use of national resources. Both methods rely on the neoclassical economics framework for estimation purposes and assume perfectly competitive industry and capital markets. These together with other assumptions may limit the reliability of the estimates (Bartelmus *et al.*, 1993, p.127).

Re: 2) Given the difficulties of assigning monetary values to changes in natural resouce stocks and the state of the environment, it has been suggested countries might do well to concentrate only on measuring the real or physical changes involved stating these in a set of 'satellite' accounts to accompany standard national accounts (SNA). This approach has been adopted in France and Norway. According to Peskin (1991, p.180) these separate or 'satellite' accounts to SNA should ideally describe 'flows of resources, materials (including pollutants), and energy that underlie any economic system', so that the physical counterpart to the economic circular flow is fully described and measured. The UNSO (United Nations, 1984) has set out a Framework for the Development of Environment Statistics (FDES) intended to produce a systematic and comprehensive coverage of environmental characteristics (United Nations, 1984, 1991).

Re: 3) The most ambitious and comprehensive approach to natural resource/

environmental accounting is one specifying physical characteristics of natural resource/environmental assets, placing valuation on these and linking these to SNA. The United Nations (1991, p.137) has developed a method for doing this which links FDES data bases to natural resource accounts and then to standard national accounts and a pilot study has been undertaken in Papua New Guinea with a view to applying this method (Bartelmus *et al.,* 1993).

Bartelmus *et al.,* (1993, p.126) reported that the PNG pilot study faced many difficulties mainly because of PNG's weak environmental data base. Furthermore, they were concerned about some of the assumptions that they needed to make to get their results and suggested that the value of doing such a relatively costly exercise would depend upon how it was proposed to use the actual results, say for environmental policy purposes. The purpose of collecting environmental/natural resource data needs to be specified in advance and systems or frameworks for this collection should be assessed in terms of this purpose.

Systems for adjusting national income aggregates such as GDP and NNP to allow for changes in the environment and natural resources may have little policy value except to sound a note of warning that natural resource stocks are falling and environmental conditions are deteriorating in an undesirable way. By the time this becomes apparent from aggregate *ex post* figures damage is likely to have been irreversibly done. There appears to be a general view that it may be a better use of limited resources to concentrate on improving physical measurement of changes in the environment and natural resource stocks along the lines indicated in the Framework for the Development of Environment Statistics than adjusting national income aggregate to allow for such factors. Paul McCarthy (1993, p.7) indicates that the Australian Bureau of Statistics has questioned 'the priority that should be given at this time to investigating 'green GDP', given the amount of statistical development required (relative to other environmental indicators). The view that further development of physical indicators is required before values can be placed on environmental factors is shared by national accountants and environmental statisticians in most countries'.

Analysis of sustainability has also had an impact on economic evaluation in other ways. Safe minimum standards have for example been suggested as a means of conserving resources and keeping options open thereby favouring sustainability. It has for example been claimed that the cost of conserving safe minimum populations of many species is low and the potential benefits of doing so are very high or alternatively the potential costs of opportunities forgone by not conserving a safe minimum population of a species can be very high. Thus risk-avoidance suggest that one should err in favour of conservation of species. Proponents of this view such as Ciriacy-Wantrup (1968) and Bishop (1978, 1979) are critical of the use of cost-benefit analysis as a basis for making decisions about natural resource conservation.

This view appears to be shared by Pearce *et al.,* (1989) who suggests that while the social selection of economic projects should make use of social or extended cost-benefit analysis, such analysis should be subject to constraint. The constraint that they propose is that economic projects as a whole should not result in a decline in the stock of natural environmental assets. This is not to say that some environmentally damaging projects cannot be undertaken but they must be **offset** by other projects which cause environmental improvement. Thus for example, an electricity company which builds a fossil fuel power station which emits greenhouse gases might be allowed to do so provided it engages in re-afforestation to provide a sink for absorbing these gases. Or, a company might be allowed 'to develop' a wetland for a housing estate provided that it creates an artificial wetland elsewhere which compensates for the loss of the natural one. Just, however, what is adequate or suitable compensation is likely to be a controversial matter. Furthermore, the constrained social CBA rule faces other difficulties some of which are discussed by Tisdell (1993, Ch. 8).

The above rule suggests that it is unsatisfactory from a sustainability point of view to let the stock of 'natural' environmental resources decline below their present value. It therefore restricts the substitution of man-made capital for natural resource-capital. It makes the maintenance of natural resource/environmental stocks central to sustainability. This, however, a very strong requirement. It raises the question of whether substitution between man-made types and natural capital is ever acceptable. A number of writers suggest that substitution of man-made capital for natural resource capital to improve knowledge (to promote technological progress) can be compatible with sustainable development. Debate continues about the extent to which natural resource depletion is compatible with sustainable development.

Despite the sustainability concerns of environmental economics, mainstream economic growth theory has been little affected. This theory was dominated by the Solow-Swan model which sees economic growth as depending on three main factors, namely, the accumulation of man-made capital, technological progress and the increase in the labour force as determined by growth in the size of the population (Jones, 1975; Tisdell, 1990, Ch. 3). In these models economic growth is not constrained by natural resource availability, let alone environmental factors. Natural resources simply play no explicit role in those models which suggest that the recipe for enhanced economic growth is a faster rate of man-made capital accumulation and a higher rate of technological progress. Whereas neoclassical theories of economic growth as typified by the Solow-Swan model assumed technological progress to be exogenous, 'new' theories of growth consider (Dowrick, 1993) it as being endogenous and subject to variation by policy. Romer (1990, 1994), for example, takes this point of view and also sees increases in human capital as important for economic growth. In these new models externalities, learning-by-doing and economies of agglomeration all become significant considerations for economic growth. However, natural resource and environmental constraints continue to be ignored as was the case in the Solow-Swan models. As far as **this** group of economic growth theorists are concerned, discussions of sustainable development appear to have been like 'water off a duck's back'.

Despite the apparent non-engagement of the above group in the environmental debate, sustainability issues have led to make other changes in economic evaluation. The importance of environmental externalities are now more widely recognized as

Economic Analysis & Policy Vol.24 No.2, September 1994

are their likely implications for the sustainability of production. There has been renewed debate about the relationship between the rate of interest and sustainability (Arndt, 1993) and appropriate methods and rates for discounting of future benefits and costs (Kula, 1992). This debate will no doubt continue.

5. ECONOMIC GROWTH, RESOURCE SHORTAGES AND ENVIRONMENTAL QUALITY – IS SUSTAINABLE DEVELOPMENT POSSIBLE?

Economic theorists have and still do hold divergent views about the sustainability of economic growth. While classical economists such as Malthus (1798) and Ricardo (1817) were very much aware of possible limits to economic growth, by the end of the nineteenth century an optimistic point of view prevailed and this has remained dominant in this century. Most economists, subject to a few minor qualifications, appear to believe that economic growth is good, that it results eventually in stationary populations and that the market system will make appropriate allowances for reductions in stocks of natural resources provided that it is allowed to operate widely and freely. Furthermore, it is expected that continuing technological progress will make for a bright future. However, continuing technological and scientific progress is accepted as a matter of **faith**. But can humanity expect the largesse from the conucopiea to continue *ad infinitum*.

Empirical evidence about the compatibility of economic growth, natural resouce availability and maintenance of environmental quality is mixed. This is evident from a recent report of the World Bank on development and the environment (World Bank, 1992). In order to see if economic growth, designed to achieve higher per capita incomes, is associated with a deteriorating or an improving environment and with increasing natural resources scarcity (1) time series or (2) cross-sectional observations may be used. The *World Bank Report 1992* uses both to come basically to the following conclusion. Economic growth and improvement in environmental quality and increased economic availability of natural resources are not only compatible but economic growth may be necessary for such results. In this context economic growth in the view of the World Bank is a blessing.

The Bank provides time-series evidence to support its view that the world is not running out of marketed non-renewable energy and raw material resources. For example, it provides data that between 1970 and 1988 proven reserves of energy and mineral reserves rose in relation to annual consumption. In addition, the World Bank has a figure (Box Figure 1.4) suggesting that the real long-run prices for nonferrous metals have shown a downward trend over the period 1900 to 1990 (World Bank, 1992, p.37). Declining real prices would indicate reduced economic scarcity. However, the data are insufficient to prove the Bank's point. In relation to non-ferrous metal prices, if the data before 1920 are ignored, there is no clear tendency for a long-run decline in such prices and the trend could easily be a precursor to rising future prices. In any case, the question needs to be answered of why it is appropriate to project the past trend to the future.

Concerning economic growth and environmental quality, the Bank mostly relies on cross-sectional data and provides evidence that for many indicators of environmental quality, environmental quality improves with the level of income achieved by the country (see for example World Bank, 1992, pp.11, 46, 55). This seems to be so for water quality (as measured by dissolved oxygen in rivers), to be so to some extent for urban air pollution levels and for access to safe water and sanitation. The main adverse environmental impacts of a high-income levels are seen as rising municipal rates (per capita) and rising carbon dioxide levels, (per capita). The latter adds to greenhouse gases but has a global rather than a local or national effect of perceived significance because of the major externality involved. The clear message of the World Bank is that the environmental benefits of economic growth can be expected to outweigh any disbenefits, for virtually all countries.

Encouraging evidence is also provided that points to a slow down in rates of global population increase suggesting that the world, as a whole, is completing its demographic transition and that levels of human population will stabilize in the next century.

A further powerful argument in favour of economic growth is the positive association between expected length of life of humans and income levels. Since mortality and morbidity appear to be significantly reduced by improved environmental quality, this suggests that from a human perspective environmental quality has improved on the whole – at least in vital respects.

However, there are also some worrying environmental trends. The living natural environment is taking a 'battering'. The rate at which humans, by their activities, are extinguishing other species and reducing biodiversity is far beyond the natural rate of extinction and has increased in every century since 1700 (Cf. World Bank, 1992, p.58). Indeed, it seems that the rate of extinctions of species being brought about by humankind exceeds the rates at which mass extinction of species have occurred in the past due to unusual natural events (Cf. Gould, 1990). Much of this extinction is coming about as a result of habitat destruction – the loss of natural wildlife habitats and their replacement with relatively uniform human-modified environments, modified to expand commercial and subsistence production and support a growing human population. A vast area of natural vegetation cover has been lost and in many developing countries (and in some more developed ones) and the loss continues. It is estimated for example that in the Indomalayan realm from 68 percent to 85 percent of the land area covered by the main vegetation types has been lost. In the Afrotropical area (excluding wetland/marsh) 55 percent to 60 percent of the land area originally covered by the main vegetation types has been lost. The loss is continuing and if anything is likely to accelerate as many less developed counties in these regions embark on efforts to increase their economic growth. The outlook from a non-anthropocentric point of view is therefore gloomy. Furthermore, there is a possibility that this loss of biological resources will limit sustainable economic growth (Tisdell, 1990, 1991).

The World Bank (1992), like the World Commission on Environment and Development (1987) is optimistic that economic growth and environmental improvement can be combined. Indeed, economic growth in less developed countries is seen as a prerequisite for environmental improvement, and it has been

Economic Analysis & Policy Vol.24 No.2, September 1994 **147**

argued that the economic growth of less developed countries need complementary economic growth in developed countries (Tisdell, 1991, Ch. 12).

To support its case, the World Bank (1992) appeals to the empirical evidence relying mainly on cross-sectional data to compare environmental conditions in low income, middle income and high income countries. Its basic conclusion is that except for one or two indicators (e.g. emissions of greenhouse gases, such as CO_2) environmental conditions are best in high income countries. This suggests that economic growth results in a better environment. But of course, environmental quality changes involve an index problem if the environment improves in some respects but deteriorates in others. Furthermore, to some extent high income countries depend upon resource imports from less developed ones which enables them to export some of their environmental problems. Biodiversity loss continues and higher incomes on a global scale *may* not be sustainable under current conditions. Also examining time series for long-run prices of nonferrous metals and other data, the World Bank concludes that we are not running out of non-renewable energy and raw materials. Whether the Report is too optimistic only time will tell.

6. CONCLUDING COMMENTS

Concepts of sustainable development and sustainability originating since the early 1970s have had a substantial impact on intellectual thought and significant consequences for policy-making, even though a small group of neoclassical economists have been little influenced by such concepts. As indicated, these concepts have added many new dimensions to economic evaluation. Unfortunately, many authors fail to realize that there are several concepts of sustainable development and sustainability and that new concepts are being developed. This often leads to confusion. It would be useful to have a systematic taxonomy of these concepts.

As to whether concepts of sustainability and of sustainable development are a help or hindrance to economics, on balance they are helpful because they provide a challenge to traditional neoclassical theory and provide a vehicle for meaningful interaction between economists and non-economists in addressing resource-use issues. This is not to say that all of the sustainability and sustainable development literature is based on firm foundations. The virtue of the concepts is that they bring a somewhat different perspective to resource-use issues and therefore have become a means to extend our knowledge in new directions. The world is complex and we shall never know it fully. The best we can hope for is to explore it from different, limited angles. Given that a pluralistic approach to theory is desirable, significant new perspectives such as those provided by sustainability considerations should be welcomed.

REFERENCES

Arndt, H.W. (1993), *50 Years of Development Studies*, National Centre for Development Studies, Australian National University, Canberra.

Barbier, E.B. (1987), "The Concept of Sustainable Economic Growth", *Environmental Conservation*, 14, pp.101-110.

Bartelmus P., E. Lutz and A. Schweinfest (1993), "Integrated Environmental and Economic Accounting: A Case Study for Papua New Guinea", in E. Lutz (ed.) *Toward Improving Accounting for Environment*, World Bank, Washington, pp.108 -143.

Bishop, R.C. (1978), "Endangered Species and Uncertainty: The Economics of a Safe Minimum Standard", *American Journal of Agricultural Economics*, 60, pp.10-18.

Bishop, R.C. (1979), "Endangered Species Irreversibility and Uncertainty: A Reply", *American Journal of Agricultural Economics*, 61, pp.377-379.

Ciriacy-Wantrup, S.V. (1968), *Resource Conservation and Policies*, 3rd ed., Division of Agricultural Science, University of California, Berkeley.

Conway, G.R. (1985), "Agroecosystems Analysis", *Agricultural Administration*, 20, pp.31-35.

Conway, G.R. (1987), "The Properties of Agroecosystems", *Agricultural Systems*, 24, pp.95-117.

Daly, H. (1980), *Economics, Ecology and Ethics*, Freeman, San Francisco, Ca.

Doessel, D. and Gounder, R. (1991), "International Comparisons of Levels of Living and the Human Development Index: Some Empirical Results", *Discussion Paper No. 72*, Department of Economics, University of Queensland, Brisbane, 4072, Australia.

Douglass, G.K. (1984), "The Meaning of Agricultural Sustainability". Pp.3-29 in G.K. Douglass (ed) *Agricultural Sustainability in a Changing World Order*, Westview Press, Boulder, Ca.

Dowrick, S. (1993), "New Theory and Evidence on Economic Growth and their Implications for Australian Policy", *Economic Analysis and Policy*, 23, pp.105-121.

El Serafy, S. (1989), "The Proper Calculation of Income from Depletable Natural Resources". In Y. Ahman, S. El Serafy and E. Lutz (eds) *Environmental Accounting for Sustainable Development: An UNDP – World Bank Symposium*, The World Bank, Washington.

Georgescu-Roegen, N. (1971), *The Entropy Law and the Economic Process*, Harvard University Press, Cambridge, Ma.

Gould, S.J. (1990), *The Individual in Darwin's World*, Edinburgh University Press, Edinburgh.

IUCN (1980), *World Conservation Strategy*, International Union for the Conservation of Nature and Natural Resources, Glands, Switzerland.

Jones, H.G. (1975), *An Introduction of Modern Theories of Economic Growth*, Nelson, London.

Keynes, J.M. (1936), *General Theory of Employment, Interest and Money*, Macmillan, London.

Kula, E (1992), *Economics of Natural Resources and the Environment*, Chapman and Hall, London.

Lynam, J.F. and R.W. Herdt (1989), "Sense and Sustainability: Sustainability as an Objective in International Agricultural Research", *Agricultural Economics*, 3, pp.381-398.

Malthus, T.R. (1798), *An Essay on the Principle of Population as it Affects the Future Improvement of Mankind*, J. Johnston, London.

McCarthy, P. (1993), "Problems and Prospects for 'Green' Gross Domestic Product (GDP) in the Australian National Accounts", Australian Bureau of Statistics, Canberra, mimeo. A paper presented to the Environmental Economics Conference, Canberra, November, 1993.

Meadows, D.L., J. Renders and W. Behrens (1972), *The Limits of Growth: A Report for the Club of Rome's Projection on the Predicament of Mankind*, Universe Books, New York.

NSESD (1993), *National Strategy for Ecologically Sustainable Development*, AGPS, Canberra.

Pearce, D.W., A. Markandya and E.B. Barbier (1989), *Blueprint for a Green Economy*, Earthscan Publications, London.

Pelikan, P. (1988), "Can the Imperfect Innovation Systems of Capitalism be Outperformed?" in G. Dosi, C. Freeman, R. Nelson, G. Silverberg and L. Soete, *Technical Change and Economic Theory*, Pinter Publishers, London, pp.370-400.

Peskin, H.N. (1991), "Alternative Environmental and Resource Accounting Approaches", in R. Costanza (ed.) *Ecological Economics: The Science and Management of Sustainability*, Columbia University Press, New York, pp.176-193 .

Rawls, J. (1971), *A Theory of Justice*, Harvard University Press, Cambridge, Ma.

Ricardo, D. (1817), *The Principles of Political Economy and Taxation*, London.

Romer, P. (1990), "Endogenous Technological Change", *Journal of Political Economy*, 98, pp.S71-S102.

Romer, P. (1994), "The Origins of Endogenous Growth Theory", *Journal of Economic Perspectives*, 8, No. 1, pp.3-22.

Smyth, A.J., J.K. Dumanski, G. Spendjian, M.J. Swift, P.K. and P.K.Thornton (1993), *FESLM: An International Framework for Evaluating Sustainable Land Management*, World Soil Resources Reports (73), Land and Water Division, Food and Agriculture Organisation of the United Nations, Rome.

Tisdell, C.A. (1990), *Natural Resources, Growth and Development*, Praeger, New York.

Tisdell, C.A. (1991), *Economics of Environmental Conservation*, Elsevier Science Publishers, Amsterdam.

Tisdell, C.A. (1993), *Environmental Economics*, Edward Elgar, Aldershot, UK.

Tisdell, C.A. (1994), "Conservation, Protected Areas and the Global Economic System: How Debt, Trade, Exchange Rates, Inflation and Macroeconomic Policy Affect Biological Diversity", *Biodiversity and Conservation*, 3, in press.

United Nations (1984), *A Framework for the Development of Environment Statistics*, United Nations, New York.

United Nations (1991), *Concepts and Methods of Environment Statistics: Statistics of the National Environment*, United Nations, New York.

WCED (World Commission on Environment and Development) (1986), *Our Common Future*, Oxford University Press, New York.

World Commission on Environment and Development (1987), *Our Common Future*, Oxford University Press, Oxford.

World Bank (1992), *World Development Report 1992: Development and the Environment*, Oxford University Press, New York.

Young, M.D. (1992), *Sustainable Investment and Resource Use*, UNESCO, Paris and The Parthenon Publishing Group, Carnforth, UK.

ELSEVIER

Ecological Economics 22 (1997) 289–291

ECOLOGICAL
ECONOMICS

FORUM

Capital/natural resource substitution: the debate of Georgescu-Roegen (through Daly) with Solow/Stiglitz

Clem Tisdell

Department of Economics, The University of Queensland, Brisbane 4072, Australia

While the exchange between Daly on the one hand and Solow and Stiglitz on the other, generates much heat, there is some light. Daly does considerable service by pressing the fundamental questions raised by Georgescu-Roegen about the absence of natural resources, including environmental resources, in the production functions used in neoclassical growth theories. The replies by Solow and Stiglitz help to clarify their position, although Solow's position is not completely clear.

Stiglitz states that neoclassical growth models are appropriate in the intermediate period, that is around 50–60 years. No claim is made for their relevance over a longer period and Solow asserts that the entropy law is of no immediate practical importance for modelling. What this implies is unclear but it may mean that the entropy law is not policy relevant within the time frame usually adopted by policy-makers for decision-making. In fact, in most cases, their planning period will be much less than 50–60 years. Nevertheless, long-run results will be dependent on their cumulative myopic decisions and would still be a legitimate subject for academic enquiry. If we are to know the nature of things, we should as academics not restrict ourselves exclusively to the outlook of most policy-makers.

While Georgescu-Roegen, in introducing the entropy law and related laws into the sustainable growth debate brings a new perspective to the economic problem (one that was badly needed at the time of his contribution), the matter of whether or not natural resources including environmental resources should specifically be included in the aggregate production function does not depend on the relevance of the law of entropy, even though it could be one reason for their inclusion (Tisdell, 1990). Economists have long recognized that production and ultimately economic welfare depends on factor proportions. The ratio between natural resource/environmental stock and man-made capital can change dramatically within a 50–60 year period as natural resources are transformed into man-made capital. China within a few decades has moved quickly down this transformation path. The extent of the transformation can be such that the level of production and economic welfare is impaired, that is, excess transformation of natural resources into man-made capital may impair economic welfare. This in itself would be enough reason not to leave

0921-8009/97/$17.00
PII S0921-8009(97)00089-X

natural resources, including environmental resources, out of the aggregate production relationship. The cake depends not only on the availability of ingredients but the ratio of ingredients.

The neglect of natural resources is not only evident in the writings of neoclassical economics but surprisingly (or maybe not so surprisingly) in the models considered by the new growth theorists such as Romer. Their reasons for this 'neglect' may be the same as those of Solow and Stiglitz but it would be useful to have the view of authors such as Romer on this subject.

By emphasising the application of the entropy law to economic activity, Georgescu-Roegen highlighted the potential or actual conflict between rapid economic growth and future resource scarcity. As pointed out by Faber et al. (1996), Georgescu-Roegen actually went beyond the entropy law which applies to the dissipation of energy to point out that most activity involves the dissipation of resources used. While for some resources, such as iron and aluminium resources, there is scope for recycling, there is dissipative loss of the resource for each cycle. So the cycles tend to be limited, and furthermore involve dissipation of energy on each recycling. In a closed system, the economic potential of the system runs down.

The biophysical system on earth is partly closed. It is however also partially open because it receives solar energy. Using this energy, ecosystems through existing mechanisms and self-organisation are able to concentrate or reconcentrate materials up to a point. Living things are therefore very important for maintenance of the long-run economic potential of the system because they have the ability (even though a limited one) to 'counteract' entropy of materials. It was probably because of this that Georgescu-Roegen suggested that as an ideal, aggregate economic demands should be limited to not more than the maximum sustainable yields from renewable resources. I do not agree with this as an ideal since it could suggest that non-renewable resources should be hoarded forever. Nevertheless, it brings attention to the fundamental importance of conserving living resources as a means to deal with future economic scarcities, even though this is not the only reason for wanting to conserve such resources. Issues of this fundamental nature are not raised in neoclassical economic growth theories. There is little doubt that this reduces their relevance.

Economic production is essentially a transformation process which at an aggregative level must be related to the biophysical environment. Economic output depends on the use of labour, on services provided by man-made capital and services from natural/environmental resources. The existence of the latter is essential for the other two. The existence of labour and man-made capital depends on transformations (mostly irreversible) of natural resources. In this sense, the Physiocrats were correct to emphasize the fundamental importance of land for economic activity.

Man-made capital consists of physical capital, e.g. machines; human capital, e.g. knowledge; and institutional capital, e.g. cultural mechanisms of governance. Man-made capital is a wasting asset—physical capital depreciates (a sign of entropy), knowledge declines without continual investment in education and its preservation and transmission and even cultural capital may decline unless there is continuing investment in its maintenance. The production, maintenance and expansion of all these forms of man-made capital require the continual use of natural resources and this involves their entropy. This is true of human capital including the expansion of scientific knowledge. Economists, including the new growth theorists, can therefore rest assured that there ain't a free lunch.

Solow has suggested that limits to natural resource availability is not a big problem for sustainable economic growth because sufficient substitutability of resources may exist in the system. However, in Solow (1974) and Solow (1956) man-made capital is assumed in effect to have an infinite life, whereas in reality it is a wasting asset and requires continual investment and natural resource use for its maintenance. Therefore, Solow (1974) and Solow (1956) appears to be of limited relevance (Ströbele, 1984; Müller and Ströbele, 1985). Similarly Hartwick's rule for investing rents from non-renewable rent extraction in the accumulation of man-made capital is not a recipe for sustainability, even though greater sustainability might be obtained by investing these rents rather than by consuming them.

Neoclassical economists sometimes use technological progress as a trump card. Such progress can reduce use of materials in relation to output and provide other advantages. Nevertheless, investment in research to foster technological progress, effort in knowledge generation in its diffusion and maintenance uses natural resources. Furthermore, the path of research and its profitability remains uncertain. It cannot be taken for granted.

While technological progress can and often does reduce material input for the same output (Stiglitz's soda can), total material use per capita appears to be growing, as is clear form recent studies by the Wuppertal Institute for Climate, Environment and Energy. Presumably because of rising aggregate demands, technological progress has not reduced material throughput. At the same time only limited comfort can be taken from the Kuznets curve of pollution intensity. While in its declining range, pollution emissions per unit of output fall, marginal pollution additions can still remain positive and so aggregate pollution emissions may rise. In addition, a country may be on the downward tail of a Kuznet's curve and its material throughput can continue to increase. Furthermore, aggregate production of global pollutants can escape notice when the environmental experiences of individual countries in relation to selected pollutants are considered.

Stiglitz suggests that improved operation of markets will help correct the situation. No doubt in some cases improvements in markets could help. But we need to be careful. There are limits to the economics of market-making, as for example Coase has pointed out, and the creation of property rights is to a large extent governed by the economics of it. Furthermore, markets are not static but dynamic as Schumpeter has stressed. In general, market-push is toward increasing consumption, e.g. through advertising and product promotion. In addition, current economic systems seem to require ever increasing throughput of materials to maintain employment. Consequently, the extension of markets rather than reducing the aggregate throughput of materials in the system does the opposite (Tisdell, 1994). More market-making need not give the perfect answer, a view shared it seems by Georgescu-Roegen and Daly. In fact, it is quite likely that we do not as yet have a perfect answer. Even perfectly extended markets fail to capture all values of importance to human-beings (Opschoor and van der Straaten, 1992). Market systems alone will not create a Utopia.

Acknowledgements

This note has benefited from information given to me by Professors Ulrich Hampicke, John Proops and Udo Simonis during my recent visit to them. The usual caveat applies.

References

Faber, M., Manstetten, R., Proops, J., 1996. Ecological Economics: Concepts and Methods, Edward Elgar, Cheltenham, UK.

Müller, K., Ströbele, W., 1985. Wachstumstheori, R. Oldenbourg Verlag, Munchen.

Opschoor, J.P., van der Straaten, J., 1992. Institutional aspects of sustainable development. In: Dietz, F.J., Simonis, U.E., van der Straaten, J. (Eds.), Sustainability and Environmental Policy, Edition Sigma, Berlin, pp. 55–67.

Solow, R., 1956. A contribution to the theory of economic growth. Q. J. Econ. 170, 65–94.

Solow, R., 1974. The economics of resources or the resources of economics, Am. Econ. Rev., May, pp. 1–14.

Ströbele, W., 1984. Wirtschaftswachstum bei begrentzen Energieressourcen, Duncker and Humblot, Berlin.

Tisdell, C.A., 1994. Conservation, protected areas and the global economic system. Biodiver. Conserv. 3, 419–436.

Tisdell, C.A., 1990. Natural Resources, Growth and Development, Praeger, New York.

Volume 13 Number 2 1997 *1*

ETHICS IN MODERN ECONOMIC THOUGHT AND THEIR CONSEQUENCES FOR ENVIRONMENTAL CONSERVATION, LAND AND RESOURCE-USE*

by A.E. Hohl and C.A. Tisdell, Department of Economics, University of Queensland

1. **Introduction**

During the very short period of cultural evolution of mankind, the world has changed dramatically. Modern humans have modified the environment not only to satisfy their needs, but also to please their greed. The forces that are united to destroy the last wildlands for short-term economic benefits seem to be overwhelming. However, at least in some developed countries, values, preferences and political majorities have been changing over the last two decades in favour of alternative approaches. A new multiplicity of goals has sprung up, and it will not be an easy task to reconcile the diverging interests. What makes it even more difficult is that the means, by which the different goals are to be achieved, are barely known. The scientists, whose task might be to provide tools of measurement to enable political decision-makers to set priorities, are facing serious methodological problems. Economists have not yet found practical and acceptable ways of valuing all commodities, biologists have not yet come up with proven environmental safety standards and sociologists and philosophers are far from providing a satisfactory method of integrating environmental values into the 'social contract'.

This paper examines the following aspects of resource use:

- the different kinds of resource-use conflicts,
- the value systems and value disputes underlying these conflicts, and
- the contribution, economics can make within a given value system in solving the resource-use conflicts.

Illustrations are provided in relation to whaling and to land use in the Cape York Peninsula region of Australia, a remaining wilderness region.

2. Classification of Land Use Conflicts

The most common resource use conflict in terrestrial regions is the competition for land. Land use conflicts arise between individuals, between different interest groups within society or between species, because land as a usable resource is scarce. There has to be some decision about which of the potential users should obtain the usufructuary of the resource and to what extent. This decision may depend on the kind of underlying preferences and values.

It is important to note that preferences are not to be identified with values. Preferences mean the setting by an individual of one thing before or above another thing because of a notion of betterness (Brown, 1984). Preferences are fleeting and variable and need not to be reasoned, whereas values are "invariable instrumentalities for reasoning about alternatives and the rationalisation of action" (Rescher, 1969). The issue of values is linked to the concept of preferability, not preference. However, this distinction is not always made. Especially economists often seem to use preference and value concepts quite indiscriminately.

Philosophers from Plato and Aristotle to modern axiologists have differentiated two general concepts of value, intrinsic and instrumental value. Intrinsic value is attributed to something that is valued as an end, for itself and in its own right. Instrumental value is attributed to something that is valued as a means, for something else. In other words, there is the superordinate 'that-for-the-sake-of-which-valued' or 'ultimate-end-value' and the subordinate 'that-valued-for- the-sake-of' or 'mediate-end-value' (Rescher, 1969). Despite some values being subordinated to others, a doctrine of end values need not take a monoistic form, like an inverted pyramid. There can be a plurality of distinct end values (Rescher, 1969).

Volume 13 Number 2 1997 3

Table 1 Conflict Categories According to Organisational Level and Instrumentality of Choice

Conflict category	Organisational level	Preference	Mediate-end value	Ultimate-end value
Interindividual	Individual	I	II	III
Intergroup	Society	IV	V	VI
Interspecies	Biosphere	VII	VIII	IX

Table 1 shows a simple way of categorising conflicts by taking into account the organisational level and the different instrumentalities of choice.

Referring to land use, an example can be given of each of the different types of conflict:

Type I: Mum wants to swim in a public pond, but Dad wants to fish in it.

Type II: Miller wants to build a five-storey house on his land, he subscribes instrumentally to the value of personal wealth. Neighbour Jones is strictly opposed to the development because it would spoil his view, i.e. he wants to preserve an aesthetic value.

Type III: Two neighbours, Miller and Jones, pursue their individual concepts of personal happiness.

Type IV: Ornithologists prefer to watch birds, hunters prefer to shoot them.

Type V: Conservationists believe their actions are means to something higher that is valued, the ecological integrity of the country. Developers, on the other hand pursue the economic prosperity of the country.

Type VI: The ultimate-end value for conservationists, e.g. the 'reverance for life', could conflict with the one for developers, e.g. the 'maximisation of human welfare'.

Type VII: Sugar cane farmers prefer dry land, brolgas prefer wetlands.

Types VIII and IX are only meaningful in a biocentric context, it being assumed that every living being has value in itself and a purpose in life. Type VIII and IX conflicts can cover not only man/non-human species conflicts, but also feral animal/native animal or native animal/native animal conflicts. Each species might have its own mediate-end and ultimate-end values.

Brown (1984) distinguishes further between three realms of value. Mediate-end and ultimate-end values belong to the conceptual realm, they are 'held values'. Value in this sense is 'an enduring conception of the preferable which influences choice and action' (Brown, 1984, p.232). In the relational realm, non-intrinsic value arises 'from a preference relationship between a subject and an object'. Value is neither a concept held by the subject nor something attributed to the object, but merely emerges from the preference of a subject for an object in a given context (Brown, 1984, p.233). Value in the relational realm is not observable and restricted to the feeling level. Finally, in the object realm, value is 'the expressed relative importance or worth of an object to an individual or group in a given context' (Brown, 1984, p.233). The relative importance of an object in relation to other objects results from a preference relationship. Such value is always relative, because we have no absolute value standard. Brown (1984) calls the value of the object realm 'assigned value'.

Held values provide a basis for the preference relationships which result in assigned values (Brown, 1984, p.234):

preference relationships

Held values ——————————————— > assigned values

Some confusion can arise from the fact that held values are objects in Brown's (1984) comprehensive sense of the term. Therefore, in the

Volume 13 Number 2 1997 5

object realm, specific held values, like all objects, can be assigned value. The assignment of value, on the other hand, is based on the personal system of held values.

So far only preference and value conflicts at the same level of organisation have been presented. However, it has to be assessed, how preferences and values at different organisational levels are related. There are value conflicts between the individual and society, between individual and biosphere and between society and biosphere. If there are preference and value conflicts at different organisational levels, does this mean these preferences and values belong to different logical categories? Is there a hierarchy of values? If a hierarchy exists, what does this mean for the bestowment of rights?

The following analysis concentrates on economically relevant value conflicts, i.e. resource allocation conflicts, and on the potential contribution of economics to resolving conflicts using different value systems. At first, a broad, philosophically based view is presented, then more applied aspects of the role of economics are discussed.

Conflicts between individuals and society are related to the liberal versus communal value dispute, conflicts between the human sphere and the biosphere are related to the anthropocentric versus biocentric value dispute.

3. Contemporary Liberalism, Communalism and Socio-economic Synthesis

Contemporary liberalism defends the primacy of the rights of the individual and his or her prerogative to choose the good. Every individual's chosen good or 'way of life' is ultimately equal (Rawls, 1971). Rawls (1971, p.3) presumes further that each 'person possesses an inviolability founded on justice that even the welfare of society as a whole cannot override'. Justice to the individual is valued as high as general welfare. In liberalism the notion of a hierarchy of values based on the organisational level is rejected.

Communalism replaces the autonomous self, independent of its personally chosen ends, with an embedded self. It seeks to establish a common good that is shared by and transcends each individual. The 'citizen' is bound to the common good. Sandel (1984, p.6) argues, that 'certain of our [social] roles are partly constitutive of the persons we are... [and we are] implicated in the purposes and ends characteristic of those communities'. For communitarians, the moral force of community is a central constituent of persons. The communal moral code is superordinated to individual values.

Sagoff (1981) argues that private and public preferences belong to different logical categories. Public preferences do not involve desires or wants, but opinions or beliefs. Private preferences are largely self-interested preferences, whereas public preferences express what the individual believes is in the public interest. Pearce and Turner (1989, p.277) accept this model by suggesting a categorisation of environmental values that locates assigned values at the individual level and held values at the public level. A third category of values is located at the level of physical processes and systems.

In other words Pearce and Turner (1989) accept the point of view that public preferences and publicly held values influence individual preferences and values. However, they do not seem to accept the communitarian position that individual values or preferences should be subordinated to communal values or preferences. Indeed most liberals are suspicious of the communitarian position and are inclined to believe either that the general will of the public is a will o' the wisp and/or there are no collective values independent of individual values and therefore all social preference is to be derived from the preferences of individuals. However, even in relation to the wishes of individuals, most liberals would constrain social choice in a manner which respects fundamental rights of individuals. Many liberal economists are suspicious of the concept of public preferences and publicly held values because collective or group values may not be uniform in society and the communitarian position may encourage one group in society if it has the power to impose its will on others arguing that it represents or distils 'the general will'. In the public economics arena, this may result in the dominant group subsidising the provision of merit good, goods judged to be meritorious from their point of view.

Etzioni (1988) appears to believe that for the functioning of a good society it is important that individuals interact socially to a sufficient extent (and presumably in an adequate but undefined manner) to ensure harmony between private and public values and reduce the likelihood of 'evil' values becoming established. For Etzioni (1988) both the individual and the community command a fundamental moral standing. The individual and the community 'penetrate' each other and require each other. There are very complex interrelationships between the individual and society, and instrumental and intrinsic values are relevant at both levels.

However, in today's large and multi-layered societies these value relationships are far from unequivocal. Coughlin (1991) points out: 'The tendency toward pluralism and rapid social change ensure that ... socialization to collective norms and values occurs at many levels and loci of society. Just as there are overlapping and cross-cutting group identities and structural interests in modern society, the normative and moral foundations of behaviour may be indistinct or even contradictory.'

The synthetic position of the socio-economists, as formulated in Etzioni's I&We paradigm (Etzioni, 1991), tries to overcome the conflict between individualistic and collectivistic values by stressing the interlocking, mutually dependent relationship of individual and community. The individual is neither seen as a primary decision-making unit nor as entirely constituted by community, but as an internally divided self. A self has preferences and meta-preferences based on moral values (Frankfurt, 1985). Etzioni's (1991) point is that these moral values are in part supported by social forces (The We) and in part developed and advanced by individuals (the I). This has strong political implications. It means that a bottom-down implementation of public preferences or values can never succeed - except maybe very superficially and for a relatively short period of time under violent totalitarian regimes - if there are no reflections and linkages at the personal preference and value level. This theoretical assumption is strengthened by empirical data suggesting the necessity of participation in development or conservation projects (Tacconi and Tisdell, 1993).

However, while socio-economists might be able to integrate the individual and the community level, they have relatively little to say about the biosphere. Coughlin (1991) thinks socio-economics may provide the basis for the definition of a new 'We', but he does not specify if this would be an anthropocentric approach by introducing the intergenerational equity principle or a biocentric approach granting rights to other species.

While the schematic preservation of environmental values put forward by Pearce and Turner (1989, p.227) is useful as a reference point, it suggests a more rigid distinction between its categories than in fact exists. For example, in principle, safe minimum standards could arise from the private preferences of individuals. If the community concerned is risk-averse or security conscious, a safe minimum standard can emerge from individual private preferences. Furthermore, in principle there is no reason why safe minimum standards could not be based on willingness to pay or to accept payment for changes in standards, for example, using contingent valuation-type techniques. This is not to say that we advocate the use of such methods.

It has been argued that objects do not have value in themselves and value only arises from a preference relationship between a subject and an object (Brown, 1983, p.233; Scheibe, 1970). It appears to us (and to many others, see Brown, 1984, p.233) that values cannot exist independently of preference relations expressed by subjects, so there can be no such thing as a non-preference value despite the claim of Pearce and Turner that non-preference values are specified in natural sciences. Taking the example of the preservation of the ecological carrying capacity, there might be a general agreement on the criteria to define and the measures to achieve this goal. But to what end is the ecological carrying capacity preserved? Is it preserved for itself, as an ultimate end, or is it preserved in order to maximize the span of existence of the human race (Georgescu-Roegen, 1971) or to guarantee the survival of the greater entity of life (Lovelock, 1979)? These questions point towards the conflict between anthropocentric and biocentric values.

Brown (1984, p.236) argues for a contextually based self- society continuum, i.e. 'the natural position [of the individual] along the continuum is altered by whomever the context of the valuation calls for the individual to represent'. With ongoing value-change the self-society continuum might be gradually extended towards all sentinent beings and finally towards a self-biosphere continuum.

4. Anthropocentrism and Biocentrism

Environmental disputes often involve clashes between mutually exclusive values. However, the aggravating ecological crisis has forced economists of very different ethical backgrounds to develop ideas about how to resolve the conflict between man and nature. One school of environmental economics, that evolved from traditional resource economics, keeps the old anthropocentric ethic, but tries to extend economic analysis to include environmental issues; the other adopts a biocentric ethic and subordinates economic reasoning to ethical decision-making. The relationship of man and nature in the first is a hierarchical one, the relationship of the second an equitable one.

All ethical systems can be characterized by three elements (Weinschenck, 1993):

- axioms,
- principles of action, and
- systems of rules and standards.

Economic systems are based on ethical systems and therefore include the same elements (Table 2).

Contrary to the individual versus society value conflict, currently there seem to be no approaches synthesising anthropocentric and biocentric values. Anthropocentrists tend to accuse biocentrists of

Table 2 Contrasting Elements of Economics Based on Anthropocentric and Biocentric Ethics after Weinschenck (1993)

	Economics based on anthropocentric ethic	Economics based on biocentric ethic
Axiomatic criterion	Sentience, position in evolution	Life
Axiom	Current and future generations of humans (and other sentient beings) have intrinsic value and purpose	All living beings have intrinsic value and purpose.
Principle of action	An action is ethically right if its consequences are optimal for the happiness of all human (and other sentient) beings, e.g. if actual or potential Pareto optimum can be achieved and the intergenerational equity principle fulfilled.	An action is good, if it preserves and promotes life; it is bad, if it destroys or hinders life ('Reverence for life' ethic, Albert Schweitzer). An action is right, when it tends to preserve the integrity, stability, and beauty of the biotic community ('Land ethic', Aldo Leopold)
System of rules and standards	Neoclassical economics	Mixture of ethical decision rules, which subordinate neoclassical economic rules
Economic valuation method	Classical and extended cost-benefit analysis, safe minimum standard	Cost-efficiency analysis within the framework of ethical constraints, safe minimum standard

Source: Based on an extension of Weinschenck (1993)

adopting theories based on moral experiences that are private, subjective and cannot be generalized. A biocentric ethic is said to impose very high moral and intellectual standards on its adherents, standards that cannot be met by 'common people'. An anthropocentric ethic, on the other hand, is broadly understandable, even if people are not environmentally interested. There is no need for a change in conscience as in the biocentric approach.

Biocentrists point out that the reduction of nature to a resource leads to the 'making of the makeable' (Weinschenck, 1993), i.e. everything that is technically possible will be realized. Nature is more than its economically valued parts. Theoretically, a very high valuation of uncertainty and irreversibility could lead to the same level of conservation as in the biocentric approach, but in reality mankind does not value these factors high enough. Humans start esteeming nature only when it starts to become scarce and biocentrists consider this to be too late to start conservation measures.

5. **Possibilities and Constraints of Economics in Resolving Resource Use Conflicts**

5.1 *Economics and Intrinsic Values*

The set of different land use conflicts related to Table 1 comprises problems that can only be partially addressed by economics. Economics is not a holistic science. The economic view of the world is restricted to certain features and problems, e.g. the optimal allocation of scarce resources. It is therefore logical that economics can only play a significant role in providing measures for decision-making for 'lower grade' preference or value conflicts. Economics cannot help to decide between ultimate-end values. The question 'What sorts of things may reasonably be taken to be valued as ends?' is the grand-prize question of classical philosophical ethics (Rescher, 1969). What is to be valued as an end can be as diverse as pleasure (the Cyrenaics), knowledge (Plato), happiness (Aristotle), virtue (the Stoics), a good will (Kant), the general welfare (the Utilitarians) or the integrity of the land (Leopold).

Economics is actually based on intrinsic values. Mainstream economics has been based on various concepts of 'welfare', that include specific subordinate instrumental values. Bentham's (1789) greatest happiness principle, defined as the 'sum total of the happiness of all the individuals in society' did allow some members of society to be made worse off, if the sum total of happiness would be increased. New Welfare Economics broke with the utilitarian concept of adding utilities and tried to establish the optimum conditions of production and exchange. The Paretian definition (Pareto, 1927) of optimal welfare did not allow any member of society to be disadvantaged, but it made any economic policy changes very difficult. In Pareto's value system 'welfare' apparently includes aspects of social equity. The Kaldor-Hicks's criterion allows for a more flexible, but also more risky approach. It is based on the assumption that an economic reform is a social improvement if those gaining from it can compensate losers and remain better off than before the change (Little, 1950; Tisdell, 1982a). This differs from the Paretian point of view because compensation might not be paid in all cases and some might be worse off than before. Newer concepts are based on the ultimate-end value of 'sustainable welfare'. This is often derived from Rawl's (1971) principle of justice or on the principle of intergenerational equity as for example presented by Pearce and co-authors (1989). It is important to note that each change in economic theory reflects a value change. Little (1950, p.274) pointed out that the 'superficially objective and factual' economic terminology often hides the underlying value dispute.

Economics can only satisfactorily deal with preference and instrumental value conflicts that fall into the realm of economic intrinsic values. Economics cannot decide whether animals should have rights, whether Aborigines should get their traditional land back or whether the natural resource stock should be preserved for future generations.

5.2 *Anthropocentric Economics*

Evidently, neoclassical economics can suggest solutions for all conflicts that are linked to the allocation of scarce marketable goods. If there are no markets for a good, e.g. a public good, then economists try to create surrogate markets by establishing the consumer's willingness to pay or willingness to accept compensation. Coming back to the classical family conflict, type I in Table 1. Mum wants to swim in a public pond, Dad wants to fish in it. The uses are mutually exclusive, because the pond is small and if Mum has her swim, she will scare all fish away. If there are no regulations on the use of the pond, Mum could be asked about her willingness to pay Dad so she can have her swim or her willingness to accept or to be compensated that she sits on the bank while he is fishing. 'Swimming' or 'fishing' are not marketable in this context, but they represent use values and therefore an exchange value, i.e. the consumer surplus from recreational use, can be quite easily established.

If conflicts arise about total non-use values as in the case of preservation of species, neoclassical economists have identified various possibilities of willingness to pay, such as the concepts of option, existence or bequest value (Tisdell, 1991, p.92). The total economic value of a resource would therefore consist of the willingness to pay for tangible and intangible values (Table 3). If a total economic value could be established then the Paretian optimality criteria could be used for decision-making. The potential facility to provide a common monetary measurement scale for such diverse costs and benefits seems very attractive. However, there are still many short-comings about the calculation of total economic values and it is not yet clear if the methodology can be developed to solve practical resource use conflicts.

Some economists such as Ciriacy-Wantrup (1952) and Bishop (1978) are critical of the total economic value approach, because they think it does not adequately take care of uncertainties and irre-

Table 3 **Tangible and Intangible Values of Conserving Natural Resources**

Value	Examples or explanations
Tangible: Material use (direct)	Meat, fur, feathers, for medicine
Material use (indirect)	Environmental spillovers or externalities. Reconditioning or improving air and water quality, commercial productivity, etc.
Intangible: Existence	The mere existence of a species may be values even when it has no material or recreational use and this attribute has pure public good characteristics. The mere existence for example of a particular species of whale may be valued though it will never be seen or used by an individual.
Bequest	Sometimes individuals express the wish that their children and their children's children should have an opportunity to enjoy wildlife and nature existing now e.g. species of the largest whales. For this reason they may place an economic value on their preservation.
Options	Keeping options open for meeting changed tastes or for better meeting existing tastes. Includes options in relation to material use, recreational use, existence and bequest value. Gene banks to improve or sustain productivity of agriculture, aquaculture, forestry and industries based on living resource productivity.
Vicarious	This involves the enjoyment of photographs, movies, stories and so on. The content of which or the relevance of which is dependent upon the existence of the wildlife involved.

Source: Based on Tisdell 1991, p.92

versibilities about future uses of species. The willingness to pay in the case of intangible values might be too small. They argue in favour of a 'Safe Minimum Standard' approach based on the minimax loss principle. This is biased towards conservation. The natural resource, e.g. a species, should be maintained unless the social costs of doing so are unacceptably high. However, the minimax loss principle does not provide a basis for all minimax decision situations (Bishop and Ready, 1991; Hohl and Tisdell, 1992). Bishop and Ready (1991) argue, the safe minimum standard could be adopted because a majority in society feels, it is 'the right thing to do'. Here a boundary between comprehensive economics and an economic that is constrained by exterior value judgements is reached. Using safe minimum standards, economics would be reduced to cost-efficiency-analysis.

Turner (1988, p.134) points out, that willingness to pay or willingness to accept may have limited usefulness because of contextual problems. Natural resources often belong to a social group or to mankind, whereas the context of willingness to pay or willingness to accept measures is usually a private not a social one. A crucial point in the extended neoclassical value concept is the endowment of property rights. Measures for willingness to pay and willingness to accept should be theoretically identical but vary greatly in empirical studies (Table 4).

Part of the difference depends on what is considered by the individual as being the 'right state'. If individuals have or think they should have the right to a resource, their valuation of environmental degradation of it will be much higher for willingness to accept compensation compared to the willingness to pay. In the first case the individuals feel they have the right to a resource that they can trade in voluntarily. In the second case the individuals are treated as if they only had right to the inferior level of welfare and can only go back to the initial, 'rightful' state via trading. Apart from this psychological phenomenon, willingness to pay is constrained by income.

Table 4 **Absolute and Relative Disparities Between Willingness to Pay and Willingness to Accept Payment in Contingent Valuation Studies**

Study	WTP	WTA	WTA relative to WTP in %
Hammack and Brown (1974)	247.00	1,044.00	422.67
Banford, Knetsch and Mauser (1977)	43.00	120.00	279.07
	22.00	93.00	422.73
Sinclair (1976)	35.00	100.00	285.71
Bishop and Heberlein (1979)	21.00	101.00	480.95
Brookshire, Randall and Stoll (1980)	43.64	68.52	157.01
	54.07	142.60	263.73
	32.00	207.07	647.09
Rowe, d'Arge and Brookshire (1980)	4.75	24.47	515.16
	6.54	71.44	1,092.35
	3.53	46.63	1,320.96
	6.85	113.68	1,659.56
Coursey, Shulze and Hovis (1983)	2.50	9.50	380.00
	2.75	4.50	163.64
Knetsch and Sinden (1983)	1.28	5.18	404.69

Source: Based on Cummings, Brookshire and Schulze (1986)

5.3 *Anthropocentric Economic Welfare Criteria and Property Rights*

5.3.1 *Values, Property Rights and Environmental Decisions*

Economists as a rule apply anthropocentric economic welfare criteria in an attempt to resolve environmental and resource-use conflicts. There is not, however, complete agreement amongst economists on the appropriate choice of a criterion.

Economists belonging to the Utilitarian School (e.g. Bentham, 1789) argued that social choice should be guided by the principle of maximising the total utility obtained by individuals in society. Where U_i represents the utility of the *i-th* individual and if there are n-individuals in society, welfare is maximised by maximising. However, to measure and identify utility and to compare it between persons was (is) a major stumbling block for this approach (Cf. Tisdell, 1972, Ch. 13).

In an attempt to side-step this problem, neoclassical economics adopted Pareto's principle (see section 5.1). Both the Utilitarian principle and Pareto's principle are grounded upon the assumption that each individual should count in relation to social decision-making, but whereas Pareto's principle does not sanction a social change which makes any individual worse off, the Utilitarian principle may do so. For example, suppose that a non-renewable resource is used up now which increases the total utility of the current generation by 100 utils but reduces that of future generations by 50 utils, the Utilitarian ethic would sanction this. But the Pareto principle would not.

Few economic or other changes can be made whereby someone does not lose. The Kaldor-Hicks criterion has been widely used in social cost-benefit analysis, in an attempt to circumvent this problem. According to this criterion, if human gainers from an economic or social change could compensate the losers, then the change is socially desirable. A potential Paretian improvement is possible. This criterion, however, is in practice usually qualified by the requirement either that the change not worsen the distribution of income, or not do so to such an extent as to annul the economic benefits otherwise obtained. Basically the Kaldor-Hicks criterion is supportive of the economic *status quo*. It refers to losers and gainers in relation to the existing situation. It does not as such relate changes in economic welfare to property rights.

However, property rights can play an important role in economic valuation. Coase (1960) argues that in the absence of transaction costs, that economic inefficiencies which might arise from environmental externalities can be eliminated by clearly assigning property rights to the parties involved. Either the polluter might be given the right to pollute (or a developer the right to destroy the environment) or the victims of such externalities may be given the right to be free of pollution (or destruction of the environment). The important thing in Coase's opinion is that property rights be assigned to one or other of the parties. If polluters or those destroying the environment have a right to do so, victims may pay them to desist to a 'socially optimal' extent. If those adversely affected by an externality have a right to be free of it, then perpetrators of the externality may pay those affected by it to allow it up to a point. A Pareto optimal solution can be obtained in latter case and Coase suggests that it will be the same solution as in the first case.

However, depending upon how the property are assigned the distribution of income will be different. Economics as such cannot determine the just assignment of property rights because this depends on ultimate values. Furthermore, it is usually not the case that every possible assignment of property rights is equally acceptable from the point of view of justice.

In practice, there is a further problem. Contrary to Coase's contention, the way in which property rights are assigned affect negotiated or traded economic and environmental outcomes. Any person assigned a property right must be paid not to fully exercise it. Any person not assigned a property right but wishing to influence the actions of a person with a property right must pay the possessor of the right not to exercise it fully. Thus the distribution of property rights determines who is to be paid or compensated, and who should pay for a change in social behaviour. Because in practice large differences exist between amounts which individuals are willing to pay and that which they are willing to accept in compensation to have an action varied (see Table 4), the assignment of rights affects the way in which resources are utilised and the *de facto* valuation of society of its use of resources. Consider some examples.

5.3.2 *The Case of Whales*

Take the case of whales. (This is discussed further in Kuronuma and Tisdell, 1993a, b, but for rather different welfare aspects). Assume for simplicity that there are two groups: whalers who want to catch whales commercially, and conservationists who want to avoid the killing of whales and maintain the natural stock of whales. Rights to the whales could either be assigned to the whalers or to the conservationists. If rights are assigned to whalers then given the Kaldor-Hicks principle, conservationists would need to be able to bribe whalers to reduce their catch if greater conservation is to occur. On the other hand, if the rights to whales is assigned to conservationists, whalers would need to be able to bribe or pay conservationists to allow whaling if whaling is to occur. So in the second case, the Kaldor-Hicks solution would be based on willingness of conservationists to accept compensation (and the willingness of whalers to pay) whereas in the first case it would be based on the willingness of conservationists to pay (and the willingness of whalers to accept compensation).

That the different assignment of rights may have materially different consequences for the use of whale-resources can be seen from Figure 1. Let line *GEH* represent the marginal evaluation of whalers for catching whales and for *simplicity* assume that it is the same whether based on their willingness to pay or on their willingness to accept compensation. Let line *ABC* represent the marginal evaluation of conservationists based on their willingness to pay to prevent catching of whales and let line *DEF* represent their marginal evaluation based on their willingness to accept compensation to permit whaling. These two lines differ. Empirically willingness to accept compensation is usually greater than willingness to pay (see Table 4). In this case if property rights are given to whalers and conservationist 'must' pay to prevent whaling, the Kaldor-Hicks optimal catch of whales is x_2 annually. But if the pattern of property rights is reversed, the Kaldor-Hicks optimal annual catch of whales is x_1. Greater conservation of whales occurs in the latter case. So even ignoring differences in transactions cost, the assignment of property rights is material for the extent of occurrence of environmental conservation if the Kaldor-Hicks or Paretian principle is adopted. While both points *E* and *B* are Paretian optimal points relative to assignment of property rights, they have differing implications for conservation. Economics as such appears powerless to chose between them.

Figure 1: Material Consequences of the Distribution of Property Rights for the Conservation of Whales

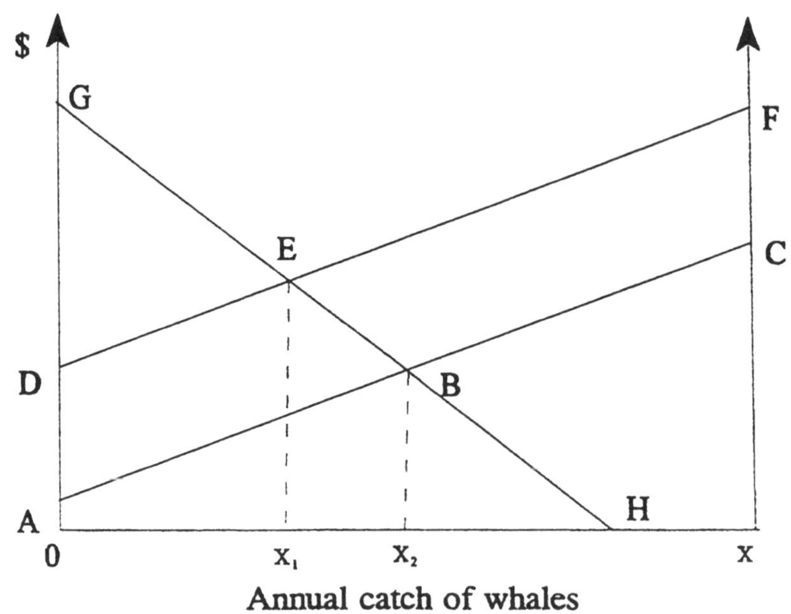

The assignment of property rights can be of crucial importance. However, one may ask why should property rights in whales be assigned to either whalers or to conservationists. A number of Third World countries have claimed that common-property resources such as whales and fish on the high seas should be assigned to them. Irrespective of whether that would be just or not, it would be likely to have different conservation consequences for whales compared to the above alternatives.

5.3.3 *The Case of Land Rights in Cape York Peninsula*

The most important outcome of any value debate on resource use is likely to be the decision on who is allocated the rights to benefit from the resources. Taking the example of Cape York Peninsula's savannas, the issue of land tenure and property rights will be assessed.

Cape York Peninsula, situated in the north of Queensland, has escaped the enormous transformations brought by 200 years of European settlement in Australia and has remained in a relatively pristine state. Its remote location, its poor soils and its adverse climate have prevented large-scale settlement. Only about 15,000 people live scattered about a huge area of almost 137,200 km^2 (Connell Wagner, 1989, p.1ff). Over fifty percent of the total population are Aborigines and Torres Strait Islanders, whereas this proportion in the national average is only one percent (WSPQ 1990, p.65). The Cape York Peninsula harbours a very diverse natural environment with rainforests, vine forests, open forests, grasslands, heathlands, dune fields, and aquatic and tidal wetlands. As a region of faunal and floral interchanges between Australia and New Guinea it supports unique biological assemblages with high endemicity rates (Connel Wagner, 1989, p.52ff). The high conservation value of this bioregion is internationally recognised.

The most important vegetation type in Cape York Peninsula is tall grass savana. Large tracts of these rangelands are devoted primarily to extensive pastoralism. Generated by the rapid expansion of non-pastoral uses, interests and values, a widening public debate has developed about the future use, management and ownership of these lands.

As discussed by Holmes (1990a, 1990b, 1991, 1992, 1993), following the general policy of British frontier settlement, from the time of the initial wave of settlement, de jure public proprietary rights have been retained by limiting the opportunities to obtain freehold title and by relying on restricted titles, such as leases, licenses and grazing permits. This has enabled governments to pursue land related policies through proprietorial as well as sovereignty powers. Lately, this approach has been questioned in the wider framework of appropriate regimes of resource property rights. Holmes (1993, p.2) pointed out that "The privatisation theorists have seized upon perceived imperfections in the administration of federal lands as evidence to support general theories on the inefficacy of public ownership of resources. Finding instances of supposedly inevitable outcomes such as: misdirected bureaucratic incentives, overbureaucratized conformity, asset hoarding and resource misallocation, agency capture and clientelism, conflict between the state's proprietarial and sovereignty responsibilities and a supposed propensity towards resource depletion... In response, the major critics of the privatisation theorists have referred to the evidence on desirable outcomes from the public administration of federal forests and range lands and the pitfalls from untrammelled privatisation."

During the period of flux in rangeland occupancy, the Australian model of rangelands leaseholds, involving 'performance standards' and limited security, with mechanism for partial resumptions, and compensation only for improvements, enabled governments to allocate land to its 'highest and best use' where this use was likely to prove only temporary, and likely to be succeeded by new forms of 'best' use. With its retention of ultimate proprietary control, the leasehold system was also an excellent mechanism for allocating rights to engage in the 'best' use while ensuring these rights also carried specified responsibilities or 'performance standards' tied to public goals (Holmes, 1993). Pastoralism was the pre-eminent land use, it gave absolute priority to Europeans to occupy all suitable lands, and was capable of being displaced only by a few 'higher' forms of land use, notably agriculture and mining. In the absence of any countervailing public interest, there was a strong propensity to agency capture and extension of property rights, barely differentiated from freehold, thus destroying the rationale for the institutional structure.

However, generated by a general change in values in the European community, the public goals, that were formerly centered on development, have been partly translated into goals of sustainable use or preservation of valued natural assets. A variety of alternative land uses, including restoration of Aboriginal land rights, nature preservation, wide-ranging recreation, water catchments, defence and quarantine, is challenging the pastoralist's domain, particularly on marginal land. The prevailing government policy towards Aborigines in the last decades has been one of protective welfare, that included elements of care as well as of control, but did not grant the Aborigines any land rights. Aboriginal groups are trying to change this policy by demanding the recognition of their principles of land tenure and their basic rights in that land. Conservationist groups are trying to extend the current system of national parks, that currently covers only 10% of the Peninsula. One of their demands is to exclude cattle graze from the most marginal and submarginal lands, especially in the far north of the Peninsula. Other interest groups, such as tourists or local developers, are not competing as drastically with pastoralism as Aborigines and conservationists but nevertheless they are making their claims. There is a growing tension between the grazing lessee's demand for expanded rights and greater security of tenure, the interests of non-pastoral groups, and the land administrator's responsibilities to reconcile diverging interests and to enforce constraints on land use.

Pastoralism is coming under more pressure as a land use because of negative externalities, such as land degradation, loss of habitat and of native species, and mounting cross-subsidies needed to support the infrastructure of the cattle industry are becoming widely acknowledged. Some resource economists argue that where an unacceptable level of 'market failure' occurs because existing or potential negative externalities are disproportionate to the modest economic benefits accruing to (pastoral) enterprises, especially in marginal areas, constraints should be placed on private property rights (Randall, 1981; Pearce and Turner, 1990).

On the other hand, Coase's (1960) theorem of social cost attempts to prove the optimality of market or negotiated exchange solutions made possible by granting of private property rights, even in circumstances where externalities are present. Coase rejects the 'polluter pays principle' (McCarthy, 1992). In the absence of transaction costs it does not matter, who has the property rights, from an economic efficiency point of view. But, if private property rights were to be given for all of Cape York Peninsula, does it really not matter who will get the land? If the major rival interest groups are compared according to their financial power, it becomes obvious that only mining companies and - to a lesser extent - tourist operators would have the means to compensate the losers, whereas pastoralists, conservationists and Aborigines generally could not pay significant amounts. Additionally, WTP and WTA can differ substantially in real world decision situations, and this is directly relevant to the question of property rights.

So, should the land- or resource-rights in Cape York Peninsula be given to the economically weaker groups, e.g. the Aborigines? They are more likely to attain their wishes for the use of resources to which they lay claim when they hold the rights to these and so do not have to pay to prevent use of these resources. This raises the difficult question to which extent Aborigines should have land rights since, despite Coase's view, the assignment of property rights seems to make a mental difference to resource-use.

If land rights are say assigned to the indigenous people of the Cape York Peninsula, how exclusive should these rights be? For example, should other Australians as well as the international community be provided with any rights in relation to the conservation and use of natural resources on Cape York. For instance, in contingent valuation analysis which groups will count? Economists seem to have provided virtually no guidelines in this respect. Political factors seem to determine the reference groups used in most empirical studies of contingent valuation, so the appropriate evaluation procedure is largely left unresolved. For instance, to what extent is the sovereignty of local people to be overridden for 'global' benefit or wider-community benefit?

Economics cannot answer this question. It rests in the responsibility of governments to balance the diverging interests. The final decision on who should benefit from a resource will depend on ethical and political reasoning.

5.4 *Biocentric Economics*

Biocentric economics relates to a different intrinsic value background. The ultimate-end value is not social welfare or human happiness, but the integrity of the land or happiness of all living beings. As Muir (1867) put it: 'The world, we are told, was made especially for man - a presumption not supported by the facts... Why should man value himself as more than a small part of the great unit of creation?'

Ethical claims cannot be justified in the way which factual claims can. But the intrinsic values underlying the anthropocentric approach are self-evident for humans, whereas the biocentric values are not. Nevertheless, the biocentric approach cannot be criticised because it has different underlying intrinsic values to the anthropocentric contention. More serious is that there are - apart from general principles as shown in Table 2 - no systems or rules about how to operationalise the approach.

Taking the example of conservation of species, there have been suggestions that species higher in the hierarchy of evolution should be valued more than others that developed earlier, e.g. vertebrates should be valued higher than invertebrates (Weinschenck, 1993). The World Conservation Strategy suggests that priority should be given to saving species where the size of the loss, defined according to

Table 5 Priorities Suggested in IUCN's 'World Conservation Strategy' document for Conserving Species

		Imminence of loss		
		Rare	Vulnerable	Endangered
Size of loss	Family	4**	2***	1***
	Genus	7*	5**	3***
	Species	9*	8*	6**

Notes: 1-9 suggested order of priority
*** Top priority
** Intermediate priority
* Lower priority

Source: Based on IUCN 1980, sec. 6.2

biological classification, is large and also imminent (IUCN, 1980; Tisdell, 1993; Table 5).

However, this system of priorities seems to be rather coarse. First of all, the classification into family, genus and species is an artificial one and subject to change. Further, no account is taken of the benefits and costs of preservation. Presumably, if the costs of saving a whole plant or animal family are very high in relation to the benefits, and the benefits of saving a separate species at the same cost are high and resources are insufficient to meet both objectives, it would be sensible to save the species rather than the family (Tisdell, 1993).

Pearce and Turner (1989) therefore have a point in saying that 'acceptance of the preservationist position would mean that interspecies and animal-natural habitat conflicts, as well as human interest conflicts, would need to be equitably and practicably resolved. Principles or rules for the settlement of such moral interest conflicts have not so far been worked out on anything like a satisfactory basis.'

If humans have introduced new species into a biosystem or if the anthropogenic change of the habitat has promoted some species and has hindered others, should the newly introduced animals be destroyed and the promoted species be controlled? In which interspecies conflicts should man actively interfere and how should humankind manage 'evolution'? Biocentrists have not yet come up with criteria prescribing how more complicated interspecies value conflicts involving non-human/human and non- human/non-human species subconflicts, such as described for the categories VIII and IX in Table 2 can be resolved. Take for example campaigns for the eradication of feral animals from Australia's rangelands, whose principle objective was disease control. Some conservationists were strongly in favour of it because feral animals do not belong to the native ecosystem, as they have been introduced by Europeans, they wander into conservation areas and can severely affect native species by competing for water and food or by altering the environment (Tisdell, 1982b). Others, especially the animal rightists, campaigned internationally against these eradication campaigns, arguing they were brutal and injust, because feral animals, such as cows, water buffaloes or brumbies, had just as much right to live in Australia as other species. Even more controversial seems the issue of the kangaroo species of large size which were favoured by anthropogenic environmental change in Australia at the expense of other, small marsupials. There is a strong debate going on in Australia, involving various anthropocentric and biocentric positions, about whether kangaroo species of larger sizes, such as red and grey kangaroos, should be rightfully culled or not.

5.4 *Intergenerational Equity and Sustainability as Overriding Principles for Resolving Land Use Conflicts*

Possibly the only contemporary value with potential to make for a compromise between biocentrists and anthropocentrists may be some kind of egoistic interest in intergenerational equity or the obligation to posterity. This perspective is at least partly shared by biocentrists, moral philosophers, neoclassical economists and green politicians. Wilson (1984, p.14) points out: 'The only way to make a conservation ethic work, is to ground it in ultimately selfish reasoning ... People will conserve land and species fiercely if they foresee a material gain for themselves, their kin and their tribe.' Most human beings feel an identity with their species, and see their descendants a kind of immortality for themselves. 'Consequently they have a personal interest in the continued existence of this earth and of humankind' (Rosenfield and Strong, 1981, p.12).

The issue of the duty to posterity, i.e. the moral obligations and responsibilities of those now living to persons who may be assumed to exist in the future, is not easily separable from the population policy question, i.e. the obligations to produce, or refrain from producing, future persons (Partridge, 1981). Persons, who will exist in the future, will be affected by the reproductive decision of the present generation. On the other hand, procreative decisions must be based, in part, upon anticipation of conditions in the future 'apart from' these decisions (Partridge, 1981). The issue of population policy is not addressed here in detail, but it might be even more difficult to assess than the obligations to posterity problem. Broome (1988, p.90) wrote almost despairingly: '... this problem of population is riddled throughout with paradoxes. No principle has yet been found for assessing population policies...'

Furthermore, intergenerational equity cannot be separated from intragenerational equity. Should the current inequalities be carried over into the next generations? As the population is already too large to enable everybody to live a Western lifestyle, equity can only be achieved on a lower level of resource use. Should there be an equal distribution of wealth, i.e. a very low standard of living for everybody, as Rawls's (1971) principle of justice implies or should there be just a guarantee of a minimum standard of living, without standards being necessarily equal (Tisdell, 1993)?

Astonishingly, there is very little theoretically sound basis for a comprehensive theory of the addressed problems, that could provide decision criteria for resolving land use conflicts. Rawls's (1971) principle of justice has been extended by Page (1977) to all generations. Justice becomes essentially an agreement to pass on 'intact' an inheritance, e.g. environmental and economic goods and services, from one generation to the next. However, sets of rules within the Rawlsian framework have been criticised for not catering for the rights of possible people and non-human species (Tisdell, 1988; Turner, 1988). Tisdell (1993) pointed out if reincarnation is assumed, the Rawlsian approach would care for all living things.

Another important approach is the 'justice as opportunity' argument (Barry, 1983; Page, 1983). Future generations are owed compensation for any reduction, due to the activities of the current generation, in their access to natural resources. If justice is to prevail, future generations have to be compensated for loss of productive potential in the form of improved technology and increased capital investment designed to offset the impacts of depletion. These trade offs, however, may not account sufficiently for uncertainties and irreversibilities.

Kavka (1978) has adopted the Lockean standard that each generation should leave 'enough and as good for the others' that follow on. This would include conservation, responsible use of renewable resources, and enhanced substitution technologies for non-renewable resources. The Lockean standard will have to be for responsibility of future generations, because current global inequities are too great. The current generation would be allowed to use more than its fair share of resources in order to allow the developing economies to pass through a demographic transition and for the world population to stabilize (Turner, 1988).

The extended stewardship principle falls into a somewhat different category. Humans should act as nature's steward and practice carefully husbandry of natural resources, independently of individualistic anthropocentric desires (Pearce and Turner, 1989).

As there is no system of criteria to establish what should be preserved for future generations, many authors concentrate on the sustainability issue. However, it should be stressed that sustainability has no purpose for itself. Sustainability simply means that something is sustained over time, there is no inherent value judgement. Tisdell (1993) pointed out that not all things are worth sustaining and that the concepts of sustainability vary considerably, even to a point where they may become contradictory. Another important issue is that sustainability does not necessarily mean conservation of the status quo. Change and evolution are the very foundations of life.

Therefore, the sustainability criteria, as for example developed by Pearce and Turner (1989) must be seen as instrumental. However, by adopting the 'Preserve the natural resource stock over time' maxim Pearce and Turner (1989) make a value judgement implicitly in favour of cautiousness and responsibility with regard to the future of current and coming generations, contrasting sharply with the 'take and run' maxim, that has been dominant over much of the history of industrialisation, and is related to entirely self-centered values.

6. Conclusions

Resource use conflicts related to environmental conservation have dimensions far beyond the realm of economics. Intrinsic value conflicts cannot be resolved by economic reasoning. However, various value systems leave sufficient scope for economists to provide instruments for decision-making. Within the anthropocentric approach, extended cost-benefit-analysis can be used where surrogate markets can be established. Within the biocentric approach at least cost-efficiency-analysis is applicable. The safe minimum standard method can be applied in both value contexts.

The use of economic methods as tools for the allocation of scarce goods will remain important. What has to change is the unreflected use of economic instruments, because the underlying value system, for example neoclassical economics, is not generally accepted anymore. The value context in which economics is applied has to be much better assessed. This relates especially to strategic resource use planning, where more emphasis may need to be placed on a participatory approach embracing all relevant interest groups and involving mutual consultation on resource use goals and dynamic review and flexible coordination of resource management plans and programmes. Several arguments can be put in favour of such an approach. One of its benefits would be its assistance to policy- makers and economists in identifying prevalent end values (or intrinsic values) in society and allowing accommodation of conflicts between initially held intrinsic (or higher-order) values by different individuals or groups in society. It should also make policy-makers and economists more sensitive to changing 'societal' values. Generally held higher-order values can change over time as, appears to have happened to 'societal' valuation of mankind's appropriate relationships with nature (Cf. Passmore, 1974).

Endnote

* This paper was written while Dr Hohl was a visiting scholar at The University of Queensland under the Australian European Awards Programme. The authors wish to thank Professor J. Holmes for considerable assistance with source materials and Tomas J.F. Riha for helpful comments on an earlier draft of this paper. Dr Hohl is grateful for financial assistance under Australian European Award Programme.

References

Barry, B. (1983) Intergenerational Justice in Energy Policy, in Brown, P.G. and MacLean, D. (eds.) **Energy and the Future**, Rowman & Littlefield, Totowa, New Jersey.

Bentham, J. (1789) **An Introduction to the Principles of Morals and Legislation**, Athlone Press (Reprint, 1970), London.

Bishop, R.C. (1978) Economics of a Safe Minimum Standard, **American Journal of Agricultural Economics** 57:10-18.

Bishop, R.C. and Ready, R.C. (1991): Endangered Species and the Safe Minimum Standard, **American Journal of Agricultural Economics**, 73/2:309-312.

Broome, J. (1988) Some Principles of Population. In Collard, D., Pearce, D. and Ulph, D. (eds.) **Economics, Growth and Sustainable Environments**, St. Martin's Press, New York.

Brown, T.C. (1984) The Concept of Value in Resource Allocation, **Land Economics**, Vol. 60, No. 3:231-246.

Ciriacy-Wantrup, S.V. (1952) **Resource Conservation: Economics and Policies**, Berkeley.

Coase, R.H. (1960) The Problem of Social Cost, **Journal of Law and Economics**, 3:1-44.

Connell Wagner (1989) **Cape York Peninsula Resource Analysis**, prepared for the Premier's Department, Cairns.

Coughlin, R.M. (1991) Mediation of Self-Interest. In Etzioni, A. and Lawrence, P.R. (eds.) **Socio-Economics - Toward a New Synthesis**, M.E. Sharpe, New York.

Cummings, R.G., Brookshire, D.S. and Schulze, W.D. (1986) **Valuing Environmental Goods: A State of the Art Assessment of the Contingent Valuation Method**, Rowman and Allanheld, Totawa, N.Y.

Etzioni, A. (1988) **The Moral Dimension: Towards a New Economics**, Free Press, New York.

Etzioni, A. (1991) Contemporary Liberals, Communitarians, and Individual Choices. In Etzioni, A. and Lawrence, P.R. (eds.) **Socio-Economics - Toward a New Synthesis**, M.E. Sharpe, New York.

Frankfurt, H.G. (1971) Freedom of the Will and the Concept of the Person, **Journal of Philosophy**, 68:5-20. Georgescu-Roegen, N. (1971) *The Entropy Law and the Economic Process.* Harvard University Press, Cambridge, Mass.

Hohl, A. and C. Tisdell (1992) How Good are the Environmental Safety Standards Used in Economics? The Example of Safe Minimum Standards for Protection of Species, **Biodiversity and Conservation** 2: 168-181.

Holmes, J.H. (1990a) Land Speculation and Lease Tenure. In **A Conservation Strategy for Cape York Peninsula, Draft for Discussion**, Wildlife Preservation Society of Queensland.

Holmes, J.H. (1990b) Ricardo Revisited: Submarginal Land and Non-Viable Cattle Enterprises in the Northern Territory Gulf District, **Journal of Rural Studies**, 6, 1, 45-65.

Holmes, J.H. (1991) Land Tenures in the Australian Pastoral Zone: A Critical Appraisal. In Moffat, I. and Webb, A. (eds.) **North Australian Research: Some Past Themes and New Directions**, North Australian Research Unit, Darwin, p.41-59.

Holmes, J.H. (1992) **Strategic Regional Planning on the Northern Frontier, Discussion Paper No.** 4, North Australian Research Unit, Darwin.

Holmes, J.H. (1993) **Land Tenures, Property Rights and Multiple Land Use: Issues for American and Antipodean Rangelands,** Paper presented at annual meeting of Western Regional Science Association, Maui.

IUCN (1980) **The World Conservation Strategy: Living Resource Conservation for Sustainable Development,** IUCN, Gland, Switzerland.

Kavka, G. (1978) The Futurity Problem. In Sikora, R.I. and Barry, B. (eds.) Obligations to Future Generations, Temple University Press, Philadelphia.

Kennedy, F. (1993) Daintree - threatened by success, **The Australian Magazine,** 09.01.1993.

Kuronuma, Y. and Tisdell, C.A. (1993a) Institutional Management of an International Mixed Good: Socially Optimal Whale Harvest, the Moratorium and the Role of the International Whaling Commission, **Discussion Paper No. 112,** Department of Economics, The University of Queensland, Brisbane, 4072.

Kuronuma, Y. and Tisdell, C.A. (1993b) International Antarctic Minke Whale Management: The Economics of a Common-Property Resource Utilised as a Consumptive Good but with Adverse Non-Consumptive Externalities, **Discussion Paper No. 113, Department of Economics, The University of Queensland, Brisbane, 4072.**

Little, I.M.D. (1950) **A Critique of Welfare Economics,** Oxford University Press, Oxford.

Lovelock, J. (1979) **Gaia: A New Look at Life on Earth.** Oxford University Press, London.

McCarthy, S. (1992) An Illustration of the Coase Theorem and the Consequences Externalities have on Legal Rights. **Discussion Paper**

No. 75. Department of Economics, The University of Queensland, Brisbane, 4072.

Muir, J. (1867), as quoted in Nash, R.F. (1989) **The Right of Nature: A History of Environmental Ethics**, University of Wisconsin Press, Madison, Wisconsin, p.37.

Page, T. (1983) Intergenerational Justice as Opportunity. In Brown, P.G. and MacLean, D. (eds.) **Energy and the Future**, Rowman & Littlefield, Totawa, New Jersey.

Pareto, V. (1927) *Manuel d'Economie Politique*, Gerard, Paris.

Partridge, E. (1981) **Responsibilities to Future Generations**, Prometheus Books, New York.

Passmore, J. (1974) **Man's Responsibility for Nature: Ecological Problems and Western Tradition**, Duckworth, London.

Pearce, D., Markandya, A., and Barbier, E.B. (1989) **Blueprint for a Green Economy**, Earthscan Publications, London.

Pearce, D. and Turner, R.K. (1989) **Economics of the Natural Resources and the Environment**, The John Hopkins University Press, Baltimore.

Randall, A. (1981) **Resource Economcs: An Economic Approach to Natural Resource and Environmental Policy**, Grid Publications, Columbus Ohio.

Rawls, J. (1971) **A Theory of Justice**, The Belknap Press of Harvard University Press, Cambridge, MA.

Rescher, N. (1969) **Introduction to Value Theory**, Prentice- Hall, Englewood Cliffs, New Jersey.

Rosenfield, E.S. and Strong, D.H. (1981) Ethics or Expediency: An Environmental Question. In Shrader-Frechette, K.S. (ed.) **Environmental Ethics**, The Boxwood Press, Pacific Grove, California.

Sagoff, M. (1981) **Economic Theory and Environmental Law**, Michigan Law Review, Vol. 79(1).

Sandel, M.J. (1982) **Liberalism and the Limits of Justice**, Cambridge University Press, Cambridge.

Scheibe, K.E. (1970) **Beliefs and Values**, Holt, Rinehart and Winston, New York.

Tacconi, L. and Tisdell, C. (1993) Holistic Sustainable Development: Implications for Planning Processes, Foreign Aid and Support for Research, forthcoming in **Third World Planning Review.**

Tisdell, C.A. (1972) **Microeconomics: The Theory of Economic Allocation**, John Wiley, Sydney, London, New York.

Tisdell, C.a. (1982a) **Microeconomics of Markets**, John Wiley, Brisbane, New York, Chichester, Toronto, Singapore.

Tisdell, C.A. (1982b) **Wild Pigs: Environmental Pest or Economic Resource?** Pergamon Press, Sydney, Oxford, New York.

Tisdell, C.A. (1988) Sustainable Development: Differing Perspectives of Ecologists and Economists, and Relevance to LDCs, **World Development**, 16:373-384.

Tisdell, C.A. (1991) **Economics of Environmental Conservation**, Elsevier, Amsterdam.

Tisdell, C.A. (1993) **Environmental Economics: Policies for Environmental Management and Sustainable Development**, Edward Elgar, Aldershot, England.

Turner, R.K. (1988) Wetland Conservation: Economics and Ethics. In Collard, D., Pearce, D., and Ulph, D. (eds.) **Economics, Growth and Sustainable Environments**, St. Martin's Press, New York.

Wilson, E.O. (1984) Million-Year Histories: Species Diversity as an Ethical Goal, **Wilderness** 48, p.12ff.

Weinschenck, G. (1993) Lectures given on '**Oekonomik von Oekologie und Tierschutz in der Landwirtschaft**', University of Hohenheim, Germany.

WPSQ (1990) **A conservation strategy for Cape York Peninsula**, draft for discussion, Wildlife Preservation Society of Queensland, Brisbane.

[9]

Local communities, conservation and sustainability

Institutional change, altered governance and Kant's social philosophy

Clem Tisdell
Department of Economics, The University of Queensland, Brisbane, Australia

Introduction

Increasing concern is being expressed about the disintegration of local communities and the loss of sense of community. To a large extent, the disintegration of local communities is due to economic "modernization" involving greater use of and widening of markets as a method of economic organization, a process facilitated by new technologies for transport and communication. Moreover, many new technologies result in economies of scale and economies of agglomeration which further add to centralization processes. A concomitant social change has been the increasing centralization of government.

The reduced economic, social and political powers of local communities, along with reduced family ties, have resulted in modern societies becoming highly impersonal. In such societies, many individuals feel alienated and "rudderless". This may be associated with high levels of mental illness and rates of suicide in several high income countries.

The socio-economic costs associated with modern economic changes may be much higher than indicated above. Centralized governments seem less well able to take account of community values than more localized governments, and centralized government may have several economic cost disadvantages often overlooked by its advocates. Advocates of centralized government on economic grounds usually argue that it yields economies of scale, avoids duplication in the supply of public facilities and allows for greater specialization in the supply of public services thereby more fully utilizing the comparative advantage of individuals involved in government. However, this is merely the possible positive side of it. This position ignores the following factors: first, a centralized government may not know or reflect the concerns and values of local communities. Second, its knowledge about local conditions and possibilities

The authors wishes to thank Dr Tomas Riha for his comments on an earlier review of this article. The usual caveat applies.

International Journal of Social Economics, Vol. 24 No. 12, 1997, pp. 1361-1375. © MCB University Press, 0306-8293 may be limited due to its separation from the local scene. Third, especially if top-down public administration occurs, local communities may feel alienated from the process of government. The latter factor can generate hostility and resentment to government policies among members of local communities. Consequently, citizens may lack any commitment to such policies and may, in fact, sabotage them by non-co-operation or by active measures. The moral power associated with locally developed policy is lost.

In this paper I want to consider the matter of communal values, local communities and their governance, discuss the role of local communities in conserving the environment, and examine environmental developments which affect the sustainability of local communities. Socio-economic and environmental developments may require changes in governance to ensure sustainability of societies. In conclusion, case material from China and India is introduced and implications of Kant's social philosophy are discussed.

Communal values, local communities and local government

How best to reconcile the rights and wishes of individuals with the values and requirements of the community, its institutions and mechanisms of governance has never been satisfactorily resolved. In fact, Immanuel Kant appears to have been less than consistent in dealing with this matter. Frolov (1984, p. 210) notes that "in ethics, contrary to the formal nature of the categorical imperative [proposed by Kant], he put forward the principle of self-value of each individual which must not be sacrificed even for the good of the community as a whole".

However, it seems, as Dr Tomas Riha has suggested to me (1996), that Frolov does not represent the views of Kant correctly because the categorical imperative is the mere form of the moral will created by the self-imposed obligation of each individual, which in itself is to be fully respected. The categorical imperative involves self-determination of the rational will, which for Kant is God's will.

Riha (1966) wrote:

> Ethics (or doctrine of morals) according to Kant deals with laws of freedom. The laws of freedom are those according to which everything ought to happen although ethics also (moral laws) consider the conditions under which what ought to happen frequently does not. Kant further subdivided ethics into (1) an empirical part (called practical anthropology), and (2) a rational part called morals. When applied to man, moral philosophy does not borrow from anthropology but gives *a priori* laws to him as a rational being for man is so liable to all kinds of corruption that he is not easily able to make the idea of a pure practical reason effective in the conduct of his life. Thus the moral law cannot be dependent upon any object of will already existing in experience, and moral action ***must not appear as means in service of other ends***. The moral command demands an act of will which has its worth in itself only.
>
> The motive which stimulates man to obey this law must be nothing but "reverence for the law itself". Thus man should do his duty not for the sake of advantage, but out of reverence for himself, and in his relations with other men he should make it his supreme maxim, never to treat others as a means for attainment of his ends, but always to honour in each the ***worth of their personality***.

The above quotation from Frolov (the one previous to that from Riha) raises the question of whether community values exist independently of the values of individuals. Communitarianism suggests that this is so. However, liberals have generally been hostile to communitarianism when it has embraced the concept of the "General Will" of society not based on the values of individuals (viewed primarily as the self-interest of individuals), or without clear rules for deriving social welfare from the values of individuals or the preferences of individuals. Critics are especially hostile when a select few profess knowledge of the "General Will" and do not share the basis of their knowledge with others. Reliance on the concept of the "General Will" is sometimes seen as a step towards the establishment of an oligarchy or dictatorship. Liberals fear that nebulous and baseless views of the General Will may be imposed by authorities on individuals contrary to their individual wishes or contrary to the wish of the majority. In this context, the agnosticism of liberals about the concept of the General Will seems justified. Acton (1970, p. 43) points out that Kant was much influenced in his thinking by the concept of the General Will as set out in Rousseau's *Social Contract*.

Yet Kant was fundamentally of the view that moral principles can be established by reason (that is, by means of transcendental rationality) and these moral principles should be categorical imperatives for human action. However, to me universal agreement about the categorical imperatives so derived seems unlikely. Although Kant may have believed such disagreement to be transitory, we appear to be always in transitory states, if for no other reason than each individual having a finite temporal life. Or if there is agreement about morality, those moral principles, say resulting in a social contract, could be so general as to be of little operational value. Furthermore, there is a danger of dogmatism by those who feel they have discovered the moral will and categorical imperatives on the basis of transcendental rationality. Thus rational sceptics, like myself, are unlikely to find Kant's approach completely satisfactory. While morality can (does) have social value, I do not accept that moral imperatives can be established solely by reason. Even if it is true, as Kant postulates, that individuals have a personality beyond the temporal existence which could put them into contact with the moral order of the universe grounded in Supreme Reason, God, there is no certainty of such contact and of others knowing who has really been in contact.

Nevertheless, there do seem to be community values which transcend those of individuals and which sometimes call for the modification of the behaviour of individuals. For example, Georgescu-Roegen (1976) argues that survival of a species, including the human species, transcends as a moral value the survival of individuals and the desires of individuals.

Although individuals may subscribe to community values, they may fail to act in their individual behaviour in accordance with these unless social intervention occurs, e.g. by offering rewards for behaviour that accords with the collective good or penalties for non-compliance. This is not uncommon in relation to use of the environment and in situations where a prisoner-dilemma problem exists. While this policy would satisfy utilitarians, it would not satisfy Kant.

Whether or not collective or community values or preferences can be derived rationally from those of individuals has been given considerable attention in the literature. However, the acceptability of any process for deriving collective values from those of individuals depends on the acceptability of the ethical values which underlie the process. Arrow (1951) has shown the impossibility of deriving a social welfare function from the preference of individuals in several circumstances, if a number of axioms, which appear reasonable on the face of it, are to be satisfied. In such circumstances, a social welfare function can only be obtained if it is imposed. Nevertheless, it may be easier to satisfy these axioms at a local level than at the national level.

In addition, decentralized government based within local communities is likely to be more responsive to the needs of a country's citizens if government is democratically based. However, not all government is democratically based and the democratic system itself can be subjected to social pressures. Some local communities are extremely hierarchical. In such societies, without intervention or imposition of new local governance structures by the centre, local élites dominate local government, and use local government to further their own self-interest at the expense of the wider local community.

This possibility appears to have been recognized in India after independence. The central government of India moved to set up locally elected village councils (*panchayats*) with a view to reducing the entrenched power of local élites. Nevertheless, local élites are still sometimes able to dominate elected village councils in India.

Digression on the structure of communitarianism

Margolis (1982) argues that if we are to model the choices made by individuals, including their economic choices, we should consider their preferences as consisting of two components: one component is a set of selfish preferences and the second component reflects the interest of the group or community. In the latter case, selfish interest is subjugated to the interest of the group. An individual's choice will be determined by the relative weight which he or she places on the group compared to self, that is the individual's weight on the "saintly" set (G-set) of preferences compared to his or her selfish set (S-set) of preferences.

It may appear that the individual is being schizophrenic in having such a dichotomous utility function but Margolis argues that there is not a dual personality present, but rather a conscious balancing decision between selfishness and altruism which he (Margolis, 1982, p. 11) defines as the sense of social responsibility or sense of community. He incorporates the latter into his model as "group interest".

While communal values undoubtedly influence individual values and choices, Margolis's model seems to be too simple a representation of reality. It assumes that group interest is known or agreed on. This is not always the case.

Frequently the matter is more complicated because perceived group interest is in a state of flux and different groups perceive different interests.

A problem for communitarianism is to define the reference group of the individual. Not all individuals have the same reference group; some may relate to more than one group or change their reference group with the passage of time. Certainly, the simple model of Margolis will not apply in this case. Indeed, it is even possible that a certain amount of inconsistency or apparent multiple personalities enter the situation as far as the individual's valuations are concerned because the individual relates to different reference groups.

Another aspect that does not appear to be fully addressed by communitarian models is the influence of roles on the preferences of individuals. Individuals often fill multiple roles in society. As they move from one role to another, their expressed preferences may alter. Their preferences are socially influenced, but are not necessarily consistent for individuals in their different roles.

Traditionally, different roles in society involve different duties and imperatives. While these customary or traditional restraints can become an impediment to social progress, they often play a useful functionary role by promoting social predicability and cohesion and limiting selfish behaviour in positions of social responsibility. Once the sense of duty and moral responsibility of those in leading social positions weakens, the chances of a society disintegrating increases.

As Etzioni (1986) points out, the mono-utility concept used in neoclassical economics is too parsimonious. It does not allow appropriately for moral acts or for moral utility nor for moral sentiments. This leads Etzioni to suggest that individuals possess not dual utility functions as claimed by Margolis (1982) but multiple ones. Several reasons why multiple utility or *value* functions may exist for individuals are suggested above, e.g. the relationship of individuals to different groups, their varied roles. Etzioni (1986, p. 181) believes that for the individual there are at least two sources of values: pleasure and morality. There could, however, be additional sources of value, or preference (see Kuperan and Sutinen, 1996). Moreover, the morality to which one is subject changes with one's role in society (and one can occupy a variety of roles) and with one's reference group or groups. Sometimes individuals have different reference groups and the moral imperatives created by each may not be entirely consistent.

The concept of the internally divided self subscribed to by Margolis (1982), Elster (1985) and Etzioni (1988, 1991) is useful. The self has selfish preferences and meta-preferences. The main source of the latter is said to be moral values, partly socially induced and to some extent individually based. These moral values modify selfish behaviour. Whether the moral dimensions of individual support a good society depends on their nature and the social group to which individuals relate. We cannot avoid giving attention to the moral dimension if we wish to promote a "good" society (Cf. Etzioni, 1988).

Kuperan and Sutinen (1996) suggest that an individual's preference function depends on three components rather than two. These are:

(1) selfish gains;

(2) moral feelings; and

(3) social approval or censure.

The last factor is able to operate with considerable force in local communities (Cf. Tisdell, 1990, Ch. 2).

It is important to emphasize that Kant's social philosophy is at variance not only with self-centred utilitarianism but with models of human behaviour which incorporate social and moral values into the *preference* functions of individuals as a basis for individual actions, that is, possibly the models proposed by many communitarians and the mixed system of Etzioni. As pointed out to me by Tomas Riha (1996), both Rousseau and Kant denied that rational self-interest is a reputable moral motive and excluded prudence from the list of moral virtues. In acting in accordance with social values, an individual might be acting prudently. This might also be so when acting in accordance with the moral precepts if the individual's motive is to avoid feelings of guilt.

Sustainability of local communities

While sustaining community and local communities is seen as important by several writers, this goal is usually not well defined. What are the characteristics of community or of local communities that should be sustained? Is it the social cohesiveness of the local community, the political control of the community over local resources or the economic viability of the local community, or all of these factors?

Douglass (1984) believes that all these factors are important. He argues that modern technologies, the extension of markets and the presence of control over resources by large and/or multinational companies erodes the power of local communities over their resource-use and makes for the reduced sustainability of local communities. A somewhat similar theme is expressed by Butler (1980) in his discussion of the local area tourism-cycle. At a significant stage in the development of this cycle, local residents lose control over major developments in their area as distant companies and entrepreneurs develop tourism enterprises in their local area.

Barbier (1987) claims that sustainable development requires sustainability in three spheres: the economic, the social and the biophysical. However, in view of the above discussion, it is possible that the political sphere should be added to this list.

It is worthwhile considering how the sustainability of local communities might be related to the economic concept of sustainable development. The most common definition of sustainable development in economics is that it is development which ensures that the income of future generations is no less than that of present generations (Cf. Tisdell, 1993, Ch. 9). Applying this to a local community, it requires the income of future generations in this community to be not less than that of the present generations. If this view is adopted, sustainable development would have a spatial-dimension as well as a time-dimension. Such an approach would be relatively restrictive as far as the economic development of a country is concerned because it would tend to maintain the economic status quo between areas or regions. In reality, given some mobility of individuals, most people are prepared to trade off some loss in the economic benefits obtained by particular communities against wider economic gains.

Local communities and conservation of natural resources

The opinions of economists differ about the extent to which conservation of natural resources is necessary for sustainable development. Those supporting strong conditions for economic sustainability argue that natural environments need to be preserved and that substitution of man-made capital for natural environmental resources may well result in unsustainable development. On the other hand, those favouring weak sustainability conditions are sanguine about such substitution. There has, however, been little discussion about the development consequences of such trade-offs locally. It is likely that the extent to which local trade-off is consistent with sustainability of *local* economic development varies from region to region and would therefore need to be assessed for each individual case.

It is sometimes argued that if local people are empowered to take care of their own affairs, they are more likely to conserve natural resources than if decisions are forced on them by a wider society. Whether this will happen may, however, vary.

Where a local community is empowered, it is more likely to pursue its own self-interest (as perceived by it) than when it is lacking in such power. If its perceived self-interest involves conservation of resources, then these resources are likely to be conserved. Not all local communities, however, may see their own self-interest as being best fostered by natural resource conservation. Local communities in some circumstances are eager to exploit natural resources for their own economic gain and do not always champion the cause of resource conservation. This is even more likely when local communities are dominated by local economic interest groups.

On the one hand, there are instances where the centralization of control over natural resources has accelerated the exploitation and deterioration of local environments, and other cases, where central control has forced local communities to conserve more natural resources than they would otherwise do. Increased exploitation of the environment as a result of centralization may occur because:

- centralization results in lack of control over the exploitation of natural resources at the local level so that such resources become to a considerable extent open-access property;
- knowledge about appropriate methods for conservation in the local environment may be lacking at the centre and inappropriate land-use strategies may be adopted by the centre out of ignorance; and

- special economic interests at the centre or outside the local community may gain from the exploitation of local natural resources. Such gain may be at the expense of the local community.

Examples of all these cases are available. For instance, central control of forests in Nepal undermined control at the village level and contributed to deforestation in Nepal (Mishra, 1982).

Nevertheless, there are cases where decentralization has had similar consequences. For example, in some areas of the former Soviet Union, devolution of power to some poor regions has resulted in reduced control over economic exploitation of protected areas. Since the benefits to the *local* community of protected areas are often small and enforcement personnel from central government for protecting such areas have been withdrawn, local communities have been able to get increased access to these resources and exploit them to meet their own immediate economic needs.

Local communities do not always adopt or know of appropriate conservation techniques. Slash-and-burn agriculture, which is still practised in many parts of the developing world, is a case in point. For low population densities, it is a relatively friendly environmental method of land-use. However, as population densities become high, it becomes a technique which seriously degrades the natural environment and one which increasingly becomes unsustainable from a economic point of view. Unfortunately, the local people know no other way of life and furthermore, institutional arrangements such as land tenure arrangements developed to support slash-and-burn agriculture do not easily allow local communities to switch to other farming techniques. Barriers to continuing co-evolution of the structure of society and the introduction of new techniques of production occur.

Finally, special economic interests are often active at local level as well as at national level. For examples, the Philippines has adopted measures to give local communities greater control over the use of their natural resources. However, some fear that this may actually result in increased and inappropriate natural resource exploitation as local government bodies are captured by those with special economic interests.

Local communities in pursuing their own self-interest may not pursue the wider interest. For example, they may fail to take account of the external effects of their actions.

The extent to which a local community should take account of the interests of a wider community and how wide that community should be defined is a matter for debate. For example, conservation effort by local communities in developing countries may involve them in economic sacrifice, but bring benefits to those in higher income countries or elsewhere in their own country. To what extent should a local community be expected to make such economic sacrifices for non-local communities? One's answer is likely to depend largely on judgements about income distribution. If the local community is poor, to expect it to make such sacrifices without economic compensation appears to be unjust, and probably also ineffective. Hence, there is now a widespread view that higher income countries which can benefit from conservation in less-developed countries should be prepared to subsidize nature conservation in the latter countries so as to compensate local communities for any economic penalty imposed on them. While this has merit, there are still problems involved in how to deliver the subsidy.

There is for instance, the issue of whether the subsidy or aid for conservation will be ineffective or inequitably distributed. For example, most of the aid, or even all of it, may not be distributed to those local individuals adversely affected by the conservation project. Part will be absorbed by aid officials from higher income countries and a high proportion may be absorbed by professionals in the country assisted and be retained in centralized localities in such countries. Little or no money may find its way to those mainly affected. Consequently, it is possible that the international aid will fail to achieve its conservation goal. Even when the distribution of aid is equitable, it may be ineffective because the design of the conservation project is defective. It may, for instance, be defective because the designers have a poor knowledge of local conditions or have failed to consult sufficiently with the local community (Tisdell, 1995).

Consultation provides information and helps to legitimize governance. Local communities are more likely to be motivated to carry out procedures to embrace natural resource management when they have been consulted and their views taken into account (Kuperan and Sutinen, 1996). Effective governance depends not only on the rules or laws promulgated but also on the procedures and processes used to devise these (Tisdell, 1996). This is one of the reasons why a technocratic approach to policy formation is liable to be ineffective and socially repugnant. Furthermore, technocrats can easily overlook simple but important facts that would have come to light with some consultation with the community involved. The technocratic approach to formulation of economic policies, which has become dominant in economics in recent decades, therefore, poses obvious dangers.

The need to determine the sustainability of community in a dynamic setting

A community remains sustainable as long as it is socially cohesive and its members are able to provide adequately for their economic needs. In fact, if the latter is not the case, the community may lose its social cohesion as a result of economic stress. Such economic stress can arise from several causes, one of which is the deterioration of the biophysical resource-base on which the economic welfare of the local community depends.

Governance of a community depends on its laws, customs, traditions and institutions, all of which in certain circumstances can be regarded as cultural assets. They may help to sustain the community and increase the overall wellbeing of its members. However, such institutional factors can become impediments to the sustainability of a community if social and environmental conditions alter. This is because institutions and customs change slowly. If biophysical or other socio-economic changes are rapid, institutions may not change quickly enough to ensure sustainability of the community. Because of inertia, the institutional framework of the community becomes a liability rather than an asset. The survival of the community can then become dependent on institutional change.

Methods of economic production or techniques of production and social institutions and customs often evolve together (Gowdy, 1994). However, this co-evolution may fail to be synchronized if economic and technological change is rapid. Consequently, social disruption can occur which threatens the long-term survival of the community involved.

As Karl Marx points out, the social structure and institutions of society are moulded, to a large extent, by the methods of its economic production. When technological and economic change is rapid, variations in social structures lag behind those in technology. At the same time, inertia in the structure of social institutions may retard the adoption or development of new production technologies which are essential for the survival of the community. In particular, existing property rights in land, or other assets, may retard the adoption of new technologies essential for the economic and social survival of communities. Parts of Asia, such as Northeast India and South West China, provide examples.

The survival of local communities in Northeast India

Many village and tribal groups in southern Asia still engage in shifting or slash-and-burn agriculture. They have evolved institutions and customs, including methods of allocating land rights, which support this method of agricultural production. Unfortunately, with rising populations and income aspirations in regions where slash-and-burn agriculture is practised (mostly in the hilly regions), this form of agriculture is becoming rapidly unsustainable from a biophysical and an economic point of view. There is a need for it to be replaced by settled agriculture designed to be of a conservation-type. On sloping lands, hedgerows with alley-cropping are one possibility (Maglinao and Sajjapongse, 1995).

Traditional land rights among tribal groups in Northeast India are an impediment to transition from shifting to settled agriculture. The Mizos for example in Mizoram in Northeast India, allocate land to villagers by ballot as the area in which the village conducts its agriculture shifts. This means that village families only have possession of an agricultural plot while an area is under cultivation. Thus their possession is temporary. When the village cycle of cultivation is completed and the village eventually returns to the same area to cultivate it again at a later time, the family may be allocated another plot by the ballot. Such a system does not allow for the development of settled agriculture or the planting of perennial crops or tea-crops. Furthermore, the Mizos have no individual incentive to invest in the conservation of their land or in its long-term productivity.

The system is becoming unsustainable from a biophysical and economic point of view. With population growth, cultivation cycles have been reduced from around 20 years to four to five years. As a result, increased exposure of the soil to the elements is accelerating soil erosion and heightening nutrient loss from the soil (Ramakrishnan, 1995). Consequently, agricultural yields per crop are falling and starchy crops, e.g. tubers, are replacing those which are high protein. Effort-yield ratios have risen markedly. Ramakrishnan (1992) reports that when cultivation cycles become as short as four to five years, yields barely cover the effort involved in shifting cultivation whereas for cycles of 20 years, this method is a very economic form of agricultural production, relatively friendly environmentally and favourable to the conservation of biodiversity. The present shifting agricultural system in Northeast India is unsustainable, especially given that population in the region continues to increase.

If agricultural transition is to occur in this region, land rights need to be altered. The Government of Mizoram has attempted to force some change in this direction through its New Land Use Policy (NLUP) (Lianzela, 1994, Section 7.4; 1995, pp. 57-63) but it has only had success in extracting a small amount of land from the traditional system and this land is mostly in the neighbourhood of the capital city of Mizoram, Aizawl.

The slash-and-burn method of cultivation also occurs in parts of Yunnan in China, in Myanmar and elsewhere in Southeast Asia. Similar issues are raised by this practice there.

The author has observed slash-and-burn agriculture in Xishuangbanna, Yunnan in China (Tisdell and Xiang, 1996). Some of the hill tribes still practise it. Frequently, steepland is planted with maize (corn) in such areas because it is a cash crop. The tribal people in some areas carry corn on their backs to the local market to sell. Their main aim is to obtain cash to enable them to participate in the cash exchange economy and purchase, in particular, consumer durables. However, the maize is usually grown without any soil conservation measures being adopted. The result is severe soil erosion. In due course, this will reduce the depth of soil cover and the land surface will consist of clayey or rocky materials. Yields become unsustainable and eventually the soil may become barren. Some of these practices are so traditional that it was even impossible in Mao's China to eliminate them.

It should be emphasized that at least two matters must be taken into account in considering transition from shifting to settled agriculture:

(1) How can land rights be appropriately altered?

(2) Are sustainable and economic methods of settled agriculture available for the region under consideration?

Many of the methods developed for settled agriculture are appropriate to flat or gently sloping land, but are not environmentally sustainable and economic on steeply sloping lands where most slash-and-burn agriculture is currently practised. In areas where slash-and-burn agriculture is practised, soils are often poor and shallow. New cultivation methods therefore need to be evolved to suit steep land for settled agriculture. Often local communities lack the resources and expertise to undertake such developments and require assistance from the wider community.

Concluding comment with some observations on Kantian philosophy

The world is becoming increasingly globalized economically, environmentally and culturally (Karunaratne and Tisdell, 1996). As the information age progresses and transport and communication barriers of all sorts are reduced, local communities are drawn into an ever widening circle of interchange of ideas and commodities. Such changes have advantages and disadvantages. Their major impact is to reduce or eliminate the identities of local communities. Local communities are losing their cohesion, identity and independence. It is now impossible for any local community to exist in splendid isolation.

The processes involved are under the control of no individual. They move forward relentlessly and blindly, driven by the economic motives of individuals and small groups. There are of course gains, but also losses. There is a loss of "community" and the sense of belonging; a factor which may help to explain the high rates of suicide and psychological disorders in a several high income countries. These countries have "dismantled" local communities to a much greater extent than lower income countries. In high income countries, "community" has increasingly become identified with workplace. However, in periods of high unemployment or uncertain employment, many are denied "community" or it is insecure in workplaces. In any case, "workplace" communities may not be very supportive of individuals and their families in the modern world.

Although electronic media can help to create a wider community, the extent to which such media can establish close personal contact is limited. This synthetic method of establishing communities may not in the end prove to be very satisfying to individuals. The above highlights the question of what is the community to which an individual belongs. Which community is to be considered when one is trying to distil community values? Individuals often relate to more than one community and sometimes they are increasingly inclusive, e.g. local community, regional community and national community. However, values of these communities may very well be in conflict. In those circumstances, Kant's social imperative is far from clear.

While values at the level of the community are important, the communal values accepted by the individual are liable to vary with the community (or communities) to which he/she relates. We can only have respect for those values, if we have respect for the community or communities which form the individual's reference group. Ultimately, communitarianism cannot obviate the need for the moral responsibility of choice by individuals about values, that is the importance of choice based on individual conscience pursued independently and even on occasions, in conflict with values espoused by a community. Thus, the conflict between the rights and values of the individual and those of the community cannot be resolved in a definitive manner. Furthermore, it may be impossible to derive community values in a definitive manner from the preferences and values of individuals. This is so apart from the logical consistency problems identified by Arrow (1951). It may be impossible to transform individual preferences into a social welfare function, for the total situation may differ from the collection of individual parts in isolation.

There is a further philosophical problem for utilitarians and neoclassical economists: do the utility of preference functions of individuals, which are the building blocks of social preferences, include the moral and social components, that is the group components? If so, they have no status *independent* of society. The total values of individuals have no independent standing, as communitarians suggest is the case. These values, therefore, have no independent moral worth. One's respect for them will be dependent on one's level of respect for the group or society that helped to form them. At least in environmental economics, some economists allow moral and social impacts on individuals to be included in the valuations placed on objects by individuals. For example, writers such as Pearce (Pearce *et al.*, 1989) extol the virtues of applying total economic valuation (TEV) to environmental conservation decisions. Since societal influences on expressed individual values using this method are bound to be strong, the resulting values only have moral legitimacy if one accepts that the moral worth of the communal values of the society in which the individual is embedded. Thus one cannot resort entirely to individualism to determine an "appropriate" social decision. Circularity gives rise to a fundamental dilemma. A social decision maker cannot avoid moral choice.

Kant's philosophy does not support the view that social welfare can be measured or gauged by synthesizing the welfare of *individuals* to obtain an estimate of collective welfare. He rejects the utilitarian view that society should be so ordered as to maximize the sum of utilities of individuals but considers that society should be ordered by the Idea of Reason and the moral principles to which it gives rise. When society is so ordered, the greatest human happiness is assured (Acton, 1970, p. 44). Kant seems to be arguing that institutions should be determined independently of an appeal to the utilities of individuals and once rationally established they will maximize utility in society. The ideal society cannot be designed by relying on the utilities of individuals because this would put the cart before the horse. This is not to say that Kant does not extol the worth of the individual, as the transcendental self. As Acton (1970, pp. 41-42) points out: "According to [Kant's] Principle of Humanity, the dignity of each individual man is an essential requirement for the moral law, and according to the Principle of Autonomy, the moral law is both actively willed by every rational being and regarded by him as the law he should submit to. These principles have a liberal, even a democratic air, and Kant's other notion of a universal Kingdom of Ends in which all men are legislating members extends the ethical into a somewhat political sphere."

As mentioned by me above, I believe it unlikely that all rational beings will agree on the moral law. If some agree and others disagree which set of individuals is to be considered right? Even if there is agreement in the moral law, it may be at such a lofty level that few operational or policy consequences can be drawn. Furthermore, are not normative or moral *assumptions* already involved in the principles put forward by Kant? If so, they (moral principles) can hardly be based on pure reason. Is there more likely to be agreement on the moral law in local communities and to what extent would it be appropriate for this law to vary between communities and with the passage of time? These matters appear not to be resolved.

A difficulty both for the utilitarian approach and for the Kantian approach is path dependence. Both desires (utilities) and perceptions of moral principles may in fact be a function of the institutions and the historical development of society. This means that utilities do not have independent status. It is dangerous therefore to rely on them to build a Utopian society. They are *situational* to some extent. Kant proposed transcendental rationalism as a means to circumvent this problem. Unlike the utilitarians, Kant recognized the situational problem. Nevertheless, it is unlikely that this problem can be circumvented by appealing to transcendental rationalism as Kant claims. Modern communitarians also appear to have no solution to this problem.

Despite the above critical remarks, Immanuel Kant was able to bring attention to some of the fundamental philosophical problems which the utilitarians face in constructing a social welfare function designed to establish a Utopian society. At the same time, the Kantian method itself is unable to provide a blueprint for an ideal society. All rational beings are unlikely to agree at operational levels on the categorical imperative and its implications because Kant's transitory phase (in which individuals are in imperfect contact with Supreme Rationality, God), is unending on Earth. Such rational scepticism could result in increased respect for the rights of individuals and local communities.

References

Acton, H. (1970), *Kant's Moral Philosophy*, Macmillan, London.

Arrow, K.J. (1951), *Social Choice and Individual Values*, Wiley, New York, NY.

Barbier, E.B. (1987), "The concept of sustainable economic development", *Environmental Conservation*, Vol. 14 No. 2, pp. 101-10.

Butler, R.W. (1980), "The concept of a tourist area cycle of evolution: implications for management of reserves", *Canadian Geographer*, Vol. 24, pp. 5-12.

Douglass, G.K. (1984),"The meanings of agricultural sustainability", in Douglass, G.K. (Ed.), *Agricultural Sustainability in a Changing World Order*, Westview Press, Boulder, CO, pp. 3-29.

Elster, J. (1985), *The Multiple Self*, Cambridge University Press, Cambridge.

Etzioni, A. (1986) "The case for multiple-utility conception", *Economics and Philosophy*, Vol. 2, pp. 159-83.

Etzioni, A. (1988), *The Moral Dimension: Toward a New Economics*, The Free Press, New York, NY.

Etzioni, A (1991), "Contemporary liberals, communitarians, and individual choices", in Etzioni, A. and Lawrence, P.R. (Eds), *Socio-economics: Toward a New Synthesis*, M.C. Sharpe, New York, NY.

Frolov, I. (1984), *Dictionary of Philosophy,* 2nd rev. English ed., translation from the Russian by Saifulin, M. and Dixon, R.R., Progress Publishers, Moscow.

Georgescu-Roegen, N. (1976), *Energy and Economic Myths: Institutional and Analytic Economic Essays*, Pergamon Press, New York, NY.

Gowdy, J.M. (1994), *Coevolutionary Economics*, Kluwer, Boston, MA.

Karunaratne, N. and Tisdell, C. (1996), "Globalization and its policy repercussions", *Intereconomics*, Vol. 31, pp. 248-60.

Kuperan, K. and Sutinen, J. (1996), "Regulatory compliance in Malaysian fisheries", in *Proceedings of Seventh International Fisheries Conference*, Taiwan Fisheries Research Institute, Keelung, Taiwan.

Lianzela (1994), *Economic Development of Mizoram,* Spectrum Publications, Guwahti and Delhi.

Lianzela (1995), *Four Decades of Planning in Mizoram*, Khuangkungi Venghvai, Aizawl, Mizoram, India.

Maglinao, A. and Sajjapongse, A. (1995), *International Workshop on Conservation Farming for Sloping Uplands in Southeast Asia: Challenges, Opportunities and Prospects*, International Board for Soil Research and Management, Bangkok.

Margolis, H. (1982), *Selfishness, Altruism and Rationality: A Theory of Social Choice*, Cambridge University Press, Cambridge.

Mishra, H.R. (1982), "Balancing human needs and conservation in Nepal's Royal Chitwan National Park", *Ambio,* Vol. 11, pp. 246-51.

Pearce, D., Markandya, A. and Barbier, E.B. (1989), *Blueprint for a Green Economy*, Earthscan Publications, London.

Ramakrishnan, P.S. (1992), *Shifting Agriculture and Sustainable Development of North-Eastern India*, Paris and Parthenon, Cornforth.

Ramakrishnan, P.S. (1995), "Sustainable rural development with people's participation in the Asian context", in Samad, S.A., Watanabe, T. and Kim, S.J., *People's Initiatives for Sustainable Development: Lessons of Experience,* Asia and Pacific Development Centre, Kuala Lumpur, Malaysia, pp. 421-39.

Riha, T. (1966), Personal communication, August.

Tisdell, C.A. (1990), *Natural Resources, Growth and Economic Development*, Praeger, New York, NY.

Tisdell, C.A. (1993), *Environmental Economics*, Edward Elgar, Aldershot.

Tisdell, C.A. (1995), "Issues in biodiversity conservation including the role of local communities", *Environmental Conservation,* Vol. 22, pp. 216-28.

Tisdell, C.A. (1996), "Agricultural sustainability and conservation of biodiversity: competing policies and paradigms", *Biodiversity Conservation Working Paper No. 33,* Department of Economics, The University of Queensland, Brisbane, 4072, Australia.

Tisdell, C.A. and Xiang, Z. (1996), "Reconciling economic development, nature conservation and local communities: strategies for biodiversity conservation in Xishuangbanna, China", *The Environmentalist*, Vol. 16.

PUBLIC ADMINISTRATION AND DEVELOPMENT, VOL. 12, 267–278 (1992)

Rural development projects in LDCs: appraisal, participation and sustainability

LUCA TACCONI and CLEM TISDELL

University of Queensland, Australia

SUMMARY

Evidence on the performance of development projects shows that sustainability is seldom achieved. Project sustainability is influenced by ecological, social, political and economic systems. However, the blueprint approach to project choice tends to incorporate sustainability into the project cycle by considering only economic and environmental systems. This is done by adopting elaborate methodologies such as expanded CBA and EIA. This approach is unlikely to lead to sustainable projects. The 'participation approach' is more sensitive to the social and political systems than the blueprint approach. It involves people in decision-making and sees the achievement of sustainable projects as the result of people's empowerment and self-reliance. However, under certain circumstances, this approach can lead to environmentally unsustainable projects. Smaller scale projects tend to bring about sustainability, but government control might be needed to ensure this. Social obstacles exist in implementing participation but occur for top-down projects as well. Problems exist in combining the bottom-up and top-down approaches.

INTRODUCTION

Over the last four decades, the impact of foreign assistance on the economic performance of developing countries has been less than satisfactory. Economic, environmental and social disruptions brought about by development activities have led some to question whether active development policies are even worthwhile adopting at all (e.g. Latouche, 1986).

In the wake of the rising concern about environmental degradation across the world and the mounting poverty and social disruption in the Third World, the concept of sustainable development has been popularized by several congresses and enquiries (e.g. IUCN: International Union for Conservation of Nature and Natural Resources, 1980; WCED: World Commission on Environment and Development, 1987).

Two approaches for including sustainability features in project aid will be considered. It will be argued that both approaches involve shortcomings that need to be overcome if sustainable benefits from projects are to be achieved. To do so, integration of the different approaches to project aid is required. This is by no means an easy task as the right balance between 'top-down' and 'bottom-up' strategies and the adequate scale of the project will vary from situation to situation.

It could be argued that achieving sustainability of benefits requires the abandon-

Luca Tacconi is a Research Scholar in the Department of Economics, and Clem Tisdell is Professor of Economics and Head, Department of Economics at the University of Queensland, Brisbane, Queensland 4072, Australia

0271–2075/92/030267–12$06.00

ment of project aid in its present typology and moving to a 'programme' style approach (e.g. Lecomte, 1986). However, project aid is still an important tool of development assistance and it will probably remain as such in the near future, eventually as part of a programme. Thus, this paper concentrates more on the aspects of project sustainability than on the examination of alternatives to project aid.

PERFORMANCE OF PROJECT AID

During the 1950s and 1960s, donor countries favoured the implementation of large infrastructural projects, mostly urban. The majority of the rural population did not benefit from this approach to development as the trickle-down effects did not eventuate (Arndt, 1983). The neglect of the rural sector has encouraged urbanization of the population in many LDCs. This has sometimes disrupted the social organization of the rural sector, with negative effects on the environment (Garcia-Barrios and Garcia-Barrios, 1990). Evidence[1] shows also that rural infrastructural projects mostly benefited the wealthier members of the rural communities, increasing income inequalities.

During the 1970s and early 1980s, donor countries increased the number of rural development projects focusing on the rural poor. Those projects, however, had limited success. Howell, studying integrated rural development projects started by the World Bank in the early 1970s in Africa, reports that 'over 54% of the projects were 'failures'—that is, they had rates of return below 10%' (Howell, 1990, p. 275). This high rate of project failure is also reported by Peek (1988). Failure of a project is judged on the basis of the internal rate of return (IRR) measured at completion of the project.

The appropriateness of measuring project success on the basis of the IRR will be considered later on. It is relevant to note here that a project should provide lasting benefits to the beneficiaries if it is to be judged successful in providing sustainability. It should continue to provide benefits after completion. The limited evidence available about project performance once the donors' support has ended is not encouraging.

Cernea (1987) carried out a sustainability[2] study on 25 World Bank agricultural projects. These projects had been found successful and with good long-term prospects by an internal audit at the time of completion. However, Cernea reports that only 12 projects out of 25 had achieved sustainability.

Evidence on the ecological and social impact of projects is anecdotal as these aspects of projects were not, until recently, of major concern to most donors. The available evidence mainly refers to large-scale projects that have sometimes had deleterious effects on the environment and on livelihoods, such as in the case of agricultural projects that deforested large areas (e.g. Roche, 1989) and the many dams built around the world. Further information on the impact of small projects is awaited but, as reported later in this paper, even small-scale projects can have negative environmental effects.

---

[1] See Peek (1988) for a brief review.

[2] Sustainability was defined as 'the maintenance of an acceptable net flow of benefits from the project's investments after its completion' (Cernea, 1987, p. 3).

DIMENSIONS OF SUSTAINABILITY

In project aid jargon, sustainability used to be associated with the 'recurrent cost problem' (Gray and Martens, 1983). Gow and Morss (1988) argue that not only recurrent costs affect project sustainability but political, technical and managerial elements should also be taken into account. Their analysis of factors influencing project sustainability is, however, deficient.

The concept of sustainable development has several dimensions. At the physical-environmental level, sustainability refers to the impact of resource use on a single resource or on the ecosystem. The sustainable use of a renewable resource is equated with the maintenance of a non-decreasing physical stock of the resource. However, at the ecosystem level such use could be unsustainable because of its negative impact on the functions and outputs of the ecosystem (Dixon and Fallon, 1989).

The geographical area over which the impact of a development activity should be considered varies according to the scale of the activity. It may range from the micro-environment to the watershed or the nation. Measuring the impact of a productive activity on the ecosystem presents several problems. The ecosystem can be seen to have a hierarchy of sub-systems (Norton, 1990) in which the development activities are located. As sub-systems are faster changing than the ecosystem in which they are embedded, the development activity can be expected to have, over time, differential impacts on the sub-system and on the ecosystem. Changes in the sub-system affect the larger system only marginally over time, thus a development activity that seems to affect the sub-system negatively may in the end have only a marginal or zero effect on the ecosystem.

Unfortunately 'ecologists ... still cannot model relationships in natural systems adequately to state confidently the degree of fragility of a system prior to human-induced disturbances' (Norton, 1990, p. 121). At present a cautious approach to development seems necessary to avoid irreversible environmental damage.

A development project impacts not only on the natural environment but also on the social, political and economic systems. In fact, recent literature on sustainable development points out that these systems are inter-related and important components of the development process (Sachs, 1987; Barbier, 1987). Development organizations often ignore the influence that the political sphere has on development activities. Simon (1989) strongly argues that political economy considerations have to be incorporated in development projects if sustainability is to be achieved. Countless projects have failed because they did not take into account the political context (Tendler, 1982). Development activities should therefore account not only for economic factors such as equity and goods production, but also for cultural diversity, social justice, genetic diversity and social relations of production.

The complex inter-relationships between the four systems influencing sustainability make it extremely difficult to measure or even to define exactly how sustainability can be achieved. Because development is a value-laden concept, so are definitions of sustainable development. Hence the goals of a development activity will depend on the world view of the development agents, i.e. development agencies and project beneficiaries. This will also determine the methodologies adopted for project planning and implementation.

INCORPORATING SUSTAINABILITY IN THE PROJECT CYCLE

The conventional blueprint approach sees a project as a means 'to push the production possibility curve outwards' (Coverdale and Healey, 1987, p. 100). The development question is a technical-managerial problem and the aim of the project is to increase the production of goods and services. An improvement in well-being is often equated with increased availability of goods and services. Sociological factors are seen as peripheral to the project but should be investigated 'so that projects introduced by "outsiders" are likely to be consistent with local "felt needs" and less likely to have perverse social effects' (Coverdale and Healey, 1987, p. 106).

Recognizing the limitations inherent to the definition of development as a sole function of income, Barbier (1987) suggests that sustainable development should be seen as the maximization of the human ascribed goals across the biological, economic and social systems through a process of dynamic trade-offs. Barbier's approach belongs to the 'resource management paradigm' (Colby, 1990), whereby ecology and sociology are 'economized'. Biological diversity, cultural diversity, institutions and participation can be traded for economic goals, and the role of economics is seen as being to assess costs and benefits of the trade-offs between the three systems.

This position implies that in order to make sustainable development operational, techniques such as cost–benefit analysis (CBA) need to be improved for analyzing the above-mentioned trade-offs (Barbier, 1987). In line with a blueprint approach it is the *donor* who, *ex ante*, will appraise the project by using techniques such as CBA (eventually extended to include environmental variables), social impact assessment (SIA) and environmental impact assessment (EIA) (e.g. van Pelt *et al.*, 1990).

Together with pre-set goals, the blueprint project comes with a time-bounded and mechanistic delivery system, most often on a large-scale basis. The emphasis on accurate planning is partly responsible for the exclusion of beneficiaries' participation in the project cycle. Participation is seen as the cause of delays in project implementation. It is also personnel intensive and this is perceived as reducing project efficiency. Furthermore, participation of beneficiaries is sometimes rejected by local bureaucrats and powerful élites because it decreases their control over the project.

In the 'participation approach' (PA) to development projects, there is an increasing emphasis on people as the ultimate purpose of the development effort. In contrast to the blueprint approach, well-being is not only a function of the quantity of produced goods and services available but it also depends on security (e.g. wealth), on non-materialistic elements such as self-esteem and empowerment and on natural environmental services.

From the identification to the evaluation of a project, people's participation is fundamental to this model. Participation is seen as an essential factor for a project's success (Kottak, 1985), and cannot be traded-off against other variables.

Participation has, however, several dimensions and definitions. Participation is sometimes viewed in the blueprint approach as involvement of beneficiaries in project costs and in sharing of benefits, but in the PA it is mainly seen as involvement by beneficiaries in decision-making, leading to their empowerment.[3] The core elements of this model can be summarized as the primacy of people, the relevance of people's knowledge and the accent on gender issues (Oakley *et al.*, 1991).

[3] See Paul (1989) for a multi-faceted description of participation.

Starting from the people and their needs will ensure, according to Chambers (1987), the sustainability of the project. The people are assumed to know and respect their environment and it is mainly the influence of external factors that causes over-exploitation of the resources. When people are empowered they will be able to fend off external pressures, and a project can bring lasting benefits as the beneficiaries have an enhanced ability to use the local human and material resources and those made available by the project, thus maintaining their increased well-being.

During project implementation social, economic, environmental and political conditions and goals often change, weaknesses in the implementation plan are exposed and side-effects emerge. In order to accommodate these changes, flexibility in project activities and a 'learning approach' (Korten, 1980) are required. Beneficiaries' participation in the decision-making process, involving a two-way continuous exchange of information between development agency and beneficiaries, is a fundamental factor in accommodating these changes.

This learning-by-doing process that taps people's knowledge is germane to the co-evolutionary development advocated by Norgaard (1988), in which human goals and activities adjust in response to changes in the natural environment and *vice versa*.

The achievement and maintenance of sustainability is seen as a continuous process. Hence, this approach tends to rely on methods that allow a fast, interactive data gathering such as 'rapid rural appraisal' (e.g. Kohn Kaen University, 1987). More emphasis is put on fast and not too expensive data gathering than on 'accurate', expensive and time-consuming data collection to be used in project identification and selection with sophisticated techniques such as CBA and EIA.

SUSTAINABILITY AND THE BLUEPRINT APPROACH

The numerous shortcomings of the blueprint approach have already been highlighted by several authors (e.g. Korten, 1980) and to a certain extent in the previous sections. Therefore, in this section we concentrate on a new aspect of the blueprint approach: the tentative introduction of sustainability in the project cycle, through the extension of CBA, in order to include environmental variables. This is of particular relevance as some aid organizations tend to adopt this methodology (e.g. AIDAB: Australian International Development Assistance Bureau, 1990).

Income distribution effects, an important feature of development projects, are often neglected by the conventional blueprint approach. CBA provides for the analysis of income distribution effects,[4] but in practice '... the effects of a project on the distribution of income are not included in the formal analysis' (Squire 1988, p. 1126).

CBA is data-intensive and often data is not available because local means of livelihood are not well known and documented. Application of CBA also has a high opportunity cost in relation to the skilled personnel who have to be diverted from other tasks. It should be noted that, even if the *ex ante* IRR is a good approximation of the actual *ex post* IRR (and it rarely happens), a positive internal rate of return does not mean that the project is successful. Peek (1988) observes that many apparently successful (on the basis of IRR) World Bank poverty-oriented projects

---

[4] This theory is, however, much disputed (e.g. Stewart, 1975).

failed to improve the living conditions of the targeted poorest members of the community. These are some drawbacks of the utilization of CBA in a conventional context that are amplified when sustainability is taken into account and new ones emerge.

CBA is purported by some economic practitioners to be a scientific method of project appraisal (McAllister, 1980). A scientific method should give results that can be replicated by other researchers, but this is not the case of CBA, where different evaluation teams usually reach different results. This problem arises because of the assumptions that have to be made when carrying out CBA. Those assumptions depend on the researchers' perceptions of the local conditions and may be influenced by political pressures. Thus, assessment of project sustainability based on CBA leaves judgement in the hands of few experts who might be subject to political pressure.

Pearce, Markandya and Barbier (1989) suggest that sustainability can be introduced into CBA by imposing as a constraint a non-decreasing natural capital stock. However, they argue that it is not feasible to preserve the natural capital stock for each project, and suggest that the 'damage' of the projects should be considered at a programme level (set of projects). It is argued that the sum of the environmental damages at the programme level, expressed in value terms, should be non-positive. Environmentally enhancing projects could be undertaken in order to compensate for the damaging ones. The perspective of this approach to development is that of 'damage and off-setting repair'.

The approach of Pearce to project sustainability takes account only of the interaction of the biological and economic systems. Impacts of projects on the social and political systems are left out of the analysis. At best, this could give a partial assessment of sustainability. But, even if we accept a definition of sustainability limited to the biological and economic systems, problems are still present. The physical damages (present and future) of each project might have synergistic effects so that the sum of project costs and benefits will not give an adequate assessment of the total impact.

It is assumed that the impact of a project on the environment can be appropriately valued. Some valuation methods (cf. Dixon and Hufschmidt, 1986) use market prices to measure the impact of development projects by looking, for example, at changes in productivity and value of output or loss of earnings. These methods give an indication of the monetary impact on production given the present use of the environment, the present technology and current prices. Other methods attempt to value the environment by testing the users' and non-users' willingness to pay (WTP) or willingness to accept compensation (WTA). These methods are even more data- and personnel-intensive than traditional CBA. Furthermore, WTP and WTA are influenced by present income distribution (McAllister, 1980). But, more importantly, they measure the present generation's perceived importance of the environment, based on limited knowledge. This can hardly be taken as an approximate 'value' of the environment. In some cases, these approaches also face problems of application from a cultural standpoint. If the land is owned collectively (e.g. customary tenure) and is not alienable, and/or there are religious-cultural bonds with the land, it is hard to see how a WTP or WTA can be expressed in money terms.

Both income and stock effects should be taken into account in appraising a project, but CBA cannot properly accommodate and evaluate the role of stocks in relation to uncertain events. The loss of a stock resource, e.g. loss of land because of mining, could be compensated for by a lump sum payment. However, lack of investment opportunities could prevent the beneficiaries from investing. For example, cultural conditions might lead to the people spending the money on consumption goods (e.g. cars or alcohol). Loss of the traditional livelihood might also result in cultural disruption but this appears difficult to evaluate.

It seems that the blueprint approach faces severe difficulties in including sustainability considerations in development projects, as it pays lip service to institutional issues and it is troubled in introducing environmental variables in the project cycle.

A CRITIQUE OF THE 'PARTICIPATION APPROACH'

Environmental implications of projects, scale issues and government role are all issues that loom large in the debate over participation, hence this section will tackle them instead of looking at project analysis methods.

The PA pays greater attention to socio-political issues than the blueprint approach, but it often assumes that starting from the needs of the people and enabling them to control their resources will automatically result in sustainable projects. This is not necessarily so. In the PA the view (borrowed from ethnographic studies) that indigenous people live in symbiosis with their environment and have a 'conservationist spirit' is sometimes implicit. Some forest people do live in harmony with the forest but others are shown to have quite destructive practices (Rambo, 1982). As a matter of fact, deforestation is a phenomenon known since ancient times (Siirianen, 1990), and indigenous people have threatened the existence of animal species (e.g. Tisdell, 1986). The intentional conservationist features of traditional tenureship systems have also been rejected (Hviding, 1989). Hviding shows that in some cases indigenous peoples' lack of concern towards the environment can lead to over-exploitation of resources.

Chambers (1987) suggests that poor people will protect the environment if their control of resources is secured. However, the fact should not be overlooked that in some cases local resources may not be sufficient for local needs because of population growth or because living standards have been artificially increased, as Bertram (1986) has documented for the Pacific. Environmentally sustainable management would not be possible unless the standard of living was lowered.

Outlining the characteristics of a participation strategy, Lecomte (1986) suggests that donors should wait for the development initiatives to spring from within the local community, and prior to external financial assistance, a lengthy period (up to 10 years) of institution building should be undertaken. That would reduce the risk of suffocating local initiative and of creating dependency, and would lead to sustainable development.

The risk of hampering local initiative and making people dependent on external assistance is actual (Hough and Sherpa, 1989; Bortei-Doku, 1991). However, Hough and Sherpa show that people participation in decision-making might lead to their empowerment and self-reliance but could create environmental damage. As noted earlier, this can arise if people's needs are greater than local resources and also if institution building requires a long period during which external forces put pressure on the natural environment. For example, in the Solomon Islands large-scale logging undertaken by foreign companies has already displaced some communities and threatens to clear the commercially exploitable forests within 10–15 years. Local communities, who are the traditional landowners, are beginning to refuse logging concessions as they are offered the alternative of ecologically sustainable small-scale sawmilling through external assistance. A long period of institution building would imply, in this case, ecological disruption and loss of livelihoods. Furthermore, it is doubtful that the initiative of finding an alternative to large-scale logging could have come from the village people without external impulse, as local people lacked the knowledge to develop small-scale sawmilling projects.

Powerlessness, arising from centuries of domination (Oakley *et al.*, 1991) and from situations that cannot be overcome without external support, is often one of the major obstacles to community initiatives and participation. Population growth and rainfall decrease can induce increasing pressure on natural resources and consequent breakdown of traditional tenure systems (Heermans, 1987), thus leading to an open access property regime. A vicious circle can start, leading to an increasing exploitation of resources as people lack the means to face the problem and feel powerless. Direct external assistance is therefore needed to solve land tenure disputes and provide the means to boost the availability of natural resources, e.g. a forestry project. Dichter (1989) argues in favour of an immediate external assistance on the basis that assessing people's needs with them, soon after starting a project, helps the beneficiaries in better focusing their problems. It is obvious that the risk of creating dependency is still present.

Following Schumacher (1974) and other populist authors, advocates of the PA often argue in favour of small-scale projects. An exception is Adams (1990) who asserts that scale is not an issue in project sustainability; people participation in decision-making and project control are the critical factors. Then, does scale affect sustainability?

Project scale can influence sustainability in different ways. Firstly, consider the 'divisibility' of project control and management. A large-scale irrigation project adopting appropriate technology can allow people participation (Uphoff, 1985), but a large-scale commercial forest plantation requires centralized management, thus excluding people participation in decision-making (Fortmann and Fairfax, 1989). One further problem with large-scale projects is that sizeable financial commitments often tend to shift the focus from people participation to quantitative targets, such as the number of villages provided with water (Therkildsen, 1991), and lack of participation can lead to project failure.

Briefly, it should also be noted that large-scale projects may be unsuitable to the local institutions; in the Solomon Islands some large-scale agricultural projects have failed because they give rise to land disputes (Frazer, 1987). Small-scale projects could better target the proposed beneficiaries (Chambers, 1978) and are more flexible than large-scale ones, thus offering reduced risk of irreversible environmental damage and better possibility of refocusing project goals.

However, at the supra-project level, the environmental benignity of small-scale projects should not be taken for granted. Contrary to Schumacher's claim that 'small-scale operations, *no matter how numerous*, are always less likely to be harmful to the natural environment than large-scale ones' (Schumacher, 1974 p. 29; emphasis added), a large number of small-scale irrigation projects can have a negative impact on the environment (Kimmage, 1991), and the same concept applies to small-scale logging operations which are individually sustainable (Sargent and Burgess, 1988).

It is evident from this argument that, to ensure environmental sustainability, it may be that a certain degree of government regulation and control of development activities is needed, even if they are undertaken on a small-scale basis.

The PA is sometimes depicted as being on a collision path with the interests of recipient governments (and of their bureaucracies) and also with village social arrangements. That governments tend to centralize decision-making processes and vest development initiatives in a rhetorical participative flavour is not new. Nevertheless, it is also evident that there are cases in which governments have promoted true people participation in development, e.g. in the Philippines (Harland, 1991) and in Thailand (von Meheren and Seo, 1987), a country that Rigg (1991) considers as particularly problematic for implementing the PA, from both a social and a political standpoint.

A case in point is the study by Huntington (1988), cited by Rigg (1991) as an example of a failed participatory project.[5] This study reports on a project termed 'participatory' that actually was top-down, went against people's wishes and social values, used inappropriate technology and was simply production driven. The socio-political conflicts generated by the project, and the cause of its demise, are essentially the same as those attributed by Rigg to projects arising from the PA. It is not of great comfort, but it is obvious that difficulties of social and political acceptance are not peculiar to the PA but also arise, perhaps even to a larger extent, in the context of a blueprint project.

DISCUSSION

While a number of advantages are seen in selecting development projects using PA, it is also important to consider some of the obstacles to its application.

A mix of the top-down and bottom-up approaches has been advocated for political economy reasons (Simon, 1989); for 'technological–organizational' motivations (Rigg, 1991); to pool the state's resources with the access of local organizations to the people (Paul, 1989); and to facilitate environmentally sustainable development. Also the importance of having government agents working with the people in PA should not be underestimated. They can learn from and appreciate the extensive knowledge possessed by local people and their potential for development. If in theory a mixture of top-down and bottom-up seems to be the appropriate solution, it has to be recognized that the appropriate balance of top-down and bottom-up is not simple to achieve. For example, government's priority of the development of market crops may not be the same as the peasant's need of subsistence food. The degree of participation in projects that the government is prepared to permit may appear as a token one to the people. Even if in theory the degree of participation can be adjusted to meet different requirements (Paul, 1989), people may reject participation in the project if they believe that their influence on the project will be minimal. This happened in relation to a conservation area project in Malawi (Hough and Sherpa, 1989).

The PA is seen by some development agencies as inappropriate to their bureaucratic apparatus, geared to a timely budgeting and delivery system. One solution could

---

[5] See Oakley (1991, pp. 270–271) for a distinction between participatory projects and participation in development.

be the reform of the agencies, but this faces several obstacles. The alternative would be to design the PA in a way that can fit into the blueprint approach. This is not an easy task but, as Roe (1991) noted, blueprint planning and the learning approach can be made complementary.

The PA is personnel intensive and personnel with appropriate skills are lacking in both donor and recipient countries. Most education in developing countries involves teaching of 'Western' knowledge rather than local knowledge. If appropriate technology has to be developed, modern (often Western) knowledge has to interact with traditional knowledge. Continued dependence on donor countries for financial assistance to improve school curricula can therefore be expected.

Scaling down the projects and adopting appropriate technology often implies a reduced capital investment component in the projects. This will probably face opposition from vested interests in both donor and recipient countries. This resistance to the introduction of the PA should not be underestimated. Funds returning to the donor country through the national companies that implement development projects amount at times to up to 95 per cent of project costs (Carew-Reid, 1989).

The obstacles facing the PA are not irrelevant. Some of the alleged obstacles, such as a tendency of the advocates of the PA to call for the withdrawal of peasants from the market, are fictitious. Others are real, such as the difficulty of fostering development through the PA in hierarchic and élitist societies.

ACKNOWLEDGEMENT

We wish to thank two anonymous referees for helpful comments on an earlier draft. The usual *caveats* apply. Research for this paper has been partly funded by Australian Centre for International Agricultural Research (ACIAR) Project 8823, 'Economics of Giant Clam Mariculture'.

REFERENCES

Adams, W. M. (1990). 'How beautiful is small scale? Scale, control and success in Kenyan irrigation', *World Development*, **18**(10), 1309–1323.

AIDAB, (1990). *Ecologically Sustainable Development in International Cooperation*. AGPS, Canberra.

Arndt, H. W. (1983). 'The trickle-down myth', *Economic Development and Cultural Change*, **32**(1), 1–10.

Barbier, E. B. (1987). 'The concept of sustainable economic development', *Environmental Conservation*, **14**(2), 101–110.

Bertram, G. (1986). ' "Sustainable development" in Pacific micro-economies', *World Development*, **14**(7), 809–822.

Bortei-Doku, E. (1991). 'People's Participation Project: Ghana'. In P. Oakley *et al.* (eds), *Project with People: The Practice of Participation in Rural Development*. ILO, Geneva, pp. 61–75.

Carew-Reid, J. (1989). *Environment, Aid and Regionalism in the South Pacific*. ANU, Canberra.

Cernea, M. M. (1987). 'Farmer organisations and institution building for sustainable development', *Regional Development Dialogue*, **8**(2), 1–19.

Chambers, R. (1987). 'Sustainable livelihoods, environment and development: putting poor rural people first'. IDS Discussion Paper No. 240.

Chambers, R. (1978). 'Project selection for poverty-focused rural development: simple is optimal', *World Development*, **6**(2), 209–219.

Colby, M. E. (1990). 'Environmental management in development: the evolution of paradigms'. World Bank Discussion Papers, 80. World Bank, Washington, DC.

Coverdale, A. G. and Healey, J. M. (1987). 'Project appraisal and project aid: a decade of experience in rural development', *Journal of Agricultural Economics*, **XXXVIII**(1), 99–106.

Dichter, T. W. (1989). 'The enterprise concept: a comment on innovations in participatory approaches to development. In W. P. Lineberry (ed.), *Assessing Participatory Development: Rhetoric Versus Reality*. Westview Press, Boulder, pp. 131–137.

Dixon, J. A. and Fallon, L. A. (1989). 'The concept of sustainability: origins, extensions, and usefulness for policy', *Society and Natural Resources*, **2**, 73–84.

Dixon, J. and Hufschmidt, M. (eds) (1986). *Economic Valuation Techniques for the Environment*. John Hopkins University Press, Baltimore.

Fortmann, L. P. and Fairfax, S. K. (1989). 'American forestry professionalism in the Third World'. *Economic and Political Weekly*, August 12, 1839–1844.

Frazer, I. (1987). 'Growth and change in village agriculture: Manakuai, North Malaita'. South Pacific Smallholder Project Occasional Paper No. 11, University of New England, Australia.

Garcia-Barrios, R. and Garcia-Barrios, L. (1990). 'Environmental and technology degradation in peasant agriculture: a consequence of development in Mexico', *World Development*, **18**(11), 1569–1585.

Gow, D. D. and Morss, E. R. (1988). 'The notorious nine: critical problems in project implementation', *World Development*, **16**(12), 1399–1418.

Gray, C. and Martens, A. (1983). 'The political economy of the recurrent cost problem in the West African Sahel', *World Development*, **11**(2), 101–117.

Harland, C. (1991). 'SARILAKAS: grass-roots participation in the Philippines'. In P. Oakley *et al.* (eds), *Project with People: The Practice of Participation in Rural Development*. ILO, Geneva, pp. 99–106.

Heermans, J. G. (1987). 'The Guessebodi experiment: bushland management in Niger'. Paper presented at the Sustainable Development Conference, 28–30 April, London, IIED.

Hough, J. L. and Sherpa, M. N. (1989). 'Bottom-up vs. basic needs: integrating conservation and development in the Annapurna and Michiru mountain conservation areas of Nepal and Malawi', *Ambio*, **18**(8), 435–441.

Howell, J. (1990). 'Rural poverty and external aid', *Development Policy Review*, **8**(3), 269–286.

Huntington, R. (1988). 'Memories of development: the rise and fall of a participatory project among the Dinka, 1977–1981'. In D. W. Attwood *et al.* (eds), *Power and Poverty: Development and Development Projects in the Third World*. Westview Press, Boulder, pp. 85–104.

Hviding, E. (1989). *The Dynamics of Customary Marine Tenure, Maroro Lagoon, Solomon Islands*. The National Research Institute, Papua New Guinea.

IUCN (1980). *World Conservation Strategy*. Gland, Switzerland.

Kimmage, K. (1991). 'Small-scale irrigation initiatives in Nigeria: the problems of equity and sustainability', *Applied Geography*, **11**, 5–20.

Kohn Kaen University (1987). *Proceedings of the 1985 International Conference on Rapid Rural Appraisal*. Kohn Kaen, Thailand.

Korten, D. C. (1980). 'Community organisation and rural development: a learning process approach', *Public Administration Review*, **40**(5), 480–511.

Kottak, C. P. (1985). 'When people don't come first: some sociological lessons from completed projects'. In M. M. Cernea (ed.), *Putting People First: Sociological Variables in Rural Development*. Oxford University Press, New York, pp. 325–356.

Latouche, S. (1986). *Faut-il Refuser le Développement?* Presses Universitaires de France, Paris.

Lecomte, B. J. (1986). *Project Aid: Limitations and Alternatives*. OECD, Paris.

McAllister, D. (1980). *Evaluation in Environmental Planning*. MIT Press, Cambridge, MA.

Norgaard, R. B. (1988). 'Sustainable development: a co-evolutionary view', *Futures*, December, 606–620.

Norton, B. G. (1990). 'Context and hierarchy in Aldo Leopold's theory of environmental management', *Ecological Economics*, **2**, 119–127.

Oakley, P. *et al.* (1991). *Projects with People: The Practice of Participation in Rural Development*. ILO, Geneva.

Paul, S. (1989). 'Poverty alleviation and participation: the case for government grassroots agency collaboration', *Economic and Political Weekly*, **24**(2), 100–106.

Pearce, D., Markandya, A. and Barbier, E. B., (1989). *Blueprint for a Green Economy*. Earthscan Publications, London.
Peek, P. (1988). 'How equitable are rural development projects?', *International Labour Review*, **127**(1), 73–89.
Rambo, A. T. (1982). 'Orang Asli adaptive strategies: implications for Malaysian natural resource development planning'. In C. MacAndrews and C. Lin Sien (eds), *Too Rapid Rural Development: Perceptions and Perspectives from Southeast Asia*. Ohio University Press, Athens, OH.
Rigg, J. (1991). 'Grass-roots development in rural Thailand: a lost cause?', *World Development*, **19**(2/3), 199–211.
Roche, L. (1989). 'Forestry and famine: arguments against growth without development', *Ecologist*, **19**(1), 16–21.
Roe, E. M. (1991). 'Development narratives, or making the best of blueprint development', *World Development*, **19**(4), 287–300.
Sachs, I. (1987). *Development and Planning*. Cambridge University Press, Cambridge.
Sargent, C. and Burgess, P. (1988). *The 'Wokabout Somil'*. IIED, London.
Schumacher, E. F. (1974). *Small is Beautiful: A Study of Economics as if People Mattered*. Sphere Books, London.
Siirianen, A. (1990). 'On the historical aspect of deforestation in the Tropics'. In M. Palo and G. Mery (eds), *Deforestation or Development in the Third World? Volume III*. Bulletin 349 of the Finnish Forest Research Institute, Helsinki, pp. 23–28.
Simon, D. (1989). 'Sustainable development: theoretical construct or attainable goal?', *Environmental Conservation*, **16**(1), 41–48.
Squire, L. (1988). 'Project evaluation in theory and practice'. In H. Chenery and T. N. Srinivasan (eds), *Handbook of Development Economics Vol II*. Elsevier North Holland, Amsterdam, pp. 1093–1137.
Stewart, F. (1975). 'A note on social cost–benefit analysis and class conflict in LDCs', *World Development*, **3**(1), 31–39.
Tendler, J. (1982). 'Rural projects through urban eyes'. *World Bank Staff Working Papers*, **532**, World Bank, Washington.
Therkildsen, O. (1991). 'The desirable and the possible: participation in a water supply project in the United Republic of Tanzania'. In P. Oakley *et al.* (eds), *Project with People: The Practice of Participation in Rural Development*. ILO, Geneva, pp. 76–88.
Tisdell, C. (1986). 'Conflicts about living medicine resources in Southeast Asia and Australian waters: turtle and dugong cases', *Marine Resources Economics*, **3**(1), 89–109.
Uphoff, N. (1985). *Optimum Participation in Irrigation Management: Issues and Evidence from Sri Lanka*. Cornell University, Ithaca.
van Pelt, M. J. F., Kuyvenhoven, A. and Nijkamp, P. (1990). 'Project appraisal and sustainability: methodological challenges', *Project Appraisal*, **5**(3), 139–158.
von Mehren, P. and Seo, J. (1987). 'The Lampang Applied Nutrition Program, Thailand', Paper presented at the Sustainable Development Conference, 28–30 April, London, IIED.
WCED (1987). *Our Common Future*. Oxford University Press, Oxford.

[11]

Integrated Regional Environmental Studies: the Role of Environmental Economics

Clem Tisdell

The University of Queensland

Introduction

The purpose of this contribution[1] is to show how environmental economics can be applied to help solve environmental problems in a regional context. This seems appropriate because Percy Harris has made many outstanding contributions to regional economics. In particular, it illustrates how environmental economics can contribute to an integrated adaptive environmental assessment and management (AEAM) program designed to bring about an environmental improvement taking *eutrophication* in the Tuggerah Lakes north of Sydney in New South Wales as an example.

Eutrophication[2] of water bodies has become an increasingly common phenomenon as human populations have increased and as land-uses have changed (Castensson, 1986). It involves increased concentration of nutrients, particularly nitrates and phosphorous, in water bodies and this stimulates aquatic plant and weed growth. Consequently, the composition of fish populations in the aquatic areas concerned may change so that fish stocks are less valuable (the proportion of bottom feeders and trash fish may increase); offensive odours may be generated by decaying aquatic vegetation to the annoyance of nearby residents and to recreationists; the use of an affected area for recreational purposes, such as swimming or fishing or boating, may be impeded or prevented; and when the water is freshwater and used for human or animal consumption, health risks can emerge as in the case of blue-green algae. While growth of *macrophytes* (large plants, see photograph 1,) rather than algae appears to be the main problem in the Tuggerah Lakes, which contain brackish water, as Herath (1996, pp. 189-190) points out:

> Algal blooms have become an important water quality problem in Australia. They have occurred more frequently in recent years causing concern among water users, water managers and the public generally. There are considerable costs to the community associated

with algal blooms. These costs occur in the form of lost recreation and drinking water supplies, loss of income from commercial activities such as provision of accommodation, transport, food in caravan and tourist parks and serious health effects. Direct costs during the 1991 bloom along the Darling River were more than $1.3 million.

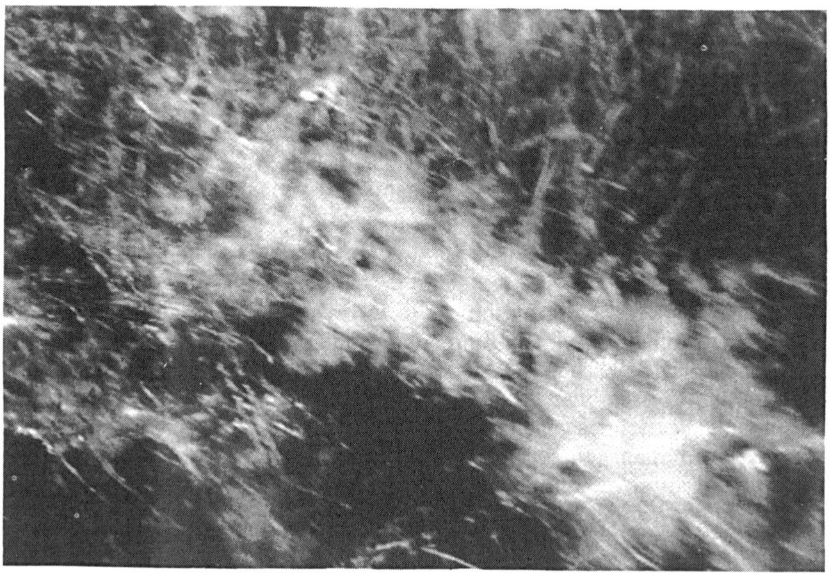

Photograph 1. An example of dense aquatic weed growth in the Tuggerah Lakes.

Problems of algal bloom are not however confined to Australia's inland waters. Coastal areas have also been affected, such as reservoirs for urban water supplies eg. in 1995 supplies of water from the Pine Rivers Dam in the Brisbane water supply system were suspended due to the presence of blue-green algae, and this has also occurred in Sydney area as well.

Tuggerah Lakes are brackish lakes located within the boundaries of Wyong Shire Council as is their catchment area. This shire is experiencing very rapid population growth which is expected to continue as Wyong is increasingly used as a dormitory area for Sydney and for retirement purposes. Furthermore, with changed technology, more people can work from this area using new electronic equipment. Serious weed problems exist in the lake system but could worsen as population densities in this shire increase. With this in mind, the Wyong Shire Council requested Macquarie Research Ltd. to investigate the situation and report to it on possible solutions. The research team decided to use an integrated adaptive environmental assessment and management approach (Holling, 1978). This is an interactive approach in which the main researchers interact with members of the community concerned to learn about the nature of the problem: the environmental interrelationships as community members perceive these and also the aspirations of local people. Parties to this process can be expected to adapt their perceptions and models as they interact. The approach is a side-by-side approach involving active community participation (Tisdell, 1995).

Adaptive assessment and management contrasts with the traditional or orthodox approaches to problem-solving commonly used in economics, reviewed by Nijkamp (1987), such as deductive or axiomatic methods and the application of econometric models based on little interaction with the community. AEEM has much in common with other methods such as Rapid Rural Appraisal and Participatory Rural Appraisal (Chambers, 1980, 1982; McCracken et al. 1988; Pido et al; 1996) but is more sustained than the former with structured results often forming part of the outcome. It was the method preferred by Macquarie Research Ltd. in giving advice to the Wyong Shire Council. It recognizes the bounded rationality of researchers (Tisdell, 1996) and the importance of community involvement in problem-solving. The latter can be important in terms of information-provision and ensuring the social acceptability of 'solutions' once determined (Berkes, 1989).

Let us consider some additional background on the environmental economics and data problems at the regional level, then consider how environmental economics can be integrated into regional environmental studies and contribute to the formulation of strategies and policies for regional environmental management, before discussing the Tuggerah Lakes and its catchment as a regional case study and raising some general policy issues about eutrophication and nutrient enrichment of water bodies.

Additional Background

Nature of Environmental Economics

Environmental economics is a relatively new specialisation in economics which has developed since the early 1970s but which has its roots in the earlier subjects of welfare economics and development economics. It is concerned with the relationships between economic systems and the natural environment, economic methods of managing this relationship as well as the economics of altering natural and degraded environments taking into account the wants of people. So environmental economics is concerned about what people want from their environment(s) as well as how they can satisfy those wants economically or efficiently.

While the focus of economics may seem very man-centred (anthropogenic), it is less so than may appear at first sight. For example, if humans value the existence of other living things or the preservation of natural environments for their own sake, this can be factored into the economic optimisation problem.

Environmental Economics and Multidisciplinary Co-operation

In order to be valuable as a management tool in practical situations, environmental economics must be combined with data and inputs from other disciplines such as engineering, biology, ecology and so on. For example, although an economist may be able to predict how industries are likely to develop in a region, he/she may not be able to identify the environmental wastes likely to be generated and their ecological impact on aquatic environments such as Tuggerah Lakes. This is where engineering, natural sciences and local knowledge assist.

Data Problems

Economists and natural scientists often have to cope with limited knowledge when undertaking a specific environmental study such as the one conducted in the Wyong Shire of weed growth in the Tuggerah Lakes. One way to help fill the knowledge-gap is to engage people in the region in an interactive process of knowledge generation such as that involved in the Adaptive Environmental Assessment and Management (AEAM) Program adopted by the Wyong Shire Council and applied by Macquarie Research Ltd. The strength of this method is that it takes advantage of local experience and expertise, makes for readier identification of locally perceived issues and problems and because it is participatory, can be expected to result in politically more acceptable solutions than a top-down approach to environmental management. This is not to say that interactive processes for generating knowledge are completely unstructured; most are semi-structured but flexible. Environmental economics can be of assistance in design of the initial structure of an enquiry and the subsequent modification of this structure so as to increase the relevance of the information obtained to the socio-economic component of a regional environmental study. It can also ensure that results are useful for environmental management or policy purposes.

Environmental Economics in Integrated Regional Environmental Studies

Holism and Links Between Socio-economic Systems and the Environment

In the past many social scientists, especially economists, have studied socio-economic systems as closed systems independent of the natural environment. This meant, for example, that circular flow diagrams representing economic interdependence between the sectors and actors in modern-day economics did not contain an environmental component. This created the impression that economic activity could sustain itself independently of natural environments. Fortunately, the spaceship analogy of the economy, as first popularised by Kenneth Boulding (1966) is now more widely accepted and economic circular flow diagrams are sprouting an extra loop which firmly links socio-economic systems with natural environments, making it clear that the performance and sustainability of economic systems as well as human welfare or standards of living cannot be divorced from the state of natural environments. This means that human welfare, the performance of economic systems the occurrence of human activities and the state of the environment must be considered as a whole (*cf.* Braat and van Lierop, 1987). This can be illustrated by Figure 1.

Figure 1. The natural environmental system and the socio-economic system are interlinked.

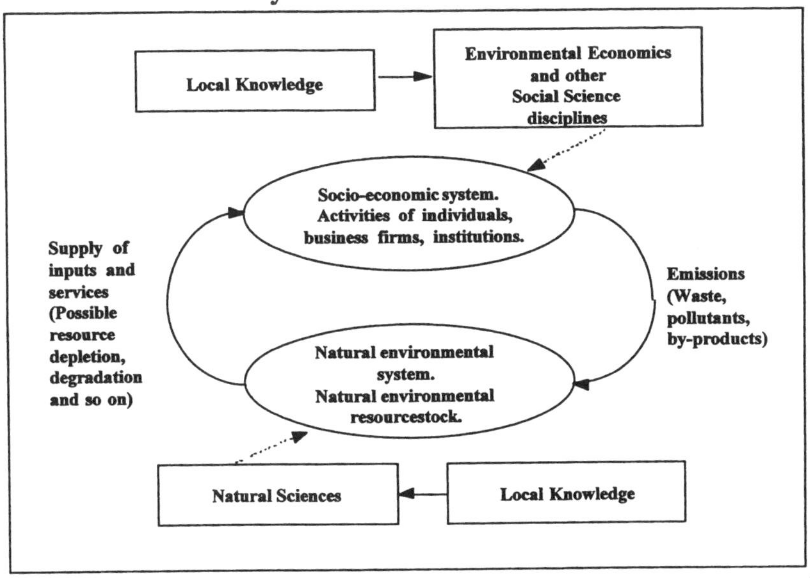

In Figure 1, the socio-economic system is represented in the top oval. It involves human activities, including economic activities of individuals, households, business firms and institutions. The bottom oval represents the natural environmental system(s). Emissions from the socio-economic system (wastes, pollutants, by-products) are received by the natural resource system which provides a 'sink' for these. Depending however on the quantity and nature of these emissions, the natural resource system may be impaired so reducing its value for sustaining economic activity and satisfying human wants.

In addition, the activities of humans often make direct use of natural resources. Natural resources may be used to provide recreational services eg. amateur fishing opportunities in Tuggerah Lakes, boating and swimming opportunities and so forth, or be used as inputs into economic production eg. fish for the professional fishery, water for power station use in the case of Tuggerah Lakes. Such activities can sometimes deplete or degrade the natural resource-base making it more difficult to sustain future human welfare. Given these interactions between the socio-economic system and the environmental system, environmental studies and the study of sustainable economic development require the simultaneous study of *both* systems and their consideration as a whole. In this regard, it is likely that environmental economics and other social science disciplines would be able to make the greatest contribution to study of the upper sphere, whereas natural sciences might be expected to make the major contribution in relation to the lower sphere, with all naturally having to be taken into account in devising environmental management strategies.

Regional Modification

Figure 1 may be modified to depict the situation for a region. A region is usually only a partially self-contained entity from an economic and environmental point of view. It often involves economic imports, inputs or contributions from outside the region (this is true of Wyong Shire) as well as in many cases environmental imports (wastes or emissions) from outside the region. Some of the possible environmental and economic interdependencies between regions are illustrated in Figure 2. The strength of these interconnections will vary with the case in hand. In the Tuggerah Lakes case, there are strong socio-economic connections with other regions eg. Sydney, but the environmental impact of other regional environments on the Lakes would appear to be small and the direct environmental spillover from the condition of the Lakes to other regions may also be small.

Figure 2. Although there may be some separation between socio-economic systems and environmental systems in different regions, a variety or myriad of links are possible as illustrated above. The strength of interconnections will vary depending upon the case being investigated.

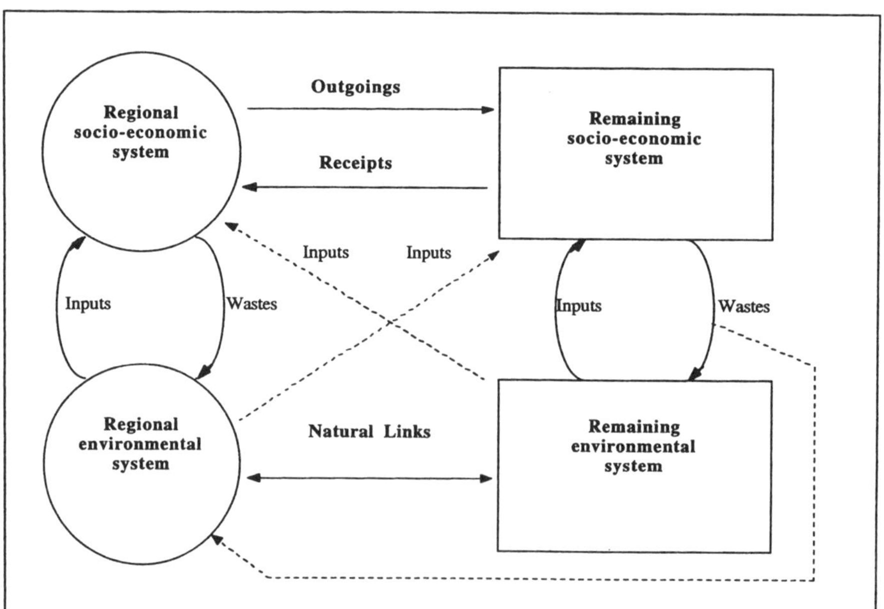

The Contribution of Economics to the Formulation of Regional Environmental Strategies and Policies

There are several ways in which economics can contribute to the formulation of regional environmental strategies. Together with other disciplines, it can establish trends in economic, demographic and other socio-economic variables for a region. This is a necessary backdrop for predicting likely demands to be made on the local environment. Secondly, it may assist in establishing community objectives and the valuation placed on environmental conservation. Thirdly, it can recommend economic policies and instruments to help manage changes to achieve the objectives desired by the community. However cut-and-dried responses to these matters are not always possible and the needed depth of analysis can vary with the particular task in hand. Initially, for example only a broad overview of the community's environmental objectives or of environmental issues of greatest concern to the community may be needed. Figure 3 indicates some ways in which economics may make a useful contribution to decision-making about the management of regional environments.

Figure 3. Some cases of regional environmental management where environmental economics can assist.

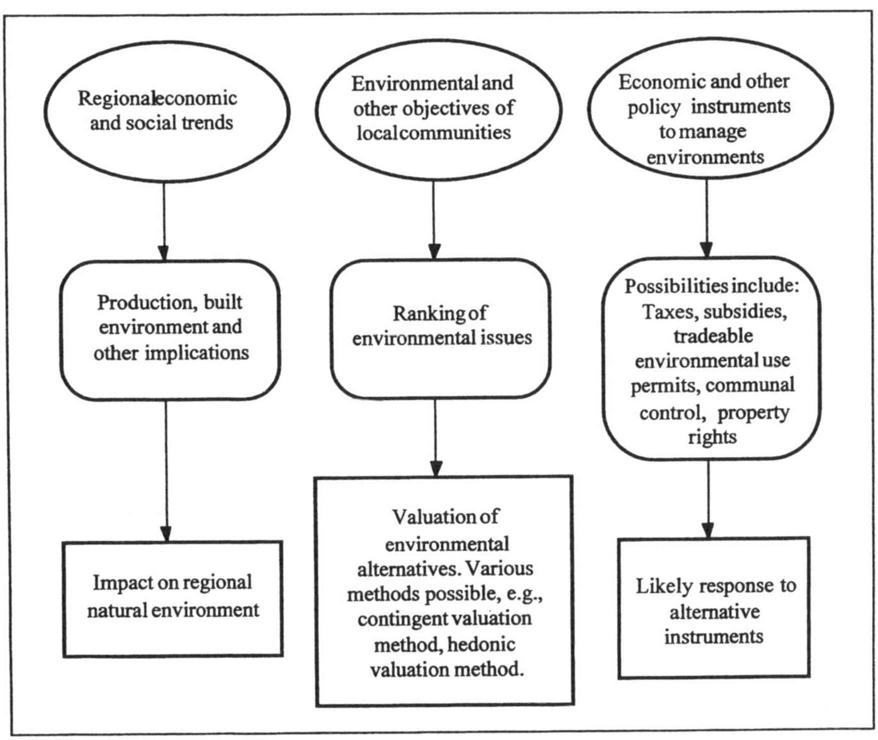

The Tuggerah Lakes Interactive Study

Accelerated eutrophication of the Tuggerah Lakes due to human activities has become severe. Effects include dense aquatic weed growth, algal blooms, sedimentation reducing the depth of water in several places and decaying plant matter, including ooze and slime along foreshores of the Lakes. Impacts include the following:

(1) The Lakes have become unsuitable for swimming in many parts (see photograph 2).

(2) Offensive smells make some areas along the foreshores of these lakes less attractive for picnicking and reduce the amenity-value of nearby residences.

(3) Boat traffic is impeded or prevented by sedimentation and weed growth in some parts of these lakes (see photograph 3).

(4) Some wharves have become unusable (see photograph 4) due to silting and/or have had to be extended.

(5) Stocks of fish for commercial and recreational fishing appear to have fallen and less valuable fish have increased as a relative proportion of fish stocks. Furthermore, line fishing has become impossible in many areas due to the growth of aquatic weeds. In addition, use of nets for commercial fishing is not practical in some weedy areas.

In order to ameliorate these problems, Wyong Shire Council has adopted a number of strategies: weeds and organic matter have been mechanically removed by the Council (see photograph 5) at considerable cost from the lakes and foreshores at points near important recreational areas eg. in an inlet near a caravan park. Public wharves have been extended and channels for boat traffic dredged. Settling ponds have been constructed at the end of a few small watercourses (with irregular flows) prior to their entry to the lakes and suitable aquatic plants have been established in the settling ponds or creek outlets (see photograph 6) to help reduce the nutrients carried into the lakes and reduce turbulence. Except for the last strategy, which is most likely not on an adequate scale to have a major impact on nutrients entering the lakes, most of the strategies are reactive. Furthermore, the mechanical removal of aquatic weeds does not have a lasting effect. Aquatic weeds soon re-establish themselves.

Given the importance of the Lakes to local residents, to tourists and recreationists and for commercial fishing, Wyong Shire Council decided to search for longer term solutions and in 1995 requested Macquarie Research Ltd. to conduct an environmental assessment and make recommendations for improved environmental management of the lakes. An adaptive assessment approach was adopted.

Photograph 2. Beach area on Tuggerah Lakes rendered unsuitable for swimming and fishing by eutrophication.

Photograph 3. Weed growth impedes boat traffic. It is now difficult to reach some parts of Tuggerah Lakes even in a flat punt.

Photograph 4. Wharf abandoned on Tuggerah Lakes due to eutrophication.

Photograph 5. Ooze and organic matter in Tuggerah Lakes mechanically removed and placed in the black heap on the side of Tuggerah Lakes. It is unsightly and smelly and not effective in preventing continuing weed growth.

Photograph 6. Wyong Shire Council is in the process of revegetating the entrance of this watercourse to Tuggerah Lakes. *Typha* species have been planted in the watercourse itself and small barriers have been constructed along its outlet.

Photograph 7. The entrance of Tuggerah Lakes to the Pacific Ocean near Toukley, N.S.W. This is a shallow and relatively narrow entrance. One option is to extend it to increase the flushing of the lakes.

Initially the process of assessment involved a number of modules; some concentrating on the physical issues, some on ecological aspects and one dealing with the socio-economic dimensions of eutrophication of the Lakes. In this stage there were interactive meetings between researchers and selected groups having local knowledge; reports on each of the modules followed. Subsequently, a meeting was convened between Council representatives, the researchers and "international experts" to formulate integrated management strategies, and a public conference was held to discuss the main findings as set out in these reports. Afterwards the research consultants and Council officers were expected to draw up feasible environmental management strategies.

The next stage envisaged was to discuss preferred feasible strategies with local communities to obtain further feedback, modify these as needed and hopefully obtain community agreement on (or acceptance of) a suitable approach.

In connection with the socio-economic module, a workshop using the adaptive environmental assessment and management process identified important socio-economic issues relating to Tuggerah Lakes and its catchment. A list of alternative community attitudes towards and objectives for the environment of the lakes were identified. The degree of community support for the alternatives was to be assessed at a later stage. Two important uses of Wyong's aquatic environment were given considerable attention: its utilisation by tourists, especially day-trippers, and its use for fishing, both recreational and commercial. Components of income of the public sector (the State Government and the Council mostly), some of which are environmentally related, were identified and a breakdown of Council's expenditure, mainly on environmentally-related items, was completed.

Environmental costs and benefits involving variations in flooding in the Lakes and their catchment, urban developments, rehabilitation of the Lakes by beach cleaning, ooze removal and by dredging were considered. Increased flushing of the lakes by major expansion of the existing entrance to the sea or provision of a second entrance were discussed. Key concerns were identified. Matters given particular attention were the likely impacts of greater flushing of the lakes on land values, the possibility of a marina development, the impact of changed environmental quality on tourism earnings, the implications of patterns of urban growth (the speed and spread of urban growth) on environmental quality, congestion and tourists diversion costs associated with this growth and with any environmental deterioration in the lakes.

An Analysis of Eutrophication in Tuggerah Lakes and Solutions to it: the Socio-Economics in Context

Discussion involved in the above-mentioned assessment procedures revealed that basically two possibilities exist for reducing eutrophication in Tuggerah Lakes:

(1) Take measures that reduce the quantities of nutrients and sediments entering the lakes and

(2) take action to ensure that there is more rapid exchange between waters in these brackish lakes and those of the Pacific Ocean.

These two strategies could also be used in combination.

Two alternatives for increasing the rate of flushing of these lakes are (a) to deepen and extend the present small channel by which the waters of these lakes enter the sea near Toukley (see photograph 7) and (b) to construct an additional channel to the sea north of Toukley in the vicinity of Marmong Point. Both could of course be done. For each of these possible constructions, there is a range of possible options with varying costs and possible environmental impacts. For example, if a second opening is envisaged would a flood gate to exclude high tides be a part of the construction? Let us consider each of the main strategies in turn.

Consider input of plant-nutrients to the lakes. It would be useful to know the following:

(1) How does aquatic plant growth in the Lakes respond to nutrient inflows? Production functions (at least primitive ones) would be useful. Inflows of nitrates and phosphorous are believed to be major stimulants of aquatic plant growth but more should be known about this relationship. However the matter is complicated because one is not interested purely in the response of a single plant species. The composition of the species in the aquatic weed population is liable to change as the mixture and total availability of plant nutrients alters. What is likely to be the impact on the weed population of reduction in all inflows of nutrients? Is the weed population more sensitive to variations in some nutrients rather than others?

(2) What are the sources of the inflows of nutrients to the Lakes? What quantities of nutrients come from the various sources and how can these quantities be controlled?

In relation to the last matter, it is believed that the main sources of inflows of plant-nutrients into the Tuggerah Lakes are as follows:

(1) Fertilization of lawns surrounding domestic dwellings.

(2) Turf farms.

(3) Soil disturbance and/or vegetation removal particularly for urban developments such as housing estates.

(4) In the past, human sewage from septic tanks.

(5) Golf courses.

Pollution from these sources is not of a single-point type but is multiple-point or diffused. This makes monitoring of actual releases from individual properties difficult. Problems of measurement and the costs involved make it impractical for the Council to introduce pollution emission changes on landholders scaled to the level of their emission of plant-nutrients.

So far Wyong Council's main approach to dealing with the problem has been to require developers of housing estates to adopt measures to reduce soil erosion during construction and to provide for vegetated watercourses with settling ponds. While this is positive, it is probably insufficient to stem the nutrient inflows to the lakes substantially, especially since rapid population increase and urbanisation is occurring in the Shire.

If it is not possible to economically measure emissions of nutrients from properties, an emission tax is not economically worthwhile. The alternative of placing taxes on inputs known to be a prime source of nutrient entry into the Lakes, such as artificial fertilizers, is also not an option available to Wyong Shire Council. It is unlikely to have legal powers to impose such taxes. It does, however, have other policy instruments available to it. These include:

(1) Higher rates for land uses which are a significant source of nutrient inputs to the Lakes, eg. turf farms. Or again, other things equal, high density housing with less lawn would be preferred to estates with medium density and rates structure could be adjusted accordingly.

(2) Zoning and permits for land use can be used to limit types of land use. Nevertheless care needs to be taken that these do not become too restrictive of enterprise.

(3) Regulations restricting vegetation removal and requiring provision of settling ponds and so on could be strengthened.

(4) Education can play a role. Householders can be encouraged to develop gardens without lawns or gardens requiring use of little fertilizer.

As for strategies to increase the rates of flushing of the Lakes, these involve considerable investment by the Wyong Council. They would necessitate some increase in rates to pay for the capital works involved. For political reasons, the Council would need to assess the willingness of ratepayers to pay for such works.

A further political problem is also foreseen: Increasing the connection of the Lakes to the sea will increase tidal influences in the Lakes. This may result in some lakeside properties being flooded during high tides, especially during above normal high tides. Higher tides in the Lakes could also impede the release of floodwaters from the catchment of the Lakes. A trade-off problem exists. This problem could be mitigated if a second entrance to the Lakes is constructed by fitting it with locks to block out high tides, but this will add substantially to costs.

The solution to the above man-induced case of eutrophication is not an easy one given the political dimension involved and the fact that a Paretian improvement (one in which all parties gain compared to the *status quo*) does not seem possible. Furthermore, a considerable amount of scientific uncertainty exists about the environmental consequences of strategies which might be adopted to deal with the problem. In addition off-the-shelf policies from standard environmental economics, such as those on pollution emissions, are impractical because most of the pollution involved is of a non-point nature.

This problem is not specific to the Tuggerah Lakes. It is present in other brackish waters in Australia eg. in Lake Macquarie and parts of Queensland. It is also a serious problem in many freshwater bodies (Herath, 1996).

Concluding Comments

Completing an integrated regional environmental study is a major task because of inadequate data for specific cases. The application of conventional methods to environmental assessment is usually not practical because of the considerable costs and long time-scale likely to be involved. At least in the shorter term and when early defensive environmental action is needed, adaptive environmental assessment processes are likely to be practical and useful. Environmental economics can assist in the design of such processes and in their adaptation as feedback is obtained from respondents. Several ways have been indicated in which this is possible. Furthermore, it is clear that an integrated regional environmental study without a significant input on the economic and social sides is likely to be of little or no value. However, at the same time, major information inputs are needed from engineering, natural sciences and the local community.

While adaptive environmental assessment is a useful approach, it is not a solution to all environmental problems. It provides some knowledge but not perfect knowledge. Furthermore, it is a useful technique for making local and regional communities aware of the nature of their environmental problems and possible solutions to these. Given political mechanisms of governance in democracies, this can improve policy formation and acceptance of policies. However, long-term progress requires sustained scientific research such as that carried out by permanent research institutions, eg. the CSIRO and the universities. Sharing of existing knowledge and community participation can only take us so far. We must not forget this in our quest for knowledge through communalism, that is through community and 'expert' participation in problem-solving. Collective participation provides a means to share our existing knowledge more effectively and disseminate it, rather than a means to increase our stock of knowledge. Long-term progress depends on the accumulation of knowledge even though dissemination and improved use of existing knowledge is not unimportant.

Endnotes

1. This is a revised and extended version of a paper presented at a conference on "Strategic Environmental Management: Managing Cumulative Environmental Impacts at the Systems Level" held August, 1995 at Toukley, N.S.W. and organised by the Wyong Shire Council. I wish to thank Mr. Brian Bell, Environmental Systems Manager, the Wyong Shire Council for inviting me to participate in the conference and to assist in the assessment of the environmental problems of Tuggerah Lakes. Thanks are also due to Professor Alistair Gilmour, Environmental Studies, Macquarie University for providing specific background material relating to the assessment of the environment of Tuggerah Lakes.
2. Castensson (1986, p.342) describes eutrophication in the following way.

   "Eutrophication is the process by which lakes age. The lake is gradually choked with vegetation and filled with sediment. This process normally takes many thousands of years. But men's activities have rapidly speeded up the process. Man has drastically shortened the life-span of lakes by addition of plant nutrients originating from human activities. The lakes are becoming more fertile. The lakes will rapidly change character. This process is usually called man-induced or man-made eutrophication".

   Man-induced eutrophication has become common in enclosed and slow flowing waters. It affects lakes, some coastal waters, ponds and slow flowing rivers and streams. It induces algal blooms, growth of aquatic plants, reduces oxygen levels in water, can cause unpleasant odours and produce offensive tastes in drinking water. It reduces the beneficial effects of water for human use. Urban water supplies, fishing and recreation are adversely affected. Algal blooms may make water consumption toxic for human and animal consumption and clog industrial and municipal water filters. Shores of lakes sometimes develop algal slimes and/or foul smelling plant matter may accumulate on their foreshores.

References

Berkes, F. (1989) *Common Property Resources: Ecology and Community-based Sustainable Development*, Belhaven, London

Boulding, K. E. (1966) 'The Economics of the Coming Spaceship Earth', pp. 3-14 in H. Jarrett (Ed.) *Environmental Quality in a Growing Economy*, Johns Hopkins Press, Baltimore, MD.

Braat, L. C. and van Lierop, W. F. J. (1987) 'Environment, Policy and Modeling', pp. 7-19 in L. C. Braat and W. F. J. van Lierop, *Economic-Ecological Modeling*, Elsevier, Amsterdam.

Castensson, R. G. (1986) 'Impact Assessment of Eutrophication on Urban Water supply: Methods and Analysis', pp. 341-350 in H. A. Becker and A. L. Porter (Eds.) *Impact Assessment Today*, Vol. 1, Uitgeverij Jan Van Arkel, Utrecht.

Chambers, R. (1980) *Rapid Rural Appraisal: Rationale and Repertoire*. Discussion Paper 155. Institute of Development Studies, Brighton, U. K.

Chambers, R. (1992) *Rural Appraisal: Rapid, Relaxed and Participatory*. Discussion Paper 311. Institute of Development Studies, Brighton, U. K.

Herath, G. (1996) 'A Review of the Costs of Removing Phosphorous to Control Algal Blooms in Waterways', *Australian Journal of Environmental Management* Vol. 3, No. 3, pp. 189-261.

Holling, C. S. (1978) *Adaptive Environmental Assessment and Management*, John Wiley, Chichester.

McCracken, J. Pretty, J. and Conway, G. (1988) *An Introduction to Rapid Rural Appraisal for Agricultural Development*. Sustainable Agriculture Program, International Institute for Environment and Development, London.

Nijkamp, P. (1987) 'Economic Modeling: Shortcomings and Projections'. pp. 20-35 in L. C. Braat and W. F. J. van Lierop, *Economic - Ecological Modeling* Elsevier, Amsterdam.

Pido, M. D. Pomeroy, R. S. Carlos, M. V. and Garces, L. R. (1996) *A Handbook for Rapid Appraisal of Fisheries Management Systems*, International Centre for Living Aquatic Resources Management, Manila.

Tisdell, C. A. (1996) *Bounded Rationality and Economic Evolution*, Edward Elgar, Aldershot, UK.

Tisdell, C. A. (1995) 'Issues in Biodiversity Conservation including the Role of Local Communities', *Environmental Conservation*, Vol. 22, No. 3, pp. 216-228.

[12]

Population, Economic Change, and Environmental Security*

by

CLEMENT A. TISDELL, PhD (ANU)

Professor & Head, Department of Economics, The University of Queensland, Brisbane 4072, Australia

INTRODUCTION

Population levels and their geographical distribution are key considerations in economic development and major influences on the state of the global environment. Virtually all economic development models include human population as a key variable, even though different theorists draw different conclusions about the implications of population increase for 'sustainable development'. Furthermore, diverse theories have evolved about socio-economic influences on population increases and the relationship of population levels with the natural environment. Such variety is to be welcomed, because it allows us to view the issues involved from varied perspectives and also reflects an expanding body of thought to meet changing circumstances. We are now better equipped than ever before to understand how socio-economic factors influence population increase, and how population increase is related to, and impacts on, the prospects for sustained economic development and for environmental security.

Population, environmental variables, economic well-being, and development, are closely interwoven (Tisdell, 1993*c*). For example, poverty may arise from an unproductive and unfavourable natural environment from a human viewpoint. In turn, poverty widely results in a high birth-rate, and consequent efforts to survive and cope with

* This updated version of 'Population, Economics, Development, and Environmental Security' (Tisdell, 1994) includes an extra case-study on biodiversity conservation in China.

population pressures can be expected to degrade the natural environment, result in its unsustainable use, and leave little or no margin for the Human community involved to develop by its own efforts. The local community is thus caught in a vicious cycle involving poverty, population pressures, and environmental deterioration, so that escape becomes more and more difficult with the passage of time. The desperate situation of the community may then become evident in terms of increased frequency of famine, heightened mortality rates, and outward migration.

However, increases in human population not only threaten the natural environment and global sustainability in low-income situations, but also pose a problem in higher-income situations. In communities with higher *per caput* incomes, the incremental impact of rising population on the natural environment tends to be greater than in low-income situations, because the quantity of natural resources transformed for human use, and the wastes and pollutants generated by production and life-style maintenance, tend to be far higher per individual. This really means that we must be aware of the significance of the human population as an environmental influence, no matter whether a community is poor or rich from an economic viewpoint.

For at least another half-century, the world will have major population problems to deal with. The German Advisory Council on Global Change has summarized the situation as follows:

> 'During the 'nineties the global population is expanding annually by nearly 100 million people, most of whom (80 millions) will settle in urban areas. Even with a drastic decrease in the current average birth-rate, the present world's population of 5.52 [thousand millions] will at least double by the middle of the next century.
>
> 'The expected *population growth*, which will mainly occur in Asia, Africa, and Latin America, will aggravate both environmental and developmental problems. Conversely, however, the solution to these problems is a crucial prerequisite for the reduction of the population growth-rate. *Rapid urbanization* and *massive migration* are two further areas of concern, both of which will affect the industrialized countries because of increasing immigration pressure' (German Advisory Council on Global Change, 1993 p. 9).

The Council emphasizes that expected population increases will add to environmental and development problems in the coming decades. Therefore, there will clearly be a need for heightened concern and policy effort to deal with such issues.

The importance which economists have placed on human population-levels and their increase as impediments or facilitators of economic development has varied over the centuries and continues to vary also between individuals and factions. In addition, a variety of views have been expressed about how or what socio-economic factors may influence family size and population growth, as well as about the likely environmental consequences of population growth. This Chapter provides an overview of population as an element in economic development models, of socio-economic influences on family size, of the dilemma raised by the 'population–environment–poverty trap' and responses to it — such as migration — and underlines the importance of wise natural-resource management.

POPULATION AS A VARIABLE IN ECONOMIC DEVELOPMENT MODELS

Population is an important variable in most economic development models, and population growth is seen by many (but not all) economists as a possible impediment to raising *per caput* incomes. Malthus (1798), for example, believed that population growth could be expected to fritter away the benefits of economic growth, whereas K. Marx and F. Engels (*cf.* Engels, 1973) were of the view that technological progress would more than compensate for any tendency of population growth to reduce *per caput* incomes. It is still the case today that those who are not especially concerned about the income-inhibiting consequences of population growth, point to technological progress and improvements in the quality of the work-force, *e.g. via* education, as important offsetting factors.

Malthus's population model has generally been interpreted to imply that there is always a strong tendency for the level of population to vary directly with the means of subsistence, so that in the long term *per caput* incomes hover around the prevalent levels of subsistence. However, the 'demographic transition' which has occurred in most Western countries since Malthus's time (and also in some non-Western ones) indicates the limitations of Malthus's theory (*cf.* Maitra, 1992). The natural rate of increase of population in most developed countries today is very small and in some cases negative, even though incomes per head are high. Indeed, high income levels often make for a reduction in the rate of population increase.

Such observations have led to the theory of the Malthusian 'population trap' or the low-level equilibrium of any subsistence-type 'population trap' (Todaro, 1981 Ch. 7). Basically, this theory holds that Malthus's model applies at low levels of *per caput* income but that if incomes can be raised enough, it is possible to escape from the Malthusian situation. At higher levels of income, population growth declines and, as a result of increased savings, higher capital investment, and related factors, forces resulting in rising incomes become stronger. Thus a situation of rising incomes and falling rates of population growth can be attained when once income per head rises to a sufficient level to escape the trap.

In simple theoretical renditions of this model, there is usually some threshold level of *per caput* income which is needed before self-perpetuating growth in *per caput* income and falling rates of population growth can be achieved. This of course is an over-simplified picture of the real world, but it does highlight the fact that a substantial improvement in the standard of living may be needed to escape a Malthusian population trap. In other words, the prescription for escaping from the trap may be an economic one, namely of economic development.

This point of view has been widely adopted by developmental policymakers. For example, the 'Brundtland Report' (World Commission on Environment and Development, 1987) accepted the view that economic improvement may be a prerequisite for many developing countries to escape the Malthusian population trap and bring their rate of population growth under control. Such an escape is also seen to have environmental advantages.

This was pointed out in the 'Brundtland Report' and further underlined by the later World Bank report on *Development and the Environment* (World Bank, 1992). Taking a number of indices of environmental quality, the World Bank in this report indicates that, in general, environmental quality tends to be better in the more developed countries. This is so for water quality and urban-air quality, as examples. Furthermore, the higher life-expectancy in more-developed countries is an additional indicator of better environmental conditions in more-developed countries compared with less-developed ones.

However, the relationship between economic development and the state of the environment is complex. For example, at intermediate levels of *per caput* income, environmental quality is often worse than at low levels, because at the intermediate stage the worst spillovers from modernization may be observed and there may be a strong push 'to modernize' or industrialize at any (environmental) cost. If a country should become 'stuck' in the transition phase, this may be worse for the environment than if it had shown less economic growth.

In addition, value judgements are required in deciding what really is an improvement in environmental quality. As is to be expected, this in practice is judged mostly from a human perspective. Often an improved environment from a human perspective means a substantially transformed natural environment.* Because of

*This reminds us of our — unpopular among conservationists — long-held contention that anthropogenic ecosystems and landscapes tend to be more attractive aesthetically, as well as far more productive economically, than natural ones. — Ed.

this and the increasing demand on resources resulting from economic growth and development, the natural environment tends to be a casualty of 'development' unless positive measures are taken to protect it. At higher-income levels it is economically easier than at low ones to take such measures, but they do commonly require positive governmental and often international action. *The developed countries are, economically, in a favourable position to adopt positive measures to protect their natural environment and to assist less-developed countries in this regard.*

One of the main casualties of development is loss of biodiversity. This is apparent from the World Bank (1992) as well as other sources (Tisdell, 1993*b*). Both economic growth and increases in human population are threats to biodiversity, and there again positive economic action is required to counter such threats.

Moreover, the thesis that economic growth and development lead to an improved environment needs to be examined critically from another point of view: to what extent have more-developed countries or regions improved their environments locally by exporting their environmental problems to less-developed ones? The developed countries are, globally, the major contributors of 'greenhouse' gases, and consequently export the risks involved to all nations. Furthermore, they sometimes locate their dirty industries offshore, or export their wastes to less-developed countries (LDCs) where they may cause serious environmental damage which would not be tolerated in a more-developed country. Consequently, it must remain doubtful whether the world, as a whole, really has the environmental capacity to sustain its current population, let alone projected levels of population for the next 50 years or so, at high-income levels such as are enjoyed for example in the USA and Switzerland on average.

What is being emphasized here is that cross-sectional data, such as those used by the World Bank (1992), may give a misleading picture of what is possible globally as far as the relationship between development and the environment is concerned. Furthermore, one has to be extremely careful in projecting past time-series data concerning the environment, as for instance is underlined by supporters of the precautionary principle in relation to planning of development and how to cope with environmental change.

The Malthusian population-trap theory has a significant consequence which has not been emphasized in the literature or in policy-making so far as I am aware. Premature and abortive attempts to escape from such a trap may, in the longer term, do more harm than good — because any growth achieved may prove basically non-sustainable, and furthermore it is likely to reduce permanently the natural resource-base, so making subsequent attempts at escape more difficult.

For simplicity, suppose that a population is in a low-level-equilibrium situation and has a low *per caput* income level of y_1. Furthermore, suppose that if income per head can be pushed above $y_2 > y_1$, sustainable economic growth will occur in accordance with the Malthusian population-trap theory. Imagine that the community tries to escape from the trap (for example by drawing on its environmental resources or using some once-and-for-all foreign assistance) and its income per head rises to *almost* y_2 but cannot be raised further. Consequently, the community eventually returns to its low-level of income per head. In this equilibrium, it may only be able to support a smaller population than previously because of its irreversible natural-resource depletion during its attempt to escape from its low-level-equilibrium trap. Furthermore, because of environmental deterioration and natural-resource depletion due to the abortive attempts of the community to achieve sustainable growth, it is likely to be more difficult for such a community to escape subsequently from its low-level-equilibrium trap. Thus the theory suggests that 'premature' attempts to escape from such a trap should be avoided.

A further policy consequence is that, as far as foreign development-aid is concerned, it is best to concentrate it in areas where there is a high prospect of pushing communities above the Malthusian threshold level of income. This may not be achieved if aid is broadly dispersed or, alternatively, concentrated in regions where prospects of breaking out of the Malthusian trap are bleakest. Those regions which would find it easiest to escape from the trap should be assisted first, with less-promising regions being helped in their turn. This suggests that a serial approach to development assistance is needed if this theory is accepted. Although in the short-term this does not appear to be very humanitarian, in the longer term it may be the most effective policy holistically.

A very simple economic model of the relationship between population and income levels has not been mentioned. Basically, this model sees population as supplying labour to be used in the production process. The model concentrates on the production function to determine the optimal level of population, and most commonly the optimal level of population is taken to be that which maximizes income per head. As economies of scale in production are considered to be important, production as a function of population is assumed at first to exhibit increasing returns to rising population, followed eventually by decreasing returns. Consequently, this implies that the graph indicating income per head as a function of the level of population is of an inverted U-shape, such as is illustrated in Fig. 1. In the case illustrated, where income per head is shown by the curve OABC, the optimal level of population is P_1.

A population level of P_0 would be too low to maximize income per head, whereas one of P_3 would be too high.

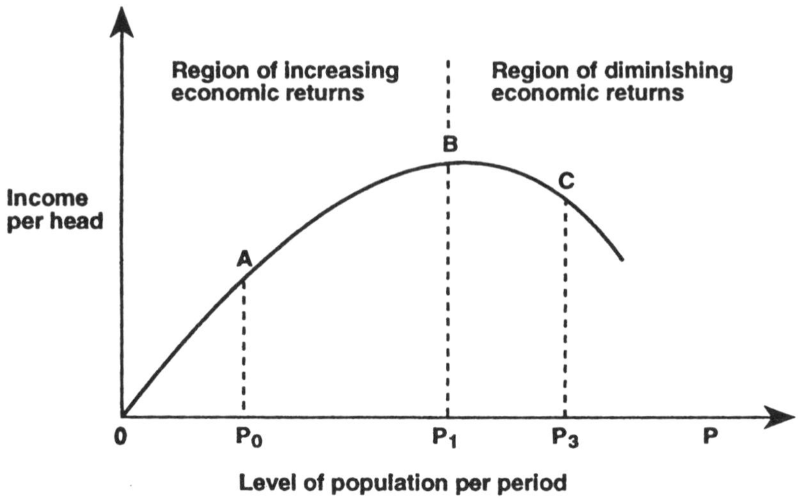

FIG. 1. *A commonly-assumed theoretical relationship between population level and income per head. It is based on the view that the productivity of a human population increases with growth in the size of the population at low levels of population, but eventually declines with increasing population because of economic constraints imposed by the limited availability of natural resources.*

While this rendition has some value, it presents a very static and partial view of population in relation to economic development, and takes population levels as being exogenously determined. Furthermore, it supposes that population is the only variable of significance for production. However, the relevant *per caput* income curve may shift, due to capital accumulation, technological progress, and/or greater education and knowledge. These shifts will usually be positive. But resource depletion and degradation may result in a negative or downward shift in the average income–population relationship.

Despite the limitations of the simple model depicted in Fig. 1, it highlights the question of what should be the criterion for determining an optimal level of human population. Should maximum *per caput* income of humans be the goal?

The answer depends in part on whether a purely anthropocentric view is taken. If expansion of human population after some point is at the expense of the survival of other species, and if it is believed that humans have some responsibility for preserving biodiversity, this would indicate that the optimal human population-level is likely to be somewhat lower than that which maximizes income *per caput* (Tisdell, 1990 Ch. 11, 1991 Ch. 11).

Another point of view which needs to be considered (even if one takes an anthropocentric viewpoint) is that the level of population which maximizes current *per caput* income may be too high from the point of view of future generations. High population levels now, because of their resource-depleting effects, may be at the expense of future generations. Thus one of the conditions for sustainability of development suggested by some economists, namely that the income levels of future generations should be no lower than those of current ones, would be violated (Pearce *et al.*, 1989; Tisdell, 1993*b*).

Georgescu-Roegen (1971), Daly (1980), and Ehrlich & Ehrlich (1990), have all called for measures to reduce the rate of population growth. Their basic fear is that, unless this is done, the time-span of survival of the human species will be shortened. Their approach is basically an anthropocentric one, but one which could coincidentally have advantages for the survival of other species. Their worries seem to be twin ones, namely that consumptive acts and reproduction rates of current generations will (i) reduce the standard of living of future generations, and (ii) shorten the time-span of human existence. Apart from other measures, Daly (1980) suggests tradeable family-size permits as a way of regulating population increases. Without going into details, under such a system each person would be issued with a permit to have a specified number of children, *e.g.* one child; but the right would be tradeable. Thus a person wishing to have two children might purchase a permit from another person opting to have none.

Another problem needs to be mentioned, namely how is *per caput* income or the standard of living to be measured? The most common approach still is to use GDP (Gross Domestic Product) *per caput* as an indication of income per head and the standard of living. However GDP, as is well known, is grossly deficient as such an indicator: it does not include the value of non-marketed goods such as clean air, clear water, and access to harmonious natural surroundings. Furthermore, some environmental costs may be included as part of GDP because they lead to market transactions to avoid or reduce environmental damage. Such costs should be deducted from the welfare measure of the standard of living rather than added to it.

Many place considerable hope in new technology (*cf.* World Bank, 1992) as a way of overcoming prevailing constraints to economic development posed by rising population levels and concomitant limitation of the natural environment. There is little doubt that such technology can be of great value in overcoming economic and environmental constraints. However, with the introduction of new technology, the scale of economic activity often expands.

Consequently, even if the new technology results in lower environmental damage per unit of activity, the expansion in the level of activity may result in the amount of *total* environmental damage actually rising. While many modern techniques are environmentally less damaging per unit of activity than earlier ones, the latter are still being used sometimes on an ever-expanding scale and with obvious environmental dangers.

As was pointed out above, a limitation of the simple static theory depicted in Fig. 1 is that it takes population as an exogenous variable, in contrast to the Malthusian theory and the Malthusian population-trap theories. In contrast to the Malthusian theory, Malthusian population-trap theories indicate that in some cases countries can escape *permanently* from subsistence equilibrium and population pressures.

In my view, Malthusian population-trap theories do deserve to be taken seriously. At the same time, it must be conceded that they are extremely crude. In particular, population growth depends on many factors other than levels of *per caput* income. This is clear from modern economic theories of family fertility and family size, which provide useful guidance on population policies and possible trends in population growth. Let us next consider the basic elements of these theories.

ECONOMIC THEORIES OF FAMILY FERTILITY AND FAMILY SIZE

Modern economic theory indicates that birth-rates and family sizes are significantly influenced by the economic circumstances of parents. One simple theory supposes that the sizes of families are largely determined by the desire of parents for children and the cost of having and raising them (Todaro, 1981 Ch. 7; Tietenberg, 1992 Ch. 5). This means that traditional economic theory can be adapted to analysing influences on family size. The demand curve of parents for children represents the value placed on extra children by parents in terms of their willingness to pay for extra children. In the case illustrated in Fig. 2, it is represented by the line marked DD.

The demand to have children will be high if local society puts considerable social value on large families, if children themselves can add to the productivity of the family as in some farming situations, or if they are essential for providing parents with income and security in their old age or if they should become handicapped. In many less-developed countries, especially in rural areas, the demand to have large families is still high because of one or more of such factors.

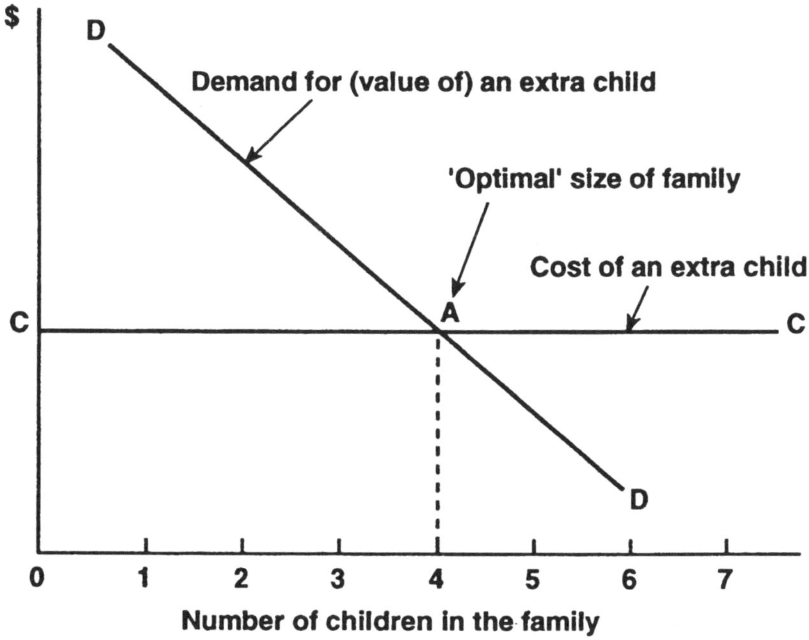

FIG. 2. *Family size determined by economic considerations, namely the value placed on an extra child and the cost of providing for it.*

The 'other side of the coin' is the cost of adding to one's family and maintaining children. In the case shown in Fig. 2, the additional cost to the family of an additional child is represented by the line marked CC. This may be relatively low in less-developed countries, because socially-required standards in provision of child-related services are usually lower in LDCs than in more developed countries. Furthermore, because of the extended-family system in most LDCs, and work being conducted in or near the home, as in many rural situations, children do not seriously interfere with the work-pattern of parents or require costly child-minding services as is the case in developed urban economies.

The size of the family, according to economic theory, is determined by the intersection of the curve showing the parents' demand for children and the additional costs involved in satisfying this demand. In Fig. 2, this occurs at the point of intersection marked 'A' and implies that the optimal size of the family from the point of view of these parents is four.

Any factor which adds to the cost of extra children will tend to reduce the size of the family. The disappearance of the extended-family system and urbanization are likely to do this — especially the former, which makes it more costly to parents to take care of children. Urbanization, where it involves work outside the home by men and women, also adds to the cost of child-care, and often children cannot be as productively employed in towns as in farming situations. Social pressures for education of children can also add to costs, and these pressures are likely to be stronger in an urban than a rural setting.

As societies develop and become more urbanized and market-oriented, the cost of having larger families rises, and the demand for, or value placed on, large families tends to fall. This trend is therefore a positive aspect of economic development from a population control viewpoint.

Furthermore, reductions in infant mortality and improvements in human health can be positive forces for reducing the birth-rate and average family size. When the probability of mortality is high among children, this can lead parents to have larger families or a greater number of childbirths to compensate for their possible loss of children after birth. Better health on the part of parents may, in addition, increase their productivity and income and reduce their need for assistance from their children, so favouring smaller-sized families.

Education, especially of women, has been identified in the literature as another positive influence in reducing family size. This may occur for a number of reasons: education may result in increased employment possibilities outside the home, improved social status (especially for females), higher incomes, and greater knowledge about methods and practice of contraception. All these factors make for families of smaller size.

Todaro (1981 p. 191) summarizes the economic theory of family size as follows:

> 'In deciding whether or not to have *additional* children, parents are assumed to weigh economic benefits against costs, where the principal benefits are, as we have seen, the expected income from child labor, usually on the farm, and their financial support for elderly parents. Balanced against these benefits are the two principal elements of "cost":
>
> 1. The "opportunity cost" of the mother's time (*i.e.* the income she could earn if she were not at home caring for her children).
>
> 2. The cost (both opportunity and actual) of educating children (*i.e.* the financial tradeoff between having fewer "high-quality", high-cost, educated children with high-income-earning potentials *versus* more "low-quality", low-cost, uneducated children with much lower earning prospects.'

Todaro (*ibid.*) goes on to elaborate on the theory and to draw policy conclusions from it. He says:

'Using the same "thought processes" as in the traditional theory of consumer behavior, the theory of family fertility as applied to LDCs concludes that when the price or cost of children rises as a result, say, of increased educational and employment opportunities for women, or a rise in school fees, or the establishment of minimum-age child labor laws, or the provision of publicly financed old-age social security schemes and so on, parents will demand *fewer* "additional" children, perhaps substituting quality for quantity or a mother's employment income for her childrearing activities. It follows that one way to induce families to desire *fewer* children is to raise the "price" of child rearing, by, say, providing greater educational opportunities and a wider range of higher-paying jobs for young women.'

Table I provides a summary of factors (mostly economic ones) which can be expected to lead to a reduction in family size. Most of these factors are positively correlated with economic growth, and can be correlated with economic development and a rising standard of living.

TABLE I

Factors Favourable to Reduced Family Size.

Demand-reducing Factors for High Birth-rates and Family Sizes	Factors Increasing Costs of Larger Families
– Social approval for small families. – Fewer opportunities for children to be productively employed. – Enhanced productivity of surviving children. – Availability of social security payments for old age or disability of parents. – Sustained health of parents, so less need for income support or other caring services.	– Rise in the social standards involved in the raising of children necessitating increased economic outlays, *e.g.* in relation to health-care and education. – Compulsory education of children where much of the cost of this education is borne by the parents. – Increased opportunity cost involved in child care, *e.g.* due to breakdown of the extended family, [and] employment of parents outside the home. – In some cases, economic penalties imposed by the State for large families (as in China), *e.g.* reduced work bonuses, increased family- support subsidies. – Increase in the cost of products used by children, *e.g.* food, clothing, and housing; medical expenses and costs for instance of schooling.

Other Influences Leading to Reduced Family Sizes
– Reduced cost of contraception, its greater reliability and acceptability. – Increased knowledge of contraception techniques and family planning. – Education appears to be positively connected with reduced family size. – Improvement in the socio-economic status of women. – Urbanization.

To regulate the size of their families, parents must know of suitable methods for this purpose and the methods must be within their economic reach. But this is not enough; they must also *want* to limit the size of their family, and exercise appropriate self-control and practised reticence. For economic or other reasons, parents may not desire a small family; consequently cheap contraception is not sufficient to ensure small-sized families, because it is only part of the decision process about family size. Self-discipline also plays a role.

The world is experiencing a rapid rate of urbanization, and this is especially apparent in LDCs. In fact, most of the increase in global population is expected to be accommodated in urban areas (German Advisory Council on Global Change, 1993). Such urbanization has been criticized as creating problems (Todaro, 1981) especially of an environmental nature. While this is true and will be a major challenge in the next few decades, urbanization also has a positive aspect in that it tends to result in smaller family sizes. This is because the costs of raising children in an urban environment are generally higher than in a rural environment, and usually the opportunities for productive employment of children are lower in towns — at least than in a countryside rich in farms.

THE NATURAL RESOURCE-BASE, ENVIRONMENT, AND POPULATION: SOME CASE-STUDIES

Particular cases enable us to consider ways in which rising population-densities can endanger the natural resource-base on which much economic production depends and likewise ultimately income-levels. Examples to be considered include shifting agriculture (which still occurs in parts of Asia, for example), farming in the Ukambani District of Kenya, and herding in the Sahel. They are indicative of a wide range of resource-problems which are emerging in rural areas owing to rising population-densities, and will now be dealt with in turn.

Shifting Agriculture

Shifting agriculture can take several different forms, but most of these forms involve a cultivation cycle where the land, after being cropped for a period of time, is allowed to return to a natural state of revegetation. The period of non-use of the land for agriculture allows for replacement of humus in the soil and a build-up of plant nutrients such as sources of nitrogen. Provided that the period allowed for natural revegetation of the cultivated land is long enough, the agricultural productivity of the land can be sustained (Ramakrishnan, 1987, 1992).

Nevertheless, as population densities rise, difficulties occur. The rotation cycle involving cultivation and fallow is altered, with the fallow-period becoming shorter in an attempt to feed more mouths by using the limited available land. Consequently, soil fertility tends to fall and with it the yields. Furthermore, the total proportion of land under cultivation at any one time rises. This usually results in an accelerated rate of soil erosion and, in wetter areas, greater water runoff. Thus flooding, siltation, and other unfavourable externalities, may occur with greater intensity or increased frequency downstream of the shifting cultivation, and with resultant economic and feeding-capacity loss. As yields decline on already cultivated land, economic pressures increase to bring even very marginal land (from an agricultural point of view) under cultivation, so adding to environmental degradation and unsustainable use of the natural resource-base, not to mention accelerated loss of biodiversity.

As a limit, shifting agriculture may give way to permanent agriculture. This may, however, not ensure sustainable yields or only do so (as practised) by the use of non-renewable resources, such as the application of nitrogenous fertilizers produced from natural gas. Furthermore, the local shifting cultivators may not have the knowledge or culture which enables them to make a smooth transition to permanent agriculture. They may therefore be displaced by migrant agriculturalists who are accustomed to permanent agriculture. This has occurred in parts of the Indian subcontinent, *e.g.* displacement of hill tribes practising shifting agriculture in Bangladesh by Bengalis who are used only to lowland permanent agriculture. In the latter case, this has often added to environmental problems in hilly areas because the Bengalis have little experience with such cultivation and tend to transfer lowland farming practices to the hilly areas, thereby accelerating soil erosion (Tisdell *et al.*, in press).

In the case of tribal people following traditional methods of rural production, including shifting agriculture, the economic plight of many is not necessarily of their own making — that is, due to their own population increase. In many cases, they are suffering encroachment on, and loss of, their traditional lands as a result of the economic expansion and population increase or explosion of other groups. This may take the form of actual appropriation of their traditional lands for farming by a dominant group, or the use of those lands for the provision of infrastructure such as dams and reservoirs for servicing the economic activities of the dominant group. For example, the building of the Kapatur Dam in the Chittagong hill tracts of Bangladesh meant the loss of a considerable amount of land by local hill-tribes. Thus the population density on the remaining land area of hill tribes in the Chittagong hill tracts increased (Tisdell *et al.*, in press). Furthermore, these losses are compounded as Bengali farmers increasingly settle in the foothills of this region (Alauddin *et al.*, 1995). This pattern is not, however, by any means unique to Bangladesh.

The acquisition (appropriation) of tribal lands by those practising more intensive forms of agriculture and rural production raises few moral qualms for those doing the appropriation. They tend to look upon such lands as wastelands or neglected lands, and consider morality to be on their side in raising the economic productivity of these lands by appropriating them and using them more intensively. However, this enhanced productivity may not be sustainable. Furthermore, those acquiring such land and using it more intensely than hitherto are likely to fail to take account of any unfavourable externalities that arise from intensification of economic activity on the land. Thus not only are tribal people marginalized, but those replacing them may also be headed for poverty due to the adoption of unsustainable land practices.

It might be noted that the appropriation of land used by tribal people and by those engaged in extensive rural land-uses, or by others who are intent on its intensive use, is not only made easier by the above moral view but also by the fact that the extensive users of the land often have no formal legal title to it. In addition, they are often not well educated and competent at making legal claims, which adds to the chances of their dispossession. Furthermore, the dominant economic group usually controls the legislature, and so expropriation may in fact proceed legally, *e.g.* all 'vacant' land may be made state property and redistributed.

It thus seems on the whole that those societies which engage in the most intensive forms of economic activity become wealthier and more powerful compared with those which are reliant on more extensive forms of economic activity, though the latter are often in greater harmony with Nature. Consequently, there has been a tendency for societies that are engaged in intensive economic activity to supplant those which are based on extensive economic activity. While 'frontiers' in which land was little-used remained, these changes could be accommodated to some extent by the emigration of those involved in the more extensive forms of economic activity. However, most such 'frontiers' have long since disappeared, so the brunt of population increase and intensification of economic activity by dominant groups now weighs very heavily on those practising extensive forms of economic activity. Of this an example is given later in this Chapter regarding nomadic herding in the Sahel.

Unsustainable Farming in the Ukambani Region of Kenya

The Akamba people live in the Machakos and Kitui districts (Ukambani) in central-southern Kenya. The area consists of low hills bordering onto plains and is very 'marginal' for agriculture. The Akamba were originally herders and shifting cultivators in more productive areas of Kenya but were displaced by the Maasai by force in competition for land and retreated to the Ukambani region. As a result of loss of land to the Maasai, and their own rising population, the Akamba have been forced to alter their land-use from one of shifting agriculture and herding to one of settled agriculture. However, yields from this agriculture are unsustainable in Ukambani.

The situation has been explained by Lee (1993 pp. 10–1) in the following terms:

> 'Towards the end of the 19th century, skirmishes between the Akamba and the Maasai subsided. As their population increased, the Akamba expanded onto the surrounding plains. Initially, they used the plains for cattle herding, but the need to grow grain brought increasing cultivation around their homesteads.
>
> 'To begin with, the farmers practised shifting cultivation. As each cultivated site became less productive, due to soil depletion, they moved to another site. But as the population pressure increased during this century, opportunities for shifting cultivation onto new desirable land diminished. The Akamba thus became more intensive cultivators on fixed locations, eventually with fixed land-titles. Today the rate of population increase in Ukambani is one of the highest in the world, but the productivity of the soil continues to fall.
>
> 'The social and economic problems of the area have been of concern for more than 70 years. There have been several cycles of rapid population growth, soil depletion, and erosion, and attempts to solve the problem. These have included emigration to new settlement areas, terracing to protect the land from erosion, and introduction of an early-maturing maize variety, called 'Katumani Composite', that produces more than the traditional maize varieties in poor seasons. Nevertheless, soil fertility has continued to decline.'

The Akamba farmers have thus been caught in a poverty trap in which population increase and economic circumstances have combined to ensnare them more and more firmly. Many different cycles are involved. The area under cropping is increasing as available land is subdivided and parcelled out to the rising population. This means that the area for livestock is shrinking and stocking densities are growing, leading to overgrazing and the need to supplement the food supply of cattle. In fact a soil degradation cycle is involved which is increasingly difficult to break out of.

The soil degradation cycle involves the following factors:

(1) Soil organic matter is declining because crop residues (mostly of Maize, *Zea mays*) must be fed to the animals and manure from the 'bomas' (livestock corrals) is not returned to the fields, mainly because of the effort involved.

(2) Because of the reduction of organic matter in the soil, useful biological processes in it are impeded and there is low infiltration of rain-water, with resultant accelerated runoff.

(3) Consequently there is a loss of soil and nutrients and crop yields fall. Hence, the incomes of the Akamba farmers are reduced and the incidence of poverty rises.

The course of this downward economic spiral is indicated in Fig. 3.

The problems faced by the farmers of Ukambani have been investigated by the Kenyan Agricultural Research Institute and Australian researchers in the CSIRO (Commonwealth Scientific and Industrial Research Organization). Their recommendation for breaking the poverty cycle is, for the Akamba:

(1) to apply commercial fertilizer in small quantities;

(2) preferably to spread manure from the bomas on the fields and include legumes* in their crop rotation; and,

(3) from the increased yield of crops that have been attended to in this way, to reserve a part of the coarser crop residues, such as corn-stalks, for return to the soil so as to provide more humus.

The suggestion is a positive one. Nevertheless, it is not certain to result in escape from the Malthusian population-trap. Its success depends on farmers supplementing their limited use of fertilizer by other sustainable practices, *e.g.* return of a portion of the increased crop residues to the soil, spreading of manure, and crop rotation using legumes.* Pressure to feed increased crop residues to livestock may be strong, and rising population levels may add to this pressure. The prospects of escape from the 'trap' may therefore be limited. Furthermore, the fertilizer will require imports, adding to Kenya's balance of payments difficulties. Further yields may become fertilizer-dependent, and in the longer term be sustained only by increasing applications of chemical fertilizer (*cf.* Tisdell, 1991 Ch. 9; 1993*a* Ch. 11). Nevertheless, if the full set of recommendations were adopted and population levels could be stabilized, the proposals would be of great assistance.

Unfortunately, there are not promising prospects for stabilizing the population in Ukambani, where females have little opportunity for off-farm employment. Although males often go to Nairobi and other urban centres for work, their womenfolk are left in the villages

---

* Members of the pea and bean family (Leguminosae), commonly fixing atmospheric nitrogen and hence of nutritional value to crops, increasing their yield. — Ed.

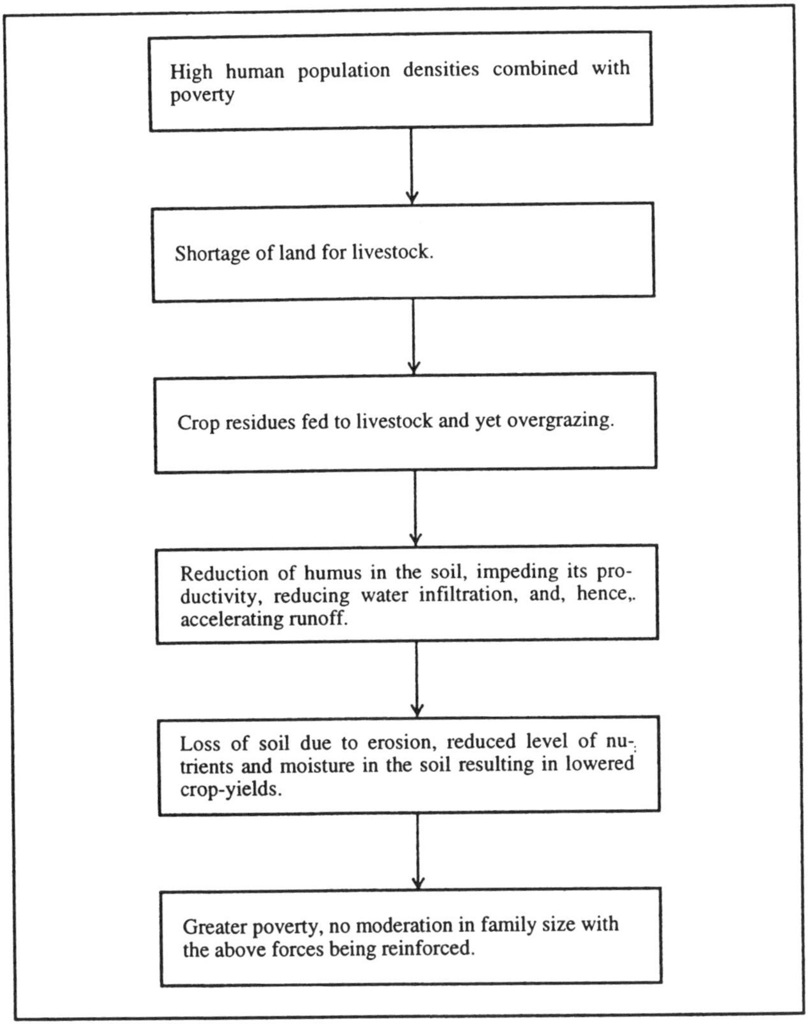

FIG. 3. *A cycle induced by poverty and population-pressure involving soil degradation. An example of a Malthusian population-trap.*

and primarily take care of the farming, with the males returning periodically. This form of partial urbanization does little to put a brake on population growth.

The Nomadic Herders of the Sahel

Another group of extensive land-users who have come under growing resource and economic pressures in recent decades are nomadic herders of livestock. This has occurred in many parts of the globe and is particularly evident in the Sahel region of northern Africa.

As population levels in the Sahel have increased, this has led to an expansion of agriculture, often supported by foreign aid, at the expense of nomadic herding. Increasingly 'fixed' agriculturalists have appropriated the traditional grazing-lands of nomads — the land which the latter had long used for grazing and access to vital drinking-water for their livestock. This is well documented by cases described in Bennett (1991).

Several consequences have followed, which include:

(1) Greater crowding of livestock on the reduced total area of land available for nomadic grazing, with accelerated environmental deterioration thereof.
(2) Greater degree of poverty and frequency of famine.
(3) Ecologically induced migration of nomads to urban areas where they often become fringe-dwellers and have great difficulty in adjusting to the urban situation.
(4) Increased violence and armed conflicts between land-users — that is, between nomadic pastoralists and settled agriculturalists, and between competing nomadic groups or tribes.
(5) Ecologically unsustainable use of the land by agriculturalists or by those engaged in pastoralism in a fixed location.

This case of nomadic herders, as well as those described above, illustrate the dangers inherent in intensification of rural land-use. One must carefully consider whether increased yields from such intensification are ecologically sustainable. It is not that intensification of land-use should never be contemplated as a strategy for economic development, but that it is necessary to consider very carefully whether a particular case is sustainable and will show a reasonable degree of internal ecological balance — bearing in mind that systems which have been heavily reliant on outside energy resources may not be sustainable in the long run.

Biodiversity Conservation in China: a Brief Case-study

China provides yet another case of conflict between environmental conservation, economic growth, and population increase. Since 1978, when China commenced its economic reforms designed to increase the use of market forces in its economy, its economic growth has been faster than that of most countries (Tisdell, 1993*d*). However, this growth, coupled with continuing population increases, has not been without environmental costs. Primarily as a result of population expansion and economic growth, China has experienced a substantial reduction in the extent of its natural forests, woodlands, wetlands, and grasslands, *e.g.* due to the encroachments of agriculture onto naturally vegetated areas, the intensification of agriculture, and the need for fuel and timber supplies. Although China has a one-child policy, this policy does not apply to minorities and is difficult to enforce in rural areas. So population increase in many rural areas continues to be a matter of concern.

Apart from that resulting from the loss of natural vegetation cover, the introduction of aggressive exotic species to China and the adoption of high-yielding varieties of agricultural crops have all led to reduced biodiversity in China. Whereas 10–15% of species of plants are considered to be threatened or endangered globally, in China 15–20% of its species are believed to be threatened or endangered nationally, which is proportionately up to twice the world's average. Consequently, a high priority needs to be given to biodiversity conservation in China. This is recognized in *China's Agenda 21 — White Paper on China's Population, Environment and Development in the 21st Century* (State Council, 1994) and in *China: Biodiversity Conservation Action Plan* (National Environmental Protection Agency and others, 1994). Both of these documents represent a search for strategies to ensure environmentally sustainable development and the maintenance of biodiversity, but not easy solutions appear to be available.

A major problem is how to provide adequate economic benefits to local people without compromising the maintenance of biodiversity. The problem can be illustrated briefly by Xishuangbanna Dai Autonomous Prefecture located in southern Yunnan. This Prefecture borders on Laos and Burma. According to Myers (1988, 1990) and Mittermeier & Werner (1990), this is a region of 'biological megadiversity' and is thus deserving of a high priority for conservation purposes. It has a rich variety of plants and contains the only remaining populations of the Asiatic Elephant (*Elephas maximus*) in China.

However, its natural environment is under continuing threat and subject to considerable modification. The rate of human population growth of this Prefecture is rapid, due to natural increase as minorities predominate outside of its towns. Currently it is reported that there is little inward migration to this Prefecture, though prior to 1978 considerable numbers of Han Chinese were relocated in this area. Rising rural populations have resulted in intensification of land-use outside of protected areas. Permanent agriculture has encroached onto ever-more marginal land and the cycles of shifting agriculture, practised by some minorities, have become shorter. These factors, combined with increased demands for fuel and timber, have — apart from increasing rates of soil erosion — severely reduced forested and naturally-vegetated areas in the Prefecture, as is clear from comparative satellite photographs. Furthermore, human pressures on protected areas within this Prefecture have mounted. Illegal hunting of animals, and removal of plants, timber, and so on, are continual problems that are exacerbated by the rising population and denudation of land areas outside of reserves and protected areas.

Strategies that are being employed, or are being considered by the Chinese government, for reducing human pressure on protected areas in this Prefecture include:

(1) The encouragement of ecotourism employing the 'user-pays' principle and involving local communities. For instance, a joint local venture has been established with a local village near Menglun to open a portion of Xishuangbanna State Nature Reserve to ecotourism.

(2) Granting of limited rights to local communities to use protected areas for extractive purposes or for restricted cultivation. For example, rights are given to some local communities within Xishuangbanna State Nature Reserve to cultivate a local 'ginger plant' that is used for medicinal purposes. This plant grows only on the forest floor, and forest use which has a minimally adverse impact on conservation can thus be legitimized.

(3) Government financial support for economic development projects in villages bordering on or located near protected areas. It is hoped that such projects, by raising the incomes of villagers, will make them less inclined to use protected areas illegally. Where this project is subsidized by the government, the subsidy can provide a lever for compliance with the law; for example, the subsidy may be withdrawn in the event of any illegal use of protected areas.

(4) Some other methods of law-enforcement include small payments to village leaders to act as 'forest guards'.

Whether or not such measures will work remains to be seen. Although the prospects cannot be discussed here, it should be noted that increasing population mobility in China could reduce human populations located in or near protected areas and so reduce pressures from this immediate source. Unfortunately, however, pressures on protected areas do not only come from local populations. For example, growing urban populations, industrialization, and 'modernization', add to demands for greater energy supplies, and there is rising demand in China for electricity, including in the urban areas of Xishuangbanna. In Xishuangbanna, electricity supplies could be expanded by constructing a dam on the Lancang River (known downstream as the Mekong River). Such a dam could also supply irrigation water for agricultural use in the dry season. But while the possibility has been seriously considered by China, no decision has yet been taken as to whether to build this proposed dam.

A major disadvantage of such a dam (given the suggested site for it) would be that it would flood a large part of Xishuangbanna State Nature Reserve and further threaten the maintenance of biodiversity in this Prefecture. In fact, the building of infrastructure throughout

China (and for that matter throughout most of Asia) as a part of its drive for 'modernization', and its efforts to raise living standards, constitutes a major threat to the preservation of biodiversity. The road to ecologically sustainable development in Asia is not likely to be easy, particularly if the maintenance of biodiversity is considered to be a desirable part of it. In Asia, urbanization is accelerating and its consequences for the environmental future need to be increasingly considered, taking into account the ecological and economic interdependence of urban and rural areas (Tisdell, 1995). Rural environments are all-too-often altered or sacrificed to satisfy the demands of urban growth, and in such cases we must look beyond rural communities to establish trends.

CONCLUDING COMMENTS

Since the time of Malthus's epoch-making *Essay* (1798), there has been considerable progress in forming an effective economic theory of population. The modern economic theory of optimal family size has proven to be useful for the purposes of both prediction and policymaking. There is an increasing need to link this theory with the prospects for environmentally sustainable development and for escape from poverty cycles that are characteristic of many LDCs, involving, as most of them do, the economically unsustainable use of natural resources and concomitant environmental degradation.

We have been able to explore the difficulties of escaping from a low-level equilibrium 'trap' involving population, poverty, and natural resources, in a general context as well as for particular cases. The particular cases, however, are not unique but are chosen to illustrate the difficulties of combining economic growth and population growth with a secure environmental future. They underline the importance of *fully exploring ecological consequences* of changes in land-use before actually embarking on such changes, so as to ensure wise resource management, sustainable land-use, and ultimately economically sustainable incomes and conditions with good prospects for population control.

REFERENCES

ALAUDDIN, M., MUJERI, M.K. & TISDELL, C.A. (1995). Technology–employment–environment linkages and the rural poor of Bangladesh: insights from farm-level data. Pp. 221–5 in I. AHMED & J.A. DOELEMAN (Eds) *Beyond Rio: The Environmental Crisis, Technological Dilemma and Sustainable Livelihoods in the Third World*. Macmillan, London, UK: xx + 390 pp., illustr.

BENNETT, O. (Ed.) (1991). *Greenwar: Environment and Conflict*. Panos Institute, London, England, UK: iv + 156 pp., illustr.

DALY, H.E. (1980). *Economics, Ecology and Ethics: Towards a Steady-state Economy.* Freeman, San Francisco, California, USA: xii + 372 pp., illustr.

EHRLICH, P.R. & EHRLICH, A.H. (1990). *The Population Explosion.* Simon & Schuster, New York, NY, USA: 320 pp.

ENGELS, F. (1973). Outlines of a Critique of Political Economy. In K. MARX *Economic and Philosophic Manuscripts of 1844,* Foreign Languages Publishing House, Moscow, Russia, also cited as 1973, Lawrence & Wishart, London, England, UK: 255 pp., but not available for checking.

GEORGESCU-ROEGEN, N. (1971). *The Entropy Law and the Economic Process.* Harvard University Press, Cambridge, Massachusetts, USA: xv + 457 pp., illustr.

GERMAN ADVISORY COUNCIL ON GLOBAL CHANGE (1993). The world in transition: basic structure of the global Man–Environment relationship. *Global Change Prisma,* **4**(2), pp. 7–10.

LEE, B. (1993). *Escaping from Hunger.* Australian Centre for International Agricultural Research, Canberra, Australia: 52 pp., illustr.

MAITRA, P. (1992). The demographic effects of technological change and capitalist transformation in a re-interpretation of the Demographic Transition Theory. *Artha Vijana,* **34**(2), pp. 125–54.

MALTHUS, T.R. (1798). *An Essay on the Principle of Population as it Affects the Future Improvements of Society.* [Reprint 1909. Macmillan, London, England, UK: xix + 134 pp.]

MITTERMEIER, R.A. & WERNER, T.B. (1990). World of plants and animals in 'megadiversity' countries. *Tropicus,* **4**(1), pp. 4–5.

MYERS, N. (1988). Threatened biota: hotspots in tropical forests. *The Environmentalist,* **8**(8), pp. 1–20.

MYERS, N. (1990). The biodiversity challenges: expanded hot-spot analysis. *The Environmentalist,* **10**(4), pp. 243–56.

NATIONAL ENVIRONMENTAL PROTECTION AGENCY AND OTHERS (1994). *China: Biodiversity Conservation Action Plan.* National Environmental Protection Agency, Beijing, China: v + 106 pp.

PEARCE, D., MARKANDYA, A. & BARBIER, E.G. (1989). *Blueprint for a Green Economy.* Earthscan Publications, London, England, UK: xvi + 192 pp., illustr.

RAMAKRISHNAN, P.S. (1987). Shifting agriculture and rainforest ecosystem management. *Biology International,* **15**, p. 17.

RAMAKRISHNAN, P.S. (1992). *Shifting Agriculture and Sustainable Development: An Interdisciplinary Study from North-eastern India.* UNESCO, France–USA–England: xvii + 424 pp., illustr., tables.

STATE COUNCIL (1994). *China's Agenda 21 — White Paper on China's Population, Environment and Development in the 21st Century.* China Environmental Science Press, Beijing, China: iv + 246 pp.

TIETENBERG, T. (1992). *Environmental and Natural Resource Economics,* 3rd edn. Harper Collins, New York, NY, USA: xxvi + 678 pp., illustr.

TISDELL, C.A. (1990). *Natural Resources, Growth and Development.* Praeger, New York, NY, USA: xvi + 187 pp., illustr.

TISDELL, C.A. (1991). *Economics of Environmental Conservation.* Elsevier Science Publishers, Amsterdam, Netherlands: xxii + 234 pp., illustr.

TISDELL, C.A. (1993*a*). *Environmental Economics.* Edward Elgar, Aldershot, England, UK: xii + 260 pp., illustr.

TISDELL, C.A. (1993*b*). *Combining Biological Conservation, Sustainability and Economic Growth: Can We Overcome Potential Conflict?* Discussion Paper No. 130, Department of Economics, University of Queensland, Brisbane 4072, Australia: 11 pp. (An invited keynote paper for the 20th Waigani Seminar on Environmental Development, 23–27 August 1993, Port Moresby, Papua New Guinea.)

TISDELL, C.A. (1993*c*). Ecological economics and the environmental future. Pp. 363–76 and following Commentary in *Surviving With The Biosphere: Proceedings of the Fourth International Conference on Environmental Future (4th ICEF), held in Budapest, Hungary, during 22–27 April 1990* (Eds NICHOLAS POLUNIN & Sir JOHN BURNETT). Edinburgh University Press, Edinburgh, Scotland, UK: xxii + 572 pp., illustr.

TISDELL, C.A. (1993*d*). *Economic Development in the Context of China*. Macmillan, London, UK: xiv + 220 pp., illustr.

TISDELL, C.A. (1994). Population, economics, development, and environmental security. Pp. 63–84 in *Population and Global Security* (Eds NICHOLAS POLUNIN & MOHAMMAD NAZIM), *Limited Geneva Edition for* United Nations Population Fund (UNFPA) *et al.* The Foundation for Environmental Conservation, Geneva, Switzerland, & Energy and Environment Society of Pakistan, Lahore, Pakistan: xi + 285 pp., illustr. and tables.

TISDELL, C.A. (1995). Asian development and environmental dilemmas. *Contemporary Economic Policy*, **13**, pp. 38–49.

TISDELL, C.A., ALAUDDIN, M. & MUJERI, M. (in press). Water resource availability, management and environmental spillovers in Bangladesh. In *Perspectives in Resource Management in Developing Countries* (Ed. A. Thakur). Concept Publishing Company, New Delhi, India.

TODARO, M.P. (1981). *Economic Development in the Third World*, 2nd edn. Longman, New York, NY, USA: xxxiv + 588 pp., illustr.

WORLD BANK (1992). *World Development Report 1992: Development and the Environment*. Oxford University Press, New York, NY, USA: xii + 308 pp., illustr.

WORLD COMMISSION ON ENVIRONMENT AND DEVELOPMENT (1987). *Our Common Future*. Oxford University Press, Oxford, England, UK: xv + 400 pp., tables.

[13]

ELSEVIER

Ecological Economics 31 (1999) 395–408

ECOLOGICAL ECONOMICS

www.elsevier.com/locate/ecolecon

ANALYSIS

Carrying capacity reconsidered: from Malthus' population theory to cultural carrying capacity

Irmi Seidl [a,*], Clem A. Tisdell [b,1]

[a] *Institut für Umweltwissenschaften, Universität Zürich, Winterthurerstrasse 190, CH-8057 Zürich, Switzerland*
[b] *Department of Economics, The University of Queensland, Brisbane Qld 4072, Australia*

Received 11 November 1998; received in revised form 24 May 1999; accepted 27 May 1999

Abstract

In this paper the concept of carrying capacity is investigated to provide an improved understanding about its contribution to solve environmental problems. Light is shed on its form, interpretation and application in biology, demography, applied and human ecology. The analysis begins with an examination of the bedrock of carrying capacity which is Malthus' population theory, and its mathematical formulation — the logistic growth equation. The investigation shows Malthus' thinking to be both political and normative. Furthermore, the rigid assumptions of the logistic equation and the uncertainty of its terms are found not to allow an unequivocal calculation and prediction of the upper limits (carrying capacity) of population growth. It is illustrated that in ecology, carrying capacity focuses on the quality of an ecosystem (pressures on it) and corresponding population numbers, and less on equilibrium of populations as in biology. It is shown that carrying capacity, when applied in fields where human activity or human aims are involved, is a complex normative concept influenced by ecological dynamics, human values and aims, institutional settings and management practices. However, it is demonstrated that the discussion about institutional settings, aims, and values does not take place as much as necessary for its useful application and operationalization in such fields. Instead, authors fall back on sustainability, environmental standards or resilience. The main contribution of carrying capacity in applied and human ecology is as a political concept generally highlighting that exponential growth and thus environmental pressures have to be curbed. Carrying capacity is far from being a universal constraint. Operationalization will continue to be hampered as long as agreements are missing about which social carrying capacity is to be opted for and when it is considered to have been transgressed. © 1999 Elsevier Science B.V. All rights reserved.

Keywords: Carrying capacity — biological, social, biophysical; Logistic growth exponential; Population growth; Equilibrium population; Malthus; Demography

* Corresponding author. Tel.: +41-1-6354803; fax: +41-1-6355711.
E-mail addresses: iseidl@uwinst.unizh.ch (I. Seidl), c.tisdell@economics.uq.edu (C.A. Tisdell)
[1] Tel.: +61-7-33656570; fax: +61-7-33657299.

PII: S0921-8009(99)00063-4

1. Introduction

In the late 1960s and early 1970s the discussion about looming limits of the Earth's carrying capacity due to population and economic growth initiated the widespread development of environmental awareness (e.g. Ehrlich, 1971; Meadows et al., 1972). Exponential growth of the human population and economy, and some of their upper limits (e.g. food availability, arable land, nonrenewable resources) were identified. Other unknown upper limits causing irreversible changes in climate, or interrupting severely vital natural processes, were alluded to or predicted. Later, this discussion also highlighted consumption patterns in industrialized countries and their technologies as further pressures on Earth's carrying capacity (e.g. Daily and Ehrlich, 1992, 1996; Srivastava and Ruesink, 1998). Presently, not many people doubt the rapid decline and deterioration of environmental resources (e.g. freshwater, fish stocks, biodiversity, soil, minerals, fossil resources), the overuse of ecological sinks (e.g. waste assimilation in air, water, soil; Brown, 1998), and the fact that such overuse deteriorates and destroys ecosystems and ultimately living conditions of humans and other species. Undoubtedly, the concept of carrying capacity has played a significant part in promoting public and political awareness and understanding of looming and existing limits to economic activity.

However, as will be demonstrated, attempts to apply the concept of carrying capacity to socio-economic sectors such as tourism or the management of natural sites, and to ecosystems have not been successful. Either the results have been unreliable or the concept of carrying capacity has been profoundly modified (as in applied ecology, human ecology) to make it operational.

The political importance of the concept on the one hand and discontent regarding its applications and modifications on the other motivated this current investigation of carrying capacity. The aim of the paper is to provide an improved understanding of the concept, its history, its aims, its characteristics, and its flaws, and to clarify where and how it can be applied.

As Malthusian thinking is still perceptible in this concept, the study begins with an examination of Malthus' treatise on the development of population. This treatise had a major influence on Darwin and, subsequently, on later biologists, as well as on the incipient science of demography. Both disciplines — biology and demography — provide the bedrock of the concept of carrying capacity as it is applied and used in environmental policy and discussion. However, major modifications of the biological and demographical understanding of the concept of carrying capacity within the fields of applied ecology and human ecology have been made. It is argued that the concept is a normative one as soon as it is applied in fields where human activity is involved. This implies a considerable role for value judgments and institutional settings in formulating carrying capacity and deducing policies.

2. Malthus and his influence on Darwin and on human demography

The Reverend Thomas Robert Malthus' (1766–1834) *An Essay on the Principle of Population* (Malthus, 1986, 1st edition of 1798) has undoubtedly been a long-lasting, broadly discussed and culturally absorbed contribution to the overall views of the 19th and 20th centuries. His theory about human population growth can be considered as providing a basis for the concept of carrying capacity. This is mainly because of Malthus' great influence on Darwin's concept of natural selection, the foundation of modern evolutionary biology and ecology, and finally because of Malthus' influence on the incipient science of human demography.

What are the essentials of Malthus' theory? There are three basic assumptions, the first being that food was considered to be necessary for the existence of man and to be the sole limiting factor on human population growth. Secondly, Malthus put major emphasis on the assumption that the human population increases geometrically (exponentially, 1, 2, 4, 8, 16, 32...) as God gave humans an unchanging force of sexual passion. However, the idea of exponential growth was deduced by Malthus from population growth in North America and was not observed elsewhere at his time.[2] Interestingly, in North America immigration largely accounted for the exponential growth, a point ignored by Malthus. Lastly, he took for granted that food production could only be increased linearly (1, 2, 3, 4, 5...) and that this would lead to food shortage given the geometrical growth of population. These three assumptions form the basis for Malthus' explication of the scarcities and misery he observed in England, and for his prediction of everlasting food shortages and poverty. Hence, he declared, paucity in food and consequent 'vice and misery', which he considered as being always with mankind as biblical texts indicate, to be 'checks' to population growth imposed by the prescribed bounds of nature (Bowen, 1954, p. 88ff.).

Malthus' *Essay* met with an approving audience and only a few suspicious critics (see Bowen, 1954, p. 81ff.). The positive reception of his *Essay* was principally because his general thesis pleased nearly everybody. Capitalist apologists as well as those who defended the landed interest agreed with Malthus' stance that population tends to outrun subsistence. Furthermore, his theory fitted in with all schools of classical economics which used it for their own ends (Worster, 1985, p. 84). Beside such rather ideologically-based support, it has to be noted that Malthus was, as Bowen puts it, "a brilliant publicist... and... a 'philosopher' who first saw the importance of the limiting factors of environment on human material progress." (Bowen, 1954, pp. 95–96).[3] Finally, it has to be stressed that Malthus' theory reflects the overall societal situation and mind of the industrializing Victorian England. So, it is not pure invention to conclude that Malthus' success is largely due to his excellently presented ideas which reflected the overall circumstances of his time and concurred even with opinions and judgments of broad public sectors otherwise opposed to one another. However, not all of Malthus' approving readership might have agreed with his ideological standpoint that measures to reduce poverty and misery are in vain.

Malthus' great success is in fact astonishing because his very rough, unrealistic assumptions were not proven by any empirical evidence. Despite criticism, Malthus initially refused to admit any restraints on human population growth and institutional influences on reproduction. It is only in the 2nd edition (1803) of his treatise that he began to admit some existing restraints on population growth, namely moral restraints, and institutional influences on these moral restraints. He did so by suggesting that income equality and common ownership of property would offset any moral restraint (Bowen, 1954, p. 93). Acknowledging the influence of institutional settings on population development made "his case... explicitly a political case... and [it] no longer rested on inexorable demological tendencies" (Bowen, 1954, p. 93). Furthermore, Malthus only considered food as a limiting factor, but other constraints also exist (e.g. housing, health, energy). Another critical point which, however, was not stressed in Malthus' time is the fact that he put humans and other species on the same level,[4] and that he

[2] Observed patterns of global population growth during the last thousand years indicate that different human populations have different exponential growth curves. Nevertheless, it is important to note that during the last 1000 years, the periods in which the global population doubles have become shorter and shorter (see Cohen, 1995a, p. 94).

[3] It has been claimed Malthus had ideological aims as a publicist. Bowen writes: "...a brilliant publicist who wished to attack existing social legislation, and also to attack 'speculations' upon possible improvement of existing institutions of government and property" (Bowen, 1954, pp. 95–96). Worster notes, that "[t]here was nothing new in the idea that there are strict limits to population capacity of any area. The Linnaean naturalists, for example, had long been emphatic about the need for restraints to keep each species within its prescribed bounds. What were unprecedented in Malthus' argument were the ironclad ratios and his warnings of impending national apocalypse." (Worster, 1985, p. 152). Also, Schumpeter states that all facts and arguments Malthus put forward had already been developed by many other authors before so that Malthus' ideas had already been widely accepted in the 1790s (Schumpeter, 1965, p. 706). It is worthwhile to note that geometrical population growth was already discussed in demographical research of the 17th and 18th century. Thus, Malthus' assumptions about population growth were not new (see the perusal of scientific demography from 17th century onwards in Hutchinson, 1979, pp. 5–21).

[4] Young (1969) (p. 129) quotes Malthus as saying: "... it is not to be supposed that the physical laws to which he [man] is subjected should be essentially different from those which are observed to prevail in other parts of animated nature."

adopted the mechanistic view of nature common among the naturalists of the 18th century. This allowed him to abstract the individual organism (including the human being) from its place in nature and society, considering it as an atomistic part with a fixed and independent set of qualities instilled by God, adapted to the environment by mere mechanical arrangements (Worster, 1985, p. 152). To sum up, it has to be stressed that Malthus' theory is based on normative assertions and on a mechanistic conception of nature and society.

Malthus' role in the formation of Darwin's ideas and his influence on the overall evolutionary thinking of the 19th century is unequivocally evident (Young, 1969). Darwin adopted Malthus' views of populations growing geometrically, and of restraints posed by limited resources. In his *Essay of 1844*, Darwin wrote:

> "Even slow-breeding mankind has doubled in twenty-five years, and if he could increase his food with greater ease, he would double in less time. But for animals, without artificial means, *on an average* the amount of food for each species must be constant; whereas the increase of all organisms tends to be geometrical, and in a vast majority of cases at an enormous ratio." (Darwin, 1958, p. 117).

The idea of population pressure was central to Darwin's development of the concept of natural selection and hence of a mechanism to explain biological diversity and evolution. In Darwin's *The Variation of Animals and Plants under Domestication [1868]*, we read: "I saw, on reading Malthus on Population, that Natural Selection was the inevitable result of the rapid increase of all organic beings" (Darwin, 1969, p. 10). Furthermore, Darwin revealed in his *Autobiography*:

> "In October 1838, that is fifteen months after I had begun my systematic enquiry, I happened to read for amusement Malthus on *Population*, and being well prepared to appreciate the struggle for existence which everywhere goes on from long-continued observation of the habits of animals and plants, it at once struck me that under these circumstances favorable variations would tend to be preserved, and unfavorable ones to be destroyed. The result of this would be the formation of new species." (Darwin, 1993, p. 120).

Darwin's reference to Malthus and his ideas clearly indicate a substantial influence of Malthus on the most influential biological theory.

However, Malthus' influence was not limited to biology as studies of human demography were also based on his ideas for a long time. In reviewing developments in demography, Back (1983, p. 123) writes:

> "...[T]he manner of reasoning he [Malthus] employed, looked at population as a practically self-propelled unit. We have the image of an expanding mass straining against the constraint of natural resources. What is missing from this picture is the characteristically human ability to plan, to think and to organize. Demography has followed this path for a long time..."

The Malthusian idea of an uncontrollable population growth only restricted by the bounds of natural resources was first put into a mathematical equation describing human population growth by Pierre F. Verhulst, Professor of Mathematics in Brussels, Belgium, in 1838 (Verhulst, 1838).[5] He checked the results of the equation with censuses of population developments in France, Belgium, Russia and in Essex, England, over 20 years in the early 19th century and found confirming results.The equation of logistic growth is:

$$\frac{\mathrm{d}N}{\mathrm{d}t} = rN\left(\frac{K-N}{K}\right)$$

where N is the population, r is the growth rate and K is the carrying capacity.

[5] Verhulst wrote: "We know that the famous Malthus established the principle that human population tends to grow in geometrical progression... This proposition is incontestable..." (Verhulst, 1838, p. 113, translation by the authors).

One term of the logistic growth introduced by Verhulst is the constant relative growth rate later called the Malthusian parameter r (r = [birth rate b − death rate d]). It represents Malthus' assumption of exponential growth (see Fig. 1). The equation is:

$$\frac{dN}{dt} = rN$$

However, the existence of permanent geometrical (exponential) growth which is what Malthus and his predecessors thought in principle about the inherent growth of populations, must be rejected as it does not include an upper limit (Hutchinson, 1979, p. 3). Such growth can only be observed for short time periods. Therefore, Verhulst's equation takes into account limits to population growth (carrying capacity K), which in Malthus' terms stands for the shortage of food. At K the birth rate equals the death rate leading to a stable or equilibrium population size ($dN/dt = rN = O$, $r = O$) (see Fig. 1). Through the introduction of the term $(K - N)/K$ the growth rate dN/dt raises to a maximum as N reaches $K/2$, and than falls asymptotically to zero as the population N approaches K.

Nearly a century later, in 1920, Raymond Pearl, Professor of Biometry and Vital Statistics in Baltimore (Maryland), and his colleague Lowell J. Reed, probably unaware of Verhulst's work, also formulated a logistic growth curve, and fitted it to US census data (Pearl and Reed, 1920). However, both Verhulst's and Pearl and Reed's applications of this curve to empirical data are doubtful because of their failure to take account of immigration (deduce it from r) and, in the case of Pearl

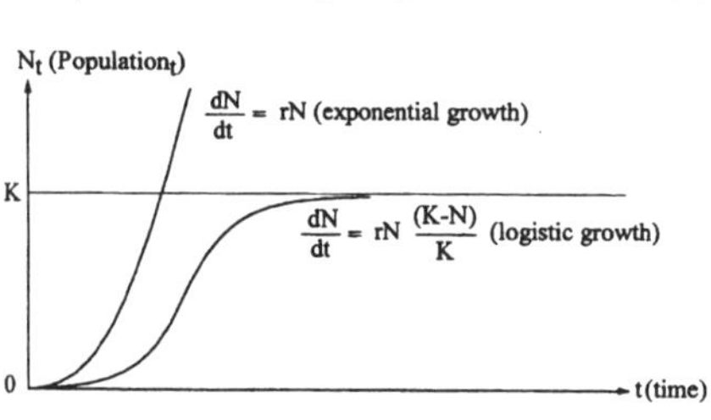

Fig. 1. Exponential and logistic population growth curve.

and Reed, the expansion of the American land frontier (Cohen, 1995a, p. 85). Other than for a short time span, their empirical data did not allow a reliable verification (a fact Verhulst admitted [1838, p. 115]). Yet, Pearl was successful in promoting his work which resulted in his and Verhulst's name being attached to the curve now widely known as the Verhulst–Pearl logistic equation. Since the development of this logistic equation, there have been numerous applications in which, however, the equation has only sometimes been confirmed by empirical data for short time periods. It seems "that the logistic curve works until it doesn't." (Cohen, 1995a, p. 87). A major reason for this missing empirical confirmation might be the rigid assumptions of the logistic growth equation; the parameters r and K are not supposed to change in time, the environment is supposed to provide a steady supply of nutrients and resources, the spatial boundaries of populations are assumed to be fixed and known, the system is closed allowing no immigration or emigration, no import or export (Cohen, 1995a, p. 84).

With the introduction of the logistic growth equation, Malthus' assumptions about population growth and limits had finally found a mathematical expression. However, empirical evidence in support of these assumptions remain slight and there is also much uncertainty about demographic and social developments, and ecological capacities and reserves. Hence, estimates about the carrying capacity of the Earth, conducted in the second half of this century, vary largely and the results range between less than 1 billion and 1000 billion people which can be supported by the Earth (Cohen, 1995b, p. 342).

Given the demographic transitions which had occurred in countries showing considerable economic growth, increasing doubts were expressed about the value of Malthus' theory as a predictor of the growth of human population. Many high-income countries have experienced low or even negative rates of net population growth. Some writers (e.g. Leibenstein, 1957) suggest that Malthus' theory may hold in the circumstances of low income but not of higher levels of income, e.g. due to escape from low-equilibrium trap (Leibenstein, 1957) or changes in the net benefit of family size (Becker, 1960).

The joining and mathematical representation of Malthus' assumptions of exponential growth and existing limits to growth was an important first step in the development of the paradigm today known as carrying capacity. In conclusion, the considerable impact of Malthus' assumptions can be attributed to their broadly favorable reception in his lifetime, to his influence on Darwin, and consequently on biology, and also to the fact that the new science of demography initially adopted Malthusian ideas.

3. Carrying capacity in biology and ecology

Logistic growth of populations is a basic assumption in population biology as '[o]ver long periods of time, in all populations of organisms... *N*, the population size, fluctuates up and down around some average value.' (Wilson and Bossert, 1971, p. 102). This logistic growth dynamic consists of an exponential population growth slowed down by an upper limit (carrying capacity).

In laboratory experiments populations of animal species often exhibit the logistic growth pattern. However, when this model with its simplified assumptions is applied in population biology, it is particularly restrictive since the basic model allows no time-lags and no interactions between species. Furthermore, it implies a carrying capacity independent of past population sizes, and finally, the prediction of the model rests on the assumption of independent life and reproduction of the individuals. However, population dynamics cannot be predicted deterministically. Rather, 'chaos', interactions between species, and environmental factors, have been attracting significant attention in the research of modern population dynamics.

In spite of its simplified assumptions, experimental evidence indicates that the logistic growth model can depict dynamics of simple populations. Nicholson showed in his now famous experiment with blowflies in population cage experiments that food availability is the sole limiting factor for their population growth and reproduction. This experiment shows that '...egglaying of population is limited by the food availability, such that a high adult population density results in a low production of eggs and a low density of adults results in a high egg production' (Christiansen and Fenchel, 1977, p. 4). Also, the doubling of K doubled the population of the blowflies as the model predicted. May (1973, p. 101) was able to model the experimental results of Nicholson by successfully fitting a logistic growth model incorporating a time lag $(t-T)$ into the equation:

$$\frac{dN(t)}{dt} = rN(t)\left(\frac{K - N(t-T)}{K}\right)$$

(For further experimental studies of logistic growth see Hutchinson, 1979, pp. 21–27.)

However, dynamics of many natural populations are much more complex than this, and consequently can only crudely be described by the logistic equation (Pulliam and Haddad, 1994, p. 142). Characteristics of natural surroundings which are not reflected in Nicholson's experiment are, for instance, the interdependence between the population and its surrounding abiotic and biotic system (e.g. weather, predators, diseases), intraspecific interactions like saturation density, changes of the environment, stochastic events, and finally differing and possibly unpredictable time lags. Also, a transgression of the initial level of carrying capacity can induce a dynamic which results in a new lower carrying capacity.

The logistic curve in biological models of population growth also builds upon the ecological concept of carrying capacity as first formulated by Hawden and Palmer in 1922 as they observed the effects of introduction of reindeer populations in Alaska. After a huge growth in the number of these animals, their population fell rapidly and eventually reached an equilibrium. Hawden and Palmer defined carrying capacity as the number of stock which a range can support without injury to the range (Pulliam and Haddad, 1994, p. 141). Their definition was an advance in that it introduced the idea of interaction between the population of animal species and the state of the environment. It shifted the attention from equilibrium population (at $dN/dt = 0$, $r = 0$) to an equilibrium quality of the environment (range). Yet, this definition of carrying capacity indicates the difficulty of evaluating objectively the interaction between a population and the environment. What qualifies as an injury, what does it mean to say 'without injury'? Normative judgments may well be inescapable in such evaluations.

A similar definition was introduced a decade later by Leopold (Hawden and Palmer, 1994, p. 141). He defined carrying capacity as the maximum density which a particular range is capable of supporting (Dhondt, 1988, p. 339). Since the definitions of Hawden/Palmer and Leopold many others have been formulated which restate, vary, or develop these basic ones (see Dhondt, 1988; Pulliam and Haddad, 1994). All these definitions, however, are, as Pulliam and Haddad (1994) point out, a poor descriptor of the dynamics of many natural populations. An important reason for this is the complexity of actual ecosystems. Their biotic interactions and multiple steady states are characterized by nonlinear dynamics and population thresholds which are all influenced and modified by environmental variations in space and time (e.g. exogenous disturbance). Hardin states: "There is no hope of ever making carrying capacity figures as precise as, say the figures for chemical valence or the value of the gravitational constant. On St. Matthew Island the growth of reindeer moss is no doubt greater in some summers than others..." (Hardin, 1986, p. 600).

In principle, there are at least three major reasons why the simple logistic model of population growth may be a poor predictor in practice:

1. Exogenous environmental forces may cause variation in the carrying capacity, *K*, or in the Malthusian parameter, *r*, or in the lag involved in the response of a population. While these variations are frequently temporary, they can also be permanent.
2. Variations in population sizes may cause *K*, *r*, or the lag-factor to alter permanently. For example, a sudden and large increase in the population of a species may permanently destroy environmental resources which the species utilizes to some extent, or populations in particular ranges may slowly and irreversibly degrade their environment. These environmental alterations are internal to the system, often exhibit hysteresis and can occur either in the absence of exogenous environmental change or due to human intrusion.
3. Exogenous environmental variation combined with certain sizes of population may bring about permanent alterations in the coefficients of the logistic model. In other words, *interactive* permanent effects can easily occur between the state of the environment and particular population sizes.

McLeod (1997) analyzed different models and methods for determining and calculating carrying capacity, and showed that complex characteristics, uncertainties and stochastic environments cannot be overcome or captured by these models. Rather, the concept of carrying capacity can only be calculated for deterministic and slightly variable systems, and only for cases where behaviour and ecological relationships of the species change slowly on the human time scale (Cohen, 1995a, p. 247). In variable environments, carrying capacity might be useful as a measurement of short-term potential densities as a function of resource availability but not of long-term equilibrium densities (McLeod, 1997, p. 540).

4. Application of carrying capacity to environmental impacts of human activity

Since the late 1960s and early 1970s, the concept of carrying capacity has been applied to capture, calculate, and express environmental limits brought about by human activity. Two main areas of application can be distinguished. First, in applied ecology (application of basic ecology to human aims and aspirations), the concept of carrying capacity is employed in relation to management of particular habitats or ecosystems like rangeland or wildlife, and to management of tourism (for example, in national parks, tourist resorts). Second, carrying capacity has been employed in human ecology (analysis of interactions between individuals, environment and society, and of demands of humans towards the environment) to discuss and illustrate the ecological impacts and limits of the growing human population and rising consumption. As will be shown, both of these new applications brought about major modifications to the concept, alienated it ever more from Malthus' initial ideas and thereby supported some of the principal criticisms. Most importantly, it has become evident that the concept has an important normative and institutional component. A judgment of an environmental situation or the decision of limits — e.g. the carrying capacity — is influenced by value-judgments and institutional settings.

Cohen (1995a, p. 248ff.) mentions at least five distinct concepts of carrying capacity that exist in applied ecology, each of which entails different aims of management or different institutional backgrounds. According to Cohen these concepts vary depending on whether the aim is to maximize (i) the standing stock of a population (plants/animals), (ii) the steady yield of the population, (iii) the number of protected plants, whether (iv) the harvested population is subject to discounting, and (v) the population is an open-access resource, subject to revenue and cost curves. Consequently, the comprehension of carrying capacity depends on the pursued aims. This becomes particularly clear from the example of rangeland management in Zimbabwe investigated by Scoones (1993). There, management decisions are based on two types of carrying capacities — an economic and an ecological one. Moreover, each category of carrying capacity itself exhibits a range of possible levels dependent on aims, farming methods and ecological features. For instance, the economic carrying capacity varies depending on productivity objectives and land availability: whether farmers aim at maximizing weight of beef produced or protein output, or whether they pursue multiple objective farming in which cattle are used as draught animals and are kept for production of meat, milk, and calf, and finally whether farmers can move them somewhere else in case of droughts. These aims and conditions determine the economic carrying capacity and the ecological one as well, and, in consequence, the most adequate management strategies. Further, farming methods affect the ecological carrying capacity. For instance, in periods of drought, farmers in Zimbabwe move their animals to other areas, and consequently relieve the pressure on pasture land. Their rotational grazing strategy and use of a few preferred grazing areas (e.g. riverbanks, drainage lines) also determine carrying capacity levels. Additionally, these ecological carrying capacities themselves vary as a function of a wide range of ecological dynamics which must be understood to assess ecological carrying capacities. This complex network of different objectives, particular farming methods and ecosystem dynamics have to be taken into account for determining carrying capacities. Therefore, as Scoones concludes, "it is essential... that planning is locally based with farmers, with local knowledge of resources and their use, being the primary participants in design and development." (Scoones, 1993, p. 114).

In a similar vein, in tourism, different definitions of carrying capacities and a multitude of aims lead to equivocal applications. Carrying capacity in tourism is conceived as a maximum number of visitors that can be tolerated without irreversible or unacceptable deterioration of the physical environment and without considerably diminishing user satisfaction (see also Mathieson and Wall, 1982, p. 21; Tisdell, 1988, p. 244; Davis and Tisdell, 1996, p. 232). Needless to say that it is difficult to determine such a number. As Mathieson and Wall (1982, p. 21) point out, separate capacities exist for each of the economic, physical (or environmental) and social subsystems of relevance (see also Davis and Tisdell, 1996, p. 232). Lindberg et al. (1997) express considerable discontentment with the concept of carrying capacity in tourism (see also Tisdell, 1988, p. 88; Davis and Tisdell, 1996). They claim that the concept is 'not adequate to address the complexity found in tourism situations'. In particular, they criticize the concept as being imprecise, a fact which hinders its operational specification. Furthermore, the subjectivity of the concept is often not realized by policy proponents who often perceive it as a scientific, objective concept. Finally, in its application to tourism planning, Lindberg et al. (1997) consider that its focus on tourist use-levels or numbers of visitors involves misguided simplicity, and instead they advocate a focus on site conditions. Mathieson and Wall (1982, p. 21) do not go as far but state nevertheless that there is a 'need for clear and precise statements of goals, and assessments of the extent to which

I. Seidl, C.A. Tisdell / Ecological Economics 31 (1999) 395–408 403

these goals are realized'. Again, the concept of carrying capacity only becomes operational if (i) the question about the desired conditions is asked and answered, if (ii) sociopolitical, economic and subjective components are taken into account, and (iii) concerned parties are involved — but, so far, this has rarely been incorporated into ideas of tourist carrying capacity. From the above discussion of the application of carrying capacity in applied ecology, it is clear that it involves normative characteristics and multiple levels often varying with objectives. Thus, carrying capacity by default is ambiguous.

Another application of carrying capacity to human society stresses that nature's bounds can be transgressed by rapidly growing population, accelerated use of natural resource and society's interference with ecological systems and cycles (Ehrlich and Holdren, 1971; Holdren and Ehrlich, 1974; Hardin, 1986). The 'little change' of the concept of carrying capacity which Hardin (1986, p. 602) considered necessary to apply it to human population and to illustrate the natural limits, in fact has to be profound if the concept is to be of any practical use in the new context. Actually, the newly titled concept of human or social carrying capacity implies a deep transformation and deviation from the initial biological and demographical positivist concept as is illustrated below.

The application of carrying capacity to the human species requires the recognition that the carrying capacity is foremost socially determined, rather than biologically fixed due to the important influence of human consumption patterns, technologies, infrastructure, and impacts on the environment or food availability. This is captured by the differentiation between biophysical carrying capacity (K_B) and social carrying capacity (cultural or human carrying capacity, K_S), and the acknowledgement that the former can only be higher or equal than the latter ($K_B \geq K_S$) (Ehrlich and Holdren 1971; Hardin, 1986; Daily and Ehrlich, 1992). Biophysical carrying capacity (K_B) expresses 'the maximal population size that could be sustained biophysically under given technological capabilities', whereas social carrying capacity (K_S) specifies 'the maxima that could be sustained under various social systems' (Daily and Ehrlich,

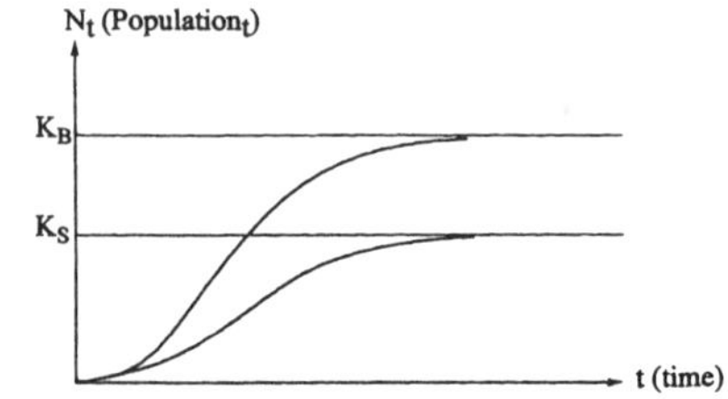

Fig. 2. Biophysical (K_B) and social (K_S) carrying capacity.

1992, p. 762). K_S represents higher (or equal) consumption and pressure on the environment and thus is lower (equal) than K_B. As Hardin (1986, p. 603) puts it: "Carrying capacity is inversely related to the quality of life." Both kinds of carrying capacity are illustrated in Fig. 2.

These two different carrying capacity levels and their consequences on optimal population size can also be illustrated by a simple model (Fig. 3) which represents a society with a given technology and which describes the relationship between income or consumption per head y, and population number N, by the function $y = f(N)$.

The function $y = f(N)$ represents a commonly-assumed theoretical relationship between population level and income or consumption per head. It is based on the assumption that the productivity and hence income and consumption of a human population increase with the growth in population size at low population level, but eventually declines with increasing population number because of economic constraints (e.g. resources, infrastructure). y_B depicts income or consumption which is

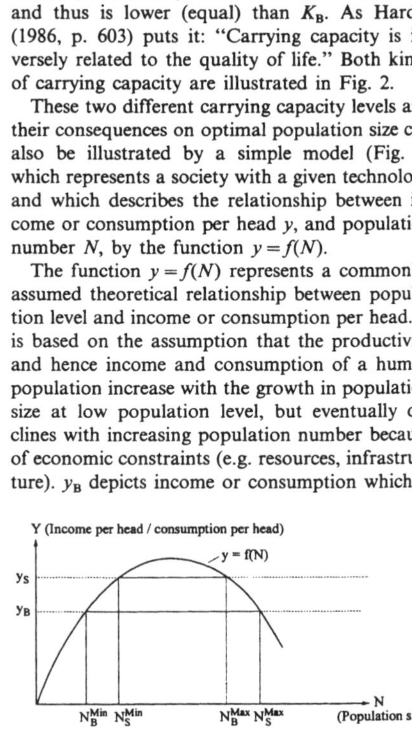

Fig. 3. Economic model allowing for biophysical and socially determined subsistence levels.

possible at biophysical carrying capacity (K_B) (minimum subsistence level). It represents a lower (equal) income or consumption compared with y_S which is the income or consumption related to social carrying capacity (K_S) ($y_B \leq y_S$). As y_S increases the maximal population number or carrying capacity declines (or remains equal). The minimum population size (N^{Min}) needed to achieve the socially determined subsistence level in this model is (N_S^{Min}), and it is higher than the biophysical minimum population (N_B^{Min}). N^{Min} as an economic concept can be compared with 'minimum viable population' in biology. This model initially exhibits economies of scale. The maximum population size which satisfies the biophysical subsistence level is N_B^{Max}, and is greater than that providing the socially determined subsistence level N_S^{Max}.

Another major variation in the concept of carrying capacity has been the introduction of *damage* or *impact* to the Earth's ecological system. These terms have been used by some authors (e.g. Daily and Ehrlich, 1992) to replace the predominance on population-number of the initial concept. These authors suggest that limits to human population are set by total damage of the global population rather than by population number per se. The new focus, *impact*, instead of maximum population *K*, stresses the significance of institutional settings, human values, traditions, economic and consumption patterns, distribution, and infrastructure even more. The normative nature and need for value judgements for the operationalization of this notion of carrying capacity is manifest.

Daily and Ehrlich (1992, p. 762) consider this impact *I* to be a product of three interdependent factors: the population's size *P*, its affluence or per-capita consumption *A*, and the environmental damage *T*, inflicted by technologies: $I = PAT$. Daily and Ehrlich's notion of impact implies that there are different levels of carrying capacity depending on value judgments and predominant system dynamics. Society can opt for different levels of carrying capacity, it can even opt for levels which allow it to stay within the limits avoiding significant irreversible degradation, but which can mean degradation of the environment nonetheless. Pulliam and Haddad (1994, p. 154) explain this with the example of biodiversity.

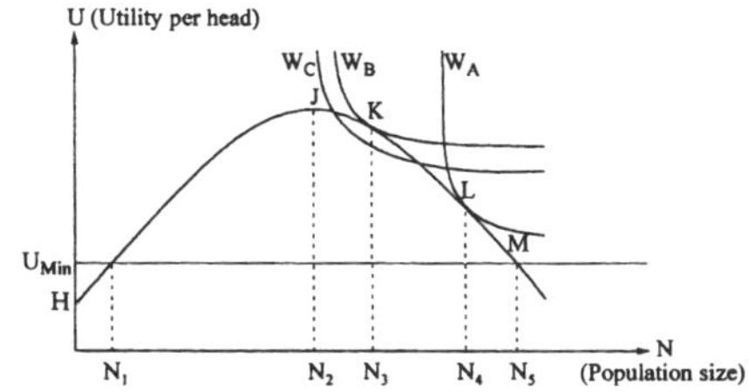

Fig. 4. Carrying capacity depends on the nature of the social welfare function.

> "Loss of biological diversity degrades the environment by lowering living standards and closing options for future improvement. However, this loss can be sustainable; life, albeit impoverished, may go on in perpetuity in the presence of fewer species."

The impact-concept illustrates the need for many far-reaching decisions. Cohen (1995a, p. 262) discusses a dozen examples of choices necessary to answer the question of how many people the Earth can support. Such questions are for instance: What average level of material well-being should we choose and how should well-being be distributed? What technology should we use? What domestic and international political institutions, economic and demographic arrangements should we adopt? Which physical, chemical, and biological environments do we want to live in? What time-scale should we consider?

If we assume that the value-laden, normative answers to these questions are expressed in a welfare function of a Bergson-type (Bergson, 1938), the resulting optimal level of human population can be graphically illustrated by a simple model as shown in Fig. 4. In this model, which is of a similar type of that in Fig. 3, utility per head rises at a decreasing rate as the population grows. Utility or well-being per head *U* is a function of population size *N*. In the case $U = g(N)$ where

$g'' < 0$, U is shown by the curve marked HJKLM. J represents the maximum individual utility and occurs at a population size of N_2. Beyond this point social utility keeps on rising up to a point N_3 if the set of social welfare functions represented by W_B apply. However, if the set of social welfare functions W_A indicated in Fig. 4 apply, social utility will rise until population reaches N_4. The socially optimal population size ('social carrying capacity') is therefore determined by the chosen social welfare contours (W_A, W_B, and so on). As Fig. 4 indicates, carrying capacities depend on normatively based social welfare functions (see also Tisdell, 1990, p. 160). If higher welfare contours as those indicated in Fig. 4 were chosen this would mean that the carrying capacity will be transgressed.

Discussions of welfare economics indicate that the welfare curve of Bergson-type cannot be established objectively by adding up individual utilities (Rothschild, 1993, p. 71). Other approaches seem necessary to bring population number and human welfare into a relationship which is socially acceptable for present and future generations.

One attempt to approach social welfare functions is to make use of ideas and expressions of society about how to live and what to aim for. This can provide an image of social carrying capacity, making this concept more concrete. Authors like Daily and Ehrlich (1992, p. 763) fall back on normative concepts which focus on conditions of the environment by calling upon sustainability and environmental standards. They stress the following connection:

> "A sustainable process is one that can be maintained without interruption, weakening, or loss of valued qualities. Sustainability is a necessary and sufficient condition for a population to be at or below any carrying capacity."

This definition of sustainability represents an equilibrium state like the concept of carrying capacity in applied ecology does. Furthermore, in order to determine the level of maximal sustainable use of resources Daily and Ehrlich (1992, p. 765) introduce the idea of a limit or threshold 'below which the constituent stocks are so small that the resource cannot be used sustainably'. Yet, sustainability requirements and acceptable standards are influenced by human choices. Thus, it has become clear that applications of the concept of carrying capacity to problems induced by humans leads to a shift from a positivist-type concept to a normative one. This shift means that there is no longer an objective, single level of carrying capacity (equilibrium population) as in the blowfly experiment. Rather it is replaced by different more or less stable states of environment dependent on value-judgements, institutional arrangements, technologies, consumption patterns, and human aims. These factors must be conciliated, be agreed upon and considered for estimating the acceptable pressure on the environment, and for developing accompanying management schemes. Therefore, political and social ideas and norms about technologies, institutions, consumption, distribution etc. have to be discussed, harmonized and agreed upon to approach a stable quality of the environment (equilibrium situation). If discrepancies become visible, in other words, if human activities will not stay within the carrying capacity, society will have to discuss its values, develop its technologies and institutions, and review its aims.

5. More on resilience and sustainability as an indicator of carrying capacity

One of the most recent developments of the concept of carrying capacity has been to relate it to ecological resilience (Arrow et al., 1995). However, some writers making this connection, such as Arrow et al., do not see carrying capacities as *particular* critical limits, but rather as normative, variable concepts which accord with the view given above. Arrow et al., (1995, p. 521) state:

> "Carrying capacities in nature are not fixed, static, or simple relations. They are contingent on technology, preferences, and the structures of production and consumption. They are also

contingent on the ever-changing state of interactions between the physical and biotic environments. A single number for human carrying capacity would be meaningless because the consequences of human innovation and biological evolution are inherently unknowable."

Thus, it is clear that these writers reject particular critical limits but they indicate that carrying capacity has been exceeded when ecosystem resilience is lost and a system flips from one locally stable equilibrium to another because the ecosystem is so altered that its resilience in relation to its original equilibrium is overcome.

Despite the above, suggestions can be found in the literature that the concept of carrying capacity is more definite than in Arrow et al. (1995), even when it is related to resilience. For example, Perrings et al. (1995) suggest that there are critical points at which ecosystems will collapse and have most 'unwelcome' (economic) consequences for the human population. They state:

> "The notions of 'carrying' and 'assimilative' capacity are indirect measures of the level of stress that is consistent with a tolerable level of resilience (what level of resilience is tolerable depends on the severity and frequency of the 'shocks' expected to occur). Since, for a given technology, human population growth implies an increasing level of stress on the ecosystems exploited under that technology, there is necessarily some point at which the associated loss of ecosystem resilience will become critical. Human population growth will at some point cause the collapse of those ecosystems." (Perrings et al., 1995, p. 8).

This view, however, raises many questions. What is a tolerable level of resilience? Does not a decision about what is tolerable involve a value-judgment, and how will social agreement be reached about such judgments? What does it mean to say the loss of ecosystem resilience will become critical? Critical in what way, or from what point of view? Does critical imply a jump or discontinuity in the system? Is there likely to be a continuous reduction in 'utility' rather than a precipitous decline in it as some ecosystems 'collapse'? What does it mean to say that an ecosystem collapses? Do they collapse or merely alter? Certainly many questions remain unanswered, even though the authors correctly stress the ability of human populations and activity to alter the nature of ecosystems and the natural environment.

6. Concluding comments: social carrying capacity and its application

The concept of social or human carrying capacity exhibits some of the major flaws which Malthus' treatise of population development has suffered from. For instance, the attempt to overcome Malthus' focus on one limiting factor for human existence by defining different carrying capacities can lead to divergent limits (e.g. carrying capacity for food, energy, water). Further, the vagueness of Malthus' indicators for transgressing carrying capacity (vice and misery) has not been solved. Finally, the influence of institutions which Malthus has began to admit in the second edition of his treatise is not captured in a satisfying way. These flaws still remain and pose the following difficulties.

The focus on one limiting factor (food) and on the heterogeneous variable 'population' hampers the application of carrying capacity in applied ecology and human ecology. Calculating different carrying capacities for different resources and species may lead to opposing aims about which upper limit is to be respected. Also, this provides little information about the state of an ecosystem. In ecological partial analysis, however, the focus on one limiting factor and one species is tenable. Further, the problem of unequivocal indicators for transgressing carrying capacity has not been solved. Often, it is unclear when carrying capacity is transgressed, i.e. what 'vice and misery' could mean in applied and human ecology. For instance, it might be difficult to decide which degree of water pollution exceeds carrying capacity (e.g. is drinking water which is filtered a few times acceptable, does the underlying pollution exceed carrying capacity)? Also in the social realm indicators for transgression of carrying capacity are elusive (e.g. does a stagnant population number in area of high industrialization mean that the latter is an indicator for transgression). Furthermore a transgression might be due to a number of factors (e.g. income, pollution, education). Taking sustainability or environmental standards (e.g. level of chemical pollution) as indicators for carrying capacity provides some guides, though usually the relationship between transgressing these indicators and carrying capacity is not scientifically proved. This, however, may not mean that measures to stay within carrying capacity have to wait until scientific evidence is provided. Different widely accepted approaches (e.g. precautionary principle, safe-minimum-standard) stress that in the case of uncertainty society should err on the safe side. Moreover, as we have seen, the attempt to use ecological resilience as an indicator for transgressing carrying capacity leaves many questions unsolved. Finally, authors discussing social carrying capacity admit the influence of institutional and cultural settings upon it. So, decisions about social carrying capacity are normative or political ones. This requires that the institutional and cultural settings are chosen deliberately or accepted when or before calculating carrying capacity and fixing environmental management objectives. Ludwig (1996) warns from basing aims or structures of social institutions and policies upon scientific objectives, as he considers scientific understanding as too limited. In such cases, ecosystem management may be unsuccessful. However, a discussion about the institutional and cultural setting within the carrying capacity discourse has hardly taken place so far even though Daily and Ehrlich (1992) discuss some institutional issues. This lack may explain why authors fall back upon normative concepts like sustainability or environmental standards as indicators for a desired condition of the environment. Seemingly, the political or normative dimension of carrying capacity, which Malthus admitted to hesitantly, are still weak points in the concept. These problems reveal the overlap of Malthus' ideas with the current concept of social/human carrying capacity with pre-existing flaws still continuing.

In some cases, the carrying capacity concept can provide reasonable estimates of the sustainable upper population level for a species in the short- to medium-term. However, one must be cautious about it for longer-term prediction. It has served a useful purpose in highlighting the limits set to population growth due to both limits of resources, sinks, and density effects. However, it fails to take account of the role which organisms especially at high population growth and densities can play in irreversibly altering their natural environment.

An academic disservice has been done by those who claim that carrying capacities in applied and human ecology are scientific and objectively determined. Only in controlled conditions does such a claim seem tenable. Here it is argued that this view is untenable as far as social carrying capacities are concerned and in relation to most applied ecology issues because value judgments inevitably become an integral part of the concept. Carrying capacities alter according to variations in value judgments and objectives. In human society, institutional arrangements are likely to alter the carrying capacities and desired levels of populations, and carrying capacities in the shorter term may differ greatly from those in the longer term. Carrying capacities are far from being universal constants.

Acknowledgements

We would like to thank Giorgina Bernasconi, Matthias Diemer, and Bernhard Schmid, Institut für Umweltwissenschaften, University of Zürich, for valuable suggestions on an earlier draft of this article, and Esther Schreier for producing the figures. The comments of the referees were greatly appreciated. The research on this paper was partly funded by the Swiss National Science Foundation.

References

Arrow, K., Bolin, B., Costanza, R., Dasgupta, P., Folke, C., Holling, C.S., Jansson, B.-O., Levin, S., Mäler, K.-G.,

Perrings, C., Pimentel, D., 1995. Economic growth, carrying capacity, and the environment. Science 268, 520–521.

Back, K.W., 1983. Malthus demography and social psychology. Hist. Eur. Ideas 4 (2), 123–133.

Becker, G., 1960. An economic analysis of fertility. In: National Bureau of Economic Research, Demographic and Economic Change in Developed Countries. Princeton University Press, Princeton.

Bergson, A., 1938. A reformulation of certain aspects of welfare economics. Q. J. Econ. 52, 310–324.

Bowen, I., 1954. Population. Cambridge University Press, Cambridge.

Brown, L.R., 1998. Facing nature's limits. In: Polunin, N. (Ed.), Population and Global Security. Cambridge University Press, Cambridge, pp. 251–270.

Christiansen, F.B., Fenchel, T.M., 1977. Theories of Populations in Biological Communities. Springer Verlag, Berlin.

Cohen, J.E., 1995a. How Many People Can the Earth Support? W.W. Norton & Co, New York.

Cohen, J.E., 1995b. Population growth and Earth's human carrying capacity. Science 269, 341–346.

Daily, G.C., Ehrlich, P.R., 1992. Population, sustainability, and Earth's carrying capacity. BioScience 42 (10), 761–771.

Daily, G.C., Ehrlich, P.R., 1996. Socioeconomic equity, sustainability, and Earth's carrying capacity. Ecol. Appl. 6 (4), 991–1001.

Darwin, C., 1958. Essay of 1844. In: Darwin, C., Wallace, A.R. (Eds.), Evolution by Natural Selection. The Syndics of the Cambridge University Press, Cambridge, pp. 91–254.

Darwin, C., 1969. The variation of animals and plants under domestication [1868]. Facsimile edition, Culture and Civilisation, Brussels.

Darwin, C., 1993. In: Barlow, N. III (Ed.), The Autobiography of Charles Darwin, 1809–1882 [Collins, London 1959]. W.W. Norton & Co, New York.

Davis, D., Tisdell, C., 1996. Economic management of recreational scuba diving and the environment. J. Environ. Manag. 48, 229–248.

Dhondt, A.A., 1988. Carrying capacity: a confusing concept. Acta Oecol. Oecol. Gen. 9 (4), 337–346.

Ehrlich, P.R., 1971. The Population Bomb. Ballantine Books, New York.

Ehrlich, P.R., Holdren, J.P., 1971. Impact of population growth. Science 171, 1212–1217.

Hardin, G., 1986. Cultural carrying capacity: a biological approach to human problems. BioScience 36 (9), 599–604.

Hawden, S., Palmer, L.J., 1994. Reindeer in Alaska. U.S. Department of Agriculture Bulletin 1089, 1–70.

Holdren, J.P., Ehrlich, P.R., 1974. Human population and the global environment. Am. Sci. 62, 282–292.

Hutchinson, G.E., 1979. An Introduction to Population Ecology. Yale University Press, New Haven.

Leibenstein, H., 1957. Economic Backwardness and Economic Growth: Studies in the Theory of Economic Development. Wiley, New York.

Lindberg, K., McCool, S., Stankey, G., 1997. Rethinking carrying capacity. Ann. Tour. Res. 24 (2), 461–465.

Ludwig, D., 1996. The end of the beginning. Ecol. Appl. 6 (1), 16–17.

Malthus, T.R., 1986. An Essay on the Principle of Population [1st ed. of 1798]. Pickering, London.

Mathieson, A., Wall, G., 1982. Tourism: Economic, Physical, and Social Impacts. Longman, Harlow, UK.

May, R.M., 1973. Stability and Complexity in Model Ecosystems. Princeton University Press, Princeton.

McLeod, S.R., 1997. Is the concept of carrying capacity useful in variable environments? OIKOS 79, 529–542.

Meadows, D.H., Meadows, D.L., Randers, J., Behrens, W.W. III, 1972. The Limits to Growth: a Report for the Club of Rome's Project on the Predicament of Mankind. Universe Books, New York.

Pearl, R., Reed, L.S., 1920. On the rate of growth of the population of the US since 1790 and its mathematical representation. Proc. Natl. Acad. Sci. USA 6, 275–288.

Perrings, C.A., Mäler, K.-G., Folke, C., Holling, C.S., Jansson, B.-O., 1995. Biodiversity Conservation: Problems and Policies. Kluwer Academic Publishers, Dordrecht.

Pulliam, H.R., Haddad, N.M., 1994. Human population growth and the carrying capacity concept. Bull. Ecol. Soc. Am. 75, 141–156.

Rothschild, K.W., 1993. Ethics and Economic Theory. Aldershot, UK.

Schumpeter, J.A., 1965. Geschichte der ökonomischen Analyse. Vandenhoeck & Ruprecht, Göttingen.

Scoones, I., 1993. Economic and ecological carrying capacity: applications to pastoral systems in Zimbabwe. In: Barbier, E.B. (Ed.), Economics and Ecology: New Frontiers and Sustainable Development. Chapman & Hall, London, pp. 96–117.

Srivastava, D.S., Ruesink, J.L., 1998. Population growth and the environmental destruction: it isn't that simple!. Bull. Ecol. Soc. Am. 79 (3), 219–221.

Tisdell, C.A., 1988. Sustaining and maximising economic gains from tourism based on natural sites: analysis with reference to the Galapagos. In: Tisdell, C.A., Aislabie, C.J., Stanton, J.C. (Eds.), Economics of Tourism: Case Studies and Analysis. Newcastle, Institute of Industrial Economics, University of Newcastle, pp. 229–251.

Tisdell, C.A., 1990. Natural Resources, Growth, and Development: Economics, Ecology and Resource-Scarcity. Praeger Publishers, New York.

Verhulst, P.F., 1838. Notice sur la loi que la population suit dans son accroissement. Correspondance Math. Phys. 10, 113–121.

Wilson, E.O., Bossert, W.H., 1971. A Primer on Population Biology. Sinauer Associates, Stamford, CT.

Worster, D., 1985. Nature's Economy: a History of Ecological Ideas. Cambridge University Press, Cambridge.

Young, R.M., 1969. Malthus and the evolutionists. Past Present 43, 109–144.

PART III

GOVERNANCE AND POLICY INSTRUMENTS FOR ENVIRONMENTAL CONTROL

THE SOUTH AFRICAN JOURNAL OF ECONOMICS . DIE SUID-AFRIKAANSE TYDSKRIF VIR EKONOMIE
VOL. 65 : 1. 1997 MARCH - MAART

GOOD GOVERNANCE, PROPERTY RIGHTS AND SUSTAINABLE RESOURCE USE

INDIAN OCEAN RIM EXAMPLES[1]

CLEM TISDELL AND KARTIK ROY [1]

THE ECONOMIC PERFORMANCE of a country and the sustainability of its resource-use depend on good governance and appropriate sets of property rights, and as explained below, these are interconnected. The 1990s has seen increasing emphasis on these aspects as far as international development policies are concerned, e.g. World Bank (1992, 1994), and the design of these policies has drawn on contemporary academic development of the economics of institutionalism, e.g. the work of the Nobel prize laureate Douglass C. North (1981, 1990, North and Thompson, 1973). The foundations of economic systems are rooted in political and legal systems and in general, in the institutional structures of a society. For most of this century, the preoccupation of mainstream economists with mathematical modelling and formal logical systems, has overshadowed institutional considerations in the formulation of policies for economic development. Fortunately, the situation is now being redressed.

1. HISTORICAL BACKGROUND

Despite the lack of emphasis on these matters for most of this century, economists have been aware of the importance of good governance and property rights for the sustainability of resource use

1 Department of Economics, University of Queensland, Brisbane 4072, Australia.

and economic welfare for a considerable time. Adam Smith clearly believed that the first step towards assuring the economic wealth of nations is good governance, or more specifically peace, order and good government. Although the term *sustainable development* was not in vogue in Smith's time, there is little doubt that he and all the great classical economic scholars were concerned both with means to achieve economic development and the sustainability of that development.

This is obvious in the works of Ricardo, Marx and John Stuart Mill. Marx was concerned with the sustainability of the capitalist market system, whereas Ricardo and Mill analysed the way in which population growth and the limited availability of land resources might restrict economic growth. Marx prophesied that the economic system would culminate in communism, a form of governance which in his view would establish a sustainable economic system. Ricardo's and John Stuart Mill's concerns were that economic growth might prove to be unsustainable and that economic systems might eventually gravitate to a stationary (sustainable) state in which the majority of the population lives at the subsistence level. As most economists - the Marxists excepted - assumed that the system of private property rights would prevail, they did not specifically explore the influence of property rights on economic activity. In fact, major interest in this issue amongst economists did not emerge until the second half of the present century (Gordon, 1954; Ciriacy-Wantrup, 1968).

Property rights and governance are closely intertwined. When individuals or groups have property rights in resources, they are usually able to govern their use and allocation. It is important to know who owns these rights and how they could be enforced, e.g. with or without state or community support. Otherwise the cost of retaining or obtaining rights may be excessive and subject to brute force rather than the rule of law. Such an uncivilized state of affairs can only have disastrous economic consequences.

Considerable debate exists in Western societies about the extent to which individuals and communities should be governed by higher authorities, especially by the central government. The debate has been sharpened in recent years by argument about whether natural resource use should be controlled by central government and its representatives or by local individuals and communities.

Berkes (1994) suggests that the desirability of central state control of natural resources has its origin in the writings of Thomas Hobbes. Hobbes argued in the *Leviathan* (1651) for the necessity of a central absolute authority such as the sovereign because left to their own free will individuals would be incapable of promoting their common good. Jean-Jacques Rousseau (1762) believed the opposite, viz. left to their own free will, individuals would organize themselves into communities to promote their common good. Local communities could effectively govern themselves and absolute central authority was unnecessary and less likely to promote the common good. Indeed, he felt that such free local communities were likely to live in harmony with nature. Centralists and those favouring the nation-state looked upon this as a romantic point of view.

It can be argued that Adam Smith introduced a third point of view in the *Wealth of Nations* (1776). He argues against Mercantilism and state monopolies, all of which are able to prosper under absolute monarchy or absolute central authority extolled by Hobbes. Smith's system is based upon private property rights and freedom for individuals rather than rights of local communities. Furthermore, the function of the state is to facilitate individuals to pursue their own self-interest subject to competition with others and within a regime of private property rights. The role of the state is to facilitate the operation of the market system by ensuring secure private titles to property, provide penalties for infringement of these rights, and enforce economic or commercial obligations as in the law of contracts or the laws relating to the sale of goods.

In addition, the state and its institutions, as well as community bodies, may find it worthwhile to foster social values which uphold this system. Some of these values for example, appear to have found expression in Protestantism and in Islam

30.

(Devahuti, 1965).

It appears, therefore, that there are three different strands of thought relating to governance in Western societies. These have consequences for property rights. Hobbes seemed to favour the ultimate allocation of property rights to the crown or absolute central authority, Rousseau favoured control of property by local communities (communal control) whereas the market system favoured by Smith, supports a system of private property rights.

2. PROPERTY RIGHTS - AN ARRAY OF POSSIBILITIES.

There are many possible dimensions to the concept of *property rights*. Four broad types can be identified from the literature:

(a) private property in which rights rest with an individual or legal entity;

(b) state property (*res publica*) in which property rights rest with the government;

(c) communal property (*res communes*) in which the resource is controlled by an identifiable community of users; and

(d) open-access property (*res nullius*) for which access is free and open to all.

In practice, the divisions between these types of property are not hard-and-fast. For example, the state may exercise some rights in relation to private property such as, say, imposing an easement on the property, or there may be rights of trespass by the general public on private or state property.

When a resource is private property, the right of exclusion exists, as is also the case for state and communal property, e.g., the local community may exclude members of other communities or individuals that do not comply with communal regulations. However, as North (1981) points out, exclusion is not always economic. Consequently, property for which exclusion exists as a legal possibility may become *de facto* open-access property or result in opportunistic use of the property by other than its owners, so that partial access occurs. Consequently, the type of market failures that occur for open-access property arise. This has happened in some cases where State ownership has replaced communal ownership. This is because the state has been less able to enforce or regulate the use of this property than the local community. An example is the transfer of community forests in Nepal to the State Forestry Department with its headquarters in Kathmandu. Whereas the villagers kept deforestation under control, the Forest Department proved to be unable to do this (Mishra, 1982). In some cases, even when property is made legally state property, it in fact remains under communal control as occurred in some parts of India, and also in some Polynesian and Melanesian communities in the Pacific. For example, marine areas adjoining villages remained under the communal control of these villages although legally they became crown or state property after colonisation.

3. WESTERN PREJUDICES AND PROPERTY RIGHTS

Westerners appear to have shown a preference for two types of property rights: those of private property and state property. They have largely dismissed communal property as a means of managing resources. In fact, they have tended to treat it synonymously with open-access, arguing that common property results in serious failures in resource allocation and conservation. As is well known, open-access can result in socially damaging abuse of natural resources, lack of investment in protection and husbandry of natural resources and the loss of resources and species which it is socially desirable to retain. This need not occur with communal governance. Indeed, there will be circumstances in which communal governance offers the best prospect for the optimal conservation and management of a natural resource, eg. fish or animals which migrate in the local community, a forest such as water-source forest which provides positive externalities to the rest of the community, and so on.

British and European practice was in the main to make all property either crown (i.e. state) property or private property. In Britain itself, the extent of communal rights was whittled away with the passing of time, communal land either being enclosed to become private property or being assigned to the crown or the state. This practice also applied in the British colonies. Forested land in India - communal property managed by local communities - was widely assigned to the crown and eventually to the Government of India or Indian state governments. It means that local communities were dispossessed of their traditional resources and their governance of the use thereof. This has often led to an accelerated environmental deterioration and deep social conflict.

Gradgil and Iyer (1989) argue that prior to the British conquest, India had developed systems of communal management that favoured a sustainable use of its natural resources. They go on to claim that "British rule led to disruption of communal organisations and converted communally managed resources into open-access resources. These have subsequently been used in an exhaustive fashion. However, pockets of good resource management under communal control have persisted and are now serving as models for the reassertion of such communal control" (Gadgil and Iyer, 1989, p. 240). The type of effects described by these authors was not peculiar to the British in India. It was repeated by them elsewhere as well as by other colonial powers. Worse still, governments of newly independent countries often continued the policies which reinforced the power of the central government of the nation state. Even in the case of the People's Republic of China, similar issues have arisen, e.g., in relation to the governance of the natural resources in Jingpo areas of China (Zhuge and Tisdell, 1996).

Although Gadgil and Iyer (1989) suggest that British colonialism in India was a major force in the creation of open-access resources in place of communally managed ones, the British system, in many cases, dispossessed local communities of their communal property which was then effectively converted into state property, not open-access property, either legally or in practice. Some central governments have continued with this process of dispossession of forest-dwelling communities and tribal groups, e.g. by attempting to establish areas for nature protection or of allowing the forest lands of minorities or tribes to become the private property of dominant groups in the country. The transmigration program in Indonesia is an example of the latter as is the incursion of Bengali farmers onto forested land in the Chittagong Hill Tracts. In Australia, the assignment of aboriginal land to the early white settlers is another example where private property rights were effectively substituted for the communal ones of the indigenous people. Both central and colonial governments were unsympathetic to communal property rights.

This may have been partly by design and partly as a result of ignorance. Even today there appear to be Western economists who believe that a resource held in common by a community is *res nullius*, a thing belonging to no one. This implies that such a resource is not appropriately managed for sustainability and suggests that there need be no moral questions about dispossession of the local community, for the resource apparently belongs to no one. It is little more than a 'convenient' fiction[2].

4. STATE, LOCAL COMMUNITIES AND CO-MANAGEMENT

All natural resources exist at a local level, and it is local people who for the main part depend most heavily on these resources for their livelihood and welfare, particularly in developing countries. But this has not prevented governments from using their power to gain control over many natural resources at the local level, and to manage these, as in the case of state forests, or to transfer these to private owners or lease these for economic use. Historically this process has diminished communal control over the management of natural resources. But there has been a reaction to this process amongst some economists and anthropologists. They see this process as undermining the sustainability of the use of natural resources.

The proponents of communalism claim that it results in practices that "influence respect, responsibility, and stewardship and are highly participatory. The planning for management of resources held as common property is carried out by those most directly affected by their decisions, decisions that are designed to contribute to the continuing sustained use of the living resources. These practices emphasize local control, self management, and to the extent possible, self sufficiency. ... They are based on co-operation rather than competition, the collective sharing of a resource rather than the individual attempting to maximize yield without reference to the commodity" (Jacobs, 1989, p. vii).

Berkes and Farvar (1989) see considerable virtue in communalism and traditional communal resource management systems. They point out (pp. 3 - 4) that they "emphasise *responsibility* to the community, rather than unbridled individualism glorified in some Western industrial cultures. Communalism is an important mode of thinking and of managing resources throughout the world from the nomads of the Arabian peninsula to native Amerindian peoples. It is no accident that traditional resource-management systems are often community-based".

For the main part they see only the positive side of communalism and in doing so, draw up a research agenda for social scientists and ecologists (pp. 5 - 6). They suggest, for example, that "the economists studying communal resource-management systems might concentrate on how joint control (by members of a community) saves scarce resources, as compared to state management or individual control" (p. 5).

In reality, the arguments in favour of communalism are far from watertight. Ideal governance is likely to call for a variety or array of forms of governance: in some cases local community control of resources may be ideal, in others formal state control of resources may be needed and in many cases, co-management by the state and local community may be called for, and in still other cases, management of natural resources is best let to individuals or households acting of their own free will. The important issue is to identify the circumstances in which these different types of governance would be socially ideal.

It is not possible to develop the theory of 'ideal' governance here but factors which should be taken into account in deciding between different forms of governance can be listed, if only to overcome preconceptions about the question of ideal forms of governance. Consideration of these factors suggests that co-management or side-by-side management (Tisdell, 1995a, 1996) of natural resources by the state and local communities is often ideal.

Difference in knowledge can affect the ideal form of management of resources. The set of knowledge of local communities differs as a rule from that available to state authorities particularly those located in central places remote from local communities. In many cases, local knowledge will be more appropriate to the sustainable management of local resources. However, the state *may* have additional valuable knowledge, e.g. as a result of research work or monitoring which it should *share* with the local community.

Local governance or involvement of communities in the formulation of rules for management of local resources is likely to result in greater compliance with these rules. This is both because the regulations will have greater acceptance, the purpose may be more easily comprehended locally as this adds to motivation to comply with the regulations and monitoring may be easier and administration costs lower, when these activities are mainly the responsibility of a local community.

In relation to the Philippines, Alcala and Vande Vusse (1994, p. 14) observe, "It is common for the personnel of the government agency interested in the protection and conservation of natural resources to assume that the agency does in fact manage them. Laws are enacted and numerous rules and regulations are promulgated by these agencies. To many, this is resource management. The government, however, does not have the capability, personnel and equipment needed to ensure that its policies, rules and regulations are enforced. The government must in reality, depend upon the people who daily use coastal resources to make proper management decisions". They go on to point out that in the Philippines fishers are the real-day-to-day managers of fishery resources and government had better co-operate at the village level if fishery resources are to be managed effectively.

There are, however, cases in which it is not socially optimal to leave the management of resources to a local community. Consider the following cases: (i) Use of natural resources by a community for its own benefit may damage other communities due to unfavourable external environmental effects. State intervention may be needed to take account of the wider community. However, this needs to be done in an appropriate way and the intervention may fail completely if it is entirely top-down. (ii) The distribution of political power, control over resources and distribution of income in some local communities are far from ideal. Without government intervention, situations of this kind can persist. It may be necessary for central government to intervene to change or modify governance structures at the local level, even though this intervention should be sensitively done if required. The actual governance processes that exist at local level are usually the result of a long period of social evolution and may be very sustainable and conducive to resource sustainability. This is why care is needed when trying to impose new social structures. Nevertheless, because of technological changes and various exogenous factors, governance and social structures of value at one time may become inappropriate later on.

5. INDIAN RIM OBSERVATIONS AND SOCIAL DYNAMICS

Despite the negative comment by Gadgil and Iyer (1989) about the role of the British in alienating communal property in India, significant amounts of communal resources remained. In Tamil Nadu for example, remaining communal lands include *poromboke* or lands incapable of cultivation and set aside for public or communal purposes, and assessed and unassessed wasteland. Blaikie, *et al.*, (1992) estimated that such land covered almost 20 per cent of the geographical area of Tamil Nadu in 1981-82. Most was forested but smaller portions were used for cultivation and permanent pasture. They find that problems arise from the bureaucratic control of common property resources (CPRs). "The bureaucratic regulation of CPRs is of particular concern in CPR-dependent villages, for this regulation is often subject to manipulation by local power to the disadvantage of poorer people" (Blaikie, *et al.*, 1992, pp. 262 - 263).

There is little doubt that 'modern' schemes for community-based resource management (CBRM) can become dominated by politicians, both local and central. This has led to some despair. Sandalo (1994, p. 180) drawing on experience in Palawan in the Philippines observes that, "Community organising has become almost like a fad, similar to the planned sprouting of NGOs. Every project proponent in an area is organising activities". He finds that much time is spent in unproductive meetings and that CBRM has become subject to political patronage and interventions. Finally, he finds that government interventions to protect the environment are inconsistent. While in one place CBRM is being fostered to rehabilitate degraded environments, in other places, the natural environment is being destroyed with state permission. He says, "in Honda Bay [Palawan], for example, mangroves are being rehabitated simultaneous with the conversion of other existing areas into fishponds, in addition to the indiscriminate and unchecked cutting of trees for housing materials and charcoal making" (Sandalo, 1994, p. 181).

Communities can vary in many different ways that depend upon variations in social customs and codes. To some extent, castes in Indian society (and tribal groups) form sub-communities, interconnected with a wider community. Gadgil and Iyer (1989) argue that this stratification of Indian society has promoted a sustainable use of resources. It divides society into economically complementary groups, so that an overall mutualism exists. They claim the caste system "promoted sustainable resource use in two ways: by restricting access to many specialised resources of any given locality to just one endogamous group, and by linking together members of different endogamous groups in a network of reciprocal exchanges and mutual obligations" (Gadgil and Iyer,

1989, p. 242). Berkes (1989, p. 237 - 238) summarises the view of these authors in the following terms: "Before colonisation, the ecological niche diversification (by varied caste access to different natural resources) ensured monopoly for a local group in the use of specific common-property resources, and was instrumental in the long-term sustainable use of these resources. The historical trend of a deteriorating resource base throughout India is traceable to the forced conversion of communal property into state and private property, increased commercialisation, and the generally increased demand for resources". While Gandhi had desired to reverse this trend, Nehru reinforced it by increasing the power of the state with the backing of urban middle and trading class (Gadgil and Iyer, 1989, p. 251). He favoured top-down policies and industrialisation and paid scant attention to the environment (Roy and Tisdell, 1995).

Nevertheless, the caste system still manages to function to some extent and there are at least remote areas of India where different groups still occupy different ecological niches and are involved in the type of exchanges indicated by Gadgil and Iyer. For example, this is so in part of Northeast India (Ramakrishnan, 1992; Tisdell, 1995b). However, these systems are under stress as a result of increasing population, demands for cash for industrial goods and growing commercialism. It is doubtful if they can be sustained. New institutional arrangements can be expected to emerge, but not necessarily in harmonious fashion.

In a world of change we also have to consider the dynamics of alterations in governance. As technology and other factors alter, the most desirable form of governance is liable to change, irrespective of whether governance is considered at the communal or state level. Major changes occur in property rights and governance over time. Thomson *et al.*, (1992) have outlined such changes in relation to land rights in Thailand. From the early 1800s onwards, there was a constant tendency in Thailand to increase the privatization of land and the security of private tenure of land, particularly in relation to arable land. Much land was also put under state ownership. Consequently, the amount of land used as common property in Thailand has been greatly reduced since the beginning of the last century, a pattern similar to the European one.

In their concluding comments based on the Thai case, Thomson *et al.* (1992, pp. 154 - 155) seem to support the evolution of private property rights by stating that 'The costs of organising collective management are extremely high and its effectiveness is problematic. Privatization does, however, risk inequality at the subdivision stage when control over the resource itself is allotted to particular individuals. If this is one-time allocation, with no easy mechanisms to rectify maldistribution, inequities can pose a serious problem. It should be noted that maintaining common-property institutions in no way avoids equity problems; they are simply pushed back a step. They reappear when annual or other increments of reduction from the resource are harvested and distributed to users. Distribution rules specify who gets what, when, and how. The potential for inequity inherent in such regulations and practices is substantial'. They also indicate that community management of common-property resources is only likely to work if the political and economic costs of such management are low.

6. CONCLUDING COMMENTS

It is only in recent times that social scientists have started to come to grips with the complexities and governance, different forms of private property rights and their relationship to sustainable resource-use and development. Most economists have been slower than other social scientists to appreciate the complexities of the situation. Some still seem quite unsophisticated in their knowledge of these subjects, even though renewed interest in institutionalism is altering the situation.

Discussion of Indian Ocean rim examples highlights the importance of considering the dynamics of variations in property rights and governance (see also Ostrom, 1990). The Indian situation has undergone a considerable change, and particularly also

Thailand's. North (1981) has argued that socially optimal patterns of property rights are likely to evolve in society and that social evolution is towards the increased creation of private property rights (Axelrod, 1984). The latter has certainly been the case in Thailand. However, it is not entirely clear that evolutionary social and political processes result in an ideal distribution of property rights. North (1981, 1990, pp. 7, 51-52) modifies his earlier position and recognizes that political mechanisms may thwart this process of evolution of ideal patterns of resource ownership. In addition, private gains may result in land becoming private property which socially would be better retained as common-property. It is not that evolutionary social processes involving property rights and governance lead invariably to perverse social consequences, but they do not necessarily result in the best of all possible worlds either. Therefore, they need to be subjected always to critical intellectual scrutiny.

NOTES

1. A revised version of a paper presented at the international conference on 'Governance Issues and Sustainable Development in the Indian Ocean Rim Countries' held at the University of Western Australia, October 28-30, 1996 and organised by the Centre for Migration and Development Studies, Department of Economics, The University of Western Australia. We want to thank the editor of this Journal for his useful editorial suggestions and Thomas Wilke of Gerhard Merkator University, Germany for a useful suggestion on the draft of this paper. The usual *caveat* applies.
2. It is unfortunately one that some Western economists still believe. For example, at the International Conference on Global Agricultural Science Policy (Melbourne, August, 1996) one of the authors (Tisdell) had a public clash with an American economist who claimed that all forested land used for slash-and-burn agriculture in Asia was open-access land. This is, of course, not so and displays considerable ignorance. In fact, communal rules, for slash-and-burn agriculture differ between village communities in different parts of Asia.

REFERENCES

ALCALA, A.C. and VANDE VUSSE, F.J. (1994) 'The Role of the Government in Coastal Resources Management'. Pp. 12 - 19 in R.S. Pomeroy (ed.) *Community Management and Common Property of Coastal Fisheries in Asia and the Pacific: Concepts, Methods and Experiences*, ICLARM, Manila.

AXELROD, R. (1984) *The Evolution of Cooperation*, Basic Books, New York.

BERKES, F. (1989) 'Multiple-Resource Cases and Integration Development'. Pp. 237 - 239 in F. Berkes (ed.) *Common Property Resources*, Belhaven Press, London.

______(1994) 'Property Rights and Coastal Fishers'. Pp. 52 - 62 in R.S. Pomeroy (ed.) *Community Management and Common Property of Coastal Fisheries in Asia and the Pacific; Concepts, Methods and Experiences*, ICLARM (International Center for Living Aquatic Resource Management), Manila.

BERKES, F. and FARVAR, M.T., (1989) 'Introduction and Overview'. Pp. 1 - 17 in F. Berkes (ed.) *Common Property Resources: Ecology and Community-based Sustainable Development*, Belhaven Press, London.

BLAIKIE, P., HARRISS, J. and PAIN, A. (1992) 'The Management and Use of Common-Property Resources in Tamil Nadu, India'. Pp. 247 - 264 in D.W. Bromley (ed.) *Making the Commons Work*, Institute for Contemporary Studies, San Francisco.

CIRIACY-WANTRUP, S.V. (1968) *Resource Conservation: Economics and Policies*, 3rd edn, Division of Agricultural Science, University of California, Berkeley, CA.

DEVAHUTI, D. (1965) *India and Ancient Malaya*, Eastern Universities Press, Singapore.

GADGIL, M. and IYER, P. (1989) 'On the Diversification of Common Property Resource Use by Indian Society'. Pp. 240 - 255 in F. Berkes (ed.) *Common Property Resources: Ecology and Community-based Sustainable Development*, Belhaven Press, London.

GORDON, H.S. (1954) 'The Economic Theory of a Common Property Resource: The Fishery', *Journal of Political Economy*, Vol. 62, pp. 124 - 144.

JACOBS, P. (1989) "Foreword". Pp. vii-viii in F. Berkes (ed.) *Common Property Resources: Ecology and Community-based Sustainable Development*, Belhaven, London.

MISHRA, H.R. (1982) 'Balancing Human Needs and Conservation in Nepal's Royal Chitwan National Park', *Ambio*, Vol. 11, No. 5, pp. 246 - 251.

NORTH, D.C. (1981) *Structure and Change in Economic History*, Norton, New York.

_______(1990) *Institutions, Institutional Change and Economic Performance*, Cambridge University Press,

_______ and THOMAS, R.P. (1973) *The Rise of the Western World: A New Economic History*, Cambridge University Press.

OSTROM, O. (1990) *Governing the Commons: The Evolution of Institutions for Collective Action*, Cambridge University Press.

RAMAKRISHNAN, P.S. (1992) *Shifting Agriculture and Sustainable Development: An Interdisciplinary Study for North-Eastern India*, UNESCO, Paris, and Parthenon Carnforth, U.K.

ROY, K.C. and TISDELL, C.A. (1995) 'Gandhi's Concept of Development and Nehru's Centralized Planning', in K.C. Roy, C.A. Tisdell and R.K. Sen (eds), *Economic Development and Environment: A Case Study of India*, pp. 1-16. Oxford University Press, Calcutta.

SANDALO, R.M. (1994) 'Community-based-Coastal Resources Management: The Palawan Experience', in R.S. Pomeroy (ed.) *Community Management and Common Property of Coastal Fisheries in Asia and the Pacific: Concepts, Methods and Experience*, pp. 165-181. ICLARM, Manila.

THOMSON, J.T., FEENY, D. and OAKERSON, R.J. (1992) 'Institutional Dynamics: The Evolution and Dissolution of Common-Property Resource Management', in D.W. Bromley (ed.), *Making the Commons Work*, pp. 129-160. Institute for Contemporary Studies, San Francisco.

TISDELL, C.A. (1995a) 'Issues in Biodiversity Conservation including the Role of Local Communities', *Environmental Conservation*, Vol. 22, No. 3, pp. 216 - 228.

________(1995b) 'Biodiversity, Conservation and Sustainable Development,Challenges for North-East India n Context,' *Biodiversity Conservation*, Working Paper No. 21, Department of Economics, The University of Queensland, Brisbane.

________ (1996) 'Reconciling Economic Development, Nature Conservation and Local Communities: Strategies for Biodiversity Conservation in Xishuangbanna, China', *The Environmentalist*, Vol. 16.

WORLD BANK (1992), *Governance and Development*, Washington D.C.

(1994), *Development in Practice; Governance: The World Bank's Experience.*

ZHUGE, R. (1996) 'Land Use Issues and Sustainable Development of the Jingpo Communities of Yunnan, China: Impacts of Governance, Institutions and Culture on Resource Management'. Paper for the conference on 'Governance Issues and Sustainable Development in the Indian Ocean Rim Countries', October, 1996 at The University of Western Australia.

[15]

Compensation for Taking of Natural Resource Interests: Principles and Practices in Recent Queensland Cases

*Clem Tisdell and Steve Harrison**

Designation of new protected areas, introduction of new environmental regulations and resumption of land for infrastructure development lead to expropriation of natural resources or limitations on private property rights. 'Takings' by government may be justified when the social gain exceeds the private loss. Important issues then arise as to compensation policy. This article examines economic aspects of takings and limitations of property rights to natural resources. Compensation decisions by government with respect to three case studies in Queensland are reviewed. The nature and extent of compensation varied widely in these cases, and lack of clearly enunciated policies by government is apparent. It is probably impractical for government to set out clear guidelines to compensation for the takings of resources interests, although some reduction in uncertainty appear to be desirable.

Introduction

The last 25 years has been a time or rapid change in land-use policy in Australia. Changing community attitudes and views on the role of government have led to a changed focus from assisting landholders to utilize land to protecting natural resources. The role of state agriculture departments in providing free management advice to farmers has declined dramatically, and natural resource, land management and environment departments and protection agencies have been developed. Tree clearing subsidies have been replaced with vegetation protection orders. Designation of new protected areas, constraints imposed by new legislation and regulations, land resumption's for infrastructure development such as highways and water storage and so on have had led to loss or attenuation of property rights of landholders.

Government takings may adversely affect a number of stakeholder groups. For example, closure of a forest to logging could affect the livelihoods of the mill operators and workers, logging contractors, firms supplying materials and services, retailers and local government (through reduced property values and rate base). Impacts on stakeholders might include loss of livelihoods or reduced income, reduced asset value, reduced incentive to invest, and acute anxiety and poorer quality of life. Given these potential costs, a number of questions may be raised about compensation policy; for example:

- under what circumstances should government compensate for taking away private property rights to natural resources?
- should those who suffer the losses have an automatic right to compensation, or should this be simply at the discretion of government?
- should governments set out clear rules for compensation, or retain flexibility to treat appellants on a case-by-case basis?
- who should be compensated - only those surrendering resources or a broader spectrum of affected stakeholders?
- how and by whom should losses from takings be assessed?
- how much compensation should be provided, e.g. full economic loss or a lesser amount?
- should compensation be confined to payments to individuals, or should regional economic stimulation packages be provided?

The formulation of socially optimal compensation policies is necessarily complex. In general, uncertainty over compensation outcomes is likely to adversely effect new investment and long-term sustainability of resource management. Hence it is appropriate to ask whether any clear patterns do or should exist with respect to compensation payments, and whether economic theory can provide useful guidelines for designing policies.

This paper examines economic issues in compensation policy, and discusses provisions which were made in three Queensland cases, viz the Wet Tropics of Queensland World Heritage listing, Fraser Island logging and dugong protection areas in the east coast

* *Clem Tisdell and Steve Harrison are with the Department of Economics at The University of Queensland.*

fishery. Some general patterns are observed from these cases. On the basis of these observations, suggestions are made for future compensation policy for natural resource takings.

Overseas and Australian provisions for compensation for takings

In the USA, there has been a long debate on government takings. Following the rather drastic superfund environmental legislation (Field and Olewiler 1995), this has become an even more highly controversial issue, as reflected by the large number of items on this topic on the World Wide Web[1]. As pointed out by Treanor (1998), the champions of the new property rights movement claim they are fighting to restore the original understanding of the Takings Clause of the Fifth Amendment of 1789. When the government exercised 'eminent domain' to compel a person to sell property, this clause asserts "nor shall private property be taken for public use, without just compensation". The original understanding of the Takings Clause was that the federal government had to compensate the property owner when it physically took property, not when regulations diminished the value of property[2]. Those who seek a 'broad reading' of the Takings Clause assert that the founders were followers of the philosopher John Locke and therefore committed the principle that the state can never diminish an individual's property (Treanor 1988, p. 5)[3]. As well, they note the US Supreme Court expanded the clause to require compensation for extreme regulations that are the functional equivalent to physical expropriations (Kendall 1998), referred to as 'regulatory takings'. Dragun (1998) provides an up-to-date critical appraisal of the 'new property rights perspective'.

There is strong concern in the USA over increasing environmental regulation and various pressure groups have arisen. Richman (1998, p. 1) of the Cato Institute states

> "The federal government has increasingly used the Endangered Species Act (ESA) and the Clean Water Act (CWA) to stop owners from developing or farming their land. If an animal on the endangered species list lives on a property, it is against the law to destroy the animal's habitat. This has been the case with farmland in California that is home to the kangaroo rat, in the Pacific Northwest forests that are home to the Spotted Owl, and with other private property. Under the Environmental Protection Agency's interpretation of the CWA, private 'wetlands ... are protected and may not be developed'".

NCBA (1998, p. 1) argues that

> "Land use regulatory regimes such as endangered species protection, wetlands designation, open space preservation, greenbelts, coastal zone protection and zoning all impact property rights. Uncertainty about permissible land uses results in declining land values, causing lenders to shy away from operating and long-term loan offers".

The forestry lobby Family Business First argues for legislation to compensate a landowner when the value of an affected portion of a property falls by at least 33 per cent as a result of agency action (Family Business First, 1998). The League of Wisconsin Municipalities (1998) reports that 21 states have enacted a requirement for *takings impact assessments* and several have specified minimum value reductions requiring compensation (which vary between states from about 20 per cent to 40 per cent). Similarly, in Canada The Western Stock Growers' Association (1998) has proposed a 'Property Rights Preservation Act' to evaluate proposed government actions that may limit the use of private property and ensure compensation.

In Australia, the debate over government takings and provision of compensation has not reached as acrimonious a level as in the USA. It is clear that the extent of compensation is unpredictable and haphazard. Often the federal and state governments have no clear liability for compensation, although there will exist moral and political reasons to provide compensation to the dispossessed.

In Queensland, the *Acquisition of Land Act* provides for compensation for land resumed by the government, at current market value (Stehn 1998). There is a provision (unproclaimed) in this Act which precludes compensation when tree-clearing permits are withdrawn. There is no provision for compensation under the *Water Resources Act* if the government takes back a license. However, the *Integrated Planning Act* does provide for compensation in relation to persons

1. A long list of references under the title of *6200 Takings* is available on the World Wide Web (Anon 1998). These include various papers on "eminent domain" (e.g Epstein 1985; McKenzie1986), economic analysis of compensation (Blume and Rubinfeld 1987; Hermalin 1995), regulatory takings (Bromley 1993), circumstances when compensation should be paid (Miceli *et al* 1994), 'just' compensation (Farber 1992; Fischel 1995), legal versus economic perspectives (Mercuro 1992), impacts for agriculture (Miceli and Sergerson 1995) and investor efficiency (Trefzger and Colwell 1996).

2. Treanor (1998 p. 3) points out that this clause provided greater protection for the property owner than England's Magna Carta (which did not require compensation for government seizure of land) and was probably intended to ensure compensation when the military seized civilian goods.

3. Critics of the move to widen the definition of compensable takings in the USA have coined the term 'givings'. They argue, for example, that if a government builds a new road which increases property values then landholders should compensate government for that service (Banz 1998). In Australia, the term 'betterment' rather than 'givings' is sometimes used (Gilpin 1990). Both relate to an unearned increment received by land-holders or other natural resource-holders.

who can no longer develop land in accordance with a superceded planning scheme, and the *Nature Conservation Act* has principles for compensation. There are no announced principles relating to compensation for matters under the jurisdiction of the Department of Natural Resources or Department of Primary Industries. A case where Cudgen Rutile carried out exploration and made discoveries of valuable minerals but was subsequently refused permission to mine by the Queensland government without compensation is reported by Schwindt (1992, p. 41).

The picture would appear to be similar in other jurisdictions. For example, it is understood that NSW does not provide compensation for changes in access rights to irrigation water. When the Commonwealth government rescinded rights to mine gold and other metals at Coronation Hill in the Northern Territory, no compensation was given to Newcrest which had spent millions of dollars on exploration and planning.

Economic perspectives on compensation for takings

The *Report of the Commission of Inquiry into Compensation for the Taking of Resource Interests* (Schwindt 1992) indicates that the availability of compensation depends upon the existence of private property rights expressed or implied. It points out (p. 17), "Property is a bundle of legally defined mutable right. The owner is free to exercise those rights and is free from interference by others in their exercise. These rights range from strong to weak, and even the strongest are subject to restrictions. When rights are modified there is commonly an effect on the value of the property". The report goes on (p. 19) to state that "Not all [government] interferences with property can possibly be compensable... the definition (whether defined by statute, judicial interpretation, or custom) of a compensable taking is influenced strongly by pragmatism. There are no hard and fast rules, but some generalisations are possible. The stronger the property right, and the greater the owner's loss, the more likely the taking will be viewed as compensable."

Economists consider that compensation usually is required on both efficiency and equity grounds. Concerning the most appropriate level of compensation on efficiency grounds, Schwindt (1992) introduced the concept of *reservation price* or the amount of compensation which leaves to private property owner indifferent about the taking. Paying more than the reservation price would encourage strategic behaviour to attract compensation. It could be argued that full compensation (the reservation price) should be paid to ensure optimal levels of private investment are achieved. Otherwise, investors will view expropriation as a risk to future profits, and investment will be redirected towards less productive but more secure ventures. Another argument for full compensation is to curb the power of government and the over-allocation of resources to public use.

A counter view is that the risk of expropriation is essentially no different to any other investment risk. Resource-based industries deal with sovereign risk constantly. Full compensation spreads the risk across all taxpayers, and creates distortions similar to other insurance schemes, particularly 'moral hazard' distortions. That is, "full compensation will lead to excessive private investment in property which is more valuable in public use" (Schwindt 1992, p. 25). At the same time, Schwindt notes the "domoralisation costs" to losers and their sympathisers from lack of compensation (in terms of personal unhappiness and reluctance to invest).

In terms of equity, it would be undesirable for the cost of adjustment of resource use to fall disproportionately on an individual or group. The implications of these efficiency and equity considerations appear to be that compensation should be something less than, but approaching, the reservation price.

In predicting whether compensation will actually be paid by the government for the taking of resource interests and the extent to which it will be actually paid, it is necessary to resort to a political economy perspective in the absence of strong legislation or clear guidelines. The occurrence and extent of compensation depends to a considerable extent on political processes. It is influenced by the political power of the parties involved (both those directly affected and the communities in which they live) and the willingness of affected parties to take political action. Compensation (as suggested by one reviewer of this article) is more likely to be paid when losers have a strong economic demand for compensation and can attract strong political sympathy from members of the relevant community. The particular political situation needs to be studied in each case. Elements of the theory, as discussed later, have been outlined by Buchanan *et al.* (1980).

Nevertheless, without detailing this theory, we can hypothesize that the demand for and likely extent of compensation can be expected to depend on the following factors:

- extent of loss, in terms of number of people affected, aggregate loss amount: the more severe and widespread the loss, the greater the welfare case for compensation.
- opportunities for alternative livelihoods: more financial assistance will be needed where there are few alternative employment opportunities.
- asset specificity of affected businesses: where resources have limited alternative uses, the equity case for compensation may be stronger.
- compensation precedents: amounts of compensation for similar takings condition the expectation by government and industry for any particular case.
- extent to which loss is concentrated on particular individuals and they can be identified.
- financial vulnerability of the affected parties: if the affected parties are a small number of large companies which have further resource interests outside the takings area, then the humanitarian case for compensation is less strong, welfare groups are less likely to enter into the debate, and the amount of compensation could be small.
- directness of relationship of takings to economic losses: those who suffer loss indirectly such as retail stores are less likely to be helped than displaced workers.
- clarity of property rights: if property rights are unclear then compensation is less likely. For example, in the case or riparian revegetation, it could be argued that landholders (or their predecessors) should not have cleared along watercourses in the first place, and hence that replanting should not be subsidised.
- community attitudes to the resource taking: if the community perceives that the taking is a necessary action to preserve a valuable resource or protect an environment, then the government can count on community support.
- negotiating strategy: hiring of legal assistance and generation of publicity about adverse effects could in general be expected to increase the level of compensation, although whether there is a net gain will be less certain. If affected firms hire consultants and produce detailed estimates of the cost of the takings to the industry, they are more likely to receive an equitable level of compensation.
- political power of losers: various factors could contribute to the ability of those losing property rights to make credible political threats on government for compensation. Some of these would include: number and financial means of affected people; strength and lobbying capacity of industry organisation; point in time within the election cycle, and marginality of affected electorates and the government's hold on power; and likely loss in rate revenue by affected local government authorities.

A review of recent government decisions on compensation sheds light on probably outcomes under new claims. Each of the three Queensland cases reviewed here involve decisions to protect natural areas, which have impacts on considerable numbers of stakeholders.

Case study 1: The Wet Tropics Structural Adjustment Packages

When the Wet Tropics of Queensland World Heritage Area (WTWHA) was declared, The Wet Tropics Structural Adjustment Package was introduced, consisting of three basic components, viz business compensation, labour adjustment assistance and alternative employment creation strategies. In formulating this package, the government was guided by two studies of Hundloe *et al.* (1987, 1988).

The *business compensation* scheme allowed for payment of up to $24.4 million to companies and businesses adversely affected by cessation of logging. Compensation was paid only to those businesses who could clearly demonstrate that the Commonwealth Government decision to cease logging in the World Heritage Listed forests resulted in:

- the closure of their operation;
- the forced rationalisation of their business; or
- a substantial reduction in their business viability (Lynch-Blosse *et al* 1991, p. 46).

About three-quarters of businesses which sought compensation were ruled to be eligible. Lynch-Blosse *et al.*, (1991 p. 47) observed: "The types of businesses which were successful in their claim for compensation include larger timber mills, factories and manufacturing establishments which were end-users of rainforest timber, contract timber cutters, sleeper cutters, and organisations which were involved in the maintenance and repairs of the timber-related equipment (e.g. Saw Doctor)". That is, businesses having a relatively direct forward or backward economic linkage with logging in the WTWHA were considered eligible for compensation.

A two-staged process was involved in determination of business compensation claims. A government body (the Rainforest Unit of the Commonwealth Department of the Arts, Sport, the Environment, Tourism and Territories -DASETT) determined whether each applicant met the criteria compensation. Then an accounting firm hired by the Commonwealth Government (Price Waterhouse) assessed the level of compensation considered to be fair and reasonable, on the basis of:

- a detailed analysis of the earnings in recent years of the business and an estimate of likely future earnings in the absence of World Heritage Listing;
- an assessment of the value of assets used by that business in deriving income from rainforest logging and milling activities; and,
- an assessment of other compensation claims made by that business.

Labour adjustment assistance for employees adversely affected by the cessation of crown rainforest operations in the WTWHA consisted of Dislocation Allowances, Early Retirement Allowances, Retraining Subsidies, and Removal and Relocation Assistance. To be eligible, applicants had to have been employed in the timber industry or a closely related business for at least 12 of the 18 months before retrenchment and have been retrenched as a result of the cessation of logging in the World Heritage Area.

In order to create alternative sources of employment for displaced timber workers, the Commonwealth Government, in addition to the above initiatives, began public sector and local community programmes and provided subsidies to the private sector to foster employment in the affected regions. Apart from providing compensation to displaced timber workers, these initiatives incidentally provided some compensation to local communities for the loss of economic injections (and multiplier effects) due to cessation of logging operations.

Alternative employment creation strategies for displaced timber workers included:

- public sector projects such as new or additional local council projects;
- tree planting projects funded by the Commonwealth Government;
- financial assistance "to individuals, private sector enterprises and other organizations who could propose feasible and economically viable initiatives which would employ eligible displaced timber workers" ($3.7 million allocated); and
- a wage subsidy payable for six months to employers *(outside* the timber industry) of eligible displaced timber workers.

Case study 2: Compensation for the Loss of Timber Rights on Fraser Island

Following the report of a Commission of Inquiry, the Queensland Government (1991) decided that logging on Fraser Island would cease by the end of 1991, and a compensation package described as 'A Special Growth and Development Package for the Great Sandy Region', was devised. In consequence, total financial assistance of $37 million was proposed for the region. Of this $21.2 million was to be contributed by the Queensland Government and $16.5 million by the Commonwealth Government. As in the case of the Wet Tropics, the package involved three basic elements:

- a Workers' Adjustment Package;
- schemes to create alternative employment opportunities; and
- compensation for businesses directly and substantially affected by phasing out of logging on Fraser Island.

However, workers were not offered a retirement allowance - emphasis was placed on obtaining alternative employment and special mortgage assistance was available to displaced workers. The Workers' Adjustment Package offered:

- dislocation assistance of up to $35,000 based on years of service;
- priority for alternative employment in government funded schemes;
- relocation assistance of up to $5,000;
- income supplement for 12 months to displaced workers sufficient to bring their income to its previous level; and
- special mortgage assistance for up to three years to ensure that repayments did not exceed 30 per cent of gross household incomes' (Queensland Government 1991, p. 3).

Government-funded initiatives were designed to provide alternative employment to displaced workers if they wished to take advantage of these. However, employment in projects resulting from these initiatives was not confined to displaced workers even though they were given priority in recruitment. The schemes were intended to compensate, or more than compensate, for any decline in regional incomes as a result of the cessation of logging on Fraser Island.

In relation to businesses directly or substantially affected by the phasing out of logging on Fraser Island, the State Government claimed that, "there is no legal obligation to pay compensation to affected businesses", (Queensland Government 1991, p. 11), but was nevertheless prepared to consider *ex gratia* payments to affected businesses. The criteria for eligibility of businesses to be considered for compensation were *narrower* than in the case of the Wet Tropics - a business had to depend heavily on the timber industry for its income:

> "To be eligible for compensation, about 50 per cent of a business's income would need to be reliant on the timber industry. The Treasurer would consider particular cases involving less than 50 per cent if it could be shown the viability of the business had been substantially affected." (Queensland Government 1991, p. 11).

The basis of compensation was intended to be the loss of value of business due to the cessation of logging on Fraser Island. To determine business loss, Price Waterhouse:

[1] valued the existing business as a going concern based on capitalisation of future maintainable earnings;

[2] deducted from this value the net book value of the physical assets retained by the business; and then

[3] adjusted for any extraordinary expenses incurred by the business relating to closure (Queensland Government 1991, p. 11).

In this case [1] - [2] - [3] would be the basis of compensation. However, the Government did not necessarily pay the loss in value of business as determined by Price Waterhouse. Compensation was decided on a case-by-case basis, taking account of Price Waterhouse's assessment and other factors such as:

- avenues available for mitigation of losses and other business opportunities;
- the commercial risks associated with operating the business in an environmentally sensitive area e.g. if expensive assets were acquired recently, it may not be appropriate to compensate the party for full loss of value; and
- the Government's overall objectives for industry rationalisation in the region.

"Compensation payments were staged to avoid the situation where a lump sum was paid up front but actual losses did not materialise in line with the original projection." (Queensland Government, 1991, p. 11). Consequently, the compensation available to businesses for the taking of resource rights was relatively uncertain.

Case study 3: Dugong Protection Areas in the Queensland East Coast Fishery

When the Commonwealth Government (Senator Hill) announced new Dugong Protection Areas (DPAs) in the Queensland east coast fishery in 1997, compensation was sought by members of the Queensland Commercial Fishermen's Organisation (QCFO) for the economic losses they faced. A consultancy report on compensation principles and the expected economic impact of DPAs on the industry was prepared for the QCFO by (Ramsay *et al* 1997). A serious concern for the fishing industry was that closures would remove more productive and accessible near-shore fishing grounds. Also, it was found that a number of fishers have quite low incomes but place high stock on lifestyle considerations. A point of contention for the industry was that habitat change brought about by spillovers from land-based agriculture and other economic activities were probably a greater cause of dugong decline than set-net fishing.

The form of compensation provided by the Commonwealth Government was an assistance package of about $4 million to affected fishers, with a subsequent competitive license buy-out scheme to reduce effort in the industry[4]. No allowance was made for fishers on-shore assets (buildings, vehicles), and no compensation was provided to fish processors or other affected firms.

Comparisons between Compensation in the three case studies

The Wet Tropics Structural Adjustment Package was comprehensive, providing compensation to all those directly or closely affected by cessation of logging in the World Heritage Area, and indirectly reducing the economic impact on local communities. It is a benchmark Australian case for the taking of resource interests by the state, in this case the Commonwealth Government.

4. An apparent risk of license buy-back arrangements is that they may take up latent rather than active effort (i.e. fishers who have the lowest willingness-to-accept values may have low catches).

The basis of eligibility for business compensation in the Fraser Island case was less generous and actual payment of compensation more restricted than for the Wet Tropics.

Whereas early retirement allowances was available to displaced labour in the Wet Tropics area, this was not so for the Great Sandy Region. In the latter case emphasis was on finding displaced workers alternative employment. To find such alternative employment in the Great Sandy Region may have been easier than in some regions affected by the Wet Tropics World Heritage listing.

The creation of alternative employment opportunities in the Hervey Bay Region were only partly intended to absorb workers displaced as a result of cessation of logging on Fraser Island. New projects also directly created employment for other workers. In the case of the Wet Tropics, more weight was placed on the absorption of displaced timber workers by the alternative employment schemes devised. Therefore, the Fraser Island Package seems to have been designed to provide greater community-wide compensation and benefits with these not all tied specifically to displaced workers.

In the DPA case, no specific compensation was provided for onshore assets, to displaced boat hands, or to firms supplying inputs to or using the catch of fishers. The level of compensation to fishers was reasonably generous, and the license buy-back scheme provided some compensation for reduction in asset values and assistance to exit from the industry.

General Observations about Compensation Arrangements

It was observed in the introduction that a good deal of pragmatism is involved in the payment of compensation for the taking of resource interest by the state. The greater the economic loss sustained by a party affected by loss of resource interest and the more established or definite are these rights, the more likely that compensation will be paid. Furthermore, "government is likely to respond to the demands of well-defined, compact interest groups whose members clearly recognise either the benefits or costs which will fall on them as a result of a particular policy, while ignoring or discounting the benefits or costs occurring to ill defined, diffused interest groups who do not clearly recognize the impact of the policy upon them" (Buchanan *et al.*, 1980). Therefore, compensation is more likely to be paid to those damaged by a resource expropriation if they form well-defined interest groups that "are capable of clearly and forcefully making their interests known to policy makers". This indicates that it is critical for those who will be adversely affected by resource takings to belong to or form such groups, if they are to avoid suffering uncompensated economic loss.

Assessing the economic loss occasioned by the taking of resource interests is a complex task not least because of the considerable economic and other uncertainties involved. Some specific matters may be raised with respect to business compensation, compensation for displaced workers and community-wide impacts and restitution.

Business compensation

The most important thing to consider in assessing the economic loss incurred by a business as a result of the taking of its resource interests is the reduction in its capitalised value. This reduction (R) is equal to the difference of net present value of its anticipated future net earnings should its resource interests be maintained (V_R) and if its resource interests are lost (V_E), i.e. $R=V_R-V_E$. It is however difficult to estimate the reduction (R) in the capitalised value of the firm due to loss of its resource interests because future income is uncertain. Furthermore, the size of R depends on the rate of interest used to discount future earnings.

The reduction of capitalised value, R, does not take account of the value of assets physical or otherwise retained by the firm. To the extent its assets can be sold they reduce the loss suffered by the business. Ideally such assets should be valued at realizable or market value once the business loses its resource interests. There does not seem to be any logic beyond ease of estimation in valuing them at net book value as in the Fraser Island case. If the business' assets are relatively *specific* to exploitation of its natural resource interests, then after loss of these resource interests these assets may have little use elsewhere. Hence, their market or realizable value may be much less than their book value after resource expropriation. It is therefore appropriate to deduct only the realizable value of the business' assets from its reduction in capitalised value in determining the business' economic loss (EL). As mentioned in the Fraser Island case, it may also be appropriate in estimating a business' economic loss, to add any special expenses (Cs) a business has to incur either because it must close down or restructure substantially due to its resource loss.

Taking these matters into account, the economic loss of

a business due to loss of resource interests would be estimated as:

$$EL = R \quad A_M + C_S$$
$$= (V_R - V_E) - A_M + C_S$$

Asset specificity needs to be given particular attention in claims for compensation for loss of resource interests. With closure of fishing grounds, boats and nets may have few alternative use opportunities. Since fishers cannot realise asset values, they may crowd into other fisheries, thereby causing over exploitation and depressing incomes in these fisheries to below normal levels. In a sense, this exacerbates the social and biological damage caused.

Asset specificity also applies to human capital. Owners and managers as well as employees embody much human capital which may be *specific* to their business operations reliant on natural resources. Their next best employment may not be able to use this capital which then becomes a sunk cost to individuals just as physical capital may have a sunk cost. The longer individuals have been operators in an industry, the more their human capital (as a rule) becomes *specific* to those operations and the greater their likely loss when those operations are no longer possible.

Compensation for displaced workers

While compensation for the taking of resource interests from businesses may have a quasi-legal basis, the case for compensating workers seems to be more a question of equity. Compensation packages have included measures to find alternative employment for displaced workers, payments to compensate for lost income in alternative employment (Fraser Island case) and allowances to cover expenses included in finding alternative employment.

Community-wide impacts and restitution

While governments have no legal requirement to compensate communities which may be adversely affected by the loss of resource-interests, political reality often requires that such restitution be made. This is especially so when a regional economy depends heavily on the exploitation of the resource, the loss of which through various multiplier effects can depress the local economy. Adverse economic effects are not, therefore, confined to those directly affected by the withdrawal of resource rights or interests.

Because of asset or capital specificity, including that of human capital, one problem that can arise when natural resource rights are restricted is that displaced businesses and workers increase their exploitation of closely related resources.

The desirability of announcing specific compensation guidelines

More precisely defined and announced compensation guidelines would reduce uncertainly for resource users, which could lead to greater investment and more sustainable resource management. Economic efficiency could also be increased through lower transactions costs (reduced litigation to resolve disputes). Lobby groups argue for such guidelines: "Clear guidelines must be established as to when compensation is required in order to clarify decades of confusing and conflicting judicial decisions and ensure that landowners are compensated when their property is taken for a public purpose" (NCBA 1988).

Clear compensation guidelines might not be achievable for a number of practical reasons. It must be recognised that a very wide spectrum of possible reductions in property rights can occur, from 'takings' in the sense of actual resource (e.g. land) resumptions or actions which effectively preclude profitable use of the resource, to minor 'limitations' on how resources can be managed. As noted by Schwindt (1992, p. 39), it is "not surprising that in the area of resource interests, few governments have well developed compensation policies given the complex differing nature of resource rights and the legal uncertainty about the status of those rights". Also, there can be a long list of affected stakeholders, and varying degrees of loss. Thus it would be extremely difficult to set up principles which covered every case in a detailed prescriptive sense.

Another impediment is that such prescriptions could lock government (and hence taxpayers) into high compensation payments, or reduce the capacity of government to react sensitively to specific circumstances, e.g. where a group is culturally disadvantaged. Enunciated guidelines could also lead to strategic behaviour by resource users designed to maximize compensation.

A further impediment is the lack of accepted international standards. According to Schwindt (1992 p. 65):

> "When formal compensation systems exist, they differ from one another in both the definition of compensable interests and in the method of valuing the interest. The options vary from no compensation to full compensation at market value. First, government may reserve for itself, either through legislation or through contractual terms, the unfettered right to vary, reduce or terminate resource

interests with no compensation. Finally, the relevant legislation may expressly state that compensation will be paid, and also go on to specify the basis of valuation."

Concluding comments

Clearly the value to the state (government), acting on behalf of the community, in taking resource interests should exceed the economic value to users of these resources of retaining the rights. However, it should be observed that the balance of net social benefit from resource takings is sometimes highly uncertain and often a matter of strong contention between conflicting interests. Community values are changing in relation to the economic exploitation of natural resources. There is now less emphasis on the direct economic benefits to be obtained from the use of these resources and more emphasis on indirect non-use values. While this may be reasonable, it may be unreasonable to expect those with specific resource-interests not to be compensated for a change in community or government attitudes affecting their previously settled interest.

The process of compensation is to a considerable extent a political process. It is influenced by the political power of the parties involved - both those directly affected and the communities in which they live. A wide variety of compensation measures and packages are possible. On cost grounds, it would not be feasible to compensate everybody who is affected in the region.

It is probably neither practical nor desirable for government to set out clear guidelines to compensation for the takings of interests to natural resources, but some reduction in uncertainty would be desirable. An examination of case studies reveals some consistency but also a good deal of variation in approaches. In general, business compensation and compensation for displaced workers are made available. Where adverse impacts are felt on a wide scale, regional economic stimuli may also be provided.

References

Anon. 1998. Encyclopaedia of law and economics, 6200 Takings, http://inprem.rug.ac.be/~gpremer/encyc/6200.html.

Banz, K. 1998. The takings debate - pro and con, http://www.wsn.org/takings.html.

Blume, L. and Rubinfeld, D. L. 1987. Compensation for takings: an economic analysis. *Research in Law and Economics.* 10:53-104.

Bromley, D. 1993. Regulatory takings: coherent concept or logical contradiction? *Vermont Law Review.* 17:647-682.

Buchanan, J.M., Tollison R. and Tullock, G. (eds). 1984. *Towards a theory of the rent-seeking society.* Texas. A. & M. University Press, College Station, Texas.

Dragun, A.K. Environmental institutional design: can property rights theory help? *International Journal of Social Sciences,* forthcoming.

Epstein, R. A. 1985. *Takings: private property and the power of eminent domain.* Harvard University Press, Cambridge, MA.

Family Business First 1998. Issue brief: private property rights. http://www.woodcom.com/woodcom/fbf-pr.html.

Farber, D. A. 1992. Economic analysis and just compensation. *International Review of Law and Economics.* 12:125-138.

Field, B.C. and Olewiler, N.D. 1995. *Environmental economics.* First Canadian Edition. McGraw-Hill Ryerson, Toronto.

Fischel, W. A. 1995. The offer/ask disparity and just compensation for takings: a constitutional choice perspective, *International Review of Law and Economics.* 15: 187-203.

Gilpin, A. 1980. *An Australian dictionary of environment and planning.* Oxford University Press, Melbourne.

Hermalin, B. E. 1995. An economic analysis of takings. *Journal of Law, Economics & Organization.* 11:64-86.

Hundloe, T.; Ware, J. and Driml, S. 1987. Regional economic impacts of listing Queensland Wet Tropical Rainforest as a World Heritage Area. A report prepared for the Department of the Arts, Sport, the Environment, Tourism and Territories, Institute of Applied Environmental Research, Griffith University.

Hundloe, T.; Driml, S. and Ware, J. L. 1988. Alternative employment creation and mitigation of impacts of listing of the Queensland Wet Tropical Rainforest as a World Heritage Area. A report prepared for Department of the Arts, Sport, the Environment, Tourism and Territories, Institute of Applied Environmental Research, Griffith University.

Kendall, D. 1998. Headwaters price far too high. Community Rights Council. http://www.portalmarket.arthportals/toohigh.html.

League of Wisconsin Municipalities 1988. A "takings" primer: position paper. http://www.lwm-info.org/legis/takings/primer.html.

Lynch-Blosse, M, Turrell, G. and Western, J. 1992. *Impact assessment: World Heritage listing,* SCRU Report No. 22.8. Resource Assessment Commission, Canberra.

McGufflog, I. and Western J.S. 1993. *Social impact assessment of the cessation of logging on Fraser Island: an evaluation of the Workers Special Adjustment Package,* Social Research Consultancy Unit, Department of Anthropology and Sociology, University of Queensland.

McKenzie, R. B. 1986. Eminent domain: a new industrial policy tool. *Journal of Institutional and Theoretical Economics,* 142:27-38.

Mercuro, N. (ed.) 1992. *Taking property and just compensation: legal and economics perspectives of the takings issue.* Kluwer Academic Publishers, Boston.

Miceli, T. J. and Segerson, K. 1994. Regulatory takings: when should compensation be paid? *Journal of Legal Studies.* 23:749-776.

Miceli, T. J. and Segerson, K. 1995. Government regulation and compensation for takings: implications for agriculture. *American Journal of Agricultural Economics.* 77:1177-1182.

NCBA (National Cattlemen's Beef Association). 1998. Property rights: position paper. http://hill.beef.org/ files/FSPP/prts.html.

Queensland Government. 1991. *The Great Sandy Region: The Queensland Government's growth and development package,* Brisbane.

Ramsay, G., et al. 1997. *Impacts of imposition of restrictions on gill nets on the Queensland East Coast Fishery: a report prepared for the Queensland Commercial Fishermen's Organisation.* Department of Economics, University of Queensland, Brisbane.

Richman, S. 1998. Takings: the evils of eminent domain. Cato Institute, Washington. http://www.halcyon.com/dick/emdomain.html.

Schwindt, R. 1992. *Report of the Commission of Inquiry into Compensation for the Taking of Resource Interests.* Resources Compensation Commission, Province of British Columbia, Vancouver.

Stehn, N. 1998. Department of Natural Resources, Brisbane, personal communication.

Treanor, W.M. 1988. The original understanding of the takings clause. Georgetown Law Centre. http://www.envpoly.org/papers/ptreanr.html.

Trefzger, J. and P. Colwell 1996. Investor efficiency in the face of takings. *Journal of Real Estate Finance and Economics.* 12(1):23-35.

Western Stock Growers' Association (1998). A suggested Property Rights Preservation Act. Calgary. http://www.cattle.ca/roo 9w6/articles/9802002.html.

[16]

Taxation versus tradable permits and alternative policies for environmental management[1]

Rationale for government intervention in environmental management

Market failure is the most common reason given by economists to justify government intervention in environmental management. However, if this intervention is to be efficient, it is also necessary for the benefits from it to exceed the costs of policy implementation, for example, the costs of policing, monitoring and enforcing the policy – that is, policy transaction costs as described by Mishan (1981). Nevertheless, market failure and economic efficiency arguments are not the only ones used to support such intervention. Sometimes income distribution arguments are used. For example, if a particular type of environmental deterioration is regressive in its impact (for instance, if reduced water quality adversely affects the health of the poor mostly through the incidence of water-borne diseases, as seems to be the case in many less developed countries) priority may be given to arresting such deterioration. Some writers associate intergenerational equity considerations with sustainability. In addition, 'non-economic' reasons for government intervention may be advanced, for example, that humankind has a responsibility for the stewardship of nature independently of individualistic human-centred desires.

Traditionally, economists have viewed market failure problems involving the environment as arising from a divergence between private marginal cost and social marginal cost and/or from a divergence between private marginal evaluation (price or value) and social marginal valuation. Within this setting, policy measures are usually designed to bring private marginal values into line with social ones (for example, by means of taxes and subsidies) or to ensure that private behaviour is in accordance with a Pigovian-type social optimum. However, the emergence of sustainability as a goal limits the application of this approach or constrains it.

While the correction of a divergence between private user-costs and social user-costs of natural or environmental resource utilization (such as is necessary when there is an open access to a resource) can be seen as an extension of the Pigovian prescription and a contribution to sustainability of economic activity, policies to ensure sustainability in terms of intergenerational equity may not be consistent with the traditional approach (Tisdell, 1993, ch. 8). When this is so, standards may be imposed, for example, the requirement may be imposed that there be no net deterioration in the availability of natural resources or the state of the environment. Nevertheless, similar sets of policies to those used in the previous case, policies such as the imposition of taxes on resource-use or the introduction of tradable permits, may be adopted to implement this conservation goal. Thus, the fiscal and other instruments discussed below have a wide range of application to environmental management. Let us consider taxes, tradable permits, property rights and other instruments in turn as means for environmental management.

Taxes

Taxes are the traditional economic prescription for dealing with unfavourable externalities. Pigou (1932) suggested, for example, that the output of industries producing unfavourable externalities should be taxed. However, taxing the output of an industry is not usually the most efficient economic method of controlling unfavourable externalities. Ignoring transaction costs, the most efficient method, if taxation is used, is to impose the tax on the item that directly causes the unfavourable externality, for example, emissions of a particular pollutant. If this is impractical, it may be economically more efficient to impose a tax on the use of particular inputs that are the prime source of the pollutants, for example, high sulphur coal, than on the output of the industry itself.

The prime purpose of such taxes is not to generate public revenue but to improve the allocative efficiency of the economy. In fact, the more successful such a tax is in reducing pollution or the extent of an unfavourable externality, the smaller is the amount of public revenue obtained. When the response is small, that is inelastic, much more revenue will be generated.

Taxes of a uniform nature on pollution or unfavourable externalities have been claimed to be relatively efficient since they ensure that the marginal costs of pollution abatement (of reducing environmental degradation) are equalized between economic agents (Tisdell, 1993, ch. 4). However, this assumes that the marginal externalities generated at all locations are the same. In many instances, they vary according to neighbourhoods and optimality will require differences in tax rates between neighbourhoods. This reduces the simplicity of this method. But the same problem also exists for the system of tradable permits or licences.

It has also been argued that taxes are unlikely to be very responsive to changing circumstances over time. They are not automatically adjusted for inflation. They do not adjust automatically to changing supply and demand conditions in an industry that may cause marginal externalities to alter.

Taxes do ensure that the polluter or user of the environment pays. However, in usual cases in industry, the tax will have incidence on firms directly degrading the environment as well as on purchasers of products produced by the industry degrading the environment. In reality, it is the purchase by consumers of products that degrade the environment that provides an incentive for such degradation and they 'should' pay. In any case, from the theory of the incidence of taxation, we know that in the market system the polluter rarely pays the full amount of the taxation revenue collected from him or her.

However, taxation is not popular with degraders of the environment because compared with some other methods, for example, restrictions on quantity of emissions, it is likely to reduce their income or rent. This it will do if the tax has an incidence on them.

One advantage of the tax system (provided it is geared to the offending externality) is to encourage innovation and technological progress to reduce the size of the unfavourable externality. This is also a feature of the tradable permit system.

Tradable permits or licences for use of the environment

Considerable support has developed amongst economists for the adoption of systems involving permits for environmental use (cf. Pearce and Turner, 1990). The support for such systems is especially strong in the USA. The system involves the creation of a market in rights to make use of the environment. It has similar efficiency consequences to a uniform taxation system. If the market in rights for use of the environment is competitive, a uniform price should prevail everywhere for such rights and costs of reducing environmental pollution should be minimized as in the taxation case. But the social optimality of this, as in the taxation case, depends upon the costs of externalities being uniform everywhere. Otherwise submarkets for rights have to be developed.

The public revenue generated by such schemes depends upon how they are administered and the conditions attaching to the permit. One possibility is for an annual fee (which could be varied by the government) to be payable to the government by permit-holders annually on a particular date. At the other extreme is the case where, after initial allocation of permits, no fee is payable to the government. If the initial allocation is made gratis on a historical basis, say on the basis of the relative use of the environment by permit-holders, no public revenue may be generated and all rents may be appropriated by initial permit-holders. *Politically* it may be expedient to allow initial users of the environment to appropriate rents from the scheme or a large share of these (so as to achieve their political support), but it may be inequitable to allow such appropriation.

The effects of the scheme will also depend upon what procedures exist for altering the total amount of rights allocated. If the rights exist in perpetuity, then the government may need to buy back rights if it 'needs' to reduce environmental use. What procedures should it adopt if it wants to increase environmental use? One way, of course, would be for the government to issue extra permits and sell these on the market or allocate them to existing holders of permits in some way. In Australia, for example, rights to catch southern bluefin tuna are uniformly increased or decreased (proportionally) for all holders of tradable permits so as to achieve the adjusted industry quota desired for any particular year.

The purpose of the above is to emphasize that one cannot generalize about the economic effects of tradable permits for using the environment *unless one is clear about the conditions that apply to such permits*, especially the extent of the entitlement granted by the permit and the rights of government in relation to the permit, for example, to impose charges and/or to vary the extent of environmental use allowed. Those who usually compare taxes and tradable permits as alternative means for environmental management often overlook these complexities. Furthermore, a government (as well as private traders) can be involved in considerable transaction costs in administering a system of tradable permits, for example, a register of holders and of transfers may be required and policing and monitoring is necessary.

As is well known, a tradable permit system is only likely to be efficient in a perfectly competitive market system. In some cases there is a danger that control over permits can be used to monopolize or to obtain a monopolistic position in an industry and restrict entry. This can happen if the environmental use covered by the permit is essential to operation in the industry and permits fall into the hands of one or a few holders. A tradable permit system can provide a barrier to entry of new firms to an industry and the price uncertainty associated with markets for permits can also have adverse economic impacts.

A comparison between taxes and tradable permits

There seems to be a perception that in a dynamic situation a system of tradable permits is likely to show more satisfactory in-built adjustment than taxation (Pearce and Turner, 1990). While the permit system will ensure that use of the environment will not exceed the aggregate permitted by the licences, failure to adjust the aggregate can lead to a greater economic loss than under an unchanged tax charge for environmental use. Social effects all depend on the prevailing parameters of the situation, as can be seen from the following example.

In Figure 16.1, let X represent the annual quantity of emissions of a pollutant and let line VV′ represent the marginal external costs imposed by these emissions. Suppose that the marginal benefit to polluters of these emissions is as represented by line AA′. The socially optimal level of emissions of the pollutant is X_2 annually. Imposing a tax of T on each unit of pollution, or selling rights to such a unit at P_2 each could achieve this as would auctioning pollution rights equal to X_2. In either case, the government would collect an equal amount of revenue.

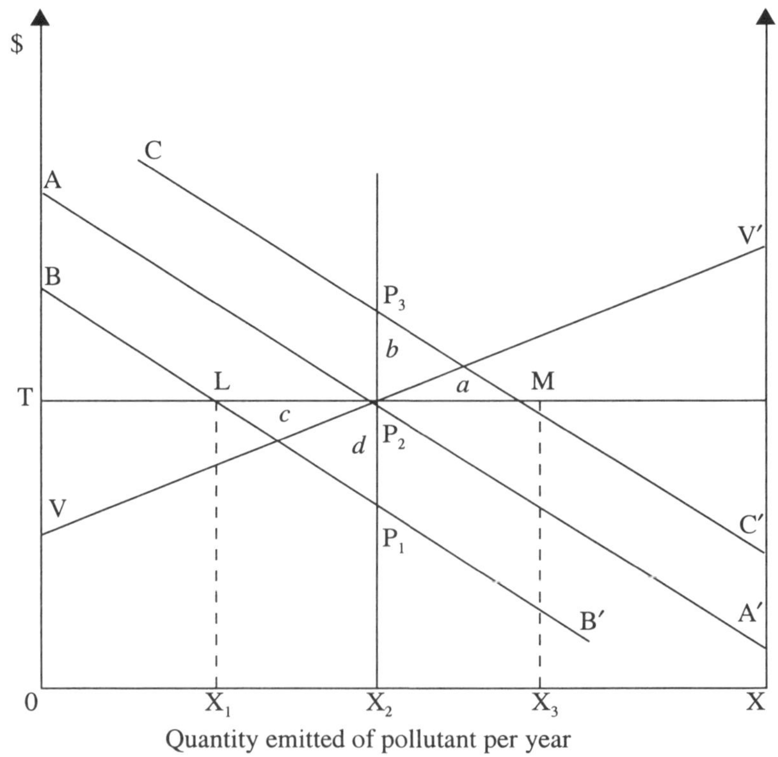

Figure 16.1 Possible differences in social deadweight arising from pollution taxes and tradable pollution permits

Now suppose that the marginal benefit to polluters of being able to emit pollutants alters. It may, for example, increase to CC′ or decrease to BB′. In the first case, if the amount of aggregate permits tradable stays at X_2, the price of permits rises to P_3 each. Price adjusts but there is a social deadweight loss equal to the triangle identified by *b*. If, on the other hand, the marginal value to polluters of emission falls to BB′, for example, due to technological progress, the price of permits falls to P_1 if the aggregate quota of allowable emissions marketed remains at X_2. The social deadweight loss is then as indicated by the triangle identified by *d*.

If, on the other hand, the tax rate remains unchanged at T, in these circumstances, in the first case (CC′ prevails) the social deadweight loss is equal to the triangle identified by *a* and in the second case (BB′ prevails) the relevant triangle is identified by *c*.

In the case illustrated, the social deadweight loss occasioned by the inflexible taxation system is less than for the system of tradable permits. This is indicated by the following: the area of triangle *a* is less than that of triangle *b*, and the area of triangle *c* is less than that of triangle *d*.

The relative welfare performance of the policy instruments depends upon the slope of the marginal external cost function. The slower is the rate of increase of the marginal external cost curve with increased levels of emissions, the more likely will the inflexible tax approach outperform the tradable permit system described. The converse also holds. The relative advantages of the alternatives vary with the circumstances. When the marginal costs of overshooting the optimal quantity of emissions rises sharply, inflexibility in quantity of emissions combined with price variation gives better welfare results than flexibility in the quantity of emissions. The opposite is the case when the marginal costs of overshooting the optimal level of emissions do not rise sharply.

Private property rights

The preferred solution of many market-oriented economists to environmental management is the creation of private property rights. Where this is practical, it is a means of attaining economic efficiency. As Coase (1960) points out, from an economic efficiency point of view, it makes little or no difference (under a range of conditions) whether the property rights are assigned to those degrading the environment or to those affected by this.[2] In such circumstances, the choice of the party to assign rights to is an ethical one. However, it is not always practical to establish such rights. Transactions costs, the costs of enforcing private property rights, may exceed the benefits to owners so even if private property rights exist *de jure*, they do not exist de facto.

Whether or not private property rights occur in practice is largely an economic question – it depends on whether it is economic for owners to enforce such rights (Demsetz, 1967). The economics of doing this can improve if the technology of exclusion, monitoring and enforcement improves and/or if the economic benefits to be had from private appropriation rise. Historically, the time must be ripe or appropriate for private property rights to be established, as has been recognized by writers such as North (1981) and Fisher (1984). Indeed, it has been argued that the set of property rights that arise in society tend to be appropriate to its historical stage. There is, therefore, an element of conflict between this laissez-faire view of a set of Chicago scholars, and another set which favours the active creation of private property rights and the making of markets.

It might be noted that the use of tradable permits or licences is in fact an exercise in market creation.

Other policies

There are, of course, other policies that may be used for environmental management. Polluters or degraders of the environment may be subsidized or bribed to reduce their degradation. Where, however, the government does this, it is a drain on its revenue. If the subsidy is paid from general public revenue, it is possible that the main beneficiaries from the environmental improvement will pay only a fraction in relation to their benefits and that a burden will be imposed on non-beneficiaries. It has also been observed in the literature that blackmail could occur – polluters could increase, or threaten to increase, their pollution so as to obtain a larger subsidy.

Prohibition is a relatively popular means of control amongst those degrading the environment. For example, it may be illegal to emit wastes with greater than a particular percentage of a chemical. This method tends to be popular amongst users of the environment because unlike taxes, tradable permits or property rights, no payment is required for using the environment provided standards are complied with. Compliance with standards also provides some legal protection to polluters and degraders of the environment. In essence, they are still able to capture substantial rents from using the environment gratis and may obtain a reduction in their risk-bearing through the legal protection afforded by government-sanctioned standards (cf. Tisdell, 1993. ch. 5).

Furthermore, this approach gives degraders of the environment an opportunity to influence officials enforcing standards. Standards may be set lower than is socially optimal and/or officials may not rigorously monitor compliance with standards. Scope exists for intervention by politicians and others in the enforcement process, for example, although pollution laws may be enacted, insufficient staff may be allocated to monitoring compliance.

Zoning and planning of economic activity provides another means of influencing environmental quality. This approach may be necessary because of neighbourhood effects and geographical influences on externalities. Economists have probably given insufficient attention to such issues, but they are especially important in an urban setting.

It might also be noted that governments in many countries have under their control club-like goods, for example, national parks. In recent years, some conservation groups have called for greater use of pricing to raise revenue from such facilities and the adoption of other means to ensure greater appropriation of revenue. By this means it is hoped to provide greater incentive for the provision of such facilities (IUCN-UNEP-WWF, 1991; McNeely, 1988). However, when such funds are returned to consolidated revenue, their incentive value may be low. Furthermore, it is not always economic to collect such fees or charges and externality factors also have to be taken into consideration. In addition, such an approach could encourage monopoly-type pricing by public authorities. While scope may exist for further development of pricing of environmental amenities as advocated by a number of conservationists, we should also be aware of the limitations to this approach.

Concluding comments

The above discussion indicates that there is no uniquely optimal public policy instrument for environmental management. One should be wary of those advocating a single policy approach. For example, whether a tradable permit system is likely to be better than traditional taxation policy for curbing environmental degradation varies according to circumstances, as already described. With increasing demands on environmental goods, there is likely to be more widespread adoption of pricing/taxation policies (cf. Commonwealth of Australia, 1992, pp. 78–9). However, in themselves, they are not sufficient for socially optimal environmental management. They need to be supplemented by zoning, the planning of economic activities in localities and the design of appropriate patterns of transport and communication infrastructure. This is specifically recognized in the Australian Strategy for Ecologically Sustainable Development (Commonwealth of Australia, 1992, pp. 40–43). Furthermore, limitations upon the growth of some macro-variables, such as the accumulation of man-made capital, may be required (Tisdell, 1991, ch. 5). My main conclusion is that a range of public policies is needed for effective environmental management. The appropriate instrument(s) will vary according to circumstances, for example, with differences in transaction costs associated with different instruments when applied in particular circumstances, with relative levels of social loss resulting from mis-specification of values for the alternative instruments, and so on.

Given present political preoccupations in Australia, one may wish to ask to what extent the environmental policies discussed above are compatible with a uniform value-added tax or a general goods and services tax. These taxes do not specifically address themselves to environmental issues. Supplementary or additional policies are required to deal with these issues. For example, taxation to curb unfavourable externalities needs to be non-uniform, that is, to vary with the extent of the marginal externality generated by different activities. However, if uniformity in the tax rate were an overriding goal, policy alternatives would be to make greater use of the tradable licences or permits or private property rights. However, there are limits to the extent to which this can be done, or sensibly done, from a social viewpoint, particularly in Australia given limited market competition.

Notes

1. This chapter originally appeared in D. Thampapillai (ed.) (1993), *Taxation and the Environment*, Australian Tax Research Foundation, Conference Series No. 14, Sydney, pp. 95–105. The content of this chapter is the same as in the original (except for minor changes) but its presentation has been improved. Consequently, pagination is no longer the same as in the original.
2. However, there are some circumstances for which economic outcomes are sensitive to the choice of parties assigned property rights (Tisdell, 1991, pp. 136–7).

References

Coase, R. (1960), 'The Problem of Social Waste', *Journal of Law and Economics*, **3**, 1–44.

Commonwealth of Australia (1992), *National Strategy for Ecologically Sustainable Development*, A.G.P.S. Press, Canberra.

Demsetz, H. (1967), 'Towards a Theory of Property Rights', *American Economic Review*, **57**, pp. 347–59.

Fisher, J. (1984), *Australia and the First Economic Revolution*, Research Report or Occasional Paper No. 96, Department of Economics, University of Newcastle, NSW 2308.

IUCN-UNEP-WWF (1991), *Caring for the Earth: A Strategy for Sustainability*, Gland, Switzerland: IUCN.

McNeely, J.A. (1988), *Economics and Biological Diversity: Developing and Using Economic Incentives to Conserve Biological Resources*, Gland, Switzerland: IUCN.

Mishan, E.J. (1981), *Introduction to Normative Economics*, New York: Oxford University Press.
North, D.C. (1981), *Structure and Change in Economic History*, New York: Norton.
Pearce, D. and R. Turner (1990), *Economics of Natural Resources and the Environment*, New York: Harvester Wheatsheaf.
Pigou, A.C. (1932), *The Economics of Welfare*, London: Macmillan.
Tisdell, C.A. (1991), *Economics of Environmental Conservation: Economics for Environmental and Ecological Management*, Amsterdam: Elsevier Science.
Tisdell, C.A. (1993), *Environmental Economics: Policies for Environmental Management and Sustainable Development*, Aldershot: Edward Elgar.

Sustainable Development
Sust. Dev. **6**, 18–22 (1998)

ECONOMIC POLICY INSTRUMENTS AND ENVIRONMENTAL SUSTAINABILITY: ANOTHER LOOK AT ENVIRONMENTAL-USE PERMITS

Clem Tisdell

University of Queensland, Australia

There has been a recent tendency to extol tradeable or marketable pollution permits or similar permits to use or exploit some natural resources, such as fish. They are often seen as a very effective way of maintaining environmental conditions in a desired way. However, considerable care is required in adopting such systems. If they are inappropriately designed, the government will lose its flexibility to control the state of the environment. Permits which give their owners absolute rights to emit certain quantities of pollution in perpetuity or entitle holders to use or appropriate a particular quantity of a natural resource in perpetuity can cause particular problems for government. They can for example, involve expensive buy-back schemes. There are, however, ways around the problem. Furthermore, holders of rights may have to pay fees to cover enforcement costs. Where tradeable permits have a very long life, the question arises of how they should be allocated and whether those allocated these rights should be allowed to capture the rents. As discussed, changing ambient conditions may have to be allowed for in designing systems involving tradeable permits. © 1998 John Wiley & Sons, Ltd and ERP Environment.

Correspondence to: Clem Tisdell, Department of Economics, The University of Queensland, Brisbane, Queensland 4072, Australia.

CCC 0968-0802/98/010018–05 $17.50

Received 30 June 1997
Accepted 1 October 1997

INTRODUCTION

The introduction of marketable environmental-use rights, such as pollution rights, are considered by many to be an efficient way of satisfying environmental standards e.g., air and water quality standards, or of achieving sustainable use of natural resources, such as fish stocks, to which there is some degree of common access. It is frequently argued that they result in environmental standards or targets being met at minimum cost because the market will ensure that rights to use the environment are distributed between users so that the marginal net benefit of each from this use is equal (Dales, 1968). Consequently, social benefits from use of the environment are maximized relative to the aggregate environmental use permitted.

In principle, a similar result could be obtained by the introduction of suitable taxes or government charges on the use of the natural environment (Dales, 1968; Tisdell, 1993a, Ch. 4). However, it is not easy to predict the level of tax or user-charges necessary to achieve a particular degree of use of the environment or to achieve an environmental standard. Marketable rights or quotas are advantageous in that regard (Pearce and Turner, 1990; Tisdell, 1993b). Secondly, in order to meet the environmental targets set, taxes or charges need to be altered with changing conditions. Politically and administratively this is not easy. Consequently, they tend to be 'sticky'. On the other hand, the price of marketable pollution permits automatically changes as the demand for these alters. Nevertheless, marketable environmental-use rights have been subjected to substantial criticism as a means of environmental regulation (Livingston *et al.*, 1996; Russell and Powell, 1996; Sterner, 1994).

POLITICAL ASPECTS

Politically it is easier in most cases to introduce marketable environmental-use rights than taxes or government charges on environmental use. This is so provided that 'grandfathering' is used to distribute rights. In this case the rights are distributed to those already involved in use of the environmental resource in question, usually in proportion to their use at no charge or at a nominal charge. Consequently, any rents from rights to use the resource are captured by the existing users and there is little or no income transfer to the government. This reduces political opposition from environmental users such as producers. However, the question of whether such a distribution of property rights is just remains unresolved.

Rents from use of environmental resources in a system of marketable environmental-use rights need not be captured by the original users of the environment. Whether they are depends on how the system for such rights is designed and operated. If, for example, rights are not in perpetuity but are auctioned, say each year, by the government, then the government would capture the rents. However such a system is likely to be unpopular with existing environmental users. There are a variety of different possible schemes involving marketable rights to use the environment. These have different consequences for income distribution, economic efficiency and flexibility of policy and this aspect will be discussed below.

MARKETABILITY OF RIGHTS

If marketable pollution or environmental-use rights are to achieve the efficiency benefits ascribed to them, then the market in such rights needs to be relatively competitive. In practice markets in these rights tend to be 'thin' because there may be few holders of such rights, particularly if rights are differentiated by region (see below).

Sale of rights can also be used to restrict competition and new entry. If rights are held by those already in an industry, they may retain them as a way of restricting new entrants. Supply in an industry could also be restricted by one or a few firms cornering environmental-use rights.

ENFORCEMENT AND AGENCY COSTS, ALLOCATION OF RIGHTS

If a system of marketable environmental-use permits is to be effective, it is necessary to ensure that only those who have permits use the environment in question and do so only to the extent allowed by their permits. Failure to enforce the rules of the system can be expected to result in increasing violations and a breakdown of control. How does one ensure compliance?

One possibility is to allow permit-holders to sue violators for damages. This will however involve costs and legal uncertainty for any permit-holder bringing a court action against a violator and other permit-holders may free ride on the litigant. The system may therefore not result in sufficient enforcement to protect property rights through permits and to achieve environmental targets. Consequently, the government or an agency of the government may be called upon to enforce the regulations.

Considerable costs of enforcement may be incurred by the agency. It may for example have to keep a register of rights including transfers, and guard against the issue of fraudulent certificates. It will also need to monitor compliance and take legal action against violators. The question arises of who should pay for those costs and how. A common practice is to impose a levy on permit-holders and a fee on transfers to meet such costs. Thus the user appears to pay although the full incidence of these charges may not fall on permit-holders because they may be passed on to some extent to others further along the economic chain e.g., the buyers of the commodities of permit-holders.

Ideally the enforcement agency should minimize its costs for the degree of enforcement achieved. However, it may fail to do so. In fact, like many public agencies, it may try to maximize its budget, although possible criticism from permit-holders may curb its behaviour in this respect. Nevertheless, its goal may be to maximize its budget subject to account being taken of the possible political pressures generated.

Another possible institutional means for obtaining compliance is co-management (Pomeroy, 1994). This approach involves the government agency and those involved in the use of the environment in co-operating to draw up and ensure enforcement of environmental regulations. This can have a number of advantages. It improves information flows between the parties involved and can reduce enforcement costs (Kuperan and Sutinen, 1996). On the other hand, there are circumstances in which it would give rise to socially unacceptable results. This may occur when not all relevant interest groups are involved in the management of environmental use. For instance if co-management only involves members of the public service and permit-holders, those damaged by pollution are unrepresented. At least this is so if only permit-holders are polluters.

Note that it is sometimes considered to be an advantage of a system of tradeable pollution or environmental use-permits that those who wish to prevent the activity can buy permits and withhold these from the market and from use. This action will be effective provided that it is not counteracted by an increased issue of permits by the government. The latter is always a political possibility. Secondly, benefits from environmental conservation are often greatly diffused and can be relatively small for each individual. No or few conservationists might find it worthwhile to buy environmental-use permits for withholding purposes, even though collectively it may be worthwhile for them to do so. Because of free riding and the cost of organizing collective action to buy environmental-use permits for withholding purposes, it is unlikely to occur. Thus the system is not fully effective in achieving conservation goals.

The buy-back proposed for conservationists also raises the question of justice. Should environmental-user rights be given to conservationists, in which case those wishing to use the environment would need to purchase rights from conservationists, or should those permits be allocated to users of the environment, or should the initial allocation involve an allocation to both parties? Despite the suggestion of Coase (1960), environmental use is likely to vary with the initial allocation of rights to use of the environment (Tisdell, 1991, 136). In addition, the nature of this allocation affects the distribution of incomes in very different ways.

LOCATIONAL FACTORS AND ENVIRONMENTAL RIGHTS

The sustainable level of environmental use or the socially optimal level of environmental use can vary from region to region. Thus different levels of environmental control may have to be executed in different regions and this calls for variation and differentiation in environmental-use rights by location (Tietenberg, 1974). Furthermore, this can be expected to result in variations in the market price of pollution rights between regions. Thus regional differentiation in pollution rights in Southern California results in permits for air pollution rights having a higher price in coastal areas than inland. Because the prevailing winds blow from the sea more damage is done by air pollutants originating near the coast in Southern California than by those emitted further inland. Similarly, it is possible that water pollutants originating upstream may do more environmental damage than those released near the mouth of a river.

While regional differences in rights to use the environment are often necessary, one problem in the case of marketable permits is that this reduces the breadth of markets for rights because it creates regional submarkets. This can affect market competition for such rights and make it easier to corner rights in some regions. Ownership of rights can be used as a barrier to entry of new regional competitors or in certain cases as a means to restrict regional supplies.

In some cases, regional rights to use the environment need to be varied seasonally, e.g., depending on the seasonal direction of prevailing wind flows or water currents. In principle, environmental-use rights can be designed to take seasonal variation into account.

DURATION OF ENVIRONMENTAL-USE RIGHTS AND THEIR NATURE

Transferable environmental-use rights can vary significantly in their direction and in their nature. The following are some of the possibilities:

- The permit-holder has the right in perpetuity to use the environment to a fixed absolute extent, e.g., the right to a specified absolute catch of a fish species annually or rights to emit a particular quantity of pollutants per year.
- Rights may be as above but for a finite period, e.g., for one year or for five years.
- The rights may be in perpetuity but only for a fixed *proportionate* level of use of the environment, e.g., rights to emit a fixed proportion of the total or aggregate level of emissions of a pollutant allowed in each period of time for instance a year or rights to a fixed proportion of the total allowable catch of a species. This method is used for example to allocate rights to catch southern bluefin tuna in Australian waters.
- Another possibility is for the above rights not to be in perpetuity but for finite duration.
- Still another possibility is for the above absolute or relative rights to be discounted or diminished in a regular fashion with the passage of time. For example, 10% of rights per year may have to be surrendered to the government. The government could re-issue these or it may decide not to do so or only re-issue a portion of the surrendered rights. A system of this type was proposed at one time for permits for amateur fishermen in New South Wales.
- In some cases, rights may be restricted in terms of their transferability, e.g., they may be restricted to use in a particular region or regions.
- The method by which permits are issued or re-issued can vary. For instance, their issue could be by open tender or auctioning with a variety of conditions applying or they may be allocated administratively, taking into account pre-existing use of the environment by the parties concerned.

From the above, it should be clear that a large range and complex set of possibilities exist for systems of transferable or tradeable environmental-use permits. Differences in these systems are liable to have different implications for economic efficiency and for the impact generally of environmental regulation. Take the first case above, absolute rights in perpetuity. This provides considerable security to permit-holders but provides the regulator with virtually no flexibility. This can create difficulties. For example, suppose that after the absolute rights are issued it becomes clear that the aggregate level of environmental use allocated is unsustainable or not optimal and needs to be reduced. Given the nature of the rights, this can only be achieved by the government buying back rights, which can be expensive. This is not just a hypothetical possibility. The New Zealand Government in a bold experiment introduced such a system for some of its fisheries. Subsequently, it was found that the total allowable catch for some species exceeded the level that was sustainable. The Government therefore, at considerable expense to New Zealand taxpayers, purchased back some of the rights and did not re-issue these.

Schemes of shorter duration or in which rights 'depreciate' or are discounted with the passage of time provide environmental regulators with more flexibility but create greater uncertainty for users of the environment. In practice a compromise between security of rights for environmental users and the need for some flexibility in regulation needs to be reached. Systems of marketable permits should be designed with this in mind. In doing this, it is important to bear in mind that businesses may have to make long-term investments to curtail pollution efficiently or limit their use of the environment. The greater the degree of uncertainty about allowable future environmental use, the less likely businesses are to commit themselves to investments reducing environmental degradation because they need to retain flexibility as a hedge against uncertainty.

AMBIENCE

In many cases, the impact of use of the environment depends upon ambient conditions. Since these can often vary considerably, ideally permitted use of the environment should be altered as their conditions change. However, the transaction costs of such variations can be high and they may be so high that it is not worthwhile trying to achieve the absolute ideal. Where it is not practical to vary user rights as ambient conditions alter, the level of use allowed by the permits may have to be adjusted to take this into account. Thus, if for example, there is expected to be a period of the year when ambient conditions are expected to be such that air pollutants cause much greater environmental damage than usual, rights to emit air pollutants may be curtailed more than otherwise for the whole period in which the rights apply. This is the most likely approach when the period of environmentally dangerous ambient conditions is uncertain and variable.

If this period is relatively certain, for example, it occurs in the summer season only, then the rights to use the environment can be specified in a regularly varying manner. For example, users of the environment may be issued with permits to emit a specified quantity of air pollutants per month but the quantity allowed in the summer period may be 20% less than in the remainder of the year. Other possibilities also exist, e.g., the 20% reduction applies only when this is announced in advance by the regulator.

CONCLUDING COMMENT

Some writers extol the virtues of marketable environmental-use rights in comparison to other means to control the use of the environment. Their argument is usually based on highly simplified models and situations. In particular, they give insufficient consideration to the complexities of systems of marketable rights to use the environment and the possible diversity of such systems. There is a need to give much more attention to the varied possibilities for such permit systems and the consequences of different types of system. Otherwise, little practical progress will be made in devising effective and efficient policies for environmental management.

REFERENCES

Coase, R. (1960) The problem of social waste, *The Journal of Law and Economics*, **3**, 1–44.

Dales, J.H. (1968) *Pollution, Property and Prices*, University of Toronto Press, Toronto.

Kuperan, K. and Sutinen, J. (1996) Regulatory compliance in Malaysian fisheries. In *Proc. 7th International Fisheries Conference*, Taiwan Fisheries Research Institute, Keelung.

Livingston, M.L., Batie, S.S. and Southgate D.D. (1996) Introduction and symposium summary. In M.L. Livingston (Ed.), *Environmental Policy for Economics in Transition: Lessons Learned and Future Directions, Proc. Resource Policy Conservation Symposium*, Washington, DC, 1996, Department of Economics, University of Northern Colorado, Greeley, 1–8.

Pearce, D. and Turner, R. (1990) *Economics of Natural Resources and the Environment*, Harvester Wheatsheaf, New York.

Pomeroy, R.S. (1994) *Community Management and Common Property of Coastal Fisheries in Asia and the Pacific: Concepts, Methods and Experience*, ICLARM, Manila.

Russell, C.S. and Powell, P.T. (1996) Choosing environmental policy tools. In M. Livingston (Ed.), *Environmental Policy for Economics in Transition: Lessons Learned and Future Directions, Proc. Resource Policy Consortium*, Washington, DC, 1996, Department of Economics, University of Northern Colorado, Greeley, 30–87.

Sterner, T. (1994) Policy instruments for a sustainable economy. In T. Sterner (Ed.), *Economic Policies for Sustainable Development*, Kluwer, Dordrecht, 1–19.

Tietenberg, T.H. (1974) On taxation and the control of externalities: a comment, *American Economic Review*, **64**, 452–466.

Tisdell, C.A. (1991) *Economics of Environmental Conservation*, Elsevier, Amsterdam.

Tisdell, C.A. (1993a) *Environmental Economics*, Elgar, Aldershot.

Tisdell, C.A. (1993b) Taxation versus tradeable permits and alternative policies for environmental management. In D. Thampapillai (Ed.), *Tax and the Environment*, Australian Tax Research Foundation, Sydney, 95–105.

BIOGRAPHY

Professor Clem Tisdell, Head of Department, Department of Economics, The University of Queensland, Brisbane, Queensland 4072, Australia.

Tel: +61 7 3365 6570.

Fax: +61 7 3365 7299.

Sust. Dev. **6**, 18–22 (1998)

ETA Volume 2, No. 2

ENVIRONMENTAL TAXATION VERSUS TRADEABLE PERMITS: PUBLIC FINANCE, ACCOUNTING AND RELATED ASPECTS

Clem Tisdell
Professor of Economics
The University of Queensland
Brisbane Australia 4072

1. Introduction

Considerable debate has occurred about the virtues of tradeable permits to use the environment compared to environmental taxation. Nevertheless, in this debate little attention has been given to the implications of these different environmental policy instruments for public finance and the necessary accounting associated with them. The purpose of this article is to focus on such issues and related aspects.

In the economics literature, proposals to tax activities giving rise to adverse environmental spillovers or externalities, such as air or water pollution predate by several decades alternative proposals to use tradeable permits to regulate the environmental impacts of such activities. For example, Alfred Marshall (1890) mentions the possibility of using taxes to restrict adverse externalities, and of employing subsidies as a means to encourage the generation of favourable externalities. It was, however, left to Arthur Pigou (1932) to develop this tax-subsidy policy approach in some detail. The distinction of developing an alternative to it goes to the Canadian economist, Dale (1968) who suggested tradeable environmental-use permits as an efficient alternative. Under this scheme, property-rights for the use of the environment are created by government and assigned to individuals or economic agents who may trade these rights. The conditions for a *market* in such rights are thereby established.

Proponents of tradeable or marketable permits argue that these are likely to be just as efficient as environmental taxes or charges in controlling environmental use in the sense that under certain conditions, they can be expected to minimize the cost to society of achieving the level of environmental control occurring or required (Tisdell, 1993a, Ch. 4). While either environmental taxation or tradeable permits can be used as a means to satisfy safe minimum environmental standards, proponents of tradeable permits argue that environmental standards are less likely to be breached when the latter system applies. Therefore, tradeable permits are seen as both being efficient, and as fostering environmental security. However, the case in favour of such permits is not as clear cut as their exponents frequently claim. Because public schemes for the issue and maintenance of a system of tradeable permits can vary widely, any comparison between the environmental taxation and tradeable permits requires the type(s) of tradeable permit systems to the specified which are to be used as the basis of comparison. Tradeable rights can vary in terms of the duration of the entitlement, conditions such as the location of the entitlement, method of the initial allocation of the rights and on whether or not annual fees or charges are imposed by public authorities on holders of rights and in terms of the extent to which fees are payable for transfer of rights. The case most commonly considered in the economic literature dealing with tradeable rights is one in which rights once issued are available in perpetuity, involve no payment of public annual fees and are transferable without transaction costs. This is a very special case indeed.

2. Public finance aspects of tradeable permits

The public finance implications of tradeable permits in comparison to environmental taxes and charges have not been extensively discussed in the literature. It is clear that environmental taxes or charges provide public revenue. This may use as an addition to general public revenues, or it may be employed for treating environmental pollutants or 'bads' or for environmental research. Such payments can either be regarded as a rental payment by businesses to the government to use the environment and/or a reimbursement for public expenses involved in treating environmental 'bads' e.g., wastes produced by businesses.

In comparison, some system of tradeable environmental-use rights generate no public revenue, which of course can make them popular with users of the environment. This will be the case for example if 'grandfathering' is used to allocate these rights initially, if the rights are guaranteed in perpetuity and can be transferred without any public fee being imposed. In this case, the user does not pay the government. 'Grandfathering' describes the practice of issuing rights initially free of change to existing users of the environment. The initial allocation may for example be in proportion to the relative use of the environment by incumbents.

Politically it is usually much easier to introduce such a scheme than one of environmental taxation because the latter involves an income transfer to the government. The former scheme ensures that those initially allocated rights can capture any resource rents. They acquire 'property' which can be sold. and which also may, in certain cases, be used as collateral for loans or financing. However, such a scheme does have the disadvantage that it does not provide any public revenue. Consequently costs to the public or public authorities are not paid for by users of the environment: so in this regard the *user does not pay* and the user-pays principle is violated in some respect.

Nevertheless, a system of tradeable permits can be combined with one involving environmental taxes or public charges, even if grandfathering is used. For example, permits may be subject to an annual tax, public change or fee. These must of course be less than the value of the permit otherwise permit-holders will surrender these permits. Such taxes or charges may be used to appropriate some of the resource rents for the public or to cover the public costs of treating environmental 'bads' created by the activities in question. They may also be used to foster research into environmental control methods. In addition, as discussed below, government administration costs are incurred in managing a tradeable permit scheme. It may be reasonable to have these charges met from levies on permit-holders.

Instead of grandfathering, a public authority could in principle auction initial entitlements or try to sell them at a market-clearing price. For rights in perpetuity, however, this would give only a one-off payment to the government. This approach is furthermore not likely to be popular with incumbent-users of the environment. In addition, because of uncertainties and financial limitations on businesses, the rent appropriated by government may be less than when annual charges are imposed on environmental users.

3. Accounting and monitoring aspects

Tradeable permits involve property rights. Transfers of such rights need to be recorded and registered. Transaction costs are involved. Purchasers of rights also must check the validity of the rights. Effective and efficient systems are required to keep records of such transfers.

When large numbers of environmental users are involved, it is necessary for the government to take an active role in monitoring use of the environment and whether or not use of the environment is covered by permits. This cost of monitoring and follow-up enforcement needs to be met. This can be done by imposing an annual levy on permit-holders.

In a small group, legitimate permit-holders might bring an action against violators, but in a large group this is unlikely because of the cost of organising collective action and its uncertainties (Tisdell, 1996, Ch. 8). In the latter case, any individual action is unlikely because the benefit to individual litigant is likely to exceed his/her cost, even though the collective benefit to all permit-holders may be well in excess of such cost. At the very least, one is faced by a 'free-riding' problem. More generally there are failures (akin to those arising for pure public goods) which prevent a large group of permit-holders from pursuing action of collective benefit to them (Tisdell, 1996, Ch. 8). As a result, government monitoring and enforcement is necessary if a system of tradeable permits is not to become completely ineffective. The costs of public administration involved in a tradeable permit scheme are not likely to be less than for environmental taxes, and may be higher given that a rights register has to be maintained and kept up-to-date.

The government may also have to perform a monitoring role in relation to the nature and operation of markets for environmental-us rights. The more competitive such markets are the more efficiently they are assumed to operate. However, sometimes these markets are 'thin'. Potentially also environmental-use rights can be used as a barrier to entry of new businesses in an industry and could be cornered so as to give the purchaser a dominant market position in relation to products or services, the supply of which is entirely dependent on the environmental use in question. Businesses can potentially use acquisition of environmental use rights as an instrument for monopolisation of product or service markets.

4. Further policy observations and concluding comments

Greater interest in adopting tradeable permits as methods of pollution control has been shown in the United States than in Europe. One the other hand, the United States has been more reluctant than either New Zealand or Australia to introduce tradeable catch permits into its fisheries.

While there has recently been a spate of economic literature extolling the virtues of tradeable permits in comparison to environmental taxes (e.g., Pearce and Turner, 1990), the superiority of systems of tradeable permits is by no means clear cut. Comparisons are frequently based on gross simplifications about the system of tradeable permits and the costs necessarily associated with it. Systems of tradeable permits can vary in the extent of the entitlement generated by the permit, and the rights of the government in relation to the permit for instance to impose changes and/or to vary the extent of environmental use allowed. Furthermore, a government can be involved in considerable transaction costs in administering a system of tradeable permits, for example, a register of holders and of transfers is required and policing and monitoring is necessary.

It is sometimes argued that in a dynamic situation systems of tradeable permits are likely to show automatic adjustment via price changes for permits whereas for political reasons tax rates are slower to adjust (Pearce and Turner, 1990). However, price is just one variable in the adjustment process. It may very well be necessary in a dynamic context as learning takes place to adjust the total allowable level of use of the environment. When a tradeable permit system is in place there may be difficulties if the government wishes to change the total level of environmental-use.

For example, the New Zealand Government entered the 'brave new world' of transferable fishing rights issuing rights to fishermen in perpetuity. It was subsequently found that in some cases the total allowable catch was not sustainable. In order to reduce the total catch to sustainable levels, the New Zealand Treasury was involved in an expensive buy back operation of permits from fishermen.

Tradeable permit systems of this type lack flexibility but schemes can be devised which are more flexible. For example, for the Australian tradeable permit scheme applying to southern bluefin tuna, rights are only to a fixed proportion of the total allowable catch. Regulatory authorities can, therefore, alter the total allowable catch as required. The scheme strikes a balance between security (for fishermen) and flexibility from a regulatory point of view.

As I have pointed out elsewhere (Tisdell, 1993b), while a permit system can be expected to ensure that use of the environment will not exceed the aggregate permitted by licences, failure to adjust the aggregate can lead to a greater economic loss than under an unchanged tax charge for environmental use. It depends upon the slopes of the marginal curve of benefits to polluters of being able to pollute and the slope of the marginal external costs imposed by pollutants, taking the emissions of pollutants as the example of environmental use in this case.

It should not be construed from the above that I am arguing that tradeable permits are inferior to environmental taxation. In fact, they can be superior from an economic policy purpose in some cases. Much depends on their design. Furthermore, in some cases they need to be designed to meet the public finance requirements as discussed above. In such cases, a mixed system emerges and the tradeable rights system convergences towards systems of environmental taxation.

It is clear from the above that a wide range of different systems of tradeable permits is possible. A taxonomy of such systems would be useful (Cf. Tisdell, 1997). At least such a taxonomy would underscore the variety of such possibilities. It should also increase awareness about the perils of simplistic comparisons between environmental taxation and tradeable permits as means of environmental regulation. A taxonomy would need to take account of variations in (1) the duration of rights; (2) location of entitlements and any other restrictive conditions on these; (3) the imposition of annual fees or levies, if any, on permit-holders by the government and (4) transfer fees.

References

DALES, J.H. (1968) *Pollution, Property and Prices*, University of Toronto Press.
MARSHALL, A. (1890) *Principles of Economics*, 1st ed., Macmillan, London.
PEARCE, D. AND TURNER, R. (1990) *Economics of Natural Resources and the Environment*, Harvester Wheatscheaf, New York.
PIGOU, A.C. (1932) *The Economy of Welfare*, Macmillan, London.
TISDELL, C.A. (1993a) *Environmental Economics*, Edward Elgar, Aldershot, England.
TISDELL, C.A. (1993b) 'Taxation Versus Tradeable Permits and Alternative Policies for Environmental Management', pp. 95-105 in D. Thampapillai (ed.) *Tax and the Environment*, Australian Tax Research Foundation, Sydney.
TISDELL, C.A. (1996) *Bounded Rationality and Economic Evolution*, Edward Elgar, Cheltenham, England.
TISDELL, C.A. (1997) 'Economic Policy Instruments and Environmental Sustainability: A Second Look at Marketable or Tradeable Pollution on Environmental-Use Permits', pp. 310-315 in *The 1997 International Sustainable Development Research Conference: Proceedings*, ERP Environment, Yorkshire, England.

6 *Int. J. Agricultural Resources, Governance and Ecology, Vol. 1, No .1, 2000*

Coevolution, agricultural practices and sustainability: some major social and ecological issues

Clem Tisdell

The University of Queensland, Brisbane, Qld 4072, Australia
E-mail: c.tisdell@economics.uq.edu.au

Abstract: This paper outlines the major social and ecological issues involved in the coevolution of social and ecological systems by initially reviewing relevant aspects of the recent literature relating to economic development and their implications for agricultural development. Coevolutionary qualitative-type models are presented. There has been a failure among advocates of structural adjustment policies (involving the extension of markets and economic globalization) to take account of coevolutionary principles and to allow for historical differences in the evolution of communities and their varied circumstances. This lack of sensitivity has had unfortunate social and ecological consequences for some communities in, for example, the Russian Federation and for subsistence agriculturalists in some less developed countries. The evolution of globalized market systems involving industrial/commercial agriculture (largely dependent on inputs external to the farm) under the 'patronage' of oligopolistic suppliers is seen to increasingly threaten the balance between social and ecological systems and as undermining the sustainability of both. Capitalistic processes of technological change, such as advances in biotechnology, play a major role in this evolution.

Keywords: coevolution; ecological systems; globalization; industrial/ commercial agriculture; property rights; social systems.

Reference to this paper should be made as follows: Tisdell, C. (2000) 'Coevolution, agricultural practices and sustainability: some major social and ecological issues', *Int. J. Agricultural Resources, Governance and Ecology*, Vol. 1, No. 1, pp. 6–16.

1 Introduction

The general idea of coevolution is by no means new to social science, that is the view that social structures change and evolve with variations in other components of mankind's environment such as climate, resource availability and technology. Karl Marx and Friedrich Engels for example were of the view that available technologies to a large extent determine the nature of societies and that societies alter in relatively predictable ways as modes of production change. At the same time, however, Marx's theory of the evolution of societies (in *Das Kapital*) was of a relatively deterministic nature. He seemed to have in mind a social system driven by inexorable internal logic until the revolution, after which positivism would presumably hold sway and be used to engineer economic and social organizations to serve the collective benefit. For Marx, the social system evolves to a final utopian state.

However, many different models exist of how evolution of economic systems occurs, a taxonomy of which has been prepared by Hodgson [1]. Furthermore, one may study evolutionary processes in relation to shorter and longer time-scales, and for this purpose different types of modelling may be appropriate and different types of phenomenon may warrant attention. Hence, the appropriate type of modelling of evolutionary processes often varies with the time-scale.

Despite the fact that a coevolutionary perspective is not new, it has received little weight in social thought and policy in modern times, possibly due to the prevalence of scientific specialization and to the widespread use of the reductionist approach to obtaining knowledge. This has encouraged a technical and mechanistic approach to social policy formation and favoured the growth of technocracies reliant on the expertise of specialized experts (cf. Norgaard [2]) which in turn has favoured (via feedback mechanisms) the development of educational systems designed to produce experts in ever narrower areas of specialization; such has happened in economics. Consequently, we have more specialized knowledge than ever before but are less able to use it well for solving social problems involving multiple dimensions because few individuals grasp the overall pattern and dimensions of social problems. While in economics the analytical importance of institutional and cultural dimensions is starting to be increasingly recognized, this recognition is often superficial. The purpose of this paper is not to produce a grand theory of the coevolution of agricultural, social systems and 'natural' systems. Rather it highlights aspects of coevolution discussed in the recent economic literature and indicates their relevance to agricultural development; points to the failure of structural adjustment policies, (promoted by the Washington consensus), to take account of important coevolutionary factors such as cultural and regional pluralism; considers possible coevolutionary consequences of rapid and widespread technological change in agriculture engineered and fostered by experts outside local communities; and takes account of the fact that technology is subject to speedier diffusion than ever before due to the forces of economic globalization.

2 Aspects of coevolution in recent economic literature and their relevance to agricultural development

Norgaard [2] has been one of the main proponents of a coevolutionary view of the social and natural world. However, it is quite difficult to find in his work any simple definition of coevolution or simple models of the operation of coevolution connecting social and environmental systems. In fact one wonders whether or not his approach amounts to little more than the proposition that social systems shape environmental systems and environmental systems shape social ones – they are interdependent. Norgaard suggests that more attention should be given to studying the nature of this interdependence, highlighted by Figure 1.

Figure 1 Richard Norgaard has argued strongly that social and ecological systems should be studied as coevolving systems

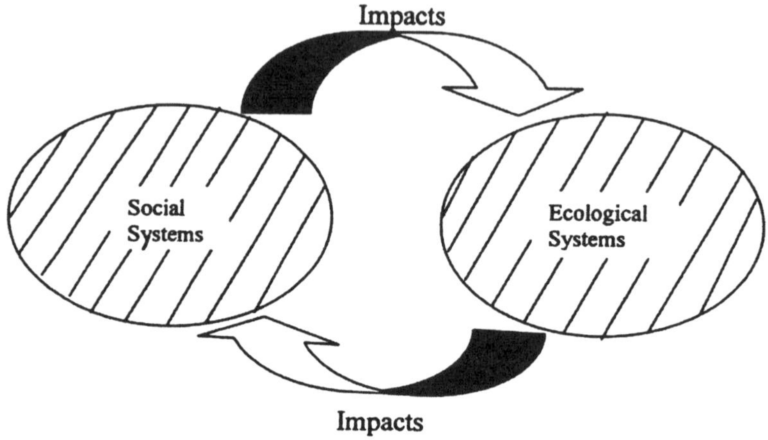

While some evolutionary processes described by Norgaard appear not to be based on forces of selection, others are. Nevertheless, he appears to be mostly concerned with selective processes of evolution. In elaborating the coevolutionary process, he states:

> "Thinking of the changes in social and environmental systems over time as a process of coevolution acknowledges that cultures affect which environmental features prove fit and that environments affect which cultural features prove fit. In this sense, coevolution accepts both environmental and cultural determinism while recasting them as a selection process." [2, p.81]

At the same time, Norgaard rejects historicism or historical determinism and appears to stress that the study of the coevolutionary processes involves a frame of mind [2, p.197] requiring that one keep in view the interdependence of social systems and ecosystems and their parts, in an evolving and changing world. While such an outlook has little operational content in itself, it can provide an important perspective when formulating economic policies.

Not all processes of evolution and change are based entirely on 'random' selective processes. In reality, a complex mosaic of mechanisms probably plays a role in determining the evolution of social and environmental systems and their interdependence. While stochastic selective processes, as in evolutionary biology, can and do play a significant role in social change, it is necessary to identify those social phenomena to which such processes are most applicable, explain exactly how these selection processes operate and be aware that mechanisms other than selective stochastic processes may play a role. While Norgaard's contribution helps to sensitize readers to a coevolutionary perspective, it is disappointing in not going much beyond this in providing an operational framework.

Partial evolutionary models have been explored in economics but little attention has been given to coevolutionary models. For example, Nelson and Winter [3] used a selective model based on profit (as an indicator of fitness) to explain the emergence of industry structures. However, it was left to Nelson [4] to develop more completely a theory of industrial evolution, even though he does not develop a coevolutionary theory. Elements of evolutionary industrial theory also are present in some of the works of Schumpeter [5].

Schumpeter's work suggests that the evolution of capitalist economics will eventually be *dominated* by oligopolies and monopolies. These large firms through their superior abilities in relation to innovation, technical change and marketing (involving in most cases the use of firm-specific assets which motivates them to become multinationals) eventually become, in the author's view, an extremely strong force for expanding the production of private economic goods (that is, marketable commodities as opposed to public or collective goods). They therefore accelerate the conversion of natural/environmental resources into man-made commodities and so may threaten economic and ecological sustainability at an earlier time than otherwise [6,7]. They do this by accelerating the depletion of the natural resource stock mainly by economic processes of transformation [8]. In addition, acting in their own self-interest, large corporations may attempt politically to reduce all those activities of the state which limit their ability to transform natural resources into marketable commodities. For this reason, they are likely to be supportive of neoliberal policies.

If the evolutionary process suggested by Schumpeter [5] is extended in its application, agriculture also becomes transformed from a socioeconomic point of view as economic development occurs. Its development is increasingly dominated by large industrial suppliers of marketed inputs for agriculture, many of these large multinational companies. In addition, agriculturalists may increasingly find, (given the changing marketing chain in agricultural products), that relatively speaking their product is sold to large companies, so that agriculturalists become ever smaller participants in determining the development of their own industry. In fact, if this scenario is correct, the business of farmers can be expected to be increasingly dominated as time passes by the interest of major agribusinesses not directly involved in farming but dependent on selling products (mostly marketed inputs) to agriculturalists, and by large intermediary companies purchasing their products. Casual observation appears to support this theory. Some possible coevolutionary consequences of this trend will be outlined later. There is another evolutionary factor in the recent economic literature worthy of attention because it has several coevolutionary consequences. Although Demsetz [9] was one of the first economists to demonstrate that the nature of property rights depends significantly on economic factors, North [10] developed the concept in an historical context. To the extent that economic development increases the economic value of resources used for private purposes and fosters techniques, which reduce the cost of exclusion from private property, private ownership of resources is increasingly liable to displace open-access communal control of resources. Thus, with economic development, we can predict that private ownership and management of natural resources is likely to grow in relative importance. To the extent that extension of markets promotes economic development and the economic significance of marketed commodities, they reinforce this trend. Private ownership stimulates private investment and is likely to accelerate the conversion of natural areas to man-made purposes as pointed out, for example, by Swanson [11]. Natural ecosystems are increasingly modified and in some cases destroyed and entirely replaced to facilitate the production of private and marketable commodities. Biological evolution becomes increasingly dominated and manipulated by human beings to select species and varieties with clear shorter-term economic value for human beings in terms of their production of private commodities. Thus domesticated animals and cultivated plants have increasingly been influenced in their evolution and selection by human beings and this in turn has impacted on natural ecosystems. Coevolution has undoubtedly been occurring as noted for example by Swanson [11]. In this regard however two sustainability problems have emerged or are emerging:

- evolutionary farming practices have reduced genetic diversity and pose a threat to long-term evolutionary possibilities by reducing future options; and
- insufficient weight has been put on the conservation of environmental resources which are not marketable but which have high public value and/or inadequate account has been taken of environmental externalities.

The first factor may be a threat to sustainable development. The second results in an inefficient economic system in satisfying human wants given that some non-marketed commodities are valued. The market system (partly because of its unavoidable gaps, gaps which cannot all be economically filled) is a considerable threat to the conservation of biological diversity. Furthermore, those who see biological diversity as having merit in itself often find that the market system does not represent their values.

Note that market systems are not alone in the above consequences as development occurs – centrally planned economies with an emphasis on material production and with a strong belief in the possibilities of social and technological engineering can (and have had) similar results.

In practice as the economic growth or development process has taken its toll on natural areas, many governments have eventually intervened to protect the last remnants of natural ecosystems by establishing protected areas under state control. In the absence of such intervention, the process of conversion would no doubt continue further.

A rough sketch of the coevolutionary process is given in Figure 2. In the early stages of human societies, most land resources are communal or open-access property but as economic growth proceeds, private or in some cases state property comes to dominate land ownership. As a result, natural ecosystems are increasingly threatened and in fact virtually all might disappear in the absence of special government or state intervention to protect them. While private ownership may effectively conserve some natural resources, it will only do so to the extent that this is profitable, and profitability depends on the marketability of commodities produced by those natural resources.

In *Development Betrayed*, Noorgaad [2] suggests that Western cultural imperialism or dominance has unfortunate economic and ecological consequences when it impinges on other societies. However, cultural imperialism is not necessarily limited to Western countries. Non-western cultures have sometimes dominated other cultures, e.g. Chinese culture in parts of Asia. Nevertheless, it is clear that the imposition of foreign cultural practices on recipient communities can have unfortunate consequences for resource conservation and management. European colonial powers, for example, gave little recognition to communal and open-access property in their colonies, and new nation states established at the end of colonial rule seem to have done likewise after their independence [12]. This has often resulted in considerable economic hardship for local communities and has eroded cultural mechanisms supporting conservation of natural resources [13]. Externally imposed social change, circumventing naturally evolving social change, can result in many unforeseen adverse consequences for environmental conservation and the welfare of local communities.

Figure 2 Alienation of natural resources by increasing private ownership or by state ownership is shown as threatening the conservation of natural ecosystems with the passage of time

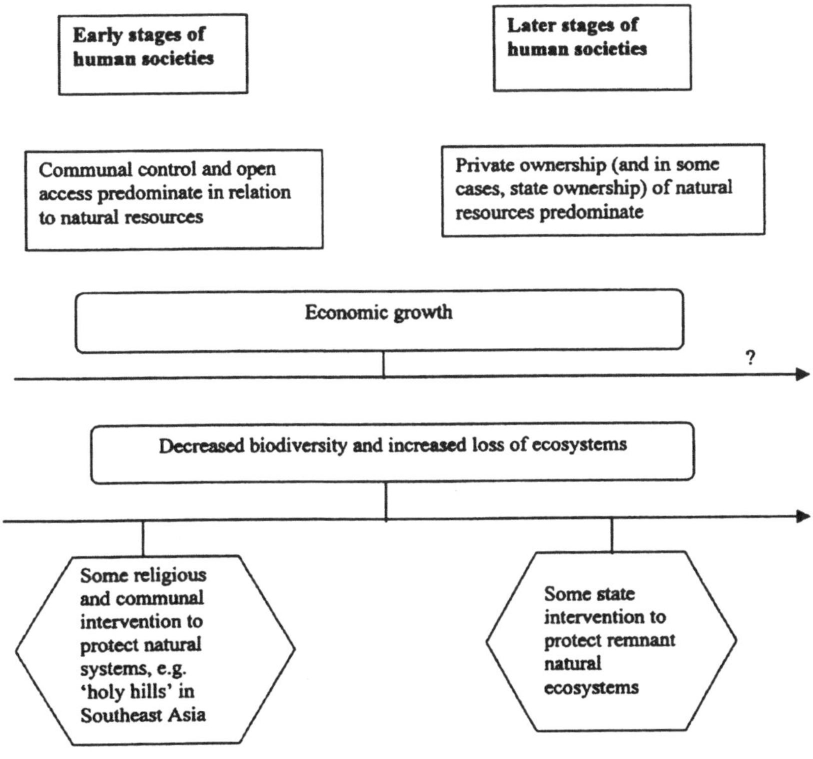

3 Economic globalization, market-making and structural adjustment policies from a coevolutionary perspective

Different local communities are frequently in differing states of coevolution and not all are able to achieve the same coevolutionary paths, partly because of different resource and cultural endowments. Consequently, a form of social organization which may be appropriate to the evolutionary stage reached by a more developed economy or society may be inappropriate to a less developed one. The rapid introduction of market systems characteristic of Western societies and their associated technologies to lower-income non-Western communities may cause considerable social disruption and sever their previous relatively harmonious relationships with their environments.

Rapid exposure to structural adjustment policies and economic globalization often destabilizes slowly evolving social processes and may do more harm than good to some communities, which have not had sufficient time to adjust their institutions and culture to such variations. The experiences of the Russian Federation in economic transition may provide an example. In many developing countries where cash cropping and market forces have been replacing subsistence agriculture, the economic situation of rural women and children has suffered [14–16]. In such societies women are responsible for and have control over food produced for subsistence purposes, but men take control of cash from commercial cropping and consequently rural women and children are often economically deprived when market and cash-based economic activities are promoted.

Increased commercial possibilities also accelerate deforestation in some developed countries. This applies both to the harvesting of timber for export and the clearing of land for commercial agricultural crops. For example, Wibowo *et al.* [17] found that one of the main reasons for the illegal clearing of Kerinci National Park in Sumatra, Indonesia, was for the purpose of growing cinnamon to supply the export market. Cinnamon growing provided a high rate of return on the investment cinnamon-growers had put into forest clearing and the establishment of cinnamon trees. Using cash income from their initial venture as finance, cinnamon-growers then engaged in further forest-clearing to expand their cinnamon production. Economic globalization (extension of markets) reduces the extent to which the economic fortunes of local communities depend on their local environment. It is likely to weaken feedback mechanisms for keeping social and ecological systems in balance. Dasmann, as discussed by Klee ([18], described this as the transformation of individuals from ecosystem people to biosphere people. Processes of market extension and economic globalization weaken the bonds between mankind and nature and impersonalize these relationships; these processes became a source of the alienation of man from nature [6, Ch.2]. Rapid response to such processes, with little time for transitional adjustment in the structure of society, can result in a severe imbalance between the economic activities of mankind and the preservation of natural ecosystems.

In terms of coevolutionary relationships, evolution of local communities from those involving ecosystem dependent people to globalized ones involving 'biosphere' people may imply the situation illustrated in Figure 3. Communities alter from those making weak demands on the resources of natural ecosystems and experiencing strong feedback from changes in natural systems to communities making strong demands on natural ecosystems and receiving weakened feedback from variations in natural systems. Consequently the risk to economic and ecological sustainability grows as economic growth and globalization proceed. International cooperation may be required to avert economic and ecological disaster once global market-directed economic systems emerge.

Nevertheless, it would be folly to believe that all traditional patterns of economic activity are sustainable. For example, slash-and-burn agriculture (swidden agriculture) while sustainable if long fallows exist between burning and cultivation, can become unsustainable if fallows become increasingly shortened under the pressure of population increases and desires for greater consumption, especially desire for cash to buy marketed commodities to supplement subsistence income. But in some hilly areas where shifting agriculture is still practiced, no economically viable alternatives to shifting agriculture may exist. If there is an alternative, transition to the alternative is sometimes a slow process, as experience in Mizoram, northeastern India indicates [19]. Change to settled agriculture requires communal property to become private property and in general a variation in the structure and cultures of local communities. Such change is not easy to engineer, can cause considerable social suffering and therefore must be sensitively considered in policy proposals. The process of social change as well as its final purpose is important from a welfare point of view – the ends do not necessarily justify the means.

Figure 3 With increasing globalization, feedback mechanisms between economic activity and natural resource systems weaken at a time when demand on these resources grows. This poses risks for ecological and economic sustainability.

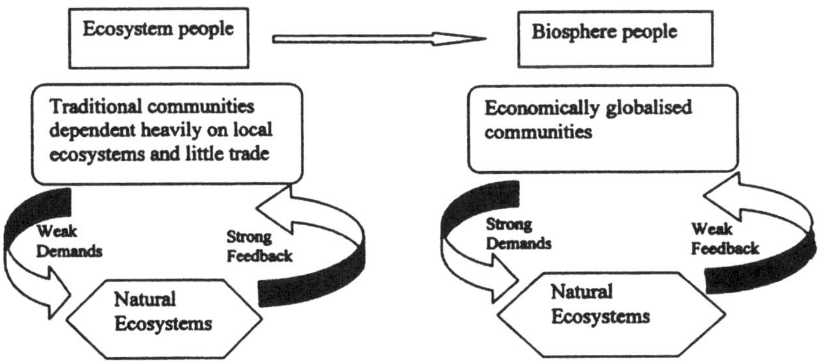

4 Globalization, technological change and dependence of agriculture on external inputs

As economic growth has proceeded, agriculture has become increasingly dependent on inputs external to the farm, that is on marketed inputs. This reflects a market-based bias in processes of economic development in which market systems become increasingly dominant. Such systems encourage market-based transactions because markets provide the main channels through which profits and incomes can be earned. Bias in favour of market-based economic activity partly reflects the efficiency of the market system in meeting wants, e.g. by utilizing comparative advantages in production, but in the longer term when combined with the rise of oligopolistic corporations such systems exhibit degenerative economic and ecological features.

Large oligopolistic firms usually arise because they have firm-specific assets such as knowledge and techniques, which give them an economic advantage over their rivals. These economic advantages may exist in relation to the techniques of their production, the special attributes or technologies embodied in their products, or occur because of their superior marketing skills or techniques, or because of all of these factors. By superior marketing methods and technological change, oligopolies relentlessly try to increase their volume of sales, thereby in the case of farmers, inducing them to purchase more of the products of oligopolistic suppliers. These external farm inputs may be substituted for internal inputs by farmers or be a net addition to their total inputs, or both. In most cases, where commercial farming develops both impacts are present. Consequently, weak (ecological) sustainability conditions grow in their relative importance in agriculture.

As indicated by Schumpeter, oligopolistic capitalism thrives on technological progress and innovation. But given the profit motive, all efforts in this direction are intended to increase the sale of private commodities, which in the case being considered here are sales of external inputs to farmers. This process in the longer term coupled with marketing promotion, further increases the dependence of agriculturalists on external inputs. Thus agriculture becomes increasingly commercialized, even industrialized, as a result of the forces generated by large suppliers of agricultural inputs, aided by competitive pressures within agriculture itself and the strengthening of profit-motives amongst commercial farmers. This process usually results in farms increasing in average size and in a radical change in the structure of local communities and their cultures. Social systems undergo radical change. Local communities can become relatively depersonalized and social alienation of individuals may increasingly occur, as commercial gain becomes the sole arbiter of activity and worth. Thus, rapid economic changes driven by forces external to local communities may undermine communal social stability and generate individual psychological stress and neurosis. In the oligopolistically-dominated market system, the following impacts are likely:

- Technological change (and associated economic change) may get severely out of balance with social systems. It is driven primarily by forces external to local communities, unlike in earlier times. Such technological change takes no account of its disruption to the 'harmony' of local communities.
- In a globalized world (and especially since many of the leading oligopolistic players are multinational), technological and economic change spreads rapidly. Thus trial-and-error mechanisms and precautionary measures may not be used as often as in the past. This may pose increasing threats to the maintenance of natural ecosystems as well as to communal life on a global scale.
- Research and development in this system tends to be biased towards the discovery of saleable private commodities (or improvements in these) with relative neglect of R&D relating to non-marketed commodities.
- Those dependent on markets for their economic gain are likely to agitate politically in favour of the extension of market mechanisms. In the longer term, this is likely to be disadvantageous to the provision of collective and public goods. Imbalance between social and ecological systems becomes increasingly likely under the above conditions.
- Weak rather than strong conditions for economic sustainability are promoted.

The interactions involved in the above scenario are complex, but this does lessen the ecological and social risks stemming from these developments. Figure 4 provides a sketch of the envisaged pattern of these changes in a coevolutionary context. Evolutionary developments are explained in its caption.

The above also suggests that agricultural development, the nature of local communities and society generally may be increasingly determined by the results of scientific and technical experts employed by large oligopolistic corporations many of which are multinational in character. The use of new technologies, such as genetic engineering of seeds, apart from possibly having an adverse impact on natural ecosystems, can also be expected to have societal impacts. Agriculturalists can be expected to become more dependent on corporations which have patents or similar rights to genetically-modified seeds or commodities. One or more companies could dominate the development of a whole industry , as demonstrated by Monsanto in relation to soyabean production [20,21], with implications for both developed and less developed countries. Such companies will also be anxious to sell their product at the earliest possible time in order to recoup development costs. Therefore, there is always a risk that 'premature' release will occur and irreversible global ecological damage may be done before environmental or health problems are observed from use of such products. One may also anticipate continued loss of biological diversity, as occurred with 'green revolution' crops, due to displacement of traditional varieties and intensification of agriculture as a consequence of the development of biotechnology. How to control such developments in a global setting is a major challenge for governance, especially since the present global thrust is towards the widespread acceptance of the global intellectual rights of corporations. Without an effective system of global government, it may be difficult (given the political predominance of neoliberal thought) to monitor and control such technological developments in the public interest.

Figure 4 Scenario in which increasing risks to ecosystems and biodiversity occur with the development of industrial/commercial agriculture under the 'patronage' of growing oligopolistic capitalism. At the same time social systems are likely to come under increasing tension or stress as a result of rapid technological and economic variations driven by forces largely external to local communities.

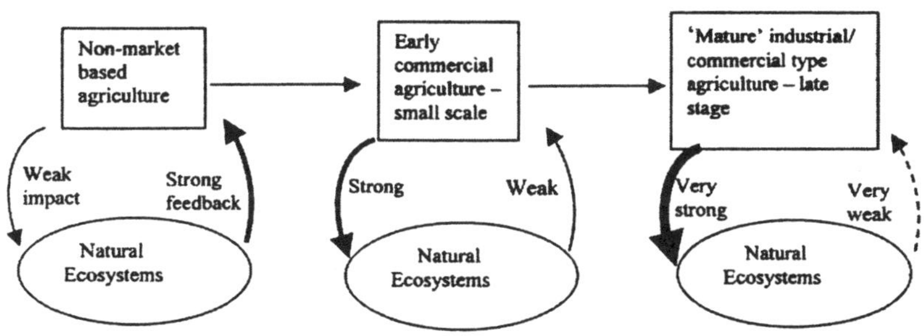

5 Conclusions

There is as yet no settled co-evolutionary theory predicting variations in social and ecological systems, nor in relation to the development of agricultural systems in both their social and ecological dimensions. In that respect, however, it is possible to have sympathy with Norgaard's view that if there was a single settled theory, it would probably be inadequate; a more pluralistic approach to social and ecological science seems desirable. Nevertheless, evolutionary and especially co-evolutionary approaches to considering society's developmental issues and to assessing its policies are of considerable value. They transcend static and mechanistic modes of thinking, which dominated economic thought in the 20th Century and which provide little or no insights into 'states of becoming', the essence of developmental concerns. Furthermore, neoclassical economic thought has impoverished economic thought by its failure to take a holistic view of development and to allow for pluralism and social diversity of communities as well as diversity of individuals within communities. This paper illustrates how a coevolutionary approach, in contrast, can provide important insights into major development issues of current concern to agricultural communities.

References

1 Hodgson, G.M. (1993) *Economics and Evolution*, Polity Press, Cambridge.

2 Norgaard, R.B. (1994) *Development Betrayed*, Routledge, London.

3 Nelson, R. and Winter, S.G. (1983) *An Evolutionary Theory of Economic Change*, Harvard University Press, Cambridge, MA.

4 Nelson, R. (1987) *Understanding Technological Change as an Evolutionary Process*, North-Holland, Amsterdam.

5 Schumpeter, J.A. (1942) *Capitalism, Socialism and Democracy*, 2nd edn., Harper Butters, New York.

6 Tisdell, C.A. (1990) *Natural Resources, Growth and Development*, Praeger, Westenport, CT.

7 Tisdell, C.A. (1999) *Biodiversity, Conservation and Sustainable Development*, Edward Elgar, Cheltenham, UK.

8 Tisdell, C.A. (1999) 'Conditions for sustainable development: weak and strong'. In A.K. Dragun and C.A. Tisdell (eds.), *Sustainable Agriculture and Environment*, Edward Elgar, Cheltenham, UK.

9 Demsetz, H. (1968) 'The cost of transacting', *Quarterly Journal of Economics*, Vol. 82, pp.33-53.

10 North, D.C. (1981) *Structure and Change in Economic History*, Norton, New York.

11 Swanson, T. (1994) *The International Regulation of Estimation*, New York University Press, New York.

12 Tisdell, C.A. and Roy, K. (1997) 'Good governance, property rights and sustainable resource-use', *The South African Journal of Economics*, Vol. 65, pp.28-43.

13 Gadgil, M. and Iyer, P. (1989) 'On the diversification of common property resource use by Indian society'. in F. Barlett (ed.) *Common Property Resources: Ecology and Community-based Sustainable Development*, Belhaven Press, London, pp.240-255.

14 Gross, D.R. and Underwood, B.A. (1971) 'Technological change and calorie cost: social agriculture in north-eastern Brazil', *American Anthropologist*, Vol. 73, pp.725-740.

15 von Braun, J. and Kennedy, E. (1986) 'Commercialisation of subsistence agriculture: income and nutritional effects in developing countries', *Working Paper on Commercialisation of Agriculture and Nutrition No 1*, International Food Research Institution, Washington DC.

16 Kennedy, E. and Oniang'o, R. (1990) 'Health and nutrition effects of sugarcane production in south-western Kenya', *Food and Nutrition Bulletin*, Vol. 12, No. 4, pp.261-267.

17 Wibowo, D.H., Tisdell, C.A. and Byron, R.N. (1997) 'Deforestation and capital accumulation: lessons from the Kevinai-Sabatt National Park, Indonesia', *Asia Pacific Journal on Environment and Development*, Vol. 4, No.1, pp.11-28.

18 Klee, G.A. (1980) *World Systems of Traditional Resource Management*, Edward Arnold, London.

19 Tisdell, C.A. (1999) 'Co-evolution in Asia: markets and globalisation'. In A.K. Dragun and C.A. Tisdell (eds.) *Sustainable Agriculture and the Environment*, Edward Elgar, Cheltenham, UK.

20 Enriquez, J. (1998) 'Genomics and the World's economy', *Science*, Vol. 281, pp.925-926.

21 Xue, D. and Tisdell, C.A. (2000) 'Safety and socio-economic issues raised by modern biotechnology', *International Journal of Social Economics* (in press).

PART IV

ENVIRONMENTAL ISSUES IN AUSTRALIA, ASIA AND TRANSITIONAL ECONOMIES

[20]

The Environment and Sustainable Development in the Asia–Pacific: Views and Policies

Clem Tisdell*

Policies in relation to the environment and sustainable development in the Asia–Pacific need to be related to the international debate about such issues. This article surveys the literature on the environmental problems to which economic development is giving rise. Attention is paid to urbanisation, agriculture, aquaculture, mining, resource depletion, energy supplies and air quality, and to Asian policy responses to environmental change and calls for sustainable development.

Introduction

The world is becoming more interdependent and not only in its economic and environmental dimensions. New views and policy approaches to development seem to sweep the world. The United Nations Conference on Environment and Development (UNCED) held in Rio de Janeiro in 1992 is an example. It proclaimed sustainable development as an important objective, emphasising the seriousness of a number of global environmental issues, such as greenhouse gas emissions and loss of biological diversity.

This paper concentrates on the environment and sustainable development in East Asia. Because the Asian-Pacific region stretches over a wide geographical area, the coverage of this paper is necessarily selective. Only incidental consideration will be given to water resources because these have been the subject of an earlier review in *Asian-Pacific Economic Literature* (Rosegrant and Meinzen-Dick 1996) and to forestry and fisheries for the same reason (Byron and Waugh 1988).

Many of the environmental and sustainability problems of the Asia–Pacific (Brookfield 1993) are of a global nature and involve issues about income distribution (Ramani et al. 1992). One cannot expect those in low-income countries in the Asia–Pacific to sacrifice their own economic welfare by conserving resources for the benefit of the rest of the world, especially to benefit those in high-income countries. Dealing with environmental problems of a global nature will require international co-operation.

Sectoral change in the Asia–Pacific, urbanisation and urban industry

Sixty years ago, Colin Clark (1940) observed that as economies develop the relative importance of their economic sectors changes. In low-income countries, agriculture predominates in terms of employment and contribution to GDP and other primary industries can be important. As income levels rise, the relative economic contribution of the agricultural sector declines and manufacturing becomes the dominant sector. At still higher income levels, service industries become the

* Professor of Economics, The University of Queensland, Brisbane.

Table 1
Labour force distribution in selected East Asia economies

Country	Percentage of labour force in								
	Agriculture			Industry			Services		
	1960	1985–88	1990	1960	1985–88	1990	1960	1985–88	1990
China	83	73.7	72	6	13.6	15	10	12.7	13
Indonesia	75	54.4	55	8	8.0	14	18	37.6	31
Korea	61	19.0	18	10	27.4	35	28	53.6	47
Lao, PDR	82	75.7	78	4	7.0	6	14	17.2	16
Malaysia	63	41.6	27	12	19.1	23	25	39.3	50
Philippines	64	43.4	46	14	9.7	15	22	46.9	39
Thailand	84	72.4	64	4	5.9	14	12	21.7	22
Vietnam	82	67.5	71	5	11.8	14	14	20.7	15

Source: Based on UNDP 1991, 1996.

Table 2
Structure of production in selected East Asian economies

Country	Distribution of GDP (%)											
	Agriculture			Industry			Manufacturing			Services		
	1970	1980	1994	1970	1980	1994	1970	1980	1994	1970	1980	1994
China	34	30	21	38	49	47	30	41	37	28	21	32
Indonesia	45	24	17	19	42	41	10	13	24	36	34	42
Korea	25	15	7	29	40	43	21	29	29	46	45	50
Lao, PDR	..	..	51	..	..	18	..	..	13	..	..	31
Malaysia	29	22	14	25	38	43	12	21	32	46	40	42
Philippines	30	25	22	32	39	33	25	26	23	39	36	45
Thailand	26	23	10	25	29	39	16	22	29	49	48	50
Vietnam	..	..	28	..	..	30	..	..	22	..	..	43

Source: Based on World Bank 1995, 1996.

largest sector. Such trends are apparent in East Asian countries. From Table 1, the decline in the percentage of the labour force employed in agriculture in East Asian countries is apparent. Structural change in terms of the composition of production is even more marked (see Table 2).

Both manufacturing and tertiary industries are predominantly located in urban areas (cf. Adachi 1996). Consequently, countries experiencing a high rate of economic growth are likely to experience rapid urbanisation. East Asia is a prime example (Jones 1991).

Both the development of new industries, as part of this sectoral change, and the geographical relocation of populations have significant environmental consequences and create new challenges for Asia and for the sustainability of its rapid economic growth. New and concentrated forms of pollution are generated in urban areas because of increasing human wastes (sewage and garbage). New industries produce air pollution and release noxious effluents; they often produce hazardous solid and other wastes and endanger the supply of safe drinking water. Considerable human effort is required to deal with these environmental changes since natural ecosystems are unable to cope with them as well as when population is scattered and industry under-developed. Without proper public authority attention to these matters, environmentally related ill health is liable to

Table 3
Urbanisation in Asia

	Urban population (% of total)		Average annual urban population change (%)
	1965	1995	1965–95
East Asia			
China	18.2	30.3	3.5
Indonesia	15.8	32.5	4.6
Philippines	31.6	45.7	3.9
Thailand	12.9	25.4	4.5
South Asia			
Bangladesh	6.2	19.5	6.7
India	18.8	26.8	3.3
Pakistan	23.5	34.7	4.2
Sri Lanka	19.9	22.4	2.1
Asia	22.2	34.0	3.5
Europe	63.8	75.0	1.0
World	35.5	45.2	2.7

Source: Based on World Resources Institute et al. 1994: Table 17.2.

Table 4
Access of urban population to safe drinking water and sanitation in Asia, 1980 and 1990 (%)

	Safe drinking water		Sanitation	
	1980	1990	1980	1990
East Asia				
China	..	72	..	100
Indonesia	35	35	29	79
Philippines	65	93	81	79
South Asia				
Bangladesh	26	39	21	40
India	73	77	27	44
Pakistan	72	82	42	53
Sri Lanka	65	80	80	68

Source: Based on World Bank 1994b: Table A.

encroach upon and even outweigh the benefits to human welfare of economic growth. It is unlikely to be economic to eliminate all diseases related to new urban environments, particularly in the early stages of development. But this is no excuse for complacency. It has to be recognised that correction of environmental externalities in large urban areas cannot be left entirely to free market forces.

In most Asian countries the percentage of the population provided with safe drinking water and with sanitation is rising (Table 4). This means of course that the absolute numbers provided with such commodities have increased greatly, given the rapid rate of urbanisation. There are, however, several countries in which provision of sanitation has failed to keep pace with rising urban populations (for example, Sri Lanka and the Philippines) and others in which safe water supplies have barely kept pace with the growth in urban population (for example, Indonesia). The percentage of urban residents supplied with safe drinking water in Indonesia is only 35 per cent (World Bank 1994b: Table A) and there is some doubt about the safety of urban water for drinking elsewhere. Cholera outbreaks from urban water supplies still occur in Manila. Much of its water is supplied from underground aquifers, many of which are often polluted with chlorine compounds and other carcinogenic agents. The latter problem is not confined to the least developed countries in Asia but is also reported from Japan. In many low-income Asian cities water supplies are limited; long queues form for supplies even in better-off suburbs, such as Salt Lake City, a suburb of Calcutta. Those living in shanty towns may have little or no supplies of reticulated water.

One of the requirements for sustainable development of cities and urban areas is trade. They obviously cannot be self-sufficient (cf. Jones 1991). Thus, with growing urbanisation, one can expect growing political support for freer trade, both within countries and internationally, as now appears to be occurring in the Asian-Pacific region with growing support for APEC.

Another important aspect of growing urbanisation is rising demand for infrastructure within a country—better roads, rail and air communications and shipping, expansion of telecommunications, provision of waterworks including dams, heightened demand for electricity and other forms of easily transferable energy and so on. Investment in infrastructure in Asia is proceeding rapidly, partly as a result of urbanisation and the extension of the market system. Adequate infrastructure is essential to urban incomes and welfare.

Many larger cities in Asia suffer from serious transportation problems. These not only include air pollution from motor vehicles (a serious problem in Bangkok and Jakarta, for example, and an increasing problem in China's major cities), but also serious traffic congestion which imposes immense economic costs. In many countries, forward planning of transportation infrastructure is limited, and politicians appear to wait until the traffic problem becomes intolerable. Taipei has only recently installed an underground railway system. Prior to its installation, severe traffic delays were common. Most of the large and growing cities in Asia, such as Bangkok, Jakarta and Manila, lack adequate forms of mass transit.

Urban areas and their associated populations and industries generate many wastes. Sewage affects water quality if not adequately treated. Heavy metals and chemicals from industry may pollute water bodies with serious health consequences for communities downstream. Solid wastes can also directly and indirectly be a source of such problems unless dealt with in an environmentally careful manner. Kaosa-ard et al. (1995) report on pollution problems in mainland Southeast Asia. In Cambodia, "solid waste and wastewater management is a serious concern in densely populated urban areas, particularly Phnom Penh" (Kaosa-ard et al. 1995) which has over a million inhabitants. Half a ton of solid waste per capita is produced in Phnom Penh, and the sewerage system is in complete disrepair. In Laos, no sanitation systems exist as yet and ground water is being seriously contaminated by wastewater in Vientiane and other urban areas. Water pollution is also serious in Vietnam. In Hanoi and many other urban areas in Vietnam, untreated sewage is dumped directly into ponds and canals. Even Thailand, the highest income country in Southeast Asia, has very serious water pollution problems, and they are getting worse. Eighteen of Thailand's 43 major rivers were found to be contaminated with heavy metals in 1989: 25 rivers were contaminated in 1991. Furthermore, the lower section of the Chao Phraya river has a dissolved oxygen level of zero. Consequently it cannot support aerobic (oxygen-using) organisms and is in a bad ecological state. Wastewater treatment in Bangkok has only recently commenced and is still on a small scale. Similar problems are reported in tourist towns such as Phuket and Pattaya (Kaosa-ard et al. 1995:35).

Agriculture, aquaculture and the environment

Agriculture affects the natural environment in two ways, through extension to land previously unused and through intensification of agriculture on land already in use. In low-income countries in Asia both types of effect have occurred. A typical pattern is that in the early stages of development both changes occur but, when incomes reach higher levels, agriculture is often abandoned on marginal areas, which revert to forest or natural vegetation. This has occurred in Japan and appears to be in process in South Korea. Since higher incomes can be earned in other sectors of the economy and living conditions are better in urban areas the young often refuse to carry on the primary activities of their parents and marginal farming areas gradually decline in population.

But in Asia as a whole, the area used for agriculture has increased in recent years (both in the case of cropland and permanent pastures for grazing), and cropping has intensified. The rate of multiple cropping has risen significantly with expansion of irrigation, improved varieties of crops with shorter maturity periods, greater mechanisation of ploughing (which has accelerated cultivation—in Thailand two-wheeled tractors have almost completely replaced buffaloes for ploughing purposes) and increased use of chemical fertilisers and pesticides.

All these changes can have adverse environmental consequences. Among them are acidification of the soil, damage to soil

Table 5

Land use in selected Asian countries, for Asia, Europe and the world as a whole— percentage change in area, 1979–91

	Cropland	Permanent pasture	Forest and woodland	Other	Forest as % of total area
East Asia					
China	-4.0	19.9	-6.5	-14.7	13.6
Indonesia	12.3	-1.5	-6.6	17.4	60.6
Philippines	2.5	24.0	-16.9	19.5	34.7
Thailand	25.5	29.7	-14.3	-16.1	27.8
South Asia					
Bangladesh	2.1	-	-13.4	9.7	14.6
India	0.7	-2.0	-0.7	-1.0	22.5
Pakistan	4.0	-	19.7	-2.8	4.4
Sri Lanka	1.5	-	17.9	-14.3	32.1
Asia	1.3	9.5	-4.9	-4.6	..
Europe	-1.8	-3.7	1.1	6.2	..
World	1.8	2.4	-7.8	5.5	..

Source: Based on World Resources Institute, UNEP and UNDP, 1994, Table 17.1.

microbes, deterioration in soil structure partly due to reduced humus levels in the soil, and depletion of some mineral and trace elements. Frequently crop yields can be sustained only by raising applications of chemical fertilisers and of pesticides to counter increasing resistance. Because of such problems, it seems that yields of green revolution rice varieties have started to decline (Pingali et al. 1990; Pingali and Rosegrant 1994; Alauddin and Tisdell 1991:Ch. 12) and doubts have been raised about the long-term economic sustainability of modern agricultural technologies (Conway 1985, 1987). Some of these technologies, moreover, have unfavourable externalities. For instance, high use of chemical fertilisers and frequent cultivation of the soil raises nitrate and phosphorus levels in water bodies. This encourages weed and algal growth, reduces the dissolved oxygen content of the water and accelerates eutrophication, the process by which water bodies become choked with vegetation and filled with sediment.

Adverse environmental consequences may also result from the infrastructure investment required by agricultural developments. The building of irrigation dams can destroy wildlife habitat and cause loss of agricultural land owing to flooding. The question of adequate compensation for those whose lands have been flooded has been a thorny point in Asia, especially since many such dams are located in remote areas inhabited by minority groups. In addition, such dams can favour disease carriers such as species of snails and mosquitoes.

The success of modern commercial agriculture depends upon good transport and communications, both for access to off-farm inputs, such as certified seed varieties, chemical fertilisers, pesticides, motor fuels and/or electricity, and for economical marketing of farm produce. Urban and rural dwellers have common interests in good roads. The same applies to dams which supply water to both urban and rural communities and may also be a source of hydro-electricity for both. The upsurge in investment in infrastructure in Asia therefore is understandable, but each large investment in infrastructure needs to be carefully assessed from an environmental point of view.

The increase in total area used for agriculture in Asia has significantly contributed to loss of natural vegetation cover and has created severe environmental problems on steeply sloping land where appropriate technologies have not been adopted. Soil erosion is a major problem on such land, on Java and elsewhere. It results in reduced yields and can eventually make farming of the affected land uneconomic. Offsite it results in siltation of dams and waterways. As more rivers and streams are stripped of natural vegetation, flash-flooding is facilitated. Streams and rivers become more variable in their seasonal waterflows. Some rivers and streams may stop running in the dry season. Social conflict between dwellers of the uplands and of the plains can arise over such issues, as has happened in Thailand.

There is a widespread belief that loss of biodiversity could result in unsustainable development and reduced welfare

Large portions of the hilly and mountainous areas of Asia are cultivated by various types of shifting slash-and-burn. While this can be a very economical and environmentally attractive system of agriculture when population densities are low (Ramakrishnan 1992), it is not sustainable at high population densities and for high income aspirations. For both reasons the cultivation cycle for this type of agriculture contracts with economic development, shortening the fallow period in which natural vegetation normally regenerates. The fertility of the cultivated land therefore falls and a greater area of cultivated land is exposed to the elements at any one time, thus increasing soil erosion and runoff of water. The economic sustainability of the system declines and adverse environmental spillovers increase. Replacing shifting cultivation by other land-use systems is by no means easy. The alternatives must be economic and reasonably sustainable. In addition, existing social customs and systems of communal property can constitute major barriers. It is difficult to alter socially based systems of property rights. In some parts of Asia, for example, in Mizoram in India, a cautious start has begun on converting some communal agricultural land into private property (Lianzela 1995).

Agricultural changes in Asia affect biological diversity. As Swanson (1994) points out, the conversion of natural habitats to agricultural use is a major source of biodiversity loss world wide. Increases in the intensity of cultivation, the shortening of cultivation cycles in shifting agriculture and the encroachment of agriculture on forested land and 'wasteland'—all of these are likely to cause biological loss. In addition, variety in cultivated crops and domesticated species is declining in Asia as they are replaced by fewer 'improved' varieties.

While there is a widespread belief that loss of biodiversity could result in unsustainable development and reduced welfare, Arndt (1990) and Beckerman (1995) are sceptical of many of the claims made in this regard. They are unconvinced that indiscriminate biodiversity is important and agree with Galbraith that it is a luxury good of the affluent middle class.

It is often suggested that Asia cannot afford to return to its traditional farming. Traditional sustainable agriculture would yield insufficient food to feed the population and expose its people to famines in years of drought. According to Koh (1992:v–vi), "many tropical countries still have a food deficit and need to increase production as their primary concern (cf. Findlay 1997). Sustainability must be a secondary consideration. Organic produce can command a very high price in industrialised countries where there are a large number of affluent urban consumers. In less industrialised countries with lower incomes, the need is for an adequate supply of cheap food which the consumer can afford". Yet there have been occasions in Asia, for instance in China under Mao, where modern agricultural practices inappropriately applied have not only resulted in reduced sustainability, but have actually reduced agricultural production in the short term (cf. Glaeser 1995:Ch. 5).

Aquaculture has many similarities to agriculture. Asia has a long established aquaculture industry, which acts as a major source of animal protein and is the world's major producer of aquaculture products. The species used have changed over the years. Recently prawn or shrimp culture has developed (often the prawns are for export) and tilapia fish have been introduced from Africa into the Philippines and other Asian-Pacific countries. These aquacultures may have adverse environmental consequences. In Taiwan, shrimp cultivation has led to land-subsidence as underground water has been withdrawn to create (mixed with saline water) brackish water for cultivation of prawns. This subsidence has damaged buildings and allowed the sea to intrude onto farm land. In other parts of Asia, aquaculture of shrimp has resulted in the removal of mangroves and the destruction of wetlands with adverse economic and environmental consequences (Alauddin and Hamid 1996).

Conversely, increasing water pollution in Asia poses a threat to aquaculture. Heavy metals in lakes and rivers increase human health risks from fish and molluscs raised in such water. Pollution of water by chemicals can kill or stunt fish and so on. Such problems are increasing, at a time when Asia's fishery harvests are declining because the sustainable catch has been exceeded in several areas (such as the Northwest Pacific).

Mining, resource depletion and the environment

Modern economies rely heavily on mineral resources to support production and maintain standards of living. Fossil fuels such as coal, oil and natural gas are the major source of their energy supply and minerals provide materials for the manufacturing industry. Minerals are essential to our way of life, but when put to economic use they are non-renewable assets. Although some minerals can be recycled, all are subject to entropy in use (Georgescu-Roegen 1971) and some, such as fuels used for combustion, permit virtually no recycling. This raises sustainability questions. In addition, the extraction and processing of minerals and their use can be a significant source of adverse environmental spillovers.

A number of writers (Repetto et al. 1989, El Serafy 1989) have pointed out that national accounts have deficiencies because they fail to take into account the diminution of stocks of natural resources as a result of their use. Consequently, estimates of net national product give an inflated impression of national welfare because, if natural resource stocks are being depleted, current levels of welfare may not be sustained. Furthermore, current accounting practice means that natural resource stocks are treated in a different way to man-made assets. The latter are depreciated in order to obtain estimates of net national product, but no similar allowance is made for any decline in natural resource stocks.

It has been argued that natural resource accounting or 'green' accounting should be adopted or at least satellite accounts should be produced that allow for depletion. It is not possible to debate the merits and drawbacks of this proposal here. However, much depends on the purpose of the accounts (cf. Tisdell and Fairbairn 1996). Are the national accounts intended to give a rough measure of welfare or sustainable welfare? Or are they intended to provide a guide to short-term employment prospects?

Adjustment of national accounts for reductions in natural resource stocks yields estimates of net national product. The reduction will be considerable when countries are fuelling their economic growth by liquidating natural resources. Rates of economic growth after such adjustment may be substantially lower as in Repetto's adjusted estimates of economic growth for Indonesia, allowing for deforestation (cf. Arndt 1993).

Note that the above-mentioned adjustments are merely in relation to sustainability of income. They do not take account of unfavourable environmental externalities. To do so would require further adjustments to the national accounts.

An interesting study has been done by Tisdale (1996) of natural gas production in Thailand relating it to natural resource accounting, but its policy relevance seems to be limited. Her main conclusion is that after allowance is made for the decline in Thailand's stock of natural gas, Thailand's net national product is over-stated by 0.4 per cent. One could be forgiven for asking, so what?

In outlining her case study, Tisdale does touch on important issues, but does not develop these for the Thai case. For example, she outlines Hotelling's rule for the optimal rate of extraction of minerals (Hotelling 1931), but does not discuss whether Thailand is following this rule in relation to its extraction of natural gas or should do so.

Bougainville Copper Pty Ltd operated from 1972 to May 1989 when it ceased mining because of the activities of the Bougainville Revolutionary Army

Much is also made of Hartwick's rule (Hartwick 1977) for investing in man-made capital in order to achieve sustainable levels of consumption to offset declining natural resource stocks. She explains as follows:

Hartwick's rule is that economies should invest their exhaustible resource rents in reproducible human capital. It turns out that rent is often the value of the decline in the stock of the resource resulting from current extraction. Hence, the investment of rents in human-made capital is a means of 'allowing for' the decline in the exhaustible stock. The depreciation of one stock is balanced off by investment in another (Tisdale 1996: 31–2).

In Thailand's case, as in several other countries in Asia and elsewhere, at least a portion of the resource rent is extracted by the government as royalty. Is there any evidence that this is being invested in the manner suggested by Hartwick? Would it be more likely to be invested in this way if it were available to the mining companies themselves rather than the government? What part of any rents left with the mining companies is used to finance 'reproducible machine capital'?

Many Asian countries have to pay attention to their declining stock of natural resources. For example, Brunei's economy is almost completely dependent on oil and natural gas extraction, the stocks of which are likely to be virtually exhausted in about thirty years' time. Several other countries in the region (Indonesia, Malaysia and Papua New Guinea, for example) are significant oil and natural gas producers, as is Australia. Many Asian-Pacific countries are significant producers of other minerals. These sustainability questions are relevant to them all. Efforts have been made to apply natural resource accounting to several economies, including Papua New Guinea (Bartelmus et al. 1993). Tisdell and Fairbairn (1996) have discussed limits to its application in Pacific island economies.

The second major problem associated with minerals is environmental degradation and pollution. This can occur during mining and beneficiation (the dressing or processing of ores or their preparation for smelting), in smelting and refining and in downstream use of mineral products, for example, combustion of fossil fuels. Papua New Guinea (PNG) may be taken as a case study of the environmental impacts of mining.

Mining in PNG has been plagued by environmental and social problems (Thompson 1990; Hyndman 1994; Schoell 1994). PNG is a major world producer of gold and copper and a medium-sized oil exporter and is believed to have considerable potential for increased production of minerals. In recent years, PNG's mining sector has accounted for up to two-thirds of PNG's export income. But the mining sector has very few local industrial linkages in PNG and is therefore an enclave-type industry (Thompson 1990:4). The government of PNG obtains a substantial income from royalties and also is a significant shareholder in most large mining projects in PNG. How such income is used is obviously important for the future economic development of PNG.

The major mining projects with controversial environmental impacts and consequences for income distribution include the Bougainville copper mine (previously operated by Bougainville Copper Pty Ltd) and the Ok Tedi gold and copper mine in which the large multi-national Australian company, Broken Hill Proprietary Co. Ltd (BHP), is a major shareholder and the operating partner.

Bougainville Copper Pty Ltd, managed by Australian mining interests, operated from 1972 to May 1989 when it ceased mining because of the activities of the Bougainville Revolutionary Army. This revolutionary group had its origins in dissatisfaction by local landowners with their share of income from the Bougainville mine, the extent of environmental damage caused by the mining and possibly also the comparatively small share of income for the provincial government. In the ten-year period 1978–87, the national government of PNG obtained 57.47 per cent of cash benefits from the mine, foreign shareholders 36.08 per cent, the provincial government 4.69 per cent and local landowners 1.37 per cent with 0.37 per cent going to other shareholders (percentages based on Thompson 1990:11).

A review completed for the National Executive Council of Papua New Guinea in 1989, reported massive environmental change as a result of seventeen years of mining (Applied Geology Associates Ltd 1989). Over 3,000 hectares of land had been covered with tailings and large amounts of tailings had entered the Jaba River creating a delta of over 900 hectares. The waters of the Jaba River are polluted, unfit for drinking or other uses, and water pollution extends into Empress Augusta Bay. The health of fish populations have been adversely affected. Although no detailed economic assessment of the environmental damage is available, local people believe it to be considerable and consider their compensation inadequate.

Some of the environmental developments that have been caused by operation of the Ok Tedi mine on the upper reaches of the Fly River in far western PNG have their origins in the closure of the Bougainville copper mine. It was feared that with falling copper prices, the Ok Tedi mine might become uneconomic if the environmental standards originally required by the PNG government for its operation were enforced. Suspension of mine development and production would result in considerable loss of government income and export revenue. Thompson (1990:15) reported that 'Government representatives have openly said that they cannot now afford to stop the Ok Tedi mine discharging larger amounts of waste into the Fly River or prevent the siltation of most of the upper tributaries'.

Serious pollution of the Fly River (one of the major rivers of PNG) and a number of its tributaries has ensued and some of the pollutants may even find their way into the Gulf of Papua. Papuans downstream of the mine have sued for compensation (Schoell 1994:9) and considerable social conflict has been generated. In addition, the Porgora gold mine on the Porgora River, which eventually flows into the Fly, is dumping tailings into the river. However, given the climatic and geological conditions of PNG, it is very difficult to dispose of mine tailings in an economical way ensuring environmental safety. There is, for instance, considerable risk of tailing dams being breached by earthquakes.

The PNG case illustrates the environmental and distributional issues involved in mining. In assessing mining developments, it is necessary not only to undertake realistic cost–benefit analyses but to consider carefully the income distribution and lifestyle consequences.

It could be argued that the basis of environmental problems is that property rights are poorly defined in a number of respects in PNG and in several Asian-Pacific countries and that the environmental and related issues could be solved by clarifying such rights. However, this may be too simplistic. If property rights are definite but believed to be unfairly or unjustly distributed, the consequence is liable to be social conflict.

Energy supply and air quality

Modern societies depend heavily on non-renewable natural resources for their energy requirements. There can be no doubt that use of such sources of energy has made human life easier, has provided humans with greater control over nature and has significantly contributed to economic abundance in high-income countries. Nevertheless, combustion of such fuels is a considerable source of air pollution in large urban areas and in several regions in Asia. In addition, according to the greenhouse gas thesis, this combustion is a major source of atmospheric warming. As is well known, developing economies in Asia such as India and China are predicted to increase their consumption of fossil fuels substantially, thereby becoming major contributors to greenhouse gas emissions. How best to deal with the threat of the greenhouse problem still remains a major issue (Tisdell 1995). It is one that will require both regional and global co-operation. At the same time, industrial activities in cities emit air pollutants affecting human health. Air pollution in many of Asia's cities, such as Shenyang, Beijing and Calcutta, is a serious and increasing problem. As Asian countries become more urbanised and expand their industrial activity, their air quality must be expected to deteriorate further unless countermeasures are adopted.

The importance of China's case will serve to illustrate the problems of energy supplies and the impact of their use on air quality. In the next century China is expected to become the world's major user of fossil fuels, overtaking the USA. According to Haugland and Roland (1994:212), "China faces two main challenges in its energy policy: (1) to provide adequate energy supplies to foster economic growth, and (2) to limit environmental damage from energy production and consumption". China is now the world's leading coal producer, having overtaken the USA in 1983. Both China's GDP and energy production and consumption have increased remarkably since the establishment of the People's Republic. Between 1953 and 1980 China's GDP grew at an average rate of 6 per cent p.a. and its energy use expanded at 9.8 per cent p.a. After China's market reforms, its GDP grew at an even faster rate averaging 9 per cent p.a. in the 1980s, but its energy use expanded at only 5.5 per cent p.a. in the 1980s.

In other words, it is clear that China's intensity of energy use in relation to its GDP rose in the 27-year period prior to 1980, but declined during the 1980s. This reflects both restructuring of China's economy and China's improving economic efficiency. Consequently, although absolute emission of pollutants increased in China in the 1980s, the intensity of this emission in relation to GDP may have declined. Nevertheless, because aggregate pollution levels in China have continued to rise, dangers to human health from pollutants have grown.

Although the intensity of China's use of energy has fallen, it is very high by world standards. In 1989, it was almost three times that of a comparable country (India), more than twice that of Japan and more than four times that of the USA (Haugland and Roland 1994:217). There may be many reasons for this. China's GDP may be under-estimated. The economy may not have fully restructured following its forced emphasis on high-energy using industries during the pre-reform era (Tisdell 1993). Technology used in its power generation industry and technology employed in industry using energy may be relatively inefficient. Proper procedures may not exist to encourage users to economise energy.

China still has a long way to go to reach the levels of per capita energy consumption of high-income countries. Its energy consumption would need to increase more than five times to reach per capita levels comparable to those of Japan and more than twelve times to reach a similar per capita level to the USA. In many parts of China electricity is still considered by local communities to be in very short supply.

The high sulphur content of Chinese coal constitutes an environmental problem. Sulphur dioxide (SO_2) emissions, with other compounds such as nitrogen oxides, from coal combustion are a serious source of air pollution in China and result in acid rain in several parts of the country. The effects are pervasive. They are not confined to the locality or province where fuel combustion occurs but extend internationally. For example, prevailing winds from China's industrial northwest bring acid rain to Japan (cf. Foell 1994:229, Fig. 2; Bleck 1996) and to and from Korea (Kim 1996). While the use of coal and other fossil fuels increases in Asia, India's emissions of SO_2 are also rising. Acid rain problems can be expected to become more serious, and will call for greater inter-regional co-operation. The inter-regional dimensions of this environmental problem (and many others) in Asia should not be neglected.

As is well known, developing economies in Asia, such as India and China, are predicted to increase substantially their consumption of fossil fuels (Drysdale and Huang 1995; Fesharaki and Wu 1992), thereby becoming major contributors to greenhouse gas emissions. How best to deal with the threat of the greenhouse problem still remains a major issue (Tisdell 1995). It is one that will require both regional and global co-operation (ABARE 1995). The potential of hydro-electricity to substitute economically for fossil fuels in electricity production and reduce greenhouse gas emissions appears to be limited, but, as discussed below, nuclear energy shows promise. Alternative energy sources can also play a larger role (Byrne and Shen 1996), but can be expected to supply only a very small fraction of Asia's energy requirements. From a social point of view, the choice of energy sources should be influenced by the externalities associated with the alternatives. The size of these is still difficult to quantify, particularly in relation to greenhouse gases. ABARE (1995:139) states that while there are considerable uncertainties associated with the science of global change, the potential risks of global warming are sufficient to justify some abatement action.

Naturally, China has considered the question of whether it can use 'cleaner' means of generating electricity than from coal. In its *Agenda 21—White Paper on China's Population, Environment and Development in the 21st Century* (State Council 1994) alternatives to using coal for energy generation, especially hydro-electricity, are discussed. While China has significant potential for expanding its production of hydro-electricity, there are some problems. The greatest potential is in the southern inland of China. This area is not well located for supplying northern and coastal areas of China which have the largest concentration of population and industry and therefore demand for electricity. Large amounts of investment are required. Furthermore, dams associated with hydro-electricity generation are not without environmental costs and risks. They may inundate areas of value for biodiversity conservation and tourism, they may flood productive farmlands, interfere with waterflows (especially if there is associated irrigation) and result in increased salting of rivers and navigation problems. The list could be extended.

In Xishuangbanna Prefecture of Yunnan, for example, there is a perceived shortage of electricity. Some local authorities favour the construction of a dam on the Lancang (Mekong) river to generate electricity and provide for irrigation. However, the dam would flood a large portion of Xishuangbanna State Nature Reserve and would reduce water supplies to Thailand, Laos, Cambodia and Vietnam.

The Three Gorges Dam to be completed in the Yangtze River (Changjiang) provides another example of a complex cost–benefit question. On the one hand, the dam will add significantly to electricity generation, provide for irrigation and flood control. On the other, it will cause the loss of cultural and natural assets, massive relocation of communities due to flooding from the water body, deterioration in important wetlands below the dam, and loss of valuable additions of silt on agricultural land below the dam. There is some concern about the risks to the dam from earthquakes. In addition, disease-patterns in environments affected by the dam are liable to alter. Schistosomiasis, the parasitic disease (Sleigh and Mott 1986; Mahmoud 1987) for which water snails are a major host (Sobhon and Upatham 1990) may well increase, as has occurred in parts of Africa following the construction of large dams. The economic costs of the disease are as yet poorly known (Huang and Manderson 1992).

Nuclear energy is probably still not, for China, an economic alternative to the generation of electricity by the use of coal

Nuclear energy is probably still not, for China, an economic alternative to the generation of electricity by the use of coal. Furthermore, while nuclear power stations avoid many of the pollution problems associated with the use of coal for electricity generation, there are still concerns about the environmental radiation hazards associated with nuclear plants.

In 1985 it was thought that China might embark on a substantial program to increase its electricity production by 2000 by building nuclear plants, and both the USA and Europe were hopeful of selling reactors, but China's ambitious plans in this regard were shelved in 1986. In fact, China has only two plants under construction. Owen and Neal (1988:28) believe that the principal reason for China's change in policy was probably the stress placed on China's relatively meagre stock of foreign exchange by the high initial cost of imported nuclear plants, although there was also scepticism regarding the purported cost advantage of nuclear power over coal.

The comparative cost of generating electricity from coal or other sources compared to nuclear varies by country and location. The Nuclear Energy Agency (1992:43) of the OECD claims that in many OECD countries electricity from nuclear energy will be at least 10 per cent cheaper than from coal for plants commissioned in 2000. However, it points out that this will not be so in the cheap coal regions of the USA, Canada, Brazil and China.

Yoda et al. (1994) suggest that in Japan the cost of electricity generation from coal and LNG was higher than from nuclear up to the mid-1980s, but from 1986 onwards the position reversed. Nevertheless, in 1994 Japan generated 28 per cent of its electricity from nuclear (Akiyama 1994) and is planning in the longer term to generate 60 per cent of its electricity from this source, but for the time being will still build more coal-fired and LNG power stations. According to Akiyama (1994:220), who is President of Kansai Electric Power Co. Inc.,

> ...utilities put aside reserve funds to cover high level radioactive costs, decommissioning costs and internalise them into revenue requirements. Electricity production is calculated at 13 yen per kilowatt hour by hydro power, at 10 to 11 yen by fossil fuels and at 9 yen by nuclear. Therefore, nuclear energy proves [to be] cost competitive.

These figures differ slightly from those of Yoda et al. (1994) but may refer to plants to be commissioned around 2000. It should be noted that in Japan much of the cost of using fossil fuels is internalised as a result of the emission standards set, which increases the cost of generating electricity from fossil fuels.

Akiyama (1994) notes that nuclear power plants are in operation in Asia, in Japan, Korea, Taiwan, India and in China a trial plant is operating and two are under construction. Indonesia has been reported to be planning to construct 12 reactors over the next 15 years with Japanese advice. However, The World Bank (1994a:265) claims that, compared to coal-based generation, nuclear is a high-cost option for Indonesia. It concludes "the nuclear option does not appear to be competitive with coal fired generation unless there is a willingness to pay a premium equivalent to about $37–64 per ton of carbon abatement".

While nuclear appears to be an economic option for some Asian countries such as Japan, it is by no means clear that it is the most economic option for all. Furthermore, nuclear is suitable only for supplying base-load electricity requirements and non-nuclear sources are needed to supply the remainder. Much depends on technological progress. While further progress in nuclear technology is to be expected, there is also a possibility of coal-fired stations recovering many of their present emissions, pro cessing these and selling them as by-products. Given Asia's large coal reserves, particularly in China, the option of cleaner coal-fired power stations needs to be vigorously pursued, especially since it is predicted that fossil fuels will still be supplying 90 per cent of the world's energy consumption in 2010 (OECD 1994:14).

Asian policy responses to the environment and sustainable development

In recent decades, less developed economies have been subject to many international pressures in relation to their policies affecting the environment and sustainable development. This is evidenced by the fact that higher income countries and multilateral agencies take increasing account of environmental impacts in deciding whether to provide aid for individual projects in developing countries or to make aid available to developing countries on a provisional basis. The United Nations Conference on the Environment and Development, held in Rio de Janeiro, adopted a number of resolutions of consequence for the Asia–Pacific. It was resolved, for example, that each nation should draw up an Agenda 21—a strategy to achieve sustainable development in the 21st century. Proposals for an international convention on biodiversity conservation were formulated and subsequently embodied in the International Convention on Biodiversity Conservation. This obliges all signatories to adopt policies to conserve biological diversity.

At the same time, bodies such as the World Bank (1992, 1994b) have increasingly emphasised good governance as a prerequisite for sustainable development and for better care of the natural environment. Good governance includes a wide range of policies—measures to reduce corruption and inefficiency in public administration, increased decentralisation of decision-making so as to increase the political power of local communities, improvements in institutions (institution building), reforms in property regimes so as, for instance, to create private property rights systems (as in transition economies) or to provide for greater security of private property rights and extension of the market system (which itself tends to decentralise economic decision-making). These policies accord with the structural adjustment policies (promoting small government and maximum use of market mechanisms) advocated by the IMF and the World Bank since the early 1980s. Opinions differ about the likely effectiveness of such policies in promoting environmental conservation and sustainable development (see Sebastian and Alicbusan 1989; Mearns 1991; Tisdell 1994). While the effects of such policies on environmental conservation obviously vary (Mearns 1991; Tisdell 1994), there are good reasons for supposing that environmental issues can be better addressed within the framework of a market system than in a centrally planned economy (Tisdell 1997). The transition of former centrally planned economies in East Asia, such as China and Vietnam, to market economies provides increased scope for environmental control and for reduction in pollution intensities in relation to their GDP. In as much as the market mechanism increases the efficiency of resource use, it also tends to reduce pollution intensities, as is apparent from European experience (Zylicz 1994).

In as much as the market mechanism increases the efficiency of resource use, it also tends to reduce pollution intensities

Market reforms in China have opened up new avenues for environmental regulation (cf. Michaelis 1992 re ASEAN). China is introducing pollution charges. The first of these were imposed in the late 1970s and have been extended geographically and in the range of pollutants covered since then. Pollution charges are imposed on water and air pollutants, solid wastes and noise emissions. However, not all geographical areas are covered. Discharge fees on sulphur dioxide emissions and sewage have been levied only on a trial basis since 1992 in nine cities in two provinces. Most of the revenue obtained from pollution charges is spent on the treatment of pollutants and on administration. There is little evidence that these charges are calculated to take full account of unfavourable externalities. Nevertheless, China has made a start with the user-pays principle and intends to extend its application by a trial-and-error approach. But decentralisation of government in China is making it difficult, if not impossible, to enforce environmental regulations at the village enterprise level.

China has drawn up its Agenda 21 for sustainable development (State Council 1994). This espouses a development philosophy different from that followed by most countries in the past. In its preface, it is claimed that:

> traditional ideas of considering economic growth solely in quantitative terms and the traditional development mode of "polluting first and treating later" are no longer appropriate when considering present and future requirements for development. It is now necessary to find a path for development, wherein consideration of population, economy, society, natural resources, and the environment are coordinated as a whole, so that a path for non-threatening development can be found which will meet current needs without compromising the ability of future generations to meet their needs. (State Council 1994: 1)

Additional policies stressed in *China's Agenda 21* include maintenance of its population control policies, institution-building including improvements in the legal system, introduction of environmentally friendly technologies and continuing international co-operation. This suggests that China would like to try to follow a development path different from that of Taiwan, South Korea, Japan and European countries. What remains to be seen is whether this will be politically possible. It will be politically difficult for China not to follow the traditional development path—one which appears to have been embraced by most Southeast Asian countries, probably most enthusiastically by Malaysia.

Concluding comments

To undertake a review of the environment and sustainable development in the Asia–Pacific is a 'tall order'. Nevertheless, the subject is directly relevant to more than half of humanity and indirectly relevant to us all. Is it possible for Asian countries to pursue the traditional economic development path (of polluting now and cleaning up later) without causing serious global environmental problems? Can a large country such as China employ the same development strategies as were successfully adopted in Europe in earlier times or in Taiwan more recently? It is far from apparent that we know the answers to these questions. Nevertheless, economic growth in the Asia–Pacific is accompanied by many predictable environmental changes and several have been outlined in this essay. Even at a pedestrian level, these call for new specific environmental policies if economic welfare is not to be lower than it need be. The economic sustainability of Asian economies as they become more urbanised and market dependent is becoming increasingly reliant on improved infrastructure. In this respect, the huge investment occurring in infrastructure in Asia is not surprising. Developing countries in Asia are undergoing rapid social and economic transformation which necessitates such investment if their economic development is to be sustained.

Economic growth in Asia is associated with expanding use of markets, increasing commercialisation of economic activity and new environmental concerns. While market systems, by encouraging efficient use of resources, can reduce pollution and improve scope for more effective environmental regulation than in planned or in subsistence-type economies, it is difficult to quantify environmental externalities and 'monetise' them, especially in a politically acceptable way. Prediction of available future technologies and their environmental consequences for as little as 30–40 years ahead (the approximate lifetime of a power plant) is fraught with fundamental uncertainties. The choices facing Asia and the rest of the world in the light of the environmental consequences of economic growth must therefore be subject to vigorous academic and public debate.

References

ABARE. 1995. *Global Climate Change*, Australian Bureau of Agriculture and Resource Economics, Canberra.

Adachi, F. 1996. Regional disparity in postwar Japan in terms of human resource distribution, paper presented at workshop on Current Issues in Regional Development and International Co-operation, 12 December 1996, United Nations Centre for Regional Development, Yokkaichi, Japan.

Akiyama, Y. 1994. 'Sustainable development and choices of electricity generating technologies', in Nuclear Energy Agency, *Power Generation Choices: costs, risks and externalities*, OECD Publications, Paris, pp. 205–49.

Alauddin, M. and Hamid, M. A. 1996. 'Economic, social and environmental implications of shrimp farming in Bangladesh', in Alauddin, M. and Hasan, S. (eds), *Bangladesh: economy, people and the environment*, University of Queensland, Brisbane, pp. 278–99.

Alauddin, M. and Tisdell, C. A. 1991. *The 'Green' Revolution and Economic Development*, Macmillan, London.

Applied Geology Associates Ltd. 1989. 'Environmental socio-economic and public health review of Bougainville Copper Mine, Panguna', a review completed for the National Executive Council of Papua New Guinea.

Arndt, H. W. 1990. 'Review of Repetto et al., *Wasting Assets: Natural Resources in the National Income Account*, Washington, DC: World Resources Institute, 1989', *Bulletin of Indonesian Studies*, 26(3):134–6.

—— 1993. 'Sustainable development and the discount rate' in *Fifty Years of Development Studies*, The Australian National University, Canberra, pp. 251–60.

Bartelmus P.; Lutz, E. and Sehweinfest, S. 1993. 'Integrated environmental and economic accounting: a case study for Papua New Guinea', in Lutz, E. (ed.), *Toward Improved Accounting for the Environment*, World Bank, Washington, DC.

Beckerman, W. 1995. *Small is Stupid: blowing the whistle on the Greens*, Duckworth, London.

Bleck, A. 1996. 'Japan air pollution (JAPANAIR)', posted on the Trade and Environment Database (TED) from the American University, Washington, DC. Internet address: http://gurukul.ucc.american.edu/TED /JAPANAIR. HTM.

Brookfield, H. 1993. 'The dimensions of environmental change and management in the South-East Asian region', in Brookfield, H. and Byron, Y. (eds), *South-East Asia's Environmental Future: the search for sustainability*, United Nations University Press, Tokyo and Oxford University Press, Kuala Lumpur, pp. 5–32.

Byrne, J. and Shen, B. 1996. 'The challenge of sustainability: balancing China's energy, economic and environmental goals', *Energy Policy*, 24(5):455–62.

Byron, N. and Waugh, G. 1988. 'Forestry and fisheries in the Asian-Pacific region: issues in natural resources management', *Asian-Pacific Economic Literature*, 2(1):46–80.

Clark, C. 1940. *The Conditions of Economic Progress*, 1st edn, Macmillan, London.

Conway, G. R. 1985. 'Agroecosystems analysis', *Agricultural Administration*, 20:31–55.

—— 1987. 'The properties of agro-ecosystems', *Agricultural Systems*, 24:95–117.

Drysdale, P. and Huang, Y. 1995. 'Growth, energy and the environment: new challenges for the Asian-Pacific economy', *Asian-Pacific Economic Literature*, 9(2):1–12.

El Serafy, S. 1989. 'The proper calculation of income from depletable natural resources', in Ahmad, Y.; El Serafy, S. and Lutz, E. (eds), *Environmental Accounting for Sustainable Development*, World Bank, Washington, DC.

Fesharaki, F. and Wu, K. 1992. 'Energy policies in Asian-Pacific developing economies', *Asian-Pacific Economic Literature*, 6(2):11–41.

Foell, W. K. 1994. 'Acid rain in Asia: regional analysis and policies', in Sterner, T. (ed.), *Economic Policies for Sustainable Development*, Kluwer Academic Publishers, Dordrecht, pp. 227–39.

Georgescu-Roegen, N. 1971. *The Entropy Law and the Economic Process*, Harvard University Press, Cambridge, Massachusetts.

Glaeser, B. 1995. *Environment, Development, Agriculture*, UCL Press, London.

Hartwick, J. M. 1977. 'Intergenerational equity and the investing of assets from exhaustible resources', *American Economic Review*, 66:972–4.

Haugland, T. and Roland, K. 1994. 'Environmental considerations for Chinese energy policy', in Sterner, T. (ed.), *Economic Policies for Sustainable Development*, Kluwer Academic Publishers, Dordrecht, pp. 212–26.

Hotelling, H. 1931. 'The economics of exhaustible resources', *Journal of Political Economy*, 39:137–75. Reprinted in Darnell, A. C. (ed.), *The Collected Economic Articles of Harold Hotelling*, Springer-Verlag, New York, 1990.

Huang, Y. and Manderson, L. 1992. 'Schistosomiasis and the social patterning of infection', *Acta Tropica*, 51(3/4):175–94.

Hyndman, D. 1994. *Ancestral Rain Forests and the Mountain of Gold: indigenous people and mining in New Guinea*, Westview Press, Boulder.

Jones, G. W. 1991. 'Urbanization issues in the Asian-Pacific region', *Asian-Pacific Economic Literature*, 5(2):5–33.

Kaosa-ard, M.; Pednekar, S. S.; Christensen, S. R.; Aksornwong, K. and Rala, A. B. 1995. *Natural Resources Management in Mainland Southeast Asia*, Thailand Development Research, Bangkok.

Kim, B. 1996. 'Korean air pollution problems (KORPOLL)', posted on the Trade and Environment Database (TED) from the American University, Washington, DC.
Internet address: http://gurukul.ucc.american.edu/TED/KORPOLL:HTM.

Koh Chin-Chao. 1992. 'Preface', in Bay-Petersen, J. (ed.), *Sustainable Agriculture for the Asian and Pacific Region*, Food and Fertilizer Technology Center for the Asian and Pacific Regions, Taipei, pp. v–vi.

Lianzela. 1995. *Four Decades of Planning in Mizoram*, Khuangkungi, Aizawl, India.

Mahmoud, A. A. F. 1987. *Clinical Tropical Medicine and Communicable Diseases: Schistosomiasis*, Vol. 2, No. 2, Baillière Tindall, London.

Mearns, R. 1991. *Environmental implications of structural adjustment: reflections on scientific method*, Discussion Paper No. 284, Institute of Development Studies, University of Sussex, Brighton.

Michaelis, P. 1992. 'Environmental policy in OECD countries: lessons for ASEAN', *ASEAN Econonic Bulletin*, 9(2):169–86.

Nuclear Energy Agency. 1992. *Nuclear Power Economics and Technology: an overview*, OECD Publications, Paris.

—— 1994. *Power Generation Choices: costs, risks and externalities*, OECD Publications, Paris.

Owen, A. D. and Neal, P. N. 1988. 'China's potential as an energy exporter', in Owen, A. D.; Neal, P. and Tong, Y., *Research Report on China's Energy Potential*, Centre for Applied Economic Research, University of New South Wales, Kensington, pp. 1–39.

Peng Chao Yang, Findlay, Christopher and Stringer, Randy. 1997. 'Food security in Asia', *Asian-Pacific Economic Literature*, 11(1):1–17.

Pingali, P.; Moya, P. F. and Velasco, L. E. 1990. *The post-green revolution blues in Asian rice production—the diminished gap between experiment station and farm yields*, Social Science Division Paper No. 90–01, International Rice Research Institute, Los Baños, The Philippines.

Pingali, P. L. and Rosegrant, M. W. 1994 . *Confronting the environmental consequences of the Green Revolution in Asia*, EPTD Discussion Paper No. 2, International Food Policy Research Institute, Washington, DC.

Ramakrishnan, P. S. 1992. *Shifting Agriculture and Sustainable Development of NorthEastern India*, UNESCO, Paris, and Parthenon, Cornforth, UK.

Ramani, K. V.; Hills, P. and George, G. 1992. *Burning Questions: environmental limits to energy growth in Asian-Pacific countries during the 1990s*, Asian Pacific Development Centre, Kuala Lumpur.

Repetto, R.; Magrath, A.; Wells, M.; Beer, C. and Rossini, F. 1989 . *Wasting Assets: national resources and national income accounts*, World Resources Institute, Washington, DC.

Rosegrant, M. and Meinzen-Dick, R. 1996. 'Water resources in the Asia–Pacific region', *Asian-Pacific Economic Literature*, 10(2):32–53.

Schoell, H. M. 1994. *Development and Environment in Papua New Guinea: an overview*, The Melanesian Institute, Goroka, PNG.

Sebastian, I. and Alicbusan, A. 1989. *Sustainable Development: issues in adjustment lending policies*, Environment Department Divisional Working Papers 1989–86, World Bank, Washington, DC.

Sleigh, A. C. and Mott, K. E. 1986. 'Schistosomiasis', *Clinics in Tropical Medicine and Communicable Diseases*, 1(3):643–69.

Sobhon, P. and Upatham, E. S. 1990. *Snail Hosts, Life-Cycle, and Tegumental Structure of Oriental Schistosomes*, UNDP/World Bank/WHO, Geneva.

State Council. 1994. *China's Agenda 21—White Paper on China's Population, Environment and Development in the 21st Century*, China Environmental Science Press, Beijing.

Swanson, T. 1994. *The International Regulation of Extinction*, New York University Press, New York.

Thompson, H. 1990. *Mining and the environment in Papua New Guinea*, Working Paper No. 39, Murdoch University, Perth.

Tisdale, P. 1996. *Natural Resource Accounting: a case study of natural gas in Thailand*, Thailand Development Research Institute, Bangkok.

Tisdell, C. A. 1993. *Environmental Economics*, Edward Elgar, Cheltenham, UK.

—— 1994. 'Conservation, protected areas and the global economic system: how debt, trade, exchange rates, inflation and macroeconomic policy affect biological diversity', *Biodiversity and Conservation*, 3(5):419–36.

—— 1995. 'Asian development and environmental dilemmas', *Contemporary Economic Policy*, 13(1):38–49.

—— 1997. 'Protection of the environment in transitional economies: strategies and practices', *Regional Development Dialogue* (in press).

Tisdell, C. A. and Fairbairn, T. I. 1996. 'The scope for applying green accounting and environmental economics to small island economies', in Gabbay, R.; Ghosh, R. and Siddique, M. A. B. (eds), *Economics of Small Island Nations*, New Age International, New Delhi, pp. 63–90.

UNDP (United Nations Development Program). 1991. *Human Development Report 1991*, Oxford University Press, New York.

—— 1996. *Human Development Report 1996*, Oxford University Press, New York.

World Bank. 1992. *Development in Practice; Governance: The World Bank's Experience*, The World Bank, Washington, DC.

—— 1994a. *Indonesia: environment and development*, The World Bank, Washington, DC.

—— 1994b. *World Development Report 1994*, Oxford University Press, New York.

—— 1995. *World Development Report 1995*, Oxford University Press, New York.

—— 1996. *World Development Report 1996*, Oxford University Press, New York.

World Resources Institute, United Nations Environment Program and United Nations Development Program. 1994. *World Resources 1994–95*, Oxford University Press, New York.

Yoda, S.; Nagano, K. and Yamaji, K. 1994. 'Current and future costs of power generation technologies', in Nuclear Energy Agency, *Power Generation Choices: costs, risks and externalities*, OECD Publications, Paris, pp. 31–55.

Zylicz, T. 1994. 'Environmental policy reform in Poland', in Sterner, T. (ed.), *Economic Policies for Sustainable Development*, Kluwer Academic Publishers, Dordrecht, pp. 82–112.

Asia Pacific J. Env. Dev., 6(1), 1999, pp. 1-16

AUSTRALIAN ENVIRONMENTAL ISSUES: AN OVERVIEW

Clem Tisdell

Australia is experiencing significant environmental problems both on land and in its marine areas and several of these problems are interconnected. Clearing of trees and woodland is still substantial and, apart from adding to CO_2 emissions, has a number of other unfavourable environmental consequences, e.g. on water systems. Australia's river systems, estuary areas, coastal lakes and lagoons are suffering from serious environmental problems, of which eutrophication is one of the more serious. Marine environments are also under stress. For example, seagrass beds have declined substantially, toxic phytoplankton blooms are of growing concern, adverse environmental impacts are experienced by some species of marine reptiles and mammals and some fisheries are adversely affected by environmental changes and excessive harvesting. Wastes from human settlements add to these environmental problems; partly because settlement occurs in dense pockets in Australia. Per capita, Australians use a high level of natural resources. Neither markets nor political mechanisms have been able to solve Australia's environmental problems in as effective a manner as many would hope for.

INTRODUCTION

Australia continues to experience significant environmental changes both on land and in its marine areas, and many of these changes are interconnected. For example, loss of tree-cover, soil erosion, increased chemical fertilizer use and sewage disposal have led to sedimentation and nutrient-enrichment of water bodies including some marine areas. Consequences have been loss of seagrass, decline in the quality of estuaries and enclosed water bodies due to eutrophication and in some cases threats to corals.

This article provides an overview of some of the most important environmental consequences of human activity in Australia. It discusses the clearing of native vegetation in Australia, the environmental state of river systems, estuarine areas, coastal lakes and lagoons, marine environmental problems and the environmental impacts of human settlements, especially urbanisation, in Australia. Although Australia has a very low average density of human population by world standards, the geographical distribution of its population has significant environmental impacts and many natural environments in Australia are vulnerable to human disturbances.

CLEARING OF NATIVE VEGETATION

Australia has a relatively high rate of clearance of native vegetation by world comparisons. It is estimated, for example, that in 1990 the rate of clearing of

The author is Professor and Head, Department of Economics, The University of Queensland, Brisbane, 4072, Australia.

native vegetation in Australia exceeded more than half of that in the Brazilian Amazon (Glanzing, 1995, p.3).

Such clearing of vegetation disrupts ecological processes:

- it often adds to soil erosion and to nutrient-enrichment of waters;
- in some areas, it contributes to dryland salinity, a serious threat in some inland areas of Australia;
- it fragments populations of native species and can add to biodiversity decline; and
- the current pattern of clearing of native vegetation in Australia has resulted in the release of large amounts of greenhouse gases. The National Greenhouse Gas Inventory Committee has estimated that in 1990 forest clearing in Australia contributed some 27.3% of Australia's total net emissions in carbon dioxide equivalent (Glanzing, 1995, p.4).

Much of Australia's land clearing in recent years has been for the purpose of expanding or maintaining beef production. A considerable amount of this beef has been exported to East Asia, which provided a buoyant and growing market prior to the Asian economic crisis. Rising incomes in Asia (Asian economic growth) stimulated the demand for Australian beef. The beef industry, however, is not the only contributor to land clearing in Australia. While both extension and intensification of agriculture are the main causes of land clearing in Australia, urban expansion, particularly along the east coast of Australia, has also increased land clearing.

The extent of clearance of native vegetation in recent times has been on a major scale. While there has been some decline in the rate of clearance, a Department of the Environment, Sport and Territories report states: "This trend [clearing of native vegetation] increased significantly in the last 50 years. Contrary to the common wisdom that most clearance occurred last century, in the last 50 years as much land was cleared as in the 150 years before 1945 (AUSLIG, 1990, p.6). Extensive clearing for agriculture occurred in the 1960s and 1970s, and significant clearing is still taking place" (Glanzing, 1995, p.1). In effect, this means that more land clearance has occurred in Australia since 1945 than in the whole of the period before European settlement in Australia. Particularly in the 1950s and 1960s, significant tax concessions existed for land clearing. Thus, the Australian Government provided economic incentives for land clearing.

It is estimated that at the time of European settlement, Australia had only 9% of forest and woodland cover. About 40% of this has been cleared for agriculture and another 40% has been subject to logging. Only a small portion is virgin. The present protected woodland cover in Australia is around 5%, much lower than that of India.

In terms of rate of forest and woodland clearing, Queensland has the highest rate as can be seen from Table 1. According to Environment Australia, 308,000 hectares of trees were cleared in Queensland in the period 1991-95 and 150,000 hectares in New South Wales in the same period (Bita, 1997). Areas of land cleared in the various Australian States are indicated in Table 1.

Table 1

Clearing rates of land in hectares per year for Australia by States

	1987-88	**1991-95**
NSW	150,000	**150,000**
Vic	10,438	**1,828**
Qld	500,000	**308,000**
WA	31,908	**8,000**
SA	4,471	-
Tas	6,000	**4,000**
NT	16,280	-
Total	719,097	**471,828**

Source : Environment Australia reproduced in Bita (1997).

Not only the rate of clearing of trees and woodland has to be considered but also its location. Some ecosystems are more fragile than others or are important for the preservation of particular species --- they contain essential habitats. Although land clearing in Western Australia may seem low in relation to its size, clearing there involves high ecological risks. Western Australia is prone to dryland salting and in some cases this has resulted in 'dead 'and silted-up rivers. Also, the rare numbat (an Australian marsupial animal) has been locally endangered by woodland clearing in Western Australia.

Australia's human population is concentrated along its coastline. This has resulted in considerable loss of wetlands and heathlands, not only in NSW in particular, but also in Queensland. Some of the urban coastal expansion has been stimulated by Australia's burgeoning tourist industry, and by the building of homes for holidays and retirement purposes. In this urban expansion, coastal wetlands have been usually undervalued in Australia and sacrificed to make way for urban development..

RIVER SYSTEMS, ESTUARINE AREAS, COASTAL LAKES AND LAGOONS

Inland Rivers

Australia's inland is extremely deficient in water. Australia's major inland water system is the Murray-Darling river system which is shared by four States: Queensland, NSW, Victoria and South Australia. Although the Murray-Darling Commission (an interstate commission) was set up to regulate use of the waters of this system, problems exist. These include:-

(1) The water, especially in the lower reaches of the system, has a very high salt content due to raised water tables as a result of irrigation and tree clearing.

(2) Increasing offtake of water upstream reduces downstream flows and further adds to salting.

(3) Vegetation clearance in the catchment area contributes to silt levels and nutrient-enrichment.

(4) Eutrophication of the water system is present periodically. At times, toxic blue-green algae occur in the system, e.g. in the Darling River. To some extent, this has been blamed on increased cotton production in the catchment of the Darling. Australia is now one of the world's major exporters of cotton. Irrigation of cotton crops reduces waterflows in streams and the fertilization of cotton adds to the nutrient-enrichment of water bodies.

(5) An additional problem is that dams and controls on waterflows prevent periodic flooding of wetlands and floodplains. This adversely affects the reproduction of some wildlife, e.g. species of ducks, and the regeneration of trees such as the Red River Gum.

These problems occur not only in the Murray and Darling Rivers but also in many of their tributaries.

Coastal Rivers and Estuaries

Coastal estuaries are in poor shape in Australia. These are considered to be critical habitats for aquatic species. "Most river catchments in eastern and southern Australia have been extensively cleared. This has resulted in land erosion, sedimentation of rivers and increased sedimentation and levels of nutrients downstream to estuaries, bays and adjacent coastal waters. High sediment levels in the water reduce light penetration which affects rates of photosynthesis. When sediments settle they can also smother seabed organisms. Sedimentation of estuaries and shipping channels causes shoaling and alters currents. Sedimentation is a major problem in ports and shipping channels, necessitating regular dredging. This resuspends sediments, creating further environmental problems" (Zann, 1995, p.10).

"The flows of many of Australia's rivers have also been significantly altered by dams and barriers, reclamation of wetlands, irrigation schemes and flood mitigation schemes, affecting the hydrodynamics or flushing characteristics of estuaries" (Zann, 1995, p.10). Reduced waterflow and larger nutrient inputs to waterways have caused nutrient loads to rise in Australian waterways. One result is excessive growth of algae and microphytes which may smother sedentary organisms and deplete oxygen levels. The presence of trash fish in comparison to more edible fish tends to increase in such conditions.

Where rivers drain disturbed acid soils, particularly in northern New South Wales and southern Queensland, acid leaches from these soils. Soil disturbance may arise from urban development or from agriculture such as cultivation of land for tea tree plantations. Low lying clayey soils are a particular risk. Runoff can cause estuaries to become periodically acidic. This process increases levels of dissolved aluminium and iron which form compounds extremely toxic to fish. Diseases such as 'red-spot' therefore occur increasingly in fish, and fish kills are increasingly common in estuaries in northern New South Wales. Aquacultured oyster production is also affected adversely.

Water quality in at least 64% of estuaries in New South Wales and 22% of those in Victoria is considered to be poor (Zann, 1995, p.10). It is claimed that poor water quality and loss of habitat in coastal estuaries have caused a decline in estuarine fisheries. "For example, fisheries are thought to be threatened in 21% of estuaries in New South Wales and 23% in Victoria. However, eutrophication of some estuaries has enhanced their value for oyster aquaculture" (Zann, 1995, p.11). The impacts often extend offshore. It is believed for example that the considerable decline in seagrass beds in Australia can be attributed to elevated levels of sediments and nutrients in water bodies.

Coastal Lakes and Lagoons Under Threat

"Of great concern in south-eastern and south-western Australia is the declining water quality and eutrophication of coastal lakes and lagoons, particularly those which are insufficiently flushed by the sea, for example, Tuggerah Lakes and Lake Macquarie (NSW), Gippsland Lakes (Vic.) and the Peel-Harvey system (WA). As coastal lakes are largely restricted to the densely inhabited south-eastern coastal strip, a significant proportion of the nation's coastal lakes has been degraded" (Zann, 1995, p.11). Most of these areas have a high value for recreational and conservation purposes and for fisheries production as pointed out in Tisdell (1998).

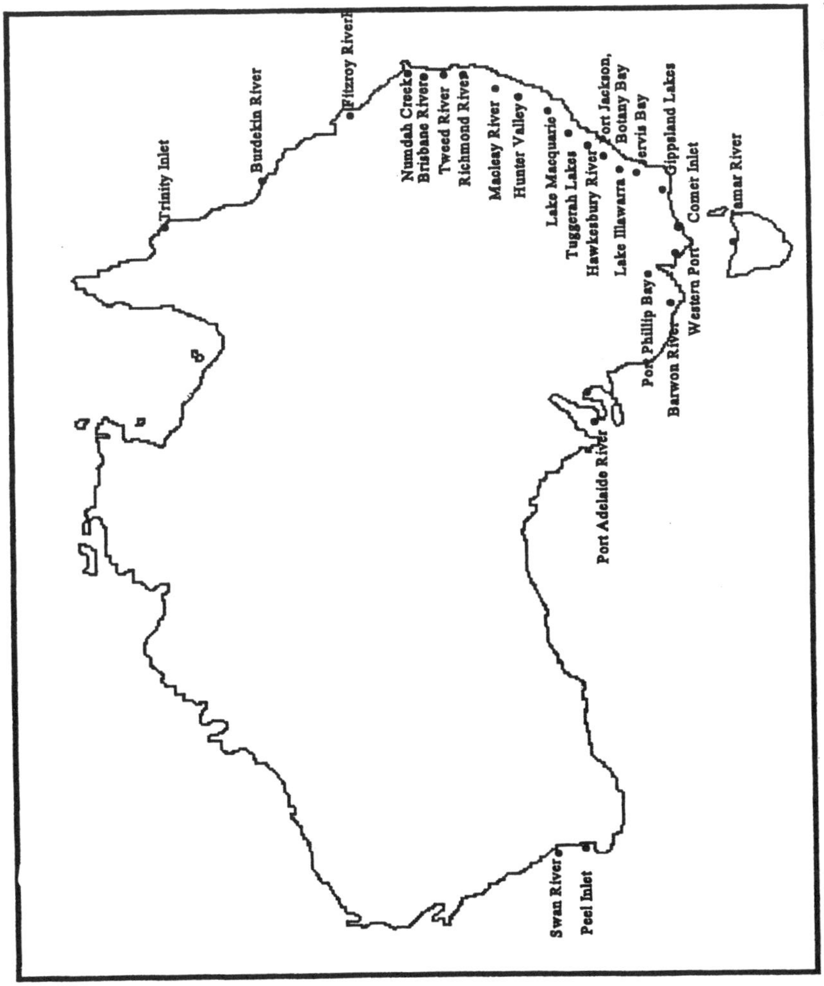

Figure 1: Estuaries and enclosed marine waters named above are environmentally threatened in Australia. (Source: Based on Zann, 1995)

MARINE ENVIRONMENTAL/ECOLOGICAL PROBLEMS

Australia has a large marine exclusive zone but the zone around continental Australia is not very productive from a fisheries point of view, mainly because ocean upwellings are absent in these waters. Despite its large marine exclusive zone, Australia is a net importer of fish. But Australia has many other marine resources, e.g. offshore oil and gas deposits, and its marine areas are attractive from a conservation and tourist point of view. For example, the Great Barrier Reef is a major tourist attraction and Australia's sandy beaches further south attract many for tourism and recreation. Australia's marine areas are also extensively used for recreational fishing.

In considering Australia's marine environmental issues, one useful approach is to concentrate on ecological and biological aspects as Zann (1995) does. In turn, let us consider inshore environments, nearshore environments such as seagrass beds, coral reefs, phytoplankton, reptiles, marine mammals and fish in Australian marine waters.

Marine Inshore Issues

Environmental threats to intertidal rocky shores, beaches and so on occur due to recreational use. Shores are often not well protected. Coastal salt marshes and wetlands have been undervalued with many such areas being reclaimed, used for landfill and for real estate development including development of canal estates. Saltmarshes and wetlands can provide breeding areas for some fish species, food sources for marine species, coastal protection, and cleanse waste waters.

Mangrove forests can perform similar environmental services. Australia has the third largest area of mangroves in the world. While losses in this area are comparatively small, losses have been significant around coastal cities and towns. For example, clearing of 20% of mangrove stands in Moreton Bay (near Brisbane) has occurred.

Seagrass Beds

Australia has the greatest biodiversity of seagrass in the world, the most extensive area of temperate seagrasses and its area of tropical seagrass is one of the largest globally (Zann, 1995, p.14). Seagrass beds are ecologically important and indirectly of considerable importance for fish catches. They trap and stabilise sediments, provide excellent habitats for fish and crustacea and for dugongs and turtles.

However, Australia's temperate seagrass beds are in a state of decline and to a large extent this is linked to increased sedimentation and nutrient releases from water catchments. A major factor in periodic losses in tropical areas is the occurrence of tropical cyclones. The extent of seagrass loss is evident from the

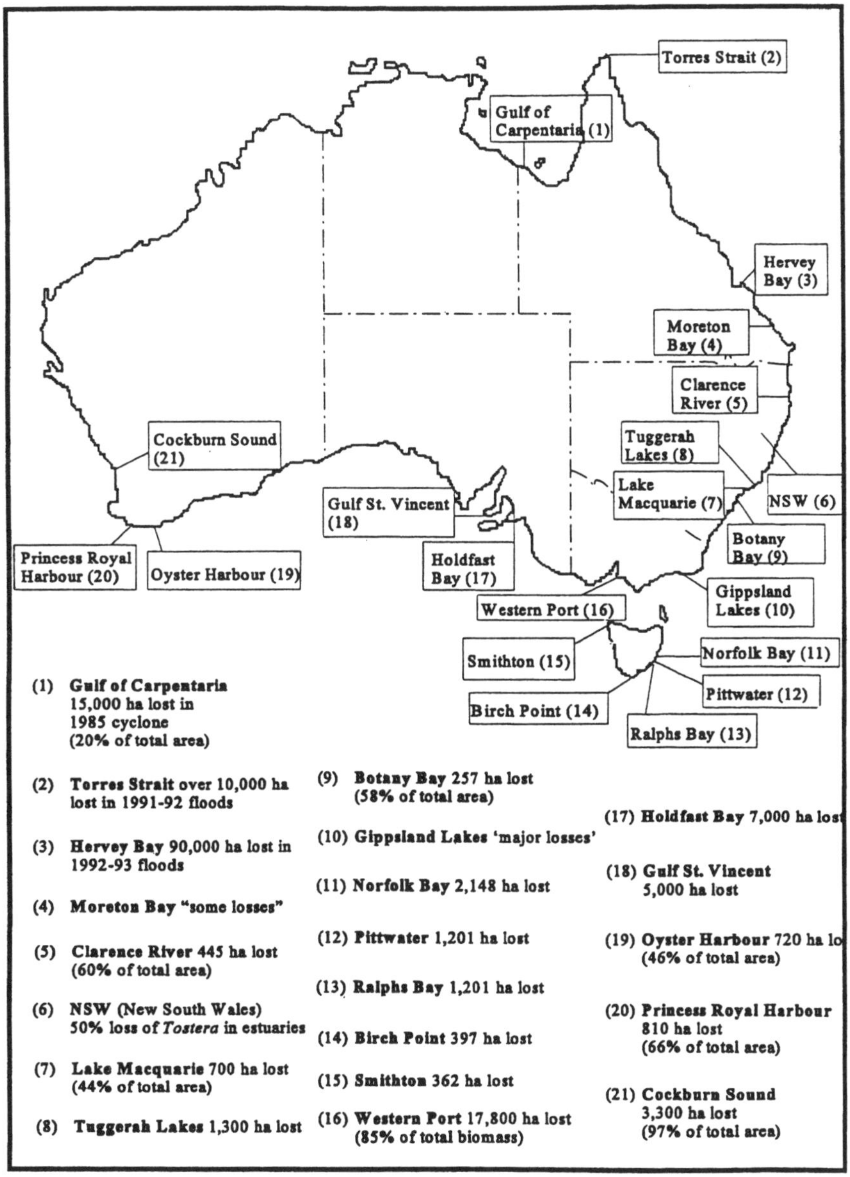

Figure 2: Areas named above are major areas of loss of seagrass in Australia. (Source: Based on Zann, 1995, p.15)

following: "New South Wales has lost half of the *Zostera* seagrass in its estuaries. In Victoria around 85% of the total biomass of seagrass in Western Port has been lost. In Tasmania there have also been declines in the Hobart and D'Entrecasteauz region, Triabunna and St. Helens on the east coast, and Tamar, Port Sorell and Duck Bay on the north-west. In South Australia's Gulf St Vincent around 5,000 hectares of seagrasses have been lost. In Western Australia around 97% of seagrass in Cockburn Sound has been lost. A serious loss of tropical seagrasses has occurred in Hervey Bay in Queensland, causing major mortality of dugongs. Once lost, seagrasses do not readily recover. The decline in temperate seagrass is one of the most serious issues in Australia's marine environment" (Zann, 1995, pp.14-15).

Coral Reefs

Globally Australia holds a very important position in relation to coral reefs. It has a greater area of coral reef than any other country and the world's major coral reef formation, the Great Barrier Reef, said to be visible from the moon. While most of these reefs are located in the extensive tropical and sub-tropical areas of Australia, some occur in temperate areas at a higher latitude than anywhere else in the world. There has been a global decline in the extent and quality of coral reefs, so the conservation values of Australian coral reefs have been growing (Zann, 1995, p.17).

"General issues affecting Australia's coral reefs include effects of sediments and nutrients, effects of fishing and tourism, and the threats of oil spills. Specific threats include elevated nutrients in the inner Great Barrier Reef; outbreaks of crown-of-thorns starfish in the outer central and northern Greater Barrier Reef and Tasman reefs; damage from the passage of tropical cyclones; and outbreaks of coral-eating *Drupella* snails in Ningaloo Reef, Western Australia" (Zann, 1995, p.17).

Phytoplankton

As is well known, the diversity of living species depends on food chains. Phytoplankton form a primary element in such a food chain for many marine species. They are minute algae which extract nutrients from water bodies, but some types of phytoplankton are toxic to animals which eat them. Toxic phytoplankton seem to be favoured by eutrophication. Furthermore, some types appear to have been introduced to Australia in the ballasts of ships. They periodically "cause serious problems in parts of Tasmania and Victoria where they kill marine life and cause the closure of shellfish farms" (Zann, 1995, p.18). The main long-term means to control toxic algae blooms is to reduce nutrient enrichment of the waters involved, e.g. by reducing sewerage discharges, artificial fertilizer use and excreta from animals in catchment areas.

Marine Reptiles

Australia has several types of marine reptiles of interest. These include snakes, saltwater crocodiles and turtles. Let us consider the situation of snakes and turtles.

"Australia has about 30 of the world's 50 species of sea snakes, around half of which are endemic. The family of aipysurids live in coral reef waters and the

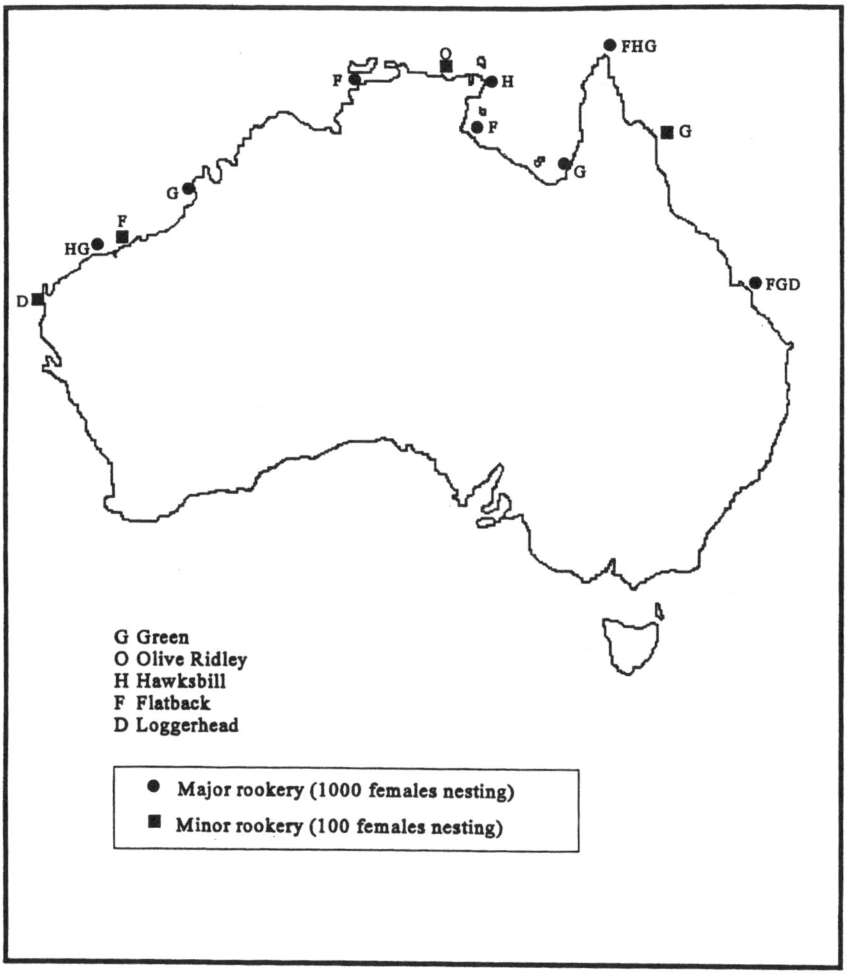

Figure 3: Status of turtle rookeries in northern Australia and adjacent islands as indicated above. Some major declines have occurred in populations of turtles in the north. (Source: Based on Zann, 1995, p.21)

family of hydrophiids live in inner-reefal waters of Australia's tropics. Sea snakes bear live young and have a relatively short lifespan; they reach sexual maturity in around three years, and live for some 10 years. The greatest human impact is from prawn trawling. Sea snakes are quite fragile animals and it has been estimated that between 10% and 40% taken in trawls die once released. For the past 20 years trawled sea snakes have been used in a small leather industry. Licences currently limit the take of sea snakes for leather to 20,000 per year" (Zann, 1995, p.20).

Australia provides breeding grounds for most species of turtles. Six of the seven species of turtles occur in Australia. This is important because turtles are threatened worldwide. Nevertheless, given the highly migratory nature of turtles, conservation of turtles which visit Australian waters is only partially under Australian control. Australian turtles visit Southeast Asia and the islands of the Southwest Pacific where they are hunted for a variety of uses.

"The main human impacts occurring while turtles are in Australian waters are: mortality of adults in prawn trawls, shark nets and gill nets, and in collisions with speedboats; subsistence hunting in indigenous communities; habitat degradation; and predation on eggs by feral animals" (Zann, 1995, p.20).

Marine Mammals

Australian waters contain several important mammal species and threats to their conservation often raise strong emotions. Let us consider three groups of these mammals - dugongs (sea cows), pinnepeds (seals and sea lions) and cetaceans (whales and dolphins).

"The tropical dugong is the only fully herbivorous marine mammal and the only Sirenian (sea cow) to occur in Australia. It is extinct or near extinct in most of its former range which extended from East Africa to South East Asia and the Western Pacific. Northern Australia has the last significant population (estimated to be over 80,000) in the world. Large, long-lived mammals, dugongs become sexually mature at around 10 years and calve every three to five years, making them vulnerable to overhunting" (Zann, 1995, p.24).

In Australia dugong populations are being adversely affected by loss of seagrass habitat, mortalities in fish gill nets and shark nets, and injuries from boat propellers. Overhunting is also occurring in the Torres Strait in the territorial waters of Papua New Guinea because populations of dugongs cross national boundaries (Tisdell, 1986). Towards the end of 1997, the Australian Government extended the coastal areas in which fishing using gill nets is banned in order to provide greater protection to dugongs and paid compensation to fishers for lost fishing rights. The major problem of declining areas of seagrass has, however, not been effectively tackled by policy-makers because it is likely to require increasing restrictions on agriculturists, especially growers of sugar cane, on their use of fertilizer.

"Three species of eared seals breed in mainland Australian waters: the endemic Australian sea lion, Australian fur seal and New Zealand fur seal. The Australian sea lion has recently been listed as 'Rare' by the IUCN. Five species of true seals and two other species of fur seals breed in Australia's subantarctic islands and the Antarctic Territories" (Zann, 1995, p.24).

In the last century seals were overharvested in Australia, but are now fully protected. Threats to their populations involve entanglement in fishing nets and plastic litter (including plastic straps for boxes), oil spills and disturbance by visitors. About 2% of seals at haul-out or at resting sites in Tasmania are entangled in net fragments and other plastic litter at any time "and it is believed that many seals drown as a result of such entanglement" (Zann, 1995, p.13).

Australia contains more than half the world's cetacean species. These include eight species of baleen whales, 35 species of toothed whales, porpoises and dolphins. The Australian whale population was severely overhunted in the past and Australia only ceased whaling in the 1960s. All cetaceans in Australian waters are now afforded protection. The main commercial use of whales in Australia today is for whale-watching tours which have given rise to a minor tourism industry.

Nevertheless, gill nets, shark nets set off bathing beaches to exclude sharks, discarded fishing nets, and ingestion of plastic litter are considered to be a threat to cetaceans, especially dolphins, within Australia. "Contamination of cetaceans by organochlorine pesticides and poly-chlorinated biphenyls (PCBs) is regarded as a significant worldwide threat" (Zann, 1995, p.24).

Fish Stocks

Stocks of several fish species are under threat in Australia due to overharvesting even though restrictions are increasingly being put limiting the level of catches by fishers. Examples include shark caught for the fish-and-chips trade and sold as 'flake' and coral trout. Serious problems exist in controlling fishing effort in relation to species which migrate outside Australia's exclusive marine zone. This has been most evident in recent years for the southern bluefin tuna. Australia and Japan are in conflict about conservation measures for this species, the stock of which has declined greatly. Australia accuses Japan of overharvesting this species in international waters and has excluded Japan (1997) from harvesting them in Australian waters. Such conflict is of long standing (Tisdell, 1983) and has been compounded by other distant water nations, apart from Japan, increasing their harvesting of southern bluefin tuna in international waters. Southern bluefin tuna are highly prized in Japan for sashimi.

In addition, fish kills due to the use of agricultural chemicals continue as a problem as do the long-term consequences for fish stocks of eutrophication of water bodies due to nutrient enrichment.

HUMAN SETTLEMENTS

"Australia is a highly urbanised nation, with about 85% of its population living in towns and cities of 10,000 or more people. Although these settlements occupy less than 1% of the country's total land area, they have a pervasive influence on the natural environment" (State of the Environment Advisory Council, 1996, p.7). Australian settlements have high livability by international standards and, in general, livability is improving.

Table 2

Trends in Resource Flows, Sydney, Australia, 1970 and 1990

	1970	1990
Population	2,790,000	3,656,500
RESOURCE INPUTS/HEAD		
Energy (MJ)	88,589	115,377
WASTE OUTPUTS/HEAD		
Solid waste (tonnes)	0.59	0.77
Sewage (tonnes)	108.0**	128.0***
Hazardous waste (tonnes)	n/a	0.04
Air waste (tonnes)	7.6	9.3
Carbon dioxide (kg)	7,210.0	9,050.0
Carbon monoxide (kg)	204.9	177.8
Sulfur oxides (kg)	20.5	4.5
Nitrous oxides (kg)	19.8	18.1
Hydrocarbons (kg)	63.1	41.3
Particulates (kg)	30.6	4.7

Notes:
- * Derived from food sales data, not consumption data. It reflects an increased use of primary foodstuffs (eg. grains) in the production of meat and processed foods
- ** Includes stormwater
- *** Waste water within sewerage systems only

Source: Based on State of the Environment Advisory Council (1996), pp.7-8.

Australian settlements are said to have higher metabolic flows - that is, they use more resources and produce more wastes - than those in other industrial nations (State of the Environment Advisory Council, 1996). These flow levels have been increasing, both in total and per person, over the past few decades, as illustrated by the following examples:

(1) Domestic water consumption has risen significantly over the past 20 years because of the rising population and increasing use per head. Sydney's total consumption per head (domestic and industrial) rose by 25% between 1970 and 1990, from 144 to 180 tonnes.

(2) Australia's primary energy consumption per head increased by 37% between 1970 and 1990.

(3) Food consumption per head (measured by energy content) increased by more than 70% between 1967 and 1992, not because Australians ate more, but probably because of more energy-intensive production and more wastage in processing.

(4) Australia produces more municipal solid wastes than other industrial nations - 681kg per person per year, compared with an OECD average of 513kg (State of the Environment Advisory Council, 1996, pp.7-8).

CONCLUDING COMMENTS

Despite growing concerns in the last two decades about the destruction of Australia's natural environments, many Australian environments continue to be undermined by human activity. Loss of trees and woodland cover continues to alter terrestrial landscapes and high levels of economic activity impact adversely on marine environments, which are also threatened by their direct human use and incidental impacts of such use.

The problem is partly a consequence of rising natural resource use per head of population, as Table 2 highlighted for Sydney. The finding of Adriaanse et al. (1997, p.12) indicate that several developed countries increased their material flow requirements per capita in the 1990s compared to those in the 1970s and 1980s. Although per capita use of materials by the USA reduced slightly, it remained higher than for other countries. Thus natural environments remain under stress from high (and in many cases increasing) levels of economic activity. This has occurred despite resource savings on average in relation to the production of individual economic items and reduced levels of pollution in relation to GDP (Gross Domestic Product) in developed countries as predicted by the Kuznets environmental curve (Barbier, 1997). The Kuznets curve shows pollution intensities (pollution levels divided by GDP) as a function of GDP per head. It predicts that as GDP per capita increases it rises at first, reaches a maximum and then declines. However, a declining Kuznets environmental curve does not guarantee a reduced level of aggregate pollution, even though this may occur (Tisdell, 1997). *A fortiori*, it does not guarantee less throughput of natural resources and a reduced rate of their transformation into man-made commodities. This continuing transformation can erode the natural resource-base and brings with it the risk of development that will not last. In addition, the use of environmental and natural resources in Australia, as in many countries, is heavily influenced by market forces. There is a bias in the use of these resources for the production of *marketable* commodities. This may rob the community of natural resources which have high non-market economic values. Although governments in Australia have often intervened to protect such resources, their interventions have often been delayed and imperfect.

Given the nature of market systems, and the objective of creating and maintaining employment in market-type economies, including the Australian one, such economies must maintain their rate of economic growth and even accelerate it as technological progress or population growth occurs (Tisdell, 1994). Thus, if market economies are to avoid rising total unemployment of labour, they need as a rule foster accelerating economic growth. This is normally accompanied by rising total throughput of materials or natural resources and not infrequently by deteriorating natural environments. Furthermore, when macroeconomic recession or depression strikes resulting in mass unemployment, long-term environmental concerns are likely to be sacrificed for employment generation if necessary. With economic recession and growing fears of economic depression in many parts of the world, including Australia, environmental conservation is liable to be sacrificed if the sacrifice means more jobs in the short to medium term.

The state of the Australian natural environment also reflects the dominance of anthropocentric values over ecocentric ones. Nevertheless, there appears to have been growing community concern about the fate of species other than human beings in the last two decades. This has been reflected to some extent in the policies of Australian governments but many conservationists believe that not enough is being done to protect threatened species, for example, the sea cow or dugong. A contentious issue in this regard has for example been the Hinchinbrook Resort Development near Cardwell in northern Queensland. This is on the edge of a Natural Heritage Area and it is believed that boat traffic to the resort will result in increased mortality amongst dugongs due to greater incidence of collision with boats.

Australia still faces significant environmental problems on land and at sea. Clearing of woodland and trees continues to have serious consequences for CO_2 emissions, for wildlife conservation and for the quality of aquatic environments. Possibly the major environmental problems for Australia itself exist in relation to its aquatic environments - salting of inland estuaries, release of acids from soils and eutrophication of water bodies as well as human damage to aquatic organisms and overharvesting of some species such as the southern bluefin tuna. These problems are partly due to market failures such as the existence of environmental spillovers from land-use and political failures. Both market and political mechanisms work imperfectly in taking into account total economic values of natural resources. In the case of the southern bluefin tuna, the problem involves international political failure rather than failure by Australia and New Zealand to adopt conservation measures. Both countries have pressed strongly for fishers from other countries exploiting this stock to adopt similar conservation measures but with less impact than hoped for.

REFERENCES

Adriaanse, A., S. Bringezu, A. Hammond, Y. Moriguchi, E. Rodenburg, D. Rogich and H. Schutz (1997), *Resource Flows:* The *Material Basis of Industrial Economics*, World Resources Institute, Washington, D.C.

Bita, N. (1997), "Ungreening Australia: 500,000ha a Year but Slowing", *The Weekend Australian,* 27-28 December.

Glanzing, A. (1995), "Native Vegetation Clearance, Habitat Loss and Biodiversity Decline: An Overview of Recent Native Vegetation Clearance in Australia and its Implications for Biodiversity Decline", *Biodiversity Series Paper No. 6*, Department of the Environment, Sport and Territories, Canberra. http:/www:environment gov.au/life/general_info/biodivser_6/biocon.html

State of the Environment Advisory Council (1996), *State of the Environment Australia: Executive Summary*, Report to Minister of the Environment, Canberra. http://www.environment.gov.au/portfolio/dest/soe/soe96/soceexec.html

Tisdell, C.A. (1983), "Economic Problems in Managing Australia's Marine Resources", *Economic Analysis and Policy*, 13(2), 113-141.

Tisdell, C.A. (1994), "Conservation, Protected Areas and the Global Economic System: How Department, Trade, Exchange Rates Inflation and Macroeconomic Policy Affect Biological Diversity", *Biodiversity and Conservation*, 3, 419-436.

Tisdell, C.A. (1997), "Protection of the Environment in Transitional Economies", *Regional Development Dialogue*, 18(1), 32-49.

Tisdell, C.A. (1998), "Integrated Regional Environmental Studies: The Role of Environmental Economics", pp. 95-111 in Claire Van Wel and John Quiggin (eds.), *Contemporary Issues in Australian Economics: Essays in Honour of Percy Harris,* Central Queensland University Press, Rockhampton, Qld.

Zann, L.P. (1995), *Our Sea, Our Future: Major Findings of the State of the Marine Environment Report for Australia,* Department of the Environment, Sport and Territories, Canberra. www.environment.gov.au/portfolio/esd/coast_marine/somer/somercon.html

Asia Pacific J. Env. Dev., **8**(1), 2001, pp. 15-35

ECONOMIC GROWTH IN CHINA: CAN CHINA COPE WITH ITS ENVIRONMENTAL CONSTRAINTS AND PROBLEMS?

Clem Tisdell

By way of background, general views about the relationships between economic growth and environmental quality are discussed. This is followed by an overview of the state of China's natural environment and a discussion of the constraints that this state imposes on China's economic growth. China's Agenda 21 is examined as a means of addressing these problems. In several respects, however, this agenda may be difficult to implement, and China's environmental policies in practice are, therefore, considered. Furthermore, particular attention is given to China's energy use and sources and its air quality, because both are closely connected. The possibility is raised that China's increasing adoption of market mechanisms will make it easier for it to control pollution.

INTRODUCTION

China's outstanding growth in recent decades and its open-door policies compared to its period of isolation have made it a growth pole in the Western Pacific. Higher-income countries, experiencing sluggish economic growth, have been vying to share in China's economic growth. They are seeking to gain from this growth through increased trade with China and greater investment opportunities in China. Consequently, along with China's economic reforms, this growth has been welcomed in Western countries. On the other hand, less attention has been given in Western countries to the environmental problems and costs involved in China's economic growth. Furthermore, China's improving economic strength has implications for its military power and its position in international political bargaining. China's advancing economic position increases its international strategic position because economic power and political power are closely intertwined. This development is capable of producing concern in Western countries as underlined by reactions to China's missile firings in the vicinity of Taiwan during Taiwan's elections in 1996, and by the types of statements made about China in 2001 by President George Bush of the United States. There are, therefore, several side-effects of China's economic growth. This essay, however, concentrates only on the environmental aspects of this growth.

Considerable debate exists in the relevant literature about the relationship between economic growth and the state of the environment. The most optimistic view sees

The author is Professor and Head, Department of Economics, The University of Queensland, Brisbane, 4072, Australia.

economic growth as leading to an improved environment whereas the most pessimistic view sees these two aspects as antagonistic. Differences of opinion exist both on the empirical and the theoretical planes. Using cross-sectional data, The World Bank (1992) for instance, suggests that with economic growth (or more particularly transition from low-income to high-income status) a country's environment at first deteriorates then improves. Economic growth is, therefore, seen as ultimately resulting in significant environmental improvement. Where is China currently placed on this U-shaped environmental quality curve? Is it still on its downward path and how much further will its environment deteriorate and in what ways? There is probably no easy answer to these questions.

One of the reasons why there is no easy answer to these questions is that environmental quality consists of multiple characteristics as also of a number of variables. Some characteristics may improve with economic growth whereas others may decline and so it can be difficult to evaluate the resulting combination. Furthermore, very long-term environmental impacts may differ from short- and medium-term ones and global environmental impacts may diverge from country-specific ones (cf. Tisdell, 1993a., Arrow *et al.*, 1995).

Actually, environmental Kuznets curves are often used to discuss the relationship between economic growth and environmental quality. Such curves usually specify observed and predicted relationships between the intensity of emission of selected pollutants (for example, level of their emissions per unit of Gross Domestic Product) and per capita levels of income. The term to descibe these curves were first introduced into the literature by Selden and Song (1994) and a widespread view became established that typically these are of a reversed U-shape. They are the reverse of the environmental quality curves mentioned above. However, empirical support for these curves is weak (see for example Harbaugh *et al.*, 2000) and it may be dangerous to use these curves to support the view that economic growth, provided that it is on a large enough scale, will ameliorate or solve environmental problems. As shown in Tisdell (2001), such an approach can lead to global environmental and economic disaster.

Nonetheless, on the theoretical level, most economists appear to agree that it is *possible* for economic growth to occur and for improved environmental quality to be achieved in the short to medium term, although some particular policy measures may be needed to make this a reality. However, there is considerable theoretical disagreement about the extent to which economic growth is sustainable in the long run. One school of thought sees economic growth as ultimately reducing the natural environmental stock and lowering it to a level where income can no longer be sustained. Advocates of this point of view argue that strong policy measures must be adopted to conserve the natural environmental stock if sustainable development is to be achieved. They are said to advocate strong sustainability conditions. (These conditions are outlined in Tisdell, 1995b.; in Alauddin and Tisdell, 1998, Ch.2.; and further discussed in Tisdell, 1999.)

On the other side of the spectrum are those who advocate weak sustainability conditions. They see man-made capital as an adequate substitute for natural environmental capital. Basically, they are supporters of traditional recipes for economic growth, whereas the strong sustainability school sees these recipes as leading ultimately to economic disaster. It should not, however, be concluded that the strong sustainability school opposes all economic growth. It merely rejects the view that man-made capital is always a suitable substitute for natural environmental capital and advocates a cautious approach to reducing the stock of natural environmental capital. It is unclear where Chinese policy-makers stand in relation to this issue, but the general importance of sustainability issues in development have been officially recognized in *China's Agenda 21 - White Paper on China's Population, Environment and Development in the 21st Century* (State Council, 1994) and this document is discussed below.

This White Paper indicates that as a result of China's economic reforms, there is now more scope for using market-related instruments (such as taxes, tradeable permits) as a means of exerting environmental control in China. While up to a point these instruments are likely to be useful in balancing economic activities in a way which takes account of their environmental externalities, they may be of little value in addressing the level of environmental impacts from the scale of economic activity and, on their own, may fail to conserve the natural environmental resource stock adequately. Price mechanisms do, it seems, have limitations in relation to environmental issues even when they are applied extensively to take account of externalities (cf. Tisdell, 1990, Ch.2).

China's environmental effects are not purely China's concern (Tisdell, 1993b). Environmental developments in China are capable of having global impacts. For example, China's increasing use of fossil fuels is likely to accelerate global warming, and loss of biodiversity in China to some extent constitutes a global loss. Furthermore, environmental changes in China can have international regional environmental impacts. Rivers from China flow into many nearby countries, and air bodies from China also circulate over nearby countries. Both have the potential of transporting pollutants to nearby countries and of causing environmental damage within these countries. Such transboundary effects will be discussed later. Furthermore, given its eagerness to attract foreign investment, China has the potential to attract polluting economic activities that would not be tolerated in many higher-income countries. Given this background, let us consider China's environmental problems.

THE STATE OF CHINA'S ENVIRONMENT AND THE SUPPLY OF ITS NATURAL RESOURCES

Compared to the world as a whole, China seems to be relatively poor in natural resources in relation to its population. This is highlighted by Table 1. In terms of availability of land and water resources in proportion to its population, China is at a serious disadvantage compared to the world as a whole.

In relation to water resources, the World Bank (1992) considers that countries with less than 2,000 cubic metres per capita have serious problems, especially in drought periods, and those with less than 1,000 cubic metres per capita face chronic water problems. Given predicted population changes, freshwater resources per capita in China are predicted to fall to less than 1,500 cubic metres by 2025 (World Bank, 1992). China's water availability problem will undoubtedly worsen. Furthermore, increasing industrial production and higher income levels will add to its demand for water. The geographical distribution of water resources in China, combined with seasonal variation in water availability, is already causing severe problems in China, especially in parts of its northeast - for example, in the Beijing-Tianjin area. Given the high value placed on China's limited freshwater resources, pollution of these can be expected to impose a heavy economic cost on China.

Table 1

Availability of Selected Natural Resources of China Compared on a Per Capita Basis with those of the World in the early 1990s

	World	**China**
Population (person/km^2)	39	117
Arable land (ha/person)	0.26	0.08
Forest (ha/person)	0.77	0.13
Grassland (ha/person)	0.62	0.20
Fresh water (m^3/person)	7744	2484

Source : Based on Wu and Flynn (1995, Table 2)

Unfortunately, many of China's water resources have become polluted. Some lakes are reported to contain unacceptable levels of heavy metals released from industry, for example, those in the Wuhan area. The organic levels and sediments carried in most rivers have increased significantly. Furthermore, high rates of use of artificial fertilizers used in agriculture and inadequate treatment of sewage has significantly added to the nitrate and phosphorous levels in rivers. It has been suggested that the discharge of these nutrient-rich waters into the China Sea is a prime factor making for the periodic occurrence of red tides which kill fish *en masse* and/or render them poisonous and therefore unfit for human consumption. These types of water pollution also threaten China' s aquaculture industry which, in terms of volume of production, is by far the largest in the world and a significant source of animal protein for China's population. Of course, the economic costs of water pollution in China are much greater than this example indicates. Its adverse consequences for health and its impact in reducing biodiversity should not be ignored.

Air quality in China has deteriorated seriously with its economic growth. Excluding township enterprises (considered by some to be a source of serious pollution), sulphur dioxide remissions in China increased by more than one-third in the period 1982-1992 and other gases contaminating the air more than doubled (estimates from figures supplied by Wu and Flynn, 1995, p.4). Most of China's large cities have air quality much lower than the standards set by the World Health Organization. For example, the air in Shenyang is heavily polluted and this has been suggested as a source of the high incidence of cancer amongst its population. Air pollution is responsible for high incidence of respiratory illnesses in many of China's cities.

In fact, because air quality is so poor, 26 per cent of all deaths in China are attributed to it, five times the U.S. level of such deaths (Bingham, 1993, p.12). Respiratory disease is the biggest single source of death in China. Acid rains are a serious problem and sometimes cause pH levels in rivers north of the Yangtze to fall below 5.6, even though alkaline loess dust helps to reduce this acidity. Inefficient boilers and small power stations are a major source of this pollution (Bingham, 1993).

China is relatively rich in coal resources, and the burning of coal in China is a serious source of local air pollution. Furthermore, the burning of fossil fuels in China is adding significantly to greenhouse gases and China's emissions of such gases are predicted to rise significantly. In 1989, China ranked third in the world in terms of greenhouse gas emissions - after the U.S. and the Soviet Union. "However by 2020, China would be the world's largest producer of carbon dioxide, releasing three times as much as the US." (Bingham, 1993, p.12.)

Solid wastes create serious problems. About 55,000 ha of land is covered with untreated solid waste, most of it industrial, and much of it contains heavy metals and toxic substances. Leaching from such waste dumps threatens aquifers and groundwater (Bingham, 1993, p.14).

Loss of forests in China has occurred on a significant scale. Estimates of the World Resources Institute *et al.* (1994, Table 17.1) indicate that the area of forest and woodland in China decreased by 6.5% between 1979 and 1991. Consequently, in 1992 only 13.6% of China's area was covered by forest and woodland. This is one of the lowest percentages for Asian countries and is slightly less than the estimated percentage of forest cover for Bangladesh (cf. Alauddin and Tisdell, 1998, Ch.2).

While forest loss is not the only source of biodiversity loss, it can be a significant source. Like several countries in Asia, China has a large number of threatened species of mammals, birds and higher-order plants. These are reported by the World Resources Institute *et al.* (1994, Table 20.4) to be 40, 83 and 3,340 respectively, and many of these species are unique to China.

Taking the situation overall, Chinese authorities estimate that almost 7% of China's

GDP is lost due to environmental pollution, about twice the estimated percentage in high-income countries (Bingham, 1993, p.10). Chinese estimates put the annual economic costs of pollution (to China) at more than 90 billion yuan, 40 billion of which is attributed to water pollution, 30 billion to air pollution and around 25 billion to pollution from solid wastes and pesticides. However, actual economic costs may be much higher than this when, for example, full account is taken of the adverse impact of pollution on human health.

ENVIRONMENTAL AND NATURAL RESOURCE CONSTRAINTS ON CHINA'S ECONOMIC GROWTH

In attempting to raise the income levels of its population to that of medium income countries in the 21st century, China faces many environmental and natural resource constraints. The question has certainly occurred to some Chinese policy-makers as to whether these constraints will prevent China from achieving its goals for increasing incomes.

According to Wu and Flynn (1995, p.5), who rely on statements in ZHN, 1992, p.305, some policy-makers in the central government believe that it would be unwise or impossible for China to repeat the Western pattern of economic development involving in the first stage economic growth and environmental degradation and in the next stage comprehensive 'clean-up' of the environment. The reason is said to be "... China does not have sufficient natural resources and environmental capacity to absorb industrial pollution. It is also impossible for China to select the 'high technology' route to control and treat industrial pollution due to its limited funding sources and great pressure for economic growth from population expansion. The best choice for China is to harmonize economic development and environmental protection to develop its economy as fast as possible under the condition of environmental stability (ZHN, 1992, p.305)". (Wu and Flynn, 1995, p.5.)

Elsewhere Wu and Flynn (1995, p.3) state that "... the relative shortage of natural resources constrains China's ability to copy the Western pattern of high-energy/ resource consumption. Thus China must explore a new kind of development path to harmonize economic growth with environmental protection". This path is believed to be one that pays more attention to protecting the environment initially then did the Western powers.

This basic policy is repeated in the preamble to *China's Agenda 21,* and has been contrasted with the approach of Taiwan to economic development. Taiwan has basically followed the Western pattern mentioned above (Tisdell, 1995a).

If the above is correct, then at least, in principle, major Chinese policy advisers lean more towards strong conditions for sustainable development in China rather than weak ones. However, in practice, China unfortunately does not have policies in place to enforce strong conditions effectively. There are many political reasons why practice differs from principles. These include the inability of central government to enforce central policies effectively at the local level. Politically, China is very decentralised and provinces and localities compete with one another for investment sometimes resulting in considerable environmental concessions being made to investors at the local level. Furthermore, laws are often not enforced. In some cases this is due to bribery and corruption and in some other cases due to lack of application by administrators. As pointed out below, some pollution control measures are only put into effect in a few locations in China. Furthermore, politicians are often keen to show quick economic results and are prepared to sacrifice environmental quality to achieve this, even though this might result in a worsened economic position in the long run. Political myopia is by no means peculiar to fully democratic systems. Hence, practice and principles of policy can diverge significantly.

The question should be pursued whether China's situation is so different that it cannot follow the pattern of Western development that seems to have been imitated by Japan and is in the process of being copied by Taiwan and South Korea. The latter three countries, like China, might also be considered to be natural resource-poor countries in relation to their populations. However, like European countries, these countries have been able to overcome their natural resource constraints mainly by reliance on international trade. Japan has made considerable progress in improving its environment and Taiwan is now undertaking considerable investment with this aim in mind.

It is possible that China faces greater problems than these countries. It is a relative latecomer in international trade and it is a very large country which means that the expansion of its trade can bring adverse reactions from trading partners. Nevertheless, because China is so short of arable land, it still has the option of importing food if it can export, say, manufactured products. It does not have to be self-sufficient in food. Thus, to some extent international trade can moderate China's environmental and natural resource constraints. Yet, its water shortage will continue and become more severe, and its air pollution and solid waste disposal problem will not be solved by international trade.

The global consequences of China's creation of pollution - for example, its contribution to greenhouse gas emissions - may also place it in a different category to South Korea and Taiwan. Thus, for environmental reasons it may not be able to initiate blindly the economic growth strategies used by other Asian countries that have significantly improved their economic lot.

CHINA'S AGENDA 21

In 1994, the Executive of the State Council of China adopted *China's Agenda 21 - White Paper on China's Population, Environment and Development in the 21st Century*. This is a wide-ranging document which, in English, consists of some 20

Chapters and is 244 pages in length. It is China's response to the United Nations Conference on Environment and Development held in Rio de Janeiro in 1992 which called on all nations to develop and put into effect their own strategies for sustainable development.

The preamble to this document states that

> "traditional ideas of considering economic growth solely in quantitative terms and the traditional development mode of 'polluting first and treating later' are no longer appropriate when considering present and future requirements for development. It is now necessary to find a path for development, wherein consideration of population, economy, society, natural resources, and the environment are coordinated as a whole, so that a path for non-threatening development can be found which will meet current needs without compromising the ability of future generations to meet their needs" (State Council, 1994, p.1).

The document goes on to elaborate on this theme.

This white paper points out that China's economic growth is hampered by its large population, relatively inadequate natural resources and fragile environment as well as its low capabilities in science and technology. It suggests that this requires holistic co-ordination of China's economic growth. At the same time as China adopts growth measures to become a middle-income country in the 21st century, China's Agenda 21 states that "it will be necessary [for it] to conserve natural resources and to improve the environment, so the country will see long-term, stable development." Consequently, the development principles outlined above are articulated in China's Agenda 21.

Continuing market reforms and opening to the outside world are seen as an important part of China's Agenda 21 presumably because these can result in more efficient use of natural resources. Maintenance of population control is regarded as essential and measures to introduce technologies that are more environmental friendly than current ones are seen as desirable. Institution building and improvements in China's legal system are desired targets, as is continuing international cooperation. All of these factors are expected to contribute to China's sustainable development. The main policies recommended for China's sustainable development have been summarised as follows:

"• Carry forward reform and expand opening to the outside, and accelerate the establishment of the socialist market economy system, with economic development as the central focus;

• Enhance capacity building for sustainable development, particularly standardize the establishment of systems of policies, laws and regulations, and indicators of the strategic objectives. It is also important to set up a management system of resources, biological monitoring system, statistical system of social and economic development, and related system of information services, and to improve the public awareness of sustainable development and the implementation of China's Agenda 21;

- Control population growth, enhance population quality, and improve population make-up;
- Popularize sustainable agricultural technology that suits local conditions;
- Develop clean coal technology, and other forms of clean and renewable energy sources;
- Adjust industrial structure and distribution, improve the rational utilization of resources, and reduce pressures on transportation and communication due to industrial development;
- Popularize cleaner production techniques, minimize the output of waste, encourage the conservation of resources and energy, and enhance the utilization efficiency;
- Speed up the construction of 'better-off building', and improve residential environment;
- Develop and popularize key technology for environmental pollution control;
- Strengthen the protection of water resources and sewage treatment, protect and expand vegetation cover, rationally utilize biological resources to safeguard biodiversity, improve regional environmental quality, increase land productivity and mitigate natural disasters."

(Administrative Centre for China's Agenda 21, 1994, pp.6-7.)

This white paper (State Council, 1994) itself, however, gives little attention to possible conflicts between objectives and how these might be best resolved. Hence, it is doubtful if it provides a workable blueprint for sustainable development. To some extent this is understandable. However, it should be observed that if a holistic approval to economic development is adopted then trade-offs between objectives will be unavoidable. To a considerable extent, the various chapters of the white paper dealing with different sectors and spheres of development read as independent entities. There is therefore some concern that much of the white paper consists of 'motherhood' statements and window-dressing. Furthermore, some may wonder if the English version of the white paper is presented to promote China as an environmental leader of less developed countries and to allay the concerns of some Westerners about the environmental consequences of China's economic growth.

On the other hand, the positive side should not be forgotten. At least China's policy leaders do recognize that an economic growth dilemma may exist which calls for positive measures to conserve China's environmental resources even in its present stage of economic growth. Recognition of a problem, while not sufficient, is necessary if concrete policy actions are to be taken to address the matter. Secondly, China appears to be one of the few countries to have followed up the UNCED resolution on Agenda 21 in a concrete manner. Possibly China's Agenda 21 will become a catalyst for more workable policies for sustainable development in the future, and that China could become a leader in that regard.

In the past, China was well known for its use of integrated diversified productive systems at the village level. These systems produced virtually no waste and were seen to accord with early Chinese philosophy stressing the importance of achieving harmony between man and nature. Even today some of its integrated agriculture-aquaculture systems may be of this nature. Such systems basically incorporate balance, stability and harmony. In reality, however, China has increasingly abandoned such naturally balanced systems and has moved towards monocultures increasingly dependent on high energy inputs typical of Western productive systems. China has been moving towards productive systems dependant on high levels of external inputs typical of those in Western countries. I have, for example, seen non-integrated aquaculture systems in China which involve the raising of a single species, for example, white eels, using imported fish meal. Furthermore, it must be a matter for environmental concern that China's consumption of artificial fertilizer is now the largest in the world (Wu and Flynn, 1995, p.4). Its application of manufactured fertilizer per hectare is now more than twice that in high income countries (Wu and Flynn, 1995, p.4). Thus, China has or is adopting production methods copied from the West which may be inappropriate to its environmental situation.

Those who advocate market-making as the solution to society's ills will be pleased to learn that special mention is made in China's Agenda 21 of the desirability of making effective use of economic instruments and market mechanisms for promoting sustainable development. The Administration Centre for China's Agenda 21 (1994, p.16) summarises the main points in this regard as:

"• Reform the unreasonable pricing system, and establish the paid use system for all kinds of resources and energy;

• Employ the taxation, financial and credit policies in promoting sustainable development;

• Endorse studies on economic policies to maintain sustainable development"

Despite this statement, reading of China's Agenda 21 white paper as a whole indicates a high degree of reliance on administrative measures rather than price-related strategies for environmental control.

CHINA'S ENVIRONMENTAL POLICIES IN PRACTICE

As mentioned earlier, principles and practice often diverge, sometimes sharply. China is continuing to lose natural resources and in several respects its environmental deterioration continues as its economic growth proceeds. The types of dilemmas that China faces are seen by its decision to proceed with the Three Gorges Dam. The dam will undoubtedly change the environment in the Yangtze Valley considerably even though it will bring economic advantages, at least in the short to medium term. However, it is hard to believe that the natural resource stock of this region will not be reduced. Hence, one could say that China in making this decision is not acting in accordance with strong sustainability conditions said to be desirable in the preamble to its Agenda 21. It will undoubtedly be forced to adopt special measures to protect desirable environmental resources in the Yangtze River basin.

Possibly, the first major moves by China to protect its environment in recent times began with the Second National Environmental Protection Work Conference in 1983. In 1984, following this conference, the Environmental Protection Commission was established under the State Council "to co-ordinate all ministries and agencies whose activities affect the environment. Similar organizations and institutions were set up at the local level" (Wu and Flynn, 1995, p.5). Thus, a relatively comprehensive administrative system for environmental management was established in China.

In the 1980s policy makers appear to have reached widespread agreement on:

(1) Use of the *precautionary principle*, that is avoiding environmental problems by means of prior planning and when necessary incorporating defensive environmental elements into projects

(2) The importance of imposing greater responsibility and liability on polluters by using the 'polluter pays' principle to internalize pollution costs which would otherwise be external to organizations

(3) *Strengthening government administration* of environmental controls. Qu and Li (1994) claim that in fact strengthening of administrative management of the environment has been the main focus of the new policy

China has considerably increased the number of persons employed in environmental protection. In 1981 only 22,000 were employed in this way but in 1992 the number was 74,898. Comparatively, however, it is still a low number and the number has failed to increase proportionately with China'sGDP because the growth in this employment has been linear rather than logarithmic (see Wu and Flynn, 1995, Table 2, p.5). Nevertheless, in 1991 China is estimated to have spent 1 percent of its GNP on environmental improvement compared to 0.7 percent of GNP in the 7th Five Year Plan (1985-1990). The National Environmental Protection Agency's target is to increase this to 1.5 percent (Bingham, 1993, p.10) which for a less developed country is a substantial investment in environmental protection.

Coming to China's practice in using economic instruments to control pollution, there can be little doubt that China has made great progress in this regard, although much still has to be done. Discharge fees on pollutants were first imposed in one form or another and with varying degrees of coverage beginning in the late 1970s - basically at the same time as China's economic reform began. They have been widened in coverage and strengthened since then. Pollutants of water and air, solid wastes and noise creation incur discharge fees. However, discharge fees on sulphur dioxide and sewage have only been levied since 1992 in nine cities in two provinces on a trial basis.

In 1994, pollution discharge fees (including fines and related items) amounted to 3.097 billion yuan. Of this 2.355 billion yuan was obtained from regular pollution charges and 0.742 billion yuan from fines, penalties and related items (Mao, 1996, p.1). Charges on emissions of water pollutants, other than sewage, were the major source of revenue, followed by charges on emissions of air pollutants, those on solid wastes, noise, and sewage.

Nearly all the revenue obtained from pollution charges was spent on treatment of pollutants and on administration. In 1994, 2.49 billion yuan was spent on the treatment of pollution and 0.54 billion yuan on government administration of pollution regulations. None of the income collected was used to compensate victims of pollution for damages caused. Nevertheless, in some cases victims can claim damages from polluters. Even when victims are not fully compensated for damage caused by the polluter, the payment is often sufficient to moderate the behaviour of the polluter. Take the example of a non-ferrous smelter which was once a serious source of cadmium poisoning.

This plant located in Daye County emitted large quantities of cadmium into the air resulting in cadmium poisoning among nearby villagers. In the latter part of the 1980s, it was required to compensate victims for their medical expenses. This was sufficient to cause the enterprise to install technology which reduced contamination of the air by cadmium. This extra investment in technology showed a substantial positive rate of social return (Zhiyong *et al.*, 1991).

In relation to compensation of victims for environmental damage, there is still scope for strengthening China's laws and their application. There are doubts about whether China's discharge fees are fairly determined and consistently applied to individual enterprises in practice.

The National Environmental Protection Agency is intending to increase the level of pollution emission fees and to apply fees to emissions at all levels rather than to those exceeding some threshold quantity as is the case for a number of pollutants at present. Some of these extra funds will be used to provide loans to enterprises for environmental protection and for treatment of pollutants.

Overall China's performance in relation to protection of natural resources and environmental protection is mixed. Even in relation to pollution control, it seems that less attention has been given to pollution prevention than to pollution treatment. So principles and practice have yet to be brought fully into line.

CHINA'S ENVIRONMENT AND THE OUTSIDE WORLD

The environments of most countries are not solely their own business. This is particularly so in China's case because of its immense size both in terms of population and land area. The main reason why a country's environment concerns the rest of the world is the presence of externalities or spillovers from the state of its environment.

China's potential level of economic activity and its possible environmental impacts are so large that they cannot be ignored by the rest of the world. Some of its impacts are global. Its possible global impacts are not restricted to its large (and potentially much larger) addition to greenhouse gases. A recent additional example was its emissions of CFCs, a threat to the ozone layer. As a result of the Montreal Agreement and subsequent international meetings, arrangements have been made to phase out the use of CFCs in countries like China and an international fund has been set up to provide financial assistance for the phase-out (Litfin, 1994). China is one of the recipients of such aid.

Regionally, China's environmental change has transboundary effects. China is the source of major rivers which are to a large extent the economic life-blood of Indo-China, Myanmar, Bangladesh and India. Environmental actions by China that pollute these rivers, reduce their waterflows, increase their sediment loads or vary the erratic nature of their flows can be expected to have considerable economic and environmental impact in China's neighbouring countries. For example, within Bangladesh, increased sediment loads in the Brahmaputra River and rising flood levels may be connected to increasing deforestation in its headwaters in China. Again, China's economic activity generates a considerable amount of acid rain. Some of this is transported to neighbouring countries. There have, for example, been complaints in parts of Japan that acid rains are responsible for the deaths of some trees in the vicinity of Hiroshima.

While not necessarily directly involving an international environmental externality element, the environmental policies of a country can influence the international location of polluting industries and international trading. Countries which have low environmental standards may attract polluting industries from abroad and have an advantage in exporting goods the production of which generates pollution. The fact that those in polluting industries do not pay the full social costs of their economic activities means that in effect they are granted a subsidy. The 'concession' benefits special economic interests but often imposes greater costs on the community than the benefits received by these special interests. Therefore, extreme care is needed in making environmental concessions to particular businesses or industries. Some polluting Taiwanese economic activities have, it is claimed, been located in China for environmental reasons. In a relatively decentralised system, particularly as in China, it is very difficult to prevent local authorities competing with one another by making environmental concessions to attract foreign investment. Increased central control may, however, be exerted as the National Environment Protection Agency becomes stronger.

ENERGY SUPPLY AND AIR QUALITY

Modern societies depend heavily on non-renewable natural resources for their energy requirements. There can be no doubt that use of such sources of energy has made human life easier, has provided humans with greater control over nature and has significantly contributed to economic abundance in high-income countries. Nevertheless, combustion of fossil fuels is a considerable source of air pollution in large urban areas and in several regions in Asia. In addition, according to the greenhouse gas thesis, this combustion is a major source of atmospheric warming. As is well known, developing countries in Asia, such as India and China, are predicted to increase their consumption of fossil fuels substantially, thereby becoming major contributors to greenhouse gas emissions. How best to deal with the threat of the greenhouse problem still remains a major issue (Tisdell, 1995a). It is one that will require both regional and global co-operation. At the same time, industrial activities in cities emit air pollutants affecting human health. Air pollution in many of Asia's cities, such as Shenyang, Beijing, Dhaka and Calcutta, is a serious and increasing problem. As Asian countries become more urbanised and expand their industrial activity, their air quality is expected to deteriorate further unless countermeasures are adopted.

The importance of China's case will serve to illustrate the problems of energy supplies and the impact of their use on air quality. In the 21st century, China is expected to become the world's major user of fossil fuels, overtaking the USA. According to Haugland and Roland (1994, p.212), "China faces two main challenges in its energy policy: (1) to provide adequate energy supplies to foster economic growth, and (2) to limit environmental damage from energy production and consumption". China is now the world's leading coal producer, having overtaken the United States in 1983. Both China's GDP and energy production and consumption have increased remarkably since the establishment of the People's Republic. Between 1953 and 1980 China's GDP grew at an average rate of 6 per cent p.a. and its energy use expanded at 9.8 per cent p.a. After China's market reforms, its GDP grew at an even faster rate averaging 9 per cent p.a. in the 1980s, but its energy use expanded at only 5.5 per cent p.a. in the 1980s.

In other words, it is clear that China's intensity of energy use in relation to its GDP rose in the 27-year period prior to 1980, but declined during the 1980s. This reflects both restructuring of China's economy and China's improving economic efficiency. Consequently, although absolute emission of pollutants increased in China in the 1980s, the intensity of this emission in relation to GDP may have declined. Nevertheless, because aggregate pollution levels in China have continued to rise, dangers to human health from pollutants have grown.

Although the intensity of China's use of energy has fallen, it is very high by world standards. In 1989, it was almost three times that of a comparable country, India, more than twice that of Japan and more than four times that of the United States (Haugland and Roland 1994, p.217). There may be many reasons for this. (1) China'sGDP may be underestimated, thereby making China's energy use in relation to the estimated GDP appear higher than it really is. (2) The economy may not have become fully restructured following its forced emphasis on high-energy using industries during the pre-reform era (Tisdell, 1993c). (3) Technology used in its power generation industry and technology employed in industry using energy may be relatively inefficient. (4) Proper procedures may not be in place to encourage users to economize on energy use.

Nevertheless, China still has a long way to go to reach the levels of per capita energy consumption of high-income countries. Its energy consumption would need to increase more than five times to reach per capita levels comparable to those of Japan and more than twelve times to reach a per capita level similar to that of the United States. In many parts of China, electricity is still considered to be in very short supply by local communities.

The high sulphur content of Chinese coal constitutes an environmental problem. Sulphur dioxide emissions, with other compounds such as nitrogen oxides from coal combustion are a serious source of air pollution in China and result in acid rains in several parts of the country. The effects are pervasive. They are not confined to the locality or province where fuel combustion occurs but extend internationally. For example, prevailing winds from China's industrial Northwest bring acid rains to Japan (cf. Foe11, 1994, p.229, Fig. 2; Bleck, 1996) and to and from Korea (Kim, 1996). India's emissions of SO_2 are also rising. As use of coal and other fossil fuels increases in Asia, acid rain problems can be expected to become more serious, and will call for greater interregional co-operation to deal with the problems. The interregional dimensions of this problem (and many other environmental problems) in Asia should not be neglected.

As is well known, developing countries in Asia, such as India and China, are predicted to increase substantially their consumption of fossil fuels (Drysdale and Huang, 1995; Fesharaki and Wu, 1992), thereby becoming major contributors to greenhouse gas emissions. How best to deal with the threat of the greenhouse problem still remains a major issue (Tisdell, 1995a). It is one that will require both regional and global co-operation (ABARE, 1995). The potential of hydroelectricity to substitute economically for fossil fuels in electricity production and reduce greenhouse gas emissions appears to be limited, but, as discussed below, nuclear energy shows promise. Alternative energy sources can also play a larger role

(Byrne and Shen, 1996), but can only be expected to supply a very small fraction of Asia's energy requirements. From a social point of view, the choice of energy sources should be influenced by the environmental externalities of spillovers associated with the alternatives. However, the size of these is still difficult to quantify, particularly in relation to greenhouse gases. ABARE (1995, p.139) states that "while there are considerable uncertainties associated with the science of global change, the potential risk covered by global warming are sufficient to justify some abatement action".

Naturally, China has considered the question of whether it can use 'cleaner' means of generating electricity than from coal. In its *Agenda 21 - White Paper on China's Population, Environment and Development in the 21st Century* (State Council, 1994), alternatives to using coal for energy generation, especially hydro-electricity, are discussed. While China has significant potential for expanding its production of hydro-electricity, there are some problems. The greatest potential is in the southern inland of China. But this area is not well located for supplying northern and coastal areas of China which have the largest concentration of population and industry and, therefore, the greatest demand for electricity. Large amounts of investment are required. Furthermore, dams associated with hydro-electricity generation are not without environmental costs and risks. They may inundate areas of value for biodiversity conservation and tourism, they may flood productive farmlands, interfere with waterflows (especially if there is associated irrigation) and result in increased salting of rivers and create navigation problems. The list could be extended.

In Xishuangbanna Prefecture of Yunnan, for example, there is a perceived shortage of electricity. Some local authorities favour the construction of a dam on the Lancang (Mekong) river to generate electricity and provide for irrigation. However, the dam would flood a large portion of Xishuangbanna State Nature Reserve and would reduce water supplies to Thailand, Laos, Cambodia and Vietnam.

The Three Gorges Dam to be completed in the Yangtze (Changjiang) River provides another example. On the one hand, it will add significantly to electricity generation, and provide water for assisting in irrigation and flood control. On the other hand, it involves loss of cultural and natural assets, massive relocation of communities due to flooding from the water body, deterioration in important wetlands below the dam, and loss of valuable additions to silt on agricultural land below the dam. There is some concern about the risks to the dam from earthquakes. In addition, disease patterns in environments affected by the dam are liable to alter. The parasitic disease schistosomiasis (Mahmoud, 1987; Sleigh and Mott, 1986), for which water snails are an important host (Sobhon and Upatham, 1990), may well increase, as has occurred in parts of Africa following the construction of large dams. The economic costs of the disease are as yet poorly known (Huang and Manderson, 1992). Dangers of the dam silting up quickly are also real due to deforestation in the headwaters of the Yangtze.

Nuclear energy is probably still not an economic alternative for China to the generation of electricity by the use of coal. Furthermore, while nuclear power stations avoid many of the pollution problems associated with the use of coal for electricity generation, there are still concerns about the environmental radiation hazards associated with nuclear plants.

In 1985, it was thought that China might embark on a substantial programme to increase its electricity production by 2000 by building nuclear plants and both the United States and Europe were hopeful of selling it reactors, but China's ambitious plans in this regard were shelved in 1986. In fact, China only has two plants under construction. Owen and Neal (1988, p.28) believe that the principal reason for China's change in policy was probably the stress placed on China's relatively meagre stock of foreign exchange by the high initial cost of imported nuclear plants, although there was also scepticism regarding nuclear power's purported cost advantage over coal.

The comparative cost of generating electricity from coal or other sources compared to nuclear energy varies by country and location. The Nuclear Energy Agency (1992, p.43) of the OECD claims that in many OECD countries electricity from nuclear energy will be at least 10 per cent cheaper than from coal for plants commissioned in 2000. However, it points out that this will not be so in the cheap coal regions of the United States, Canada, Brazil and China. One can also add Australia to this list.

Yoda *et al.* (1994) suggest that in Japan the cost of electricity generation from coal and LNG was higher than from nuclear power up to the mid-1980s, but from 1986 onwards the position reversed. Nevertheless, in 1994 Japan generated 28 per cent of its electricity from nuclear power (Akiyama, 1994) and is planning in the longer term to generate 60 per cent of its electricity from this source, but for the time being will still build more coal-fired and LNG power stations. According to Akiyama (1994, p.220), who is President of Kansai Electric Power Co. Inc.,

> "utilities put aside reserve funds to cover high level radioactive costs, decommissioning costs and internalise them into revenue requirements. Electricity production is calculated at 13 yen per kilowatt hour by hydro power, at 10 to 11 yen by fossil fuels and at 9 yen by nuclear. Therefore, nuclear energy proves [to be] cost competitive".

These figures differ slightly from those of Yoda *et al.* (1994) but may refer to plants to be commissioned around 2000. It should be noted that in Japan much of the cost of using fossil fuels is internalised as a result of the emission standard set, which increases the cost of generating electricity from fossil fuels.

Akiyama (1994) notes that nuclear power plants are in operation in Japan, Korea, Taiwan, and India, and in China a trial plant is operating and two are under construction. Furthermore, Indonesia is planning to construct 12 reactors over the next 15 years with Japanese advice. However, The World Bank (1994, p.265) claims that compared to coal-based generation, the nuclear option is a high cost option for Indonesia. It concludes that "the nuclear option does not appear to be competitive with coal fired generation unless there is a willingness to pay a premium equivalent to about $37-64 per ton of carbon abatement".

Differences of opinion exist about the comparative costs of generating electricity from nuclear sources compared to coal and about the size of the environmental externalities associated with each and how these should be monetised. While nuclear power appears to be an economic option for some Asian countries, for example, Japan, it is by no means clear that it is the most economic option for all. Furthermore, nuclear power is only suitable for supplying base-load electricity requirements and non-nuclear sources are needed to supply the remainder. Much depends on technological progress. While further progress in nuclear technology is to be expected, there is also a possibility of coal-fired stations recovering many of their present emissions, processing these and selling these as by-products. Given Asia's large coal reserves, particularly China's, the option of cleaner coal-fired power stations needs to be vigorously pursued, especially since it is predicted that fossil fuels will still be supplying 90 per cent of the world's energy consumption in 2010 (OECD, 1994, p.14).

CONCLUDING COMMENTS

China's growing importance in the world should not be judged purely in terms of its rapid economic growth and the spin-off of economic benefits to the rest of the world. The environmental and social consequences of its economic growth must be considered, including the sustainability of its growth. China does face considerable difficulties in achieving sustainable development. The Chinese themselves have posed the question of whether it is sensible for them to follow the Western and Japanese pattern of economic development involving economic growth first and environmental clean-up later.

Although the Chinese have expressed doubts about the desirability of such a pattern of growth for China, there is little evidence that they have to date been following a different pattern. On the other hand, there are some signs that this could change. Consider the position outlined in *China's Agenda 21* and the increasing control of pollution by the National Environment Protection Agency. Nevertheless, politically and especially taking into account the influence of local politics, China will find it difficult to pursue an environmentally friendly development path. In addition, in order to follow this alternative path effectively, China may need new production techniques which are environmentally appropriate and must be careful only to transfer those techniques from abroad which have suitable environmental and sustainability characteristics. Otherwise, the articulation of China's *new development path* may amount to no more than lip service. On the other hand, if the new path is earnestly sought and found, China's economic resurgence may not only be sustainable but China will re-emerge as a world leader, in technology and in intellectual thought, as it was in the Tang period.

It might be noted that the introduction of the market system in China seems to have helped in reducing pollution intensities in relation to its GDP. It also provides scope for the use of market-related instruments as a means to control pollution, and China has made a cautious start in applying such instruments. Furthermore, politically, it may be easier to control pollution in a market system than in a centrally planned economy. Social pressure towards environmental ends is, however, likely to be strongest in a fully democratic society with freedom of the press and of expression. How far China will proceed down the latter path remains to be seen. Social, economic and biophysical aspects of sustainable development are all interrelated.

ACKNOWLEDGEMENTS

This is a revised version of a seminar paper presented at the University of Duisburg, Germany. I am grateful to Professor Dieter Cassell for arranging this seminar and for useful comments received. The usual *caveat* applies.

REFERENCES

ABARE (1995), *Global Climate Change*, Australian Bureau of Agriculture and Resource Economics, Canberra.

Administration Centre for China's Agenda 21 (1994), *Introduction to China's Agenda 21*, China Environmental Service Press, Beijing.

Akiyama, Y. (1994), "Sustainable development and choices of electricity generating technologies", pp. 205-249 in OECD *Power Generation Choices: Costs, Risks and Externalities*, OECD, Paris.

Alauddin, M. and C. A. Tisdell (1998), *The Environment and Economic Development in South Asia: An Overview Concentrating on Bangladesh*, Macmillan, London.

Arrow, K., B. Bolin, R. Costanza, P. Dasgupta, C. Fölke, C.S. Holling, B. Jansson, S. Levin, K. Mäler, C. Perrings and D. Pimental (1995), "Economic Growth Carrying Capacity, and the Environment", *Science*, 268: 520-521.

Bingham, A. (1993), "China's Phenomenal Growth Has Environmental Tag", *Pollution Prevention* (Asia/Pacific edition) 1(4): 10-22.

Bleck, A. (1996), "Japan air pollution (JAPANAIR)", Internet:http:/ gurukul.ucc.american.edu /TED/JAPANAIR.HTM.

Byrne, J. and B. Shen (1996), "The challenge of sustainability: balancing China's energy, economic and environmental goals", *Energy Policy*, 24:455-462.

Drysdale, P. and Y. Huang (1995), "Growth, energy and the environment: new challenges for the Asian-Pacific economy", *Asian-Pacific Economic Literature*, 9(2):1-12.

Fesharaki, F. and K. Wu (1992), "Energy policies in Asian-Pacific developing economies", *Asian-Pacific Economic Literature*, 6(2):11-41.

Foell, W.K. (1994), "Acid rain in Asia: regional analysis and policies", pp. 227-239 in Sterner, T. (ed.), *Economic Policies for Sustainable Development,* Kluwer Academic Publishers, Dordrecht.

Harbaugh, W., A. Levinson and D. Wilson (2000), "Re-examining the Evidence for an Environmental Kuznets Curve", *NBER Working Paper No.7711*, National Bureau of Economic Research, Cambridge, MA.

Haugland, T. and K. Roland (1994), "Environmental considerations for Chinese energy policy", pp. 212-226 in Sterner, T., *Economic Policies for Sustainable Development*, Kluwer Academic Publishers, Dordrecht.

Huang, Y. and L. Manderson (1992), "Schistosomiasis and the social patterning of infection", *Acta Tropica,* 51:175-194.

Kim, B. (1996), "Korean airpollution problems (KORPOLL)", Internet: http:/ gurukul.ucc.american.edu/TED/KORPOLL:HTM.

Litfin, K.T. (1994), *Ozone Discourses*, Columbia University Press, New York.

Mahmoud, A.A.F. (1987), *Clinical Tropical Medicine and Communicable Diseases: Schistosomiasis,* Vol. 2, No. 2, Baillière Tindall, London.

Mao, Yushi (1996), "Economic Instruments adopted in China to Control Pollution", *Personal Communication*, March 26.

Nuclear Energy Agency (1992), *Nuclear Power Economics and Technology: an overview*, OECD, Paris.

OECD (1994), *Power Generation Choices: costs, risks and externalities*, OECD, Paris.

Owen, A.D. and P.N. Neal (1988), "China's potential as an energy exporter", pp. 1-39 in Owen, A.D., P. Neal and Y. Tong, *Research Report on China's Energy Potential*, Centre for Applied Economic Research, University of New South Wales, Kensington, NSW.

Qu, G. and T. Li (1994), *Population and the Environment in China*, Paul Chapman, London.

Selden, T. and D. Song (1994), "Environmental Quality and Development: Is there a Kuznets Curve for Air Pollution Emissions?", *Journal of Environmental Economics and Management*, 27: 157-162.

Sleigh, A.C. and K.E. Mott (1986), "Schistosomiasis", *Clinics in Tropical Medicine and Communicable Diseases*, 1(3):643-669.

Sobhon, P. and E.S. Upatham (1990), *Snail Hosts, Life-Cycle, and Tegumental Structure of Oriental Schistosomes,* UNDP/WORLD BANK/WHO, Geneva.

State Council (1994), *China's Agenda 21 - White Paper on China's Population, Environment, and Development in the 21st Century*, China Environmental Science Press, Beijing.

Tisdell, C.A. (1991), *The Economics of Environmental Conservation*, Elsevier, Amsterdam.

Tisdell, C.A. (1993a), "Combining Biological Conservation, Sustainability and Economic

Growth: Can We Overcome Potential Conflict?", *Discussion Paper No. 130*, Department of Economics, The University of Queensland, Brisbane, 4072.

Tisdell, C.A. (1993b), *Economic Development in the Context of China*, Macmillan, London.

Tisdell, C.A. (1993c), *Environmental Economics,* Edward Elgar, Aldershot, England.

Tisdell, C.A. (1995a), "Asian Development and Environmental Dilemmas", *Contemporary Economic Policy*, 13: 38-44.

Tisdell, C.A. (1995b), "The Environment, Biodiversity and Asian Development", *Biodiversity Conservation*, Working Paper No. 20, Department of Economics, The University of Queensland, Brisbane, 4072.

Tisdell, C. A. (1999), "Conditions for Sustainable Development: Weak and Strong", pp.23-36 in Dragun, A. K. and C. Tisdell (eds.), *Sustainable Agriculture and Environment*, Edward Elgar, Cheltenham, UK.

Tisdell, C. A. (2001), "Globalisation and Sustainability: Environmental Kuznets Curve and the WTO", *Ecological Economics* (in press).

World Resources Institute, United Nations Environment Programme and United Nations Development Programme (1994), *World Resources 1994-95*, Oxford University Press, New York.

World Bank (1992), *World Development Report: Development and the Environment*, Oxford University Press, New York.

World Bank (1994), *Indonesia: environment and development*, The World Bank, Washington, D.C.

Wu, B. and A. Flynn (1995), "Sustainable Development in China: Seeking a Balance Between Economic Growth and Environmental Protection", *Sustainable Development,* 3(1): 1-8.

Yoda, S., K. Nagano and K. Yamaji (1994), "Current and future costs of power generation technologies", pp. 31-55 in OECD, *Power Generation Choices: costs, risks and externalities*, OECD, Paris.

Zhiyong, H., B. Keguang and C.A. Tisdell (1991), "Cadmium Exposure in Daye County, China: Environmental Assessment and Management, Health and Economic Effects", *Environmental Management and Health*, 2(2): 20-25.

ZHN (1992), *Zhongguo Huanjing Nianjian* (China's Environment Yearbook), Chinese Environmental Science Press, Beijing.

[23]

PROTECTION OF THE ENVIRONMENT IN TRANSITIONAL ECONOMIES
Strategies and Practices

Clem A. Tisdell

INTRODUCTION

Transition from planned to market-based economies has now been in progress in former Soviet-style economies for several years, and in some cases for at least two decades, as in China. Even in those economies which have moved relatively rapidly to adopt market systems, transition takes time. "Big bang" instantaneous transitions to market economies remain mythical because the past continues to influence the present for some time. Even in the case of the former German Democratic Republic (GDR) (which could not be regarded as typical because of its speedy integration as a region into the already well-established market economy of the Federal Republic of Germany, with considerable aid from West Germany), replacement of equipment and infrastructure is gradual. This means that reduction in the unfavourable environmental side effects of the industrial capital stock is not immediate.

There is little doubt that former Soviet-style centrally-planned economies (CPEs) suffered high pollution and environmental degradation intensities in relation to their levels of production. There are several reasons for this, but social and economic ones appear to be very important. This article will explore the reasons involved, examine difficulties for environmental regulation of transitional economies, and then specifically discuss the Eastern European and Russian situation, together with that of China. An analytical and descriptive approach is taken.

POLLUTION INTENSITIES AND ENVIRONMENTAL DEGRADATION IN SOVIET-STYLE CENTRALLY-PLANNED ECONOMIES

Zylicz[1/] points out that it is "well documented that Centrally Planned Economies (CPEs) used to exert a significantly greater pressure on their environmental resources than comparable market economies." For instance, the pollution intensities of the former group are significantly higher. Comparing six Central and Eastern European countries (Bulgaria, Czechoslovakia, GDR, Hungary, Poland, and Rumania) with the European Community (EC) at the end of the 1980s, he found that solid wastes in tonnes per US$1,000 of gross domestic product (GDP) were 1.0 in the former and 0.4 in the latter, wastewater in m^3 was 83 in the former and 24 in the latter per US$1,000 of GDP, gases 51 kg and 24 kg,

Regional Development Dialogue, Vol. 18, No. 1, Spring 1997

respectively, and dust 13 kg and 1 kg, respectively, for every US$1,000 of GDP produced.[2] The difference could partly be due to differences in GDP per capita between the economies, but Zylicz suggests that even for economies with comparable incomes per capita, pollution intensities were higher in the CPEs, as was their intensity of energy and water use.

The matter can be clarified by use of a Kuznets-type of environmental degradation curve. It is widely believed that as economic growth occurs and income per head in a country rises, pollution intensities and environmental degradation at first rise and then, at high enough income levels, decline. The relationship involved might therefore be of the type shown in figure 1, by the curve **ABCDE**. There may be several reasons for the inverted-U shape of this curve. For example, at lower income levels, industries that are energy-intensive may dominate an economy (in the early growth stages, secondary industry becomes relatively important), whereas less energy-intensive industries and ones consuming fewer natural resources, such as service industries, become more important at higher-income levels. Stages of relative sectoral development in an economy[3] affect the nature of this curve.

In addition, as the size of the economy increases, greater scope may exist for utilizing wastes (by-products) for productive purposes and technologies because the economy-of-scale may more often be of a type which utilizes resources more fully in the production process, thereby generating fewer wastes. In addition, as incomes rise, there is likely to be greater demand for cleaner and more agreeable natural environments.

Figure 1. Kuznets-type Pollution and Environmental Degradation Curves

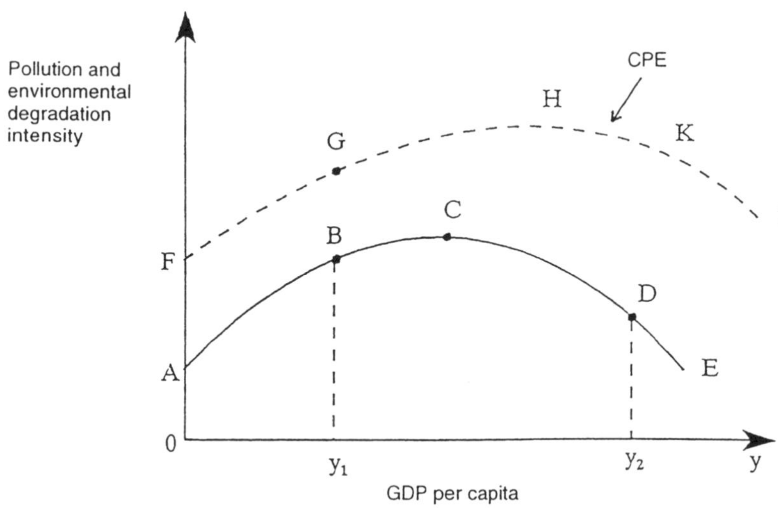

Given the type of relationship shown by the curve **ABCDE**, one would expect CPEs to have higher pollution intensities than market economies if per capita incomes in the latter are considerably higher than in the former, for example at $\mathbf{y}_2$ compared to $\mathbf{y}_1$ in the former case.

However, as Zylicz indicates, CPEs may typically experience higher intensities of pollution and environmental degradation for the same level of GDP per capita as market economies. Thus, while in figure 1, curve **ABCDE** may be the Kuznets-type pollution curve for market economies, that for CPEs might be more like that indicated by the broken curve **FGHKL**. The reasons for the difference include the following:

(1) Poor allocation methods add to resource use per unit of output in CPEs. This results in more resources being "wasted," or if pollution is a positive function of resource use, other things being equal, there is generation of greater pollution per unit of output;
(2) Managerial inefficiency in CPEs and failure to adopt or develop technologies which economize on resource use further add to the problem;
(3) Social factors also play a role. Stalinism emphasized material production as a source of wealth, ignoring the importance of the service industries including the significance of environmental services;
(4) State-owned enterprises (SOEs) were often in a position to use political power to avoid compliance with environmental regulations or block their introduction; and
(5) Restriction of international trade in CPEs, for the most part its restriction to other communist countries, often resulted in the availability of only highly-polluting fuels and resources, for example, the use of coal high in particulate matter and sulphur.

Let us now consider what might happen if a CPE is at a point such as **G** in figure 1, and then begins transition to a market economy. It will not move instantaneously from point **G** to **B**. Its environmental transition path is unclear. For instance, pollution intensities might initially increase before converging towards those of market economies. However, if transition does occur, pollution intensities in the longer term, in the transformed economy, must be lower than was so for a CPE which starts at point **G**, as in the case shown in figure 1. This is because point **G** is above all points on curve **ABCDE**. However, in the case shown in figure 2, pollution intensities may actually increase in the CPE once it transforms to a market economy. It may, for example, start initially from point **G** with per capita income of $\mathbf{y}_1$. Market reforms may raise per capita income in the economy to $\mathbf{y}'_1$ and it may transit to point **B'** on the market Kuznets curve. It will experience both increased income and a high intensity of pollution. However, in the very long term, once its income has increased sufficiently for it to be beyond point **C** in figure 2, say at **D**, decreased pollution intensities are experienced. The environmental prognosis for a former CPE depends on where the country is located in relation to the Kuznets-type curves shown in figure 2. In the case of a country such as China, for example, successful transition might for a time be accompanied by rising pollution intensities, but intensities much lower than would have been experienced under a CPE system for the same level of income or growth.

Figure 2. Potential Increase in Pollution Intensity in a Transitional Economy

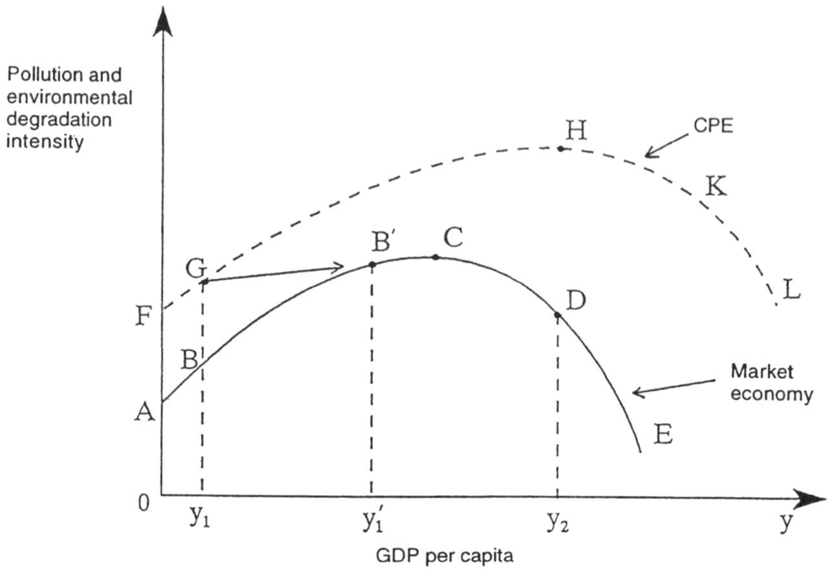

Note: A CPE in transition to a market economy may experience increasing pollution intensity.

ENVIRONMENTAL PROBLEMS IN THE TRANSITIONAL PHASE

It is possible for CPEs to experience considerable environmental difficulties in their transitional phase to a market economy. These may be such that environmental problems initially increase rather than decrease. At the very least, new environmental problems and issues emerge. Let us consider some of these difficulties.

In the early stages of transition, euphoria may exist about the potential of market systems. This can result in market advocates being blind to the possibility of market failures such as the presence of unfavourable environmental externalities. Again, politicians (and some economists) may take the view that the main priority should be to establish the market system and not to worry too much in the early stages about its imperfections. Once the system is established, imperfections can be corrected in due course. Basically, such corrections are viewed as fine tuning, and are matters of subsidiary concern.

During the process of transition to a market economy, property rights may become fuzzy or uncertain. This can result in those who control the use of such resources and who can benefit from their exploitation, accelerating their rate of exploitation. Moreover, relaxation of state control over resources can result in them becoming *de facto* open-access property. For example, reduced control by the Government of Russia over the management of protected areas because of its lack of funds has resulted in their illegal exploitation at the local level.

In some transitional economies, the power of central government over local governments has diminished. Apart from the problem mentioned above, this can result in local authorities permitting polluting activities which adversely affect neighbouring regions and thereby reduce overall national production or welfare. This may, for example, have already occurred in parts of China and Russia.

Again there is a risk of a breakdown of law and order in transitional economies as has been occurring to some extent in the former Soviet Union, because of the speed of the social change involved. In addition, law reforms and the introduction of new laws do not always keep pace with the economic transformation of the economies involved. As pointed out by Coase,[4] legal uncertainty can be a significant source of unfavourable externalities.

At the same time as transition raises new environmental issues, it creates new opportunities for controlling pollution. It provides scope for establishing new sets of property rights and for ensuring that the managers of production units obtain economic rewards which increase with the profitability of their unit. Such rewards provide incentives to economize on natural resource use and to adopt cost-saving innovations which indirectly result in greater output per unit of input and therefore are likely to reduce the pollution intensity of production. Scope also emerges for using economic instruments to control pollution which have little or no role in a centrally-planned system, especially in one which emphasizes targets for quantities of output as prime goals. Taxes or charges on pollution emissions become a policy option as do tradeable or marketable pollution permits. Furthermore, managers are likely to take greater care with new investment to ensure that equipment installed is profitable and economically efficient. Indirectly, this is likely to result in a fall in the intensity of pollution and environmental degradation. Improvements in the operation of capital and financial markets will reinforce this effort.

Even if market failures exist under a market system, it is to be expected that the market system will reduce the intensity of pollution (in comparison to a CPE for the same GDP) once it has been in operation for some time. It cannot, however, be concluded that the absolute level of pollution or environmental degradation will be lower under a market system. If, for example, introduction of the system results in greater economic growth, the absolute level of pollution and environmental degradation may rise, and even the intensity of pollution may increase, as illustrated in figure 2.

The fact that the absolute level of pollution in an economy may rise at the same time as the intensity level of its pollution falls, may not always be appreciated. However, it is a consequence of the Kuznets-type curve which is assumed to relate pollution intensities to the per capita level of income. This curve, such as the one shown by **ABCDE** in figure 1, can be interpreted as an average curve to which a marginal curve of pollution corresponds. Figure 3 indicates the type of relationship which exists between the average or intensity curve **ABCDE** and its corresponding marginal curve **MNRS**. Total pollution is indicated by the summation of the area under the latter curve and is found mathematically by integration. We observe that if per capita income should rise from $\mathbf{y_1}$ to $\mathbf{y_2}$, that the pollution intensity falls, but the total level of pollution in the country rises. **Only** when income levels move into the range beyond $\mathbf{y_3}$ (and marginal pollution is negative) does the total level of pollution begin to fall.

Figure 3. Apparent Pollution Disparities as Incomes Rise

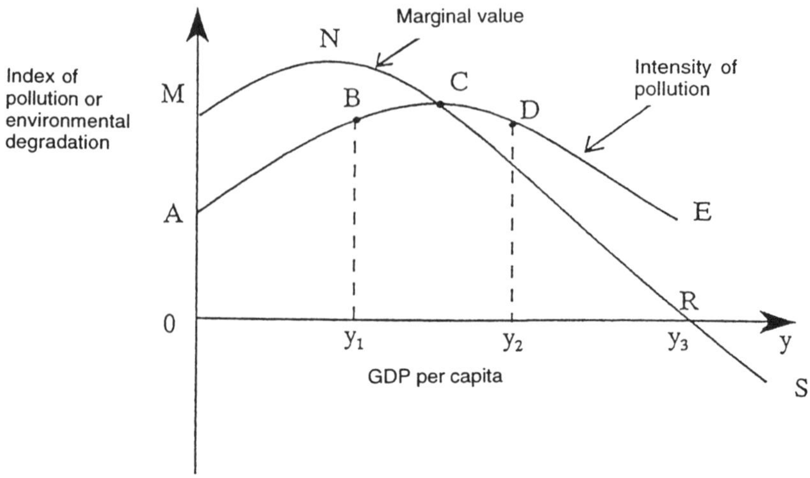

Note: As income levels rise, the intensity of pollution may eventually fall, but the total amount of pollution may continue to rise because the marginal level of pollution remains positive. Whether the latter will eventually become negative as income levels rise is unclear, but it is possible.

Applying the above to a CPE which is in transition to a market economy may achieve greater income growth as a result. Both because of a more efficient economy and economic growth, its pollution intensity may eventually fall. Nevertheless, its **total** contribution to pollution and environmental degradation can be expected to rise for some time if its income levels go up. Where the pollutants involved are of global consequence, such as greenhouse gases, this can be expected to exacerbate global environmental problems. Thus, the conversion of CPEs to successful market economies (and bearing in mind that market economies are likely to be engines of economic growth given the stage of development of many CPEs) is likely to add to global environmental concerns, as for example has the economic growth of China.

Note that the Kuznets-type curves used in this discussion should be cautiously interpreted even though they are useful for the purpose of exposition. Considerable argument, for example, is possible about how best to construct an environmental pollution and degradation **index** because a wide range of environmental variables are involved, and these may assume different degrees of relative importance to different people. These difficulties, however, should not prevent us from thinking about these issues, particularly since local activities often have global environmental consequences.

ENVIRONMENTAL PROBLEMS AND PRACTICES IN EASTERN EUROPE AND RUSSIA, BEFORE AND DURING TRANSITION

There is no doubt that the former CPEs neglected the environmental impacts of material production to the serious detriment of nature, human health, and the quality of life. Environmental disasters and disaster areas were all too frequent such as the one around Norva and Kohtla-Järve in Estonia where oil-shale mining, power stations, and chemical industries give rise to serious air and water pollution and cause serious human health problems.[5]

The reason for such an appalling environmental situation was not purely the relatively low level of economic development of the CPEs and their low levels of per capita income, which would have placed them towards the bottom of the Kuznets-type pollution and environmental degradation curve, but the nature of the economic system itself. Soviet-dominated CPEs had a number of factors which meant that environmental considerations were neglected in planning economic activity.

Stalinism gave priority to the development of heavy industries (steel and metal industries, chemical and power), all of which were major sources of pollutants and held back the growth of light industry. Furthermore, the service industries, which tend to have the lowest pollution intensities, were retarded on the traditional Marxist basis that they are unproductive. The distorted sectoral composition was thus one factor making for a high-pollution intensity in relation to production levels.

The system was unable to take full advantage of the laws of comparative advantage and the scope for beneficial trade and exchange which resulted in high input-output ratios and greater use of locally-available polluting material than was feasible. High input-output ratios were a source of higher pollution intensities and of accelerated natural resource depletion. High levels of investment and use of resources compensated for allocative inefficiency, and the presence of obsolete or backward technologies.

Marxist views appear to have influenced policies on charging for the use of natural resources. There was a tendency not to charge for, or to underprice, their use. This meant that they were not appropriately valued and were indiscriminately used as inputs in production and as sinks for pollution from industry. User-pays and polluter-pays principles were not part of the culture of the CPEs.

So-called economic branches dominated groups concerned with regional affairs and management. Broad production plans tended to emanate from the centre, mostly from Moscow, and showed little or no sensitivity to local environmental problems. Virtually no local communal input was possible. The distance between the centre and the localities or regions became a source of social and environmental insensitivity. Often the environmental problems of one region spilt over to another, or the combination of the environmental impacts of several regions magnified their total regional impact. Such issues were largely ignored or were only starting to come under serious consideration towards the end of the CPE system.

Not only did the system have allocative and social shortcomings, it was also not a strong source of invention, innovation, and technological progress generally. While not all new technology is necessarily always more environmentally friendly than that of older vintage, it frequently is. Oftentimes, for example, input or cost-saving or product innovation may replace a product that is more material-intensive than the new product. If use of the environment and natural resources are appropriately priced, and factored into economic rewards such as profits, this encourages the development and adoption of environmentally-friendlier technology. These incentives were absent in the CPEs. As Kallaste[6] points out, "for many years there was no significant incentive for investments in environmentally benign technologies or waste production equipment."

A further factor contributing to the continuation of serious environmental problems in the CPEs was the lack of freedom of the communication media and the absence of a multiparty democratic government. Thus, grass-roots and regional political action to rectify these problems was stifled. State-owned industrial firms were in a position to generate horrific environmental destruction with relative impunity. The environmental problems generated were to a considerable extent due to the **whole** Stalinist system, not just purely economic aspects.

Nevertheless, there was some attention to environmental problems under communism in the Soviet Union. In the 1970s, *Gosplan* allowed for greater investment in the protection of water resources, mainly to deal with health problems; various official committees were set up to consider environmental protection and make recommendations. Considerable administrative and legal changes occurred for protection of the environment throughout the 1980s and into the 1990s. But as Ählander[7] observed:

> ...laws and resolutions do not automatically achieve anything. While production plans generally are accompanied by the allocation of resources required to fulfil them, regulations are not. If necessary inputs and technical equipment are not provided, even enterprises actually motivated to comply might not be able to do so.

Nevertheless, in the early stages of transition in the Soviet Union, useful philosophies and tools for environmental management were identified as a part of *perestroika* which were to become the cornerstone for environmental protection in the period 1991-2005, for Russia at least. These tools, however, were also adopted by some other members of the former Soviet bloc, e.g., Estonia and Poland.

As described by Ählander,[8] these are: (a) the use of (social) cost-benefit analysis for environmental decision making; (b) the introduction of pollution charges and payments for using natural resources such as water; and (c) the introduction of self-financing systems for environmental protection measures taken at the regional or national level.

On the surface, the framework appears to be an almost ideal one for addressing the type of environmental issues besetting the former CPEs. However, cost-benefit analysis is mainly restricted to "objective" evaluation and used more widely at lower than at higher levels for environmental policy determination. According to Ählander, "payments for utilization of natural resources such as land, water, forests and minerals, were introduced in 1991,"[9] and "pollution charges were established for all principal pollutants emitted; air, water and solid wastes."[10]

It seems, however, that the mode of payment of fees (prices) for natural resources and pollution emissions was such as to provide no incentive for firms to economize on natural resource use or on their emissions of pollutants. This is because the fees were not paid out of the 30 per cent of a firm's profit left for its discretionary use, but from the 70 per cent of profit payable to the state. Thus, the opportunity cost to an enterprise of paying these charges was **zero**. It had no incentive to **economize** on its use of scarce natural and environmental resources, and this reduced the effectiveness of the scheme.

On the other hand, the scheme did result in funds becoming available for regional and national protection. Income from environmental and natural resources charges was paid into funds to finance regional and national environmental protection authorities and providers of some natural resources. Thus, greater funds were available for treating wastes, for the purification of water, and for supplying some natural resources. In addition, enterprises could be allowed to retain some of the pollution-fee income for their investment in pollution reduction. The scheme on the whole turned out to be more reactive than preventative; one of treating the symptoms rather than addressing causes. In fact, Ählander[11/] argues that the "so-called 'economic incentives' that were introduced are not likely to be effective until the whole economy is built on the basis of economic incentives." While this may be an exaggeration, it is easy to see why the environmental policy measures were far less effective than they might appear to be on the surface.

It seems that Poland[12/] and Estonia[13/] moved in a similar direction to Russia as far as environmental policy is concerned. In this regard, Zylicz[14/] observes that pollution fees and natural resources charges in Poland are substantial. Nevertheless, they are far from optimal and they will need to be adjusted as enterprises move from soft to hard budget conditions, as seems inevitable if market reforms are to run their full course.

Once market reforms have been fully completed, environmental and pollution charges will have to be deducted from the profit of enterprises. They will reduce pollution emissions and natural resource use if they are positive at the margin of these activities. However, in the short term, there may be little scope for variation. The main impact is likely to be in the longer term as new investment is undertaken.

As reforms proceed and prices are adjusted, some enterprises may find it difficult or impossible to make a profit. To impose significant charges on these firms for use of the environment may cause them to become bankrupt, even though they may be in a position to cope with these charges in the longer run. In order not to add significantly to unemployment in the short term, an easing up of these charges may be required.[15/]

Opinion is divided about the best policy instruments to use to control pollution and environmental resource use in former European CPEs. There are differences of opinion about whether to use fees, quotas, or standards, or have a system of tradeable or marketable permits based on quotas or standards[16/] to control pollution emissions and natural resource use. Even the polluter-pays principle has been questioned.[17/] Practices in existing market economies provide little guidance because none has settled exclusively on one method or another, although the US appears to have made greater use of marketable pollution permits than most other countries. Furthermore, there are also other policies that can be used as part of a set of environmental policy measures, e.g., zoning of industries according to the environmental externalities which they create; and changes in the law, so that rights are more carefully defined and provide scope for negotiation or legal remedies.

It is not possible to debate the pros and cons of these alternative policy instruments here, but it may be optimal to use an array of these instruments. It is unlikely that one single instrument will be best in all circumstances, and in some cases a combination may be required, e.g., fees or taxes on emissions and zoning.

CHINA: AN INTRODUCTION TO ITS TRANSITION AND ENVIRONMENT

Commencing around 1978, China began a process of **gradually** transforming itself into a market economy. Gradualism and cautious experimentation are the keystones of China's transitional process: it has adopted the approach of reforming its economic system first while delaying change in its political system.

Many of the environmental problems which China experienced were similar to those of European CPEs and had similar roots. Under Mao, however, there seemed to be an even greater obsession with the idea of self-sufficiency at the regional level, and even down to smaller units. By reducing the possibilities for beneficial exchange, this increased the use of resources in relation to the volume of output. Mao's personal rejection of the laws of comparative advantage was to no avail, as indicated by the dismal failure of "The Great Leap Forward". The whole system resulted in a high level of pollution intensity and environmental degradation in relation to GDP.

Apart from the self-sufficiency doctrine, distorted prices for commodities created problems. Some prices for natural resources encouraged their wasteful use. Little control existed on the use of the environment for waste disposal.

China has progressively moved in the reform period to improve its regulation of natural resource use and to control environmental pollution. This was necessary because of previous neglect, the environmental impacts and demands for rapid economic growth, and its perceived shortage of natural resources. Let us consider the last two matters, then outline China's *Agenda 21* which is intended as a long-term framework for sustainable development, and then examine China's environmental regulation in practice.

China has a serious shortage of water. The World Bank[18/] considers that countries with less than 2,000 m^3 of water per capita have serious problems especially during drought periods, and those with less than 1,000 m^3 per capita face chronic water problems. Given predicted population changes, freshwater resources per capita in China are predicted to fall to less than 1,500 m^3 by 2025.[19/] China's water availability problem will undoubtedly worsen. Furthermore, increasing industrial production and higher income levels will add to the demand for water. The geographical distribution of water resources in China combined with seasonal variation in water availability, are already causing severe problems in China especially in parts of the northeast, for example, in the Beijing-Tianjin area. It might also be noted that given the high value placed on China's limited freshwater resources, pollution of these can be expected to impose a heavy economic cost.

Unfortunately, many of China's water resources have become polluted. Some lakes are reported to contain unacceptable levels of heavy metals released from industry, e.g., those in the Wuhan area. The organic levels and sediments carried in most rivers have increased significantly. Furthermore, high rates of artificial fertilizers used in agriculture and inadequate treatment of sewage have significantly added to the nitrate and phosphorous levels in rivers. It has been suggested that the discharge of these nutrient-rich waters into the East China Sea is a prime factor causing the periodic occurrence of red tides which kill fish en masse and/or make them too poisonous for human consumption. It ought to be noted that all these types of water pollution threaten China's aquaculture industry which, in terms of volume of production, is by far the largest in the world and a significant source of animal protein for China's population. Of course, the economic costs of water pollution are much wider than this example indicates, and its health consequences and impact in reducing biodiversity should not be ignored.

Air quality in China has deteriorated seriously with its economic growth. Excluding township enterprises (considered by some to be a source of serious pollution), sulphur dioxide emissions in China increased by more than one-third in the period 1982-92 and other gases contaminating the air more than doubled.[20] Most of China's large cities have air quality much lower than the standards set by the World Health Organization (WHO). For example, the air in Shenyang is heavily polluted and this has been proposed as a reason for the high incidence of cancer among its population. Air pollution is responsible for a high incidence of respiratory illness in many of China's cities.

In fact, because air quality is so poor, 26 per cent of all deaths in China are attributed to it, five times the US level of such deaths,[21] with respiratory disease constituting the biggest single source of death. Acid rain is a serious problem and sometimes causes pH levels in rivers south of the Yangtze to fall below 5.6 even though alkaline loess dust helps to reduce this acidity. Inefficient boilers and small power stations are a major source of this pollution.[22]

China is relatively rich in coal resources, and the burning of coal in China is a serious source of local air pollution. Furthermore, the burning of fossil fuels is adding significantly to greenhouse gases and China's emissions of such gases are predicted to rise significantly. In 1989, the country ranked third in the world in terms of greenhouse gas emissions, after the US and the Soviet Union. "However by 2020, China would be the world's largest producer of carbon dioxide, releasing three times as much as the US."[23]

Solid wastes create serious problems. About 55,000 ha of land is covered with untreated solid waste, most of it industrial, and much of it contains heavy metals and toxic substances. Leaching from such waste dumps threatens aquifers and groundwater.[24]

Loss of forests in China has occurred on a significant scale. Estimates[25] indicate that the area of forest and woodland in China decreased by 6.5 per cent between 1979 and 1991. Consequently, in 1992 only 13.6 per cent of China's land area was covered in forest and woodland. This is one of the lowest percentages for Asian countries and is slightly less than the estimated percentage forest cover for Bangladesh.[26]

While forest depletion is not the only source of biodiversity loss, it can be a significant source. Like several countries in Asia, China has a large number of threatened species of mammals, birds, and higher order plants. These are reported by the World Resources Institute[27] to be forty, eighty-three, and 3,340 respectively, and many of these species are unique to China.

Taking the situation overall, Chinese authorities estimate that almost 7 per cent of China's GDP is lost due to environmental pollution, about twice the estimated percentage in high-income countries.[28] Chinese estimates put the annual economic costs of pollution (to China) at about 95 billion *yuan*, 40 billion of which is attributed to water pollution, 30 billion to air pollution, and around 25 billion to pollution from solid wastes and pesticides. However, actual economic costs may be much higher than this when, for example, full account is taken of the adverse impact of pollution on human health.

CHINA'S AGENDA 21: A STRATEGY FOR THE LONG TERM

China is aiming to become a middle-income country in the next century. It is clear that its increasing income and levels of production will bring greater environmental problems. It is even possible that China's quest could be thwarted if it does not adopt appropriate development and environmental strategies. It requires strategies which will facilitate sustainable economic development. In order to address this issue, China has drawn up *Agenda 21*.

In 1994, the State Council of China adopted *Agenda 21*[29] which is a wide-ranging document, in English, consisting of some twenty chapters and is 244 pages in length. It is China's response to the United Nations Conference on Environment and Development (UNCED) held in Rio de Janeiro in 1992 which called on all nations to develop and put into effect their own strategies for sustainable development.

The preamble to this document states that:

> ...traditional ideas of considering economic growth solely in quantitative terms and the traditional development mode of 'polluting first and treating later' are no longer appropriate when considering present and future requirements for development. It is now necessary to find a path for development, wherein consideration of population, economy, society, natural resources, and the environment are coordinated as a whole, so that a path for non-threatening development can be found which will meet current needs without compromising the ability of future generations to meet their needs.

The document goes on to elaborate on this theme.

The white paper points out that China's economic growth is hampered by its large population, relatively inadequate natural resources and fragile environment as well as its low capabilities in science and technology. It suggests that this requires holistic coordination of China's economic growth. At the same time as China adopts growth measures to become a middle-income country in the twenty-first century, China's *Agenda 21* states that "it will be necessary [for it] to conserve natural resources and to improve the environment, so the country will see long-term, stable development." Consequently, the development principles outlined above are articulated in China's *Agenda 21*.

Continuing market reforms and opening to the outside world are seen as an important part of China's *Agenda 21*, presumably because these can result in more efficient use of natural resources. Maintenance of population control is regarded as essential and measures to introduce technologies that are more environmentally friendly than current ones are seen as desirable. Institution-building and improvements in China's legal system are desired targets, as is continuing international cooperation. All of these factors are expected to contribute to China's sustainable development, the main policies recommended for which have been summarized as follows:[30]

- Carry forward reform and expand openings to the outside, and accelerate the establishment of the socialist market-economy system, with economic development as the central focus;
- Enhance capacity-building for sustainable development, particularly standardize the establishment of the systems of policies, laws, and regulations, and indicators of the strategic objectives. It is also important to set up a management system of resources,

biological monitoring system, a statistical system of social and economic development, and related system of information services, and to improve public awareness of sustainable development and the implementation of China's *Agenda 21*;
- Control population growth, enhance population quality, and improve population make-up;
- Popularize sustainable agricultural technology that suits local conditions;
- Develop clean coal technology, and other forms of clean and renewable energy sources;
- Adjust industrial structure and distribution, improve the rational use of resources, and reduce pressures on transportation and communication due to industrial development;
- Popularize cleaner production techniques, minimize the output of waste, encourage the conservation of resources and energy, and enhance their efficient use;
- Speed up the construction of "better-off building," and improve the residential environment;
- Develop and popularize key technology for environmental pollution control; and
- Strengthen the protection of water resources and sewage treatment, protect and expand vegetation cover, rationally use biological resources to safeguard biodiversity, improve regional environmental quality, increase land productivity, and mitigate natural disasters.

The white paper[31/] itself, however, gives little attention to possible conflicts between objectives and how these might be best resolved. Hence, it is doubtful if it provides a workable blueprint for development. To some extent, this is understandable. However, it should be observed that if a holistic approval of economic development is adopted, then trade-offs between objectives will be unavoidable. To a considerable extent, the various chapters of the white paper dealing with different sectors and spheres of development read as independent entities. There is therefore some concern that much of it consists of "motherhood" statements and window-dressing. Furthermore, some may wonder if the English version was presented to promote China as an environmental leader of less-developed countries and to allay the concerns of some Westerners about the environmental consequences of China's economic growth.

On the other hand, the positive side should not be forgotten. At least China's policy leaders do recognize that an economic growth dilemma may exist which calls for positive measures to conserve China's environmental resources even in its present economic growth stage. Recognition, while not sufficient, is necessary if concrete policy actions are to be taken to address the matter. Secondly, China appears to be one of the few countries to have followed up the UNCED resolution on *Agenda 21* in a concrete manner. It is possible that *Agenda 21* will become a catalyst for more workable policies for sustainable development in the future, and that China could become a leader in that regard.

In the past, China was well known for its use of integrated diversified production systems at the village level. These systems produced virtually no waste. Even today, some of its integrated agriculture-aquaculture systems may be of this nature. Such systems basically incorporate balance, stability, and harmony. In reality, however, China has increasingly abandoned such naturally-balanced systems and has moved towards monocultures increasingly dependent on high-energy inputs typical of Western production systems. China has been moving towards production systems dependent on high levels of external inputs typical of those in Western countries. I have seen, for instance, nonintegrated aquaculture systems in China which involve the raising of a single species, e.g., white eels, using imported fish meal. Furthermore, it must be a matter for environmental concern that China's consumption of artificial fertilizer is now the largest in the world.[32] Its application of manufactured fertilizer per ha is now more than twice that in high-income countries.[33] Thus, it seems that China has, or is adopting, production methods copied from the West which may be inappropriate to its environmental situation.

Economists who advocate market-making as the solution to society's ills will be pleased to learn that special mention is made in China's *Agenda 21* of the desirability of making effective use of economic instruments and market mechanisms for promoting sustainable development. The Administration Centre for China's *Agenda 21*[34] summarizes the main points in this regard as:

- Reform the unreasonable pricing system, and establish the user-pays system for all kinds of resources and energy;
- Employ taxation, financial, and credit policies in promoting sustainable development; and
- Endorse studies on economic policies to maintain sustainable development.

Despite this statement, a reading of China's *Agenda 21* white paper as a whole indicates a high degree of reliance on administrative measures rather than price-related strategies for environmental control.

CHINA'S ENVIRONMENTAL POLICIES IN PRACTICE

As mentioned earlier, principles and practice often diverge, sometimes sharply. China is continuing to lose natural resources and, in several respects, its environmental deterioration continues as its economic growth proceeds. The types of dilemmas that China faces are seen by its decision to proceed with the Three Gorges Dam. The dam will undoubtedly change the environment in the Yangtze Valley considerably even though it will bring economic advantages, at least in the short to medium term. However, it is hard to believe that the natural resource stock of this region will not be reduced and so one could say that China, in making this decision, is not acting in accordance with strong sustainability conditions said to be desirable in the preamble to its *Agenda 21*.

Possibly the first major moves by China to protect its environment in recent times began with the Second National Environmental Protection Work Conference in 1983. In 1984, following this conference, the Environmental Protection Commission was established under the State Council "to co-ordinate all ministries and agencies whose activities affect the environment. Similar organizations and institutions were set up at the local level."[35] Thus, a relatively comprehensive administrative system for environmental management was established in China.

In the 1980s, policymakers appear to have reached widespread agreement on: (a) use of the **precautionary principle**, that is, avoiding environmental problems by means of prior planning and, when necessary, incorporating defensive environmental elements into projects; (b) the importance of imposing greater responsibility and liability on polluters by using the **polluter-pays principle** to internalize pollution costs which would otherwise be external to organizations; and (c) **strengthening government administration** of environmental controls. Qu and Li[36] claim that, in fact, strengthening of administrative management of the environment has been the main focus of the new policy.

China has considerably increased the number of people employed in environmental protection. In 1981, only 22,000 people were employed in this way but, in 1992, the number was 74,898 people. Comparatively, however, it is still a small number and it has failed to increase proportionately with China's GDP because the growth in this employment has been linear rather than logarithmic.[37] Nevertheless, in 1991, China is estimated to have spent 1 per cent of its GNP on environmental improvement compared to 0.7 per cent of GNP in the *Seventh Five-Year Plan (1985-90)*. The National Environmental Protection Agency's target is to increase this to 1.5 per cent,[38] which for a developing country is a substantial investment in environmental protection.

Regarding China's practice of using economic instruments to control pollution, there can be little doubt that China has made great progress in this regard, although much still has to be done. Discharge fees on pollutants were first imposed in one form or another and with varying degrees of coverage beginning in the late 1970s — basically at the same time as China's economic reform began. They have been widened in coverage and strengthened since then. Pollutants of water and air, solid wastes, and noise creation incur discharge fees. However, discharge fees on sulphur dioxide and sewage have only been levied since 1992 in nine cities in two provinces on a trial basis.

In 1994, pollution discharge fees (including fines and related items) amounted to 3.097 billion *yuan*. Of this, 2.355 billion *yuan* was obtained from regular pollution charges and 0.742 billion *yuan* from fines, penalties, and related items.[39] Charges on emissions of water pollutants other than sewage were the major source of revenue, followed by charges on emissions of air pollutants, and those on solid wastes, noise, and sewage.

Nearly all the revenue obtained from pollution charges was spent on treatment of pollutants and on administration. In 1994, 2.49 billion *yuan* was spent on the treatment of pollution and 540 million *yuan* on government administration of pollution regulations. None of the income collected was used to compensate victims of pollution for damages caused. Nevertheless, in some cases, victims can claim damages from polluters and the payment, even when they are not fully compensated for the damage by the polluter, is often sufficient enough to moderate the behaviour of the polluter. Take the example of a nonferrous smelter which was once a serious source of cadmium poisoning. This plant located in Daye County emitted large quantities of cadmium into the air, resulting in cadmium poisoning among nearby villagers. In the latter part of the 1980s, it was required to compensate victims for their medical expenses. This was sufficient to cause the enterprise to install technology which reduced contamination of the air by cadmium. This extra investment in technology showed a substantial positive rate of social return.[40]

In relation to compensation of victims for environmental damage, there is still scope for strengthening China's laws and their application. There is still some doubt as to whether China's discharge fees are fairly determined and consistently applied to individual enterprises in practice.

The National Environmental Protection Agency is intending to increase the level of pollution emission fees and to apply fees to emissions at all levels, rather than to those exceeding some threshold quantity as is the case for a number of pollutants at present.

Some of these extra funds will be used to provide loans to enterprises for environmental protection and for treatment of pollutants.

Overall, China's performance in relation to protection of natural resources and environmental protection is mixed. Even in relation to pollution control, it seems that at least up to now, less attention has been given to pollution prevention than to pollution treatment. So principles and practice have yet to be brought fully into line. Furthermore, it has proven difficult at the village and township level to enforce environmental regulations, but it is at this level that growth in industrial production has been especially rapid. Greater attention will need to be given to control the pollution from village enterprises in the future, and this is likely to require greater devolution of control of pollution to regional bodies, but with some central surveillance being necessary to set guidelines and monitor compliance. Ideally, its approach to regulation should be an interactive side-by-side one rather than top-down.[41/]

CONCLUDING COMMENTS

Transitional economies raise major policy challenges as far as the regulation of the use of natural resources and the environment is concerned. These are not free goods and need to be appropriately priced or valued. This was neglected for too long by the former CPEs. Policymakers in the European CPEs only officially recognized environmental problems and began reacting to them in the years leading up to transition. It was not until the late 1980s and early 1990s that a holistic approach to regulating the use of natural resources and the environment was adopted. While on the surface the new approach seemed valuable, it did not provide an effective means for controlling the level of pollution emissions, but their level was a source of funds for treating emitted waste. More attention is needed now for providing economic incentives for reductions in pollution levels. However, it is necessary to adopt a long-term point of view in relation to such regulations. Scope for altering such emissions in the short run may be relatively limited, given the nature of existing equipment and infrastructure. Greater scope exists for modification as new investment proceeds. This is not to say that no scope for modification exists in the short to medium term, just that one must be realistic about what is economically possible.

Former European CPEs appear to have tried to enforce their environmental controls throughout their territory by the establishment of regional and national environmental funds to support environmental agencies. China appears to have taken a more cautious approach. In the first instance, it has restricted the main enforcement of its environmental regulations to a limited number of cities or regions, extending the number of regions under control, as experience with environmental regulations is obtained and China's authorities are convinced of the value of the regulations. This is the "crossing the river by touching the stones" method. To date, the main emphasis in China has not been on pollution prevention, but the situation is changing, and it will change further as its socioeconomic system evolves. Such an approach is likely to cause less social disruption than a big bang approach and may in the end be more successful. And it ought to be kept in mind that market economies are still searching for the best ways to deal with their environmental problems. They do not have an off-the-shelf answer since environmental regulation has only become a major focus of their policy in recent decades, and is still subject to controversy. However, there is widespread agreement that natural resources and the environment are not free goods, and they must be valued or priced appropriately.

NOTES

1/ T. Zylicz, "Environmental Policy Reform in Poland" in T. Sterner, ed., *Economic Policies for Sustainable Development* (Dordrecht: Kluwer Academic Publishers, 1994), p. 89.

2/ *Ibid.*

3/ C. Clark, *The Conditions of Economic Progress* (London: Macmillan, 1957).

4/ R. H. Coase, "The Problem of Social Cost," *Journal of Law and Economics* (1960):1-44.

5/ T. Kallaste, "Economic Instruments in Estonian Environmental Policy" in Sterner, ed., *Economic Policies for Sustainable Development*, pp. 134-5.

6/ *Ibid.*, p. 153.

7/ A. S. Åhlander "Environmental Policies in the Former Soviet Union" in Sterner, ed., *Economic Policies for Sustainable Development*, p. 79.

8/ *Ibid.*, pp. 68-81.

9/ *Ibid.*, p. 74.

10/ *Ibid.*, p. 75.

11/ *Ibid.*, pp. 68-81.

12/ Zylicz, "Environmental Policy Reform in Poland," pp. 82-112.

13/ Kallaste, "Economic Instruments in Estonian Environmental Policy," pp. 132-47.

14/ Zylicz, "Environmental Policy Reform in Poland," p. 97.

15/ Refer to A. E. Steenge, "A Survey of Environmental Problems in Eastern Europe," *Structural Change and Economic Dynamics* 2 (2:1991):315-32.

16/ T. Sterner, "Policy Instruments for a Sustainable Economy" in Sterner, ed., *Economic Policies for Sustainable Development*, pp. 1-19; and Zylicz, "Environmental Policy Reform in Poland," pp. 82-112.

17/ J. Van der Straaten and W. Hufkamp, "The Polluter Pays Principle and Sustainable Development: The Case of Eastern Europe" in W. Heijman and J. J. Krabbe, eds. *Issues of Environmental Economic Policy* (Wageningen: Agricultural University, 1992), pp. 7-18.

18/ International Bank for Reconstruction and Development (IBRD), *World Development Report: Development and the Environment* (New York: Oxford University Press, 1992).

19/ *Ibid.*

20/ Estimates from figures supplied by B. Wu and A. Flynn, "Sustainable Development in China: Seeking a Balance between Economic Growth and Environmental Protection," *Sustainable Development* 3 (1:1995):4.

21/ A. Bingham, "China's Phenomenal Growth has Environmental Tag," *Pollution Prevention* (Asia/Pacific edition) 1(4:1993):12.

22/ *Ibid.*:10-22.

23/ *Ibid.*:12.

24/ *Ibid.*:14.

25/ World Resources Institute, United Nations Environment Programme (UNEP), and United Nations Development Programme (UNDP), *World Resources 1994-95* (New York: Oxford University Press, 1994), see table 17.1.

26/ Clem A. Tisdell, "The Environment, Biodiversity and Asian Development" (Biodiversity Conservation Working Paper; no. 20) (Brisbane: University of Queensland Press, 1995).

27/ World Resources Institute, UNEP, and UNDP, *World Resources 1994-95*, table 20.4.

28/ Bingham, "China's Phenomenal Growth":10.

29/ State Council of China, *China's Agenda 21 — White Paper on China's Population, Environment, and Development in the 21st Century* (Beijing: China Environmental Science Press, 1994), p. 1.

30/ Administrative Centre for China's Agenda 21, *Introduction to China's Agenda 21* (Beijing: China Environmental Services Press, 1994), pp. 6-7.

31/ State Council of China, *China's Agenda 21*.

32/ Wu and Flynn, "Sustainable Development in China":4.
33/ *Ibid.*
34/ State Council of China, *China's Agenda 21*, p. 16.
35/ Wu and Flynn, "Sustainable Development in China":5.
36/ G. Qu and T. Li, *Population and the Environment in China* (London: Paul Chapman, 1994).
37/ See Wu and Flynn, "Sustainable Development in China":5, table 2.
38/ Bingham, "China's Phenomenal Growth":10.
39/ Yushi Mao, "Economic Instruments adopted by China to Control Pollution" (Personal communication, 26 March 1996), p. 1.
40/ H. Zhiyong, B. Keguang, and Clem A. Tisdell, "Cadmium Exposure in Daye County, China: Environmental Assessment and Management, Health and Economic Effects," *Environmental Management and Health* 2 (2:1991):20-5.
41/ Clem A. Tisdell, "Reconciling Economic Development, Nature Conservation and Local Communities: Strategies for Biodiversity Conservation in Xishuangbanna, China," *Environmentalist* 16 (1996):203-11.

PART V

ENVIRONMENTAL HEALTH

The management of cadmium-exposed populations in an industrial locality in China is studied.

Cadmium Exposure in Daye County, China:

Environmental Assessment and Management, Health and Economic Effects

Zhiyong Hong, Keguang Bao and Clem Tisdell

Environmental Management and Health, Vol. 2 No. 2, 1991, pp. 20-5

Introduction

This article aims to summarise the effects on human health of environmental exposure to cadmium (Cd) in Daye County, Hubei Province, in China; put forward some new opinions on the management of cadmium-exposed populations; and to undertake a cost benefit analysis of measures to reduce cadmium emissions from the non-ferrous smelting works in Daye County.

The authors wish to thank Dr D. Doessel for useful suggestions on an earlier draft of this article but the usual caveat applies.

Available data on human exposure to cadmium pollution are limited, but a start has been made. Ultimately, human exposure to cadmium from air, water and food together with environmental quality will be studied in a closely co-ordinated way, on a continuing basis at some 10-15 locations apart from Daye County in different parts of the world.

Materials and Methods

Of the target population in Daye County, all the subjects investigated for subclinical symptoms of cadmium poisoning between August 1987 and March 1989 were resident in cadmium-polluted areas. They came from seven villages and had lived for over 20 years in cadmium-polluted areas. The total number of persons investigated in these seven polluted villages and the control village was 1,730, of whom 817 were men and 913 were women aged between 30-75 years.

Pollutant sources: Cadmium pollution was caused by emissions from the Daye Non-ferrous Smelting Factory in smelting copper from copper ore. Cadmium was discharged into the village environment, both in waste gas and waste water from the works.

Biological Monitoring

Exposure to cadmium was investigated by analysing urinary cadmium, hair cadmium, urinary calcium, low molecular weight proteinuria and total proteinuria. Urinary cadmium was directly measured with a Zeeman effect flameless atomic absorption spectrometer (Hitachi Co, Japan) without ashing or extraction[1]. Urinary calcium was measured by atomic absorption spectrophotometry[2]. Low molecular weight proteinuria (mol. wt. below 40,000) was measured by electrophoresis on agarose gel of about 100-fold concentrated urinary proteins from the control and exposed villagers.

Cadmium Concentration in Air

Samples of suspended particle matter (SPM) and dust settlement for the determination of cadmium were taken from the polluted areas and the control area. Sampling took place at a height two to three metres above ground level, at some distance from the direct influence of the local sources of emission. SPM samples were collected on Whatman 40 ash-free paper filters using a pump with a yield of $1.5m^3$/day, which guaranteed collection of particles smaller than $20\mu m$.

Environmental-economic management: The Chinese government, as an economic lever for environmental improvement, has required the Daye Non-Ferrous Smelting Factory to contribute to the costs of the primary public health stations/hospitals, the doctors or public health personnel caring or searching for the patients and persons in the early stages of cadmium poisoning. We have collected data on these costs.

Results

Environmental Cadmium Loading

The mean annual Cd concentration in the atmosphere in the seven polluted villages surveyed was equal to 107.9 mg/m^3, about 38.5 times higher than in the control village, Qianjin, which is 36km away from the polluted villages (Table I).

The maximum concentration of Cd in the air over the polluted villages was 242.2 mg/m^3. This value exceeds the maximum (legally) permissible concentration in protected areas of China by a factor of 2.42. This concentration was found to be higher during the cooler half of the year and this can be attributed to greater stability of the atmosphere in the cooler season, which fosters greater local air pollution.

The mean annual Cd content in soil in the polluted villages was 0.91 mg/kg, about 13 times higher than that in the control village.

The polluted villages were divided into three sets and the results for all the villages were also pooled. On the basis of soil and air samples taken, Liaoyuan and Binshan were considered to experience the lowest level of Cd pollution; Xioushan, Hongguan and Hongfong a medium degree of pollution; and Jinwang and Shihong a heavy degree of Cd pollution. Soil samples (56 observations) from the heavily polluted villages had an average cadmium content of 1.41 mg/kg. This exceeds the maximum permissible concentration (standard) in the protected areas of China by a factor of 1.41.

The mean annual Cd concentration in surface water in the polluted villages was equal to 17.2 μg/L, about 4.10 times higher than that in the control village. Furthermore, the set of concentrations of Cd in surface water in the most polluted villages averaged 24.8 μg/L. This value exceeds the maximum permissible concentration (standard) in protected areas of China by a factor of 4.96. Such water may be the main source of human intake of Cd.

The urinary mean Cd concentration of the exposed villagers was 2.63 μg/L, which exceeds the accepted "normal" maximum of 2 μg/L for non-occupationally exposed persons[3]. The respective value of 1.81 μg/L for the control villages was lower than those for the medium-polluted and heavily-polluted villages (see Table II). The differences between the control villages and medium- and heavily-exposed villages were significant (t = 3.33, $p < 0.01$; t = 8.45, $p < 0.01$).

The maximum Cd content of the heavily-exposed villagers' hair was 0.41 μg/g, the respective value of 0.07 μg/g for the control villagers was lower, and the difference between them was significant (t = 43.50, $p < 0.01$).

From this comparison of urinary Cd and hair Cd, urinary Cd appears to be a better parameter for reflecting the degree of Cd uptake and impact of pollution on human body functions. Urinary Cd reveals human body Cd burden better than hair Cd in environmental epidemiological investigation.

Health Effects of Cd on Exposed Populations

The main symptoms of cadmium poisoning in the subclinical phase are back pain, pain in the limb joints, difficulty in moving limbs, kidney disease and a high incidence of respiratory infection in children.

We put stress on the early detection of cadmium proteinuria though there are many parameters, such as urinary β-Microglobulin (BMG), N-acetyl-B-d-glucosaminidase (NAG) and retinal-binding protein (RBP) etc. Given the practical limitations of methods in field investigation, however, urinary calcium and low molecular

Table I. *Environmental Cadmium Loads in Daye County, September 1987-March 1989*

Sampling site	Cd content of soil (mg/kg)			Cd concentration in atmosphere (mg/m3)			Cd concentration in surface water (μg/L)		
	n	*x*	SD	*n*	*x*	SD	*n*	*x*	SD
Control village	32	0.07	0.01	36	2.8	0.41	20	4.2	0.38
Polluted villages:									
Mild	52	0.48*	0.02	15	6.8*	0.83	22	9.2*	0.68
Medium	64	0.82*	0.02	15	74.8*	2.42	20	17.6*	1.60
Heavy	56	1.41*	0.02	15	242.2*	12.70	22	24.8*	1.47
Total	172	0.91*	0.02	45	107.9*	5.32	64	17.2*	1.24

Notes: * $p < 0.01$
n = number of samples or observations
x = average
SD = standard deviation

Table II. *Indicators of Human Body Cadmium Content in Daye County, September 1987-March 1989*

Sampling site	Urinary Cd (μg/L)			Hair Cd (μg/g)		
	n	gm	SD	*n*	gm	SD
Control village	251	1.81	0.73	254	0.07	0.01
Polluted villages:						
Mild	87	1.87	0.37	77	0.07	0.02
Medium	103	2.10**	0.78	109	0.07	0.01
Heavy	94	3.90**	0.97	98	0.14**	0.02
Total for polluted villages	284	2.49**	0.67	284	0.09**	0.02

Notes: ** $p < 0.01$
n = number of villagers observed or tested
gm = geometric mean
SD = standard deviation

weight proteinuria, and mixed type proteinuria were considered to assess the health effects induced by cadmium pollution (see Table III).

The mean calcium concentration in the urine of exposed villagers was 237.9 mg/L, about 1.37 times higher than that of the control villagers. The maximum average calcium concentration in the urine was 270.8 mg/L, which presented in the heaviest polluted Shihong village. Liaoyuan village and Binshan village were located in the mildly-polluted area; Xioushan village, Hongguang village and Hong-fong village were located in the medium-polluted area; Jinwang village and Shihong village were located in the heavily-polluted area. Urinary calcium concentration seems to be correlated with the health of Cd-exposed populations. It could be a useful indicator of Cd exposure.

The mean positive rate of low molecular weight proteinuria among the exposed was 25.6 per cent, about two to three times higher that than of control villages. There was a significant difference between heavily-exposed villagers and control villagers in the low molecular weight proteinuria ($p < 0.01$).

No difference was found between any Cd-exposed villagers and the control villagers in mixed proteinuria, so the measurement of urinary mixed proteinuria could not be used as the early monitoring indicator for reflecting health effects of Cd-exposed population.

Medical Discussion

The renal cortex is a critical organ after long-term exposure to cadmium. The excretion of low molecular weight protein in the urine after tubular dysfunction is considered to provide the earliest sign of cadmium poisoning[4]. Although β-microglobulin, retinal-binding protein, and N-acetyl-B-d-glucosaminidase (NAG) are superior indicators of such dysfunction, in practical environmental epidemiological investigation, the application of the above three indicators is limited by the availability of technical equipment. The study reported here revealed that the main biological indicator of health effects induced by cadmium exposure are higher levels of urinary calcium (U-Ca > 6ppb) and a higher positive rate of low molecular weight proteinuria. Furthermore, the measurements of

Table III. *Indicators of Health Effects of Cd on Exposed Population in Daye County, September 1987-March 1989*

Sampling site	Urinary Cd			Low molecular weight		Mix proteinuria		
	n	*x*	SD	*n*	Positive rate	*n*	*x*	SD
Control village	101	173.4	21.4	33	9.1	84	11.42	1.40
Polluted villages:								
Liaoyuan	76	179.2	8.6	37	16.2	76	7.15	1.12
Binshan	78	174.4	18.4	28	14.3	77	9.90	1.32
Xioushan	80	157.6	18.8	25	16.2	79	11.34	2.14
Hongguan	303	190.2	20.6	150	18.7	225	11.10	2.14
Hongfong	495	207.4**	21.8	327	22.0	453	10.80	1.48
Jinwang	163	249.6**	20.6	95	28.4*	126	8.23	1.36
Shihong	434	270.8**	22.8	293	33.0*	426	10.90	1.46
Total	1730	217.3**	20.8	988	25.6*	1546	10.50	1.56

Notes: * $p < 0.05$
** $p < 0.01$
n = number of villagers observed or tested
x = average
SD = standard deviation

both indicators are feasible and practicable. It is recommended that urinary calcium and urinary low molecular weight protein be used as biological indicator for the detection of the early-stage of renal dysfunction among cadmium-exposed populations.

Environmental Policy — Economic Discussion

Environmental management of cadmium pollution is an ecological-economic problem, which involves the control of pollution emissions, treatment of pollutants, detection of and appropriate therapy for cadmium poisoning. We regard prevention and treatment of the cadmium-induced health hazard to be a part of primary health care. Chinese environmental protectionists suggest that polluters should pay for their environmental damage. This suggests that, at the least, polluters should contract with primary health workers for a certain responsibility period, paying them money to treat patients, to search actively for patients in the early stages among the high-risk population and to reduce the incidence of cadmium poisoning by medical advice to the exposed population. But it may be more economic to eliminate or reduce emissions of cadmium at their source. In this case, literally, prevention is better than the cure of treatment of symptoms. As discussed below, methods to reduce or eliminate Cd emissions at the Daye Non-ferrous Smelting Works are economic from a social cost-benefit viewpoint.

Various engineering methods are available to remove cadmium in effluent, such as chemical precipitation and flotation, ion exchange, absorption osmosis as well as other effluent improvement techniques which are applied to both industrial discharges and municipal waste water. Among them alkaline precipitation is by far the most cost-effective treatment process[5]. However, ion exchange and the carbon absorption process offer the opportunity to recover cadmium and water for re-use which could offset some of the costs[6].

Economic Social Cost-benefit Analysis of Cd Emission Control in Daye County

It is important to assess the economic merits of control of Cd emissions at the Daye smelting works. We shall show that measures to control Cd emissions at these works have been economic and that the decision to install in 1989, the alkaline precipitation process to treat waste-water is economically justified from an environmental health viewpoint. But even prior to this, some measures were in place to reduce Cd emissions, e.g. settling tanks for waste-water and electrical "air scrubbing". During the period of the study, in 1987-89, 534 cases of Cd poisoning were detected in the county. It has been estimated by Dr Zhiyong and Dr Keguang that, without such prior control measures, 995 cases, or an extra 361 cases, would have occurred.

With the installation of the alkaline precipitation process in 1989, the cadmium concentration of waste-water after disposal from the works has been reduced to 0.025 ppm which is below the US Environmental Protection Agency (EPA) guideline of 0.10 ppm. (EPA Development Document 440/81-80/0246). Approximately, 230kg of Cd was released in 1989 in waste-water into 5-7 million tonnes of flowing water.

Particles are also released from the factory via the air but these emissions are reduced by an electric process. About 140kg of Cd is released into the air annually.

Note that water-borne cadmium appears to be a greater source of human intake than air-borne cadmium. But of course, air-borne particles on settling may enter water supplies or soil and be ingested with food.

The method used here for estimating the economic benefits of controlling environmental emissions of cadmium is the averted cost method, i.e. the economic costs saved by such control, as for example applied by Karlman[7] and by Weisbrod[8,9] and as discussed by Butler and Doessel[10]. Drummond *et al.*,[11, p. 149] refer to the method used here as the market valuation method of assessing costs, in that it takes account of actual valuations where these exist or imputes them by reference to the market price of similar commodities. This of course assumes that such prices are reasonable indicators, which in some cases may not be so[10]. The method, however, provides a useful starting point for assessments. When estimated benefit to cost ratios of an environmental change are greatly in excess of unity or below, minor qualifications are unlikely to change the essential result[11]. The economic costs of Cd emissions include as a result of Cd poisoning:

(1) Direct costs:
- medical treatment costs
- special diet costs

(2) Indirect costs:
- time (wages) lost from work by relatives in caring for affected children
- working days (wages) lost by those in the workforce poisoned by Cd. (The number of economic days lost in the polluted villages in the period August 1987 — March 1989, as a result of the 534 cases diagnosed as having Cd poisoning, are set out in Table IV.)

The total economic cost as a result of these cases can be estimated as follows:

(1) Direct medical expenditure
$= Y286.74 \times 534$
$= Y153,119.16$
where Y286.74 is the medical cost per patient. (This may be an underestimate of total medical costs since it does not include extra capital costs such as provision of extra hospital space for patients.)

Table IV. *Days of Hospitalisation of Patients and Number of Working Days Lost in Seven Villages in Daye County, August 1987-March 1989*

Category of patient	Days in hospital	Work days lost by accompanying relatives	Work days lost by patients
Pre-school children	84	1,176	0
School pupils	125	875	0
Peasants	258	0	11,868
Other	67	0	201
Total	534	2,051	12,069

(2) Nutrient expenditure

= Y82.74 × 554

= Y44,183.16

where Y82.74 is the nutritient cost per patient.

(3) On average the net value of output lost as a result of a working day is about Y10. Relatives lost 2,051 working days as a result of the need to provide child care to sick children. The total loss on this account is Y20,510.

(4) Patients directly lost 12,069 work days in the period studied. This resulted in a total economic loss of Y120,690.

Thus the total direct cost is Y197,302.32 and the indirect cost is Y141,200. Altogether the total cost of Cd emissions to the local community was Y338,502 (see Table V).

It is believed that the addition of the alkaline precipitation process, as described above, will virtually eliminate cases of Cd poisoning in the future. The investment required for this addition is Y102,479 and no significant additional maintenance and labour costs are involved. Even if benefits only for the period evaluated are considered, and if the waste-water plant only lasted for that period, the benefit-cost ratio of this *additional* investment would be Y338,502/102,479 = 3.3. Clearly the benefit to cost ratio for waste-water treatment is even more favourable in practice because this investment will last for some time and bring benefits which are a multiple of Y338,502. The benefit to cost ratio for this *additional* investment will exceed 3:1, even after some discounting.

All measures taken at the works to control Cd emissions should result in the elimination of Cd poisoning. Their total cost in the period was Y215,530 (see Table V). This means, in a stationary population, that 995 cases of Cd poisoning would be avoided. Assuming that the same ratios apply as before between the categories of costs imposed by Cd poisoning, a cost of

(995/534) × Y338,502 = Y603,729

would be avoided by these control measures. This can be regarded as the benefit from overall control of Cd emissions in a 20-month period. This suggests a benefit-cost ratio of Y630,729/Y215,530 = 2.926, if the reduction in cases occurs without a time-lag.

In practice, the appropriate benefit-cost ratio is higher than 2.926 because the capital investment will last for several years and benefits will also be obtained over this period. For example, undiscounted benefits for, say, ten periods of 20 months of Cd poisoning prevention would be Y6,307,290. Total costs over this period would be capital

Table V. *Costs and Benefits of Controlling Cadmium Pollution from the Daye Non-ferrous Smelting Works for Period August 1987-March 1989 (Yen)*

Costs		Added benefits (when these costs are avoided by installation of waste-water treatment plant)	
Investment costs:		*Direct economic costs averted:*	
1. Waste-water treatment plant	102,479	1. Medical costs	153,119
2. Electrical dust removal apparatus	75,625	2. Nutrient expenses	44,183
Associated operating:		*Indirect economic costs averted:*	
1. Maintenance	24,788	3. Loss of income by accompanying relatives	20,510
2. Wages	12,637	4. Income lost by patients	120,690
Total	215,530*	Total	338,502

* Does not add exactly because of rounding.

costs (Y102,479 + Y75,625) plus current costs (Y247,880 + Y126,370), which equals Y552,354. This gives a benefit-cost ratio of 11.42 in the absence of discounting. Even after a reasonable rate of discounting, the benefit-cost ratio would be well in excess of unity. However, ideally, lag factors should also be taken into account, e.g. between changes in rates of emission of Cd and the incidence of Cd poisoning.

Note that if the smelting works *only* pays the cost of medical services on account of Cd poisoning plus nutrient costs it would be economic for it to control emissions to current levels, which virtually eliminate the risk of Cd poisoning. From an economic viewpoint, however, account should be taken of all social costs, spillover or external costs. When this is done, the economic case for Cd emission control, as has now been instituted, is very strong in Daye county.

By adopting the "polluter pays" principle the government will encourage socially optimal decisions

By adopting the "polluter pays" principle and by making the payments of polluters equal to the costs which they impose on others, the government will encourage socially optimal decisions. While the Daye Non-ferrous Smelting Works did not pay the full cost of its environmental impact on health, the fact that the Works were required by the Chinese Government to pay the medical costs associated with Cd poisoning undoubtedly hastened its decision to install an alkaline precipitation process to treat its waste-water.

It should be noted that the costs to the affected community of Cd poisoning were most likely higher than indicated above. For example, reduced efficiency during working time due to Cd poisoning is not taken into account and, of course, no allowance has been made for pain and suffering of for reduced longevity. However, from the point of view of the exercise, the valuation procedure has been pursued far enough to establish the main points regarding the economic benefits of Cd pollution control in Daye County[11].

Until such times as adequate emission reduction can be undertaken and takes effect, it is important to be able to detect Cd poisoning in the early stages in the field. A method has been suggested for doing this.

References

1. Kido, *et al.*, "The Association between Renal Dysfunction and Osteopenia in Environmental Cadmium-exposed Subjects", *Environmental Research,* Vol. 52 No. 1, 1990, pp. 71-82.
2. Nogawa, *et al.*, "A Dose-response Analysis of Cadmium in the General Environment with Special Reference to Total Cadmium Intake Limit", *Environmental Research,* Vol. 48 No. 1, 1989, pp. 7-16.
3. Friberg, L., *et al., Cadmium in the Environment,* CRS Press, Cleveland, Ohio, p. 248.
4. Lauwreys, R.R. and Bernard, A.M., "Cadmium and the Kidney", *British Journal of Independent Medicine,* Vol. 43, 1986, pp. 433-5.
5. US Environmental Protection Agency, "Control and Treatment Technology for the Metal Finishing Industry — Sulfide Precipitation", *US EPA Report,* No. 625/8-80-63, 1989.
6. Poon, C.P.C., "Removal of Cadmium from Waste Waters", *Experientia,* Vol. 40, 1984, pp. 127-36.
7. Klarman, H.E., "Application of Cost-benefit Analysis to Health Services and the Special Case of Technological Innovation", *International Journal of Health Services,* Spring 1974, pp. 325-52.
8. Weisbrod, B.A., *Economics of Public Health: Measuring the Economic Impact of Diseases,* University of Pennsylvania Press, Philadelphia, 1961.
9. Weisbrod, B.A., "Costs and Benefits of Medical Research: A Case Study of Poliomyelitis", *Journal of Political Economy,* May/June 1971, pp. 527-44.
10. Butler, J.R.G. and Doessel, D.P., "Measuring Benefits in Health: A Clarification", *Scottish Journal of Political Economy,* Vol. 28 No. 2, 1981, pp. 196-205.
11. Drummond, M.F., Stoddart, G.L. and Torrance, G.W., *Methods for the Economic Evaluation of Health Care Programmes,* Oxford University Press, Oxford, 1987.

Zhiyong Hong and Keguang Bao are based at the Institute of Environmental Medicine, Tengji Medical University, Wuhan, China, and Clem Tisdell is based in the Department of Economics, at the University of Queensland, Australia.

Health, safe water and sanitation: a cross-sectional health production function for Central Java, Indonesia

D. Wibowo[1] & C. Tisdell[2]

The study describes the development of health production functions and their application in the evaluation of the health impacts of investments in safe water and sanitation. For this purpose, data on the morbidity of waterborne diseases and diarrhoea were collected from medical records in the province of Central Java, Indonesia. A reciprocal production function was found to fit the data best. The health production functions exhibit constant return to scale, i.e., a simultaneous m*-fold increase in both safe water and sanitation coverage produces a 1–1/*m *decrease in morbidity. Safe water was found to be more important for health than the sanitary disposal of excreta.*

Introduction

Although safe water supply and sanitation (WSS) have long been accepted as basic necessities for healthy living, measuring the health benefits that result from their availability remains controversial. Some studies indicate that improved WSS facilities are not efficacious in improving health status and not particularly cost-effective (*1*). In contrast, a review of 67 studies from 28 countries found that WSS investments can reduce diarrhoea morbidity and mortality rates by a median of 22% and 21%, respectively (*2*). Most of the studies reviewed, however, appear to have serious methodological deficiencies, e.g., inadequate health indicators and failure to control for confounding variables (*3*). These controversies, along with the introduction of selective primary health care (SPHC) (*1*), have placed greater emphasis on the use of oral rehydration therapy (ORT). WSS policies and ORT should nevertheless both be adopted, since the benefits of WSS extend far beyond its role in improving health status (*4*).

The health benefits resulting from investment in WSS have been measured by a number of case–control studies since the end of the 1980s. Such studies have been carried out in Malawi (*5*), the Philippines (*6*) and Lesotho (*7*), where it was reported that WSS investments can produce a 20%, 20%, and 24% reduction, respectively, in the incidence of diarrhoea.

Despite these findings, doubts remain about the benefits of WSS since the 95% confidence intervals (CI) of both the crude and adjusted odds ratios in the studies in Malawi and the Philippines included the value for the null hypothesis. The 95% CI of the adjusted odds ratio in the Lesotho study also included the null hypothesis value. In other words, at the 95% CI the WSS investments may not be efficacious in reducing diarrhoea incidence.

We describe here an alternative approach to measuring the effects of WSS on health, using a production function. Such functions have been used in agriculture and industry for some time (*8, 9*). Specification of the production function permits analysis of how health inputs interact to produce a particular level of health status. The importance of specifying health production functions is underlined if a cost–benefit analysis of WSS investments is carried out; failure to specify production functions is a serious methodological flaw in most health care cost–benefit analyses (*10*).

The present study takes the community as the unit of analysis instead of the individual or household and implicity assumes that the health status of individuals and households is strongly affected by community environments. Community health indicators such as morbidity, mortality, infant mortality rates or life expectancy can be used as a measure of health status. In this study we have adopted morbidity as the dependent variable, based on the premise that the health benefits of safe water and sanitation are better reflected by morbidity rather than by mortality rates (*4, 11*). Morbidity from diarrhoea and

[1] Researcher, Centre for Policy and Implementation Studies (CPIS), P.O. Box 1520, Jakarta 10015, Indonesia. Currently: Postgraduate Fellow, Department of Economics, University of Queensland, Brisbane, Australia.

[2] Professor and Head, Department of Economics, University of Queensland, Brisbane, Qld 4072, Australia. Requests for reprints should be sent to Professor Tisdell at this address.

Reprint No. **5379**

morbidity from all waterborne diseases were taken as dependent variables.

In addition to safe water and sanitation, a number of other factors may affect diarrhoea morbidity (or mortality). Water quality is a significant determinant of diarrhoea incidence in Quindio, Colombia (*12*); and socioeconomic conditions, e.g., per capita income, occupation, or literacy rate, are often important factors that affect morbidity (*5–7, 11*).

Level of formal education can also influence the incidence of diarrhoea (*13*), although a specially designed education programme for personal hygiene and diarrhoea prevention seems to be more effective in this respect (*12, 13*). Nutritional status may affect diarrhoea mortality in developing countries, where the condition is a predominant cause of infant death (*14*). The following factors that affect the incidence of diarrhoeal diseases have also been identified: breast-feeding behaviour (*15*), food hygiene (*16*), cholera and rotavirus immunizations (*17*), measles immunization (*16*), and human and animal/livestock populations (*12*). Diarrhoea incidence increases during warm rainy seasons (*5, 6, 12*). Furthermore, the availability of health services in a community, as indicated by the ratio—number of health centres or medical staff: population size—can also influence measured health status (*11*).

The above-mentioned variables can influence morbidity from waterborne diseases and diarrhoea; however, inadequate data (either not available or inaccurate) precluded their inclusion in the study. Data on per capita income and water quality, for example, were not available for most subdistricts in the study area. In addition, data on breast-feeding behaviour and food hygiene were not readily available. Therefore we focused on safe water supply and sanitation as the only independent variables.

Methods

Model specification

The model is specified by the following general production functions:

$$MWB = f(WTR, SAN) \quad (1)$$

$$MDR = f(WTR, SAN) \quad (2)$$

where *MWB* = morbidity of waterborne diseases, including recorded incidences of diarrhoea, cholera, bacillary dysentery, typhoid fever, paratyphoid fever, and viral hepatitis A from January to December 1990 per 1000 population;

MDR = diarrhoea morbidity, i.e., the recorded incidence of diarrhoea from January to December 1990 per 1000 population;

WTR = safe water supply coverage, i.e., the percentage of the population with access to a safe water supply; and

SAN = sanitation (sanitary excreta disposal) coverage, i.e., the percentage of the population with access to excreta disposal facilities.

In contrast to the production functions used in industry, where output normally increases when the quantities of the inputs increase, the morbidity of disease(s) will presumably decrease as the quantities of the inputs included in the model increase. This has the following consequences: first, the expected sign of each independent variable is the opposite of that for the usual production function (Table 1); second, the marginal productivity and the elasticity of production are negative (see Annex for definitions of the production economics terms used in this article and also ref. *8, 9, 18*). To avoid complications, we will use the absolute values in this article.

Definitions

The definitions shown below were used in the study.

"Waterborne diseases" were taken to refer to all diseases resulting from pathogens in water that can be transmitted by direct and by indirect faecal–oral routes, for example via food prepared with or washed in contaminated water. The usual definition of diarrhoea is three or more watery stools passed in the last 24 hours.

The definitions of "safe water supply" and "sanitation" used by WHO, and adopted by the Indonesian Ministry of Health, were employed in the study. Safe water supply includes treated surface water or untreated but uncontaminated water such as that from protected boreholes, springs and sanitary wells, either in the home or within 15 minutes walking distance of it (*19, 20*).

Because data on sanitation facilities such as solid waste disposal were inadequate, we used only sanitary excreta disposal as the sanitation variable. Sanitary excreta disposal includes collection and disposal, with or without treatment, of human excreta and wastewater by waterborne systems or the use of pit latrines and similar installations (*19*).

Data collection

Data for the period January–December 1990 were collected in June–July 1991 from 14 districts (*kabupaten*) and municipalities (*kotamadya*), including 194 subdistricts (*kecamatan*) in Central Java province, Indonesia. Subdistricts were used as the unit of analysis, and there were therefore 194 observations. Data on the variables shown below were collected.

— Population.

- Recorded incidences of waterborne diseases, including diarrhoea, cholera, bacillary dysentery, typhoid fever, paratyphoid fever, and viral hepatitis A. There may have been some unrecorded cases within the community in remote villages because the villagers failed to visit medical facilities or because medical centres did not diagnose the condition accurately.
- The number of people having access to safe water facilities, both piped and non-piped systems. Piped systems supply water to various service outlets such as public taps and homes; water distributed by government enterprises and community groups is covered. Non-piped water included all other systems of providing safe water, i.e., shallow wells, deep wells, spring captations, rainwater collectors and household treatment systems.
- The number of people with access to adequate sanitation (sanitary excreta disposal) facilities, including those with access to improved pit latrines, pour-flush latrines, septic tanks with or without latrines, and public latrines.

To ensure that data of adequate quality were collected, discussions were held with the officers responsible for medical records at the district level. If inconsistencies were found (either inadequacy of definition or misrecording), the data were revised. Site visits were also made to health centres and district hospitals.

Econometric procedures

Six basic production functions (linear, quadratic, reciprocal, log-linear, reciprocal log-linear, and double-log (Cobb–Douglas)) were fitted to the data (*8*). The properties of each function's estimators (parameters) are shown in Table 1. The SHAZAM econometrics package was used (*21*).

The ordinary least square (OLS) method was employed initially. Since a plot of the data indicated both vertical and horizontal asymptotes, however, regressions without a constant term (β_o=0) were also examined. In this case, the sum of squares was calculated from zero instead of from the mean value, resulting in a raw moment of R^2 instead of the usual R^2 adjusted (*21–23*).

Use of cross-sectional data could result in heteroscedasticity, and in consequence the OLS estimates of the parameters β_i would no longer be the best obtainable. The tests of hypotheses would no longer be valid in this case because the OLS method produces a biased variance estimator (*22, 23*).

To test for heteroscedasticity, we first applied the multiplicative heteroscedasticity test. If this test failed, the Breusch–Pagan test was used (*22*). If heteroscedasticity was detected, we employed the generalized least squares (GLS) method to estimate the values of β_i (*21–23*).

To compare specifications, we used R^2 adjusted, generalized cross validation (GCV), the Hanan and Quinn criterion (HQ), the Rice criterion (RICE), the SHIBATA criterion, the Schwarz criterion (SC), and the Akaike information criterion (AIC) (*23*). Preferred specifications were those having a higher value of R^2 adjusted or, if the total sum of squares was equal, a lower value of the measures of the other criteria; however, such criteria should not be used to compare specifications having a constant term with those that do not (*23*). In those cases where there was no constant term, the raw moment of R^2 always increases if a new variable is added to the model. Thus, we did not use this criterion to compare the goodness of fit of the quadratic function with that of the others.

Table 1: **Expected signs of estimates of the parameters, β_i, in the models**

Specifications[a]	β_0	β_1	β_2	β_3	β_4
Linear	(+)	(−)	(−)	N.A.[b]	N.A.
Quadratic					
First alternative	(+) or 0	(−)	(+)	(−)	(+)
Second alternative	(+) or 0	(+)	(−)	(+)	(−)
Reciprocal	(+) or 0	(+)	(+)	N.A.	N.A.
Log-linear	(+) (−) or 0	(−)	(−)	N.A.	N.A.
Log-linear reciprocal	(+) (−) or 0	(+)	(+)	N.A.	N.A.
Double-log	(+)	(−)	(−)	N.A.	N.A.

[a] The general mathematical form of each specification is as follows:
Linear: $Y = \beta_0 + \beta_1 X_1 + \beta_2 X_2$.
Quadratic: $Y = \beta_0+\beta_1 X_1+\beta_2 X_2+\beta_3 X_1{}^2+\beta_4 X_2{}^2$.
Reciprocal: $Y = \beta_0 + (\beta_1/X_1) + (\beta_2/X_2)$.
Log-linear: $Y = \exp[\beta_0+\beta_1 X_1+\beta_2 X_2)]$.
Log-linear reciprocal: $Y = \exp[\beta_0+(\beta_1/X_1)+(\beta_2/X_2)]$.
Double-log: $Y = \beta_0 X_1{}^{\beta_1} X_2{}^{\beta_2}$.
[b] N.A. = not available.

Results

The data collected in this study relate to approximately 11.24 million people (about 40% of the population of Central Java). The incidence of morbidity from waterborne diseases in the study area in 1990 was estimated to be about 31 per 1000, while that for diarrhoea was 23.1 per 1000 (Table 2). Thus, on average, in each subdistrict about 150 incidents of waterborne diseases and 111 of diarrhoea were recorded each month.

Diarrhoea accounted for 75% of the total recorded waterborne diseases and bacillary dysentery for about 18%. In comparison, the incidence of other diseases was very low. Although the mean incidences of typhoid fever and paratyphoid fever in most subdistricts were very low or even zero, the maximum incidences of these diseases were relatively high (Table 2). Thus these diseases pose a serious health problem in certain subdistricts.

The mean level of safe water coverage in the study sample was 56%, slightly lower than the level of 61% for the whole province of Central Java. About 39% of the population had access to sanitation facilities (excreta disposal), compared with 37% for the province as a whole. Sanitation coverage had a more uneven distribution than that of safe water, as indicated by the differences in their standard deviations.

Using the OLS method, we found that the specifications that included a constant term exhibited inferior statistical performance. This arose because the values for R^2 adjusted and the F-ratio were low, and neither safe water coverage nor sanitation coverage was statistically significant for those specifications. Application of the OLS method to specifications without a constant term indicated that reciprocal functions exhibited the best statistical performance, having the lowest values of GCV, HQ, RICE, SHIBATA, SC, and AIC. For the *MWB* and *MDR* regressions, the R^2 values were 0.54 and 0.55, respectively, which are reasonably acceptable for a cross-sectional analysis. In addition, only the reciprocal functions showed the significance of both the safe water and sanitation variables. The general form of the reciprocal function without a constant term is as follows:

$$Y = (\beta_1/X_1) + (\beta_2/X_2) \quad (3)$$

Multiplicative heteroscedasticity occurred in the *MWB* regression at the 2.5% significance level. For the *MDR* regression, multiplicative heteroscedasticity existed at the 11% significance level. Thus, the GLS method was used to estimate β_i.

Table 3 shows the regression results for the reciprocal functions obtained using the OLS and GLS methods. It is clear that the GLS method produced better specifications than the OLS method; the R^2 for the GLS specifications were higher, while those for GCV, HQ, RICE, SHIBATA, SC, and AIC were lower than those for the OLS specifications. Also, the OLS results underestimated β_i.

The preferred estimated reciprocal production functions (eq. (3)) for *MWB* and *MDR* are shown below:

$$MWB = 1346.6/WTR + 136.1/SAN \quad (4)$$

$$MDR = 938.5/WTR + 101.5/SAN \quad (5)$$

For the *MWB* and the *MDR* regressions, the standardized coefficients for *WTR* were about twice those for *SAN* (Table 3). This implies that increased safe water coverage can produce a greater reduction in *MWB* and *MDR* than that resulting from increased sanitation coverage, i.e., safe water has a greater effect than sanitation on the incidence of waterborne diseases and diarrhoea.

The properties of eq. (4) and (5) can be explored using an isoquant map (a set of isoquant curves). The following morbidity levels were chosen for this purpose: the mean value + 0.5 standard deviations (SD), the mean value, the mean value –0.5 SD, and the best case. The best case represents the lowest morbidity level achievable at the maximum coverage of safe water and sanitation. The isoquant maps for *MWB* and *MDR* are shown in Fig. 1 and 2, respectively. The abscissa represents safe water coverage and the ordinate, sanitation coverage. The further a curve is from the origin the lower is the morbidity level.

A number of important conclusions can be drawn from the isoquant maps, as discussed below.

- To achieve a given level of morbidity, a minimum coverage of safe water or sanitation is required. For example, to maintain the morbidity of waterborne

Table 2: **Summary statistics of the variables examined in the study**[a]

	Mean	Max.	Min.
Morbidity (per 1000 population)			
Diarrhoea	23.1 (15.8)[b]	105.4	0.0
Cholera	0.0 (0.1)	0.5	0.0
Bacillary dysentery	5.8 (7.6)	39.1	0.0
Typhoid fever	1.2 (3.6)	38.3	0.0
Paratyphoid fever	0.6 (2.3)	24.7	0.0
Viral hepatitis A	0.2 (0.3)	2.2	0.0
Total waterborne diseases	31.0 (21.5)	146.2	0.0
% of population with access to:			
Safe water supply	56.3 (20.3)	100.0	14.1
Sanitation	38.9 (22.0)	98.4	3.0

[a] No. of observations = 194 subdistricts; population covered in the study = 11 236 798.
[b] Figures in parentheses are the standard deviations.

Table 3: **Results of the regression analysis of morbidity from waterborne diseases (*MWB*) and morbidity from diarrhoea (*MDR*): reciprocal specifications**

	MWB regression[a]		*MDR* regression[a]	
	OLS	GLS	OLS	GLS
Estimated coefficients				
Safe water supply	1133.7	1346.6	846.1	938.5
	(9.1175)[b]	(8.6036)[c]	(9.2580)	(8.6273)[c]
Sanitation	79.8	136.1	60.8	101.5
	(1.8940)	(2.1970)[d]	(1.9623)	(2.3082)[d]
Standardized coefficients				
Safe water supply	0.491	0.583	0.498	0.552
Sanitation	0.167	0.284	0.173	0.288
Specification comparisons				
R^2	0.54	0.57	0.55	0.57
F-ratio	111.92	127.93	116.07	126.15
GCV	671.00	291.02	362.45	197.91
HQ	680.14	294.99	367.39	200.61
RICE	671.07	291.05	362.49	197.94
SHIBATA	670.78	290.93	362.34	197.85
SC	693.91	300.96	374.83	204.67
AIC	670.92	290.99	362.42	197.89

[a] OLS = ordinary least squares method; GLS = generalized least square method.
[b] Figures in parentheses are *t*-statistics.
[c] Significant at α = 2.5%.
[d] Significant at α = 0.5%.

diseases at a level of 31 per 1000 (the mean value of our data), it is necessary to have a safe water coverage of 45% at a sanitation coverage of 100% or a sanitation coverage of 8% at a safe water coverage of 100%. These minimum values can be seen in Fig. 1 by drawing a perpendicular from the 45% point on the abscissa, indicating the minimum value of safe water coverage, or a horizontal line from the 8% point on the ordinate, indicating the minimum value of sanitation coverage. Table 4 shows the minimum values of safe water and sanitation coverage for the four morbidity levels selected.

- There is a limit to the reduction in the morbidity of waterborne diseases and diarrhoea that can be produced by safe water supply and sanitation interventions only. These limits are illustrated by the isoquants that are furthest from the origin (15 per 1000 for *MWB* and 10.5 per 1000 for *MDR*).
- If any one input is held constant at the current coverage level, i.e., at the mean value of *WTR* or *SAN*, it is impossible to reach the most distant isoquant curve (the lowest morbidity level) by increasing the coverage of the other variable to 100%. Fig. 1 (points A, B, and P) and Fig. 2 (points C, D, and P) show that the existing mean coverage (*WSS*: 56%; and *SAN*: 39%) is well below the level needed to minimize morbidity if the only controlled variables are provision of safe water and sanitation.

Fig. 1. **Isoquant curves of morbidity from waterborne diseases** (points A, B, and P are explained in the text).

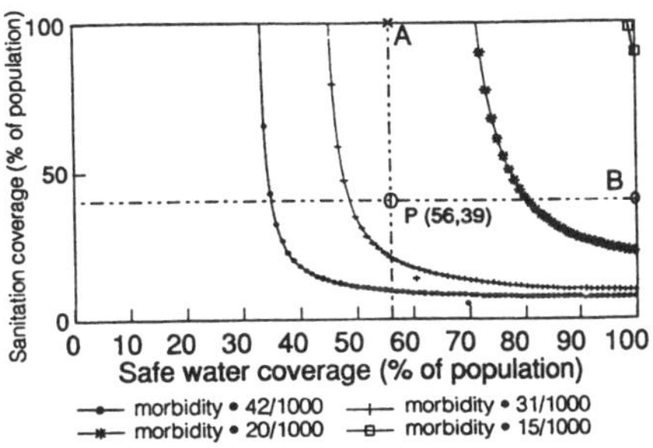

WHO 921087

Fig. 2. **Isoquant curves of morbidity from diarrhoea** (points C, D, and P are explained in the text).

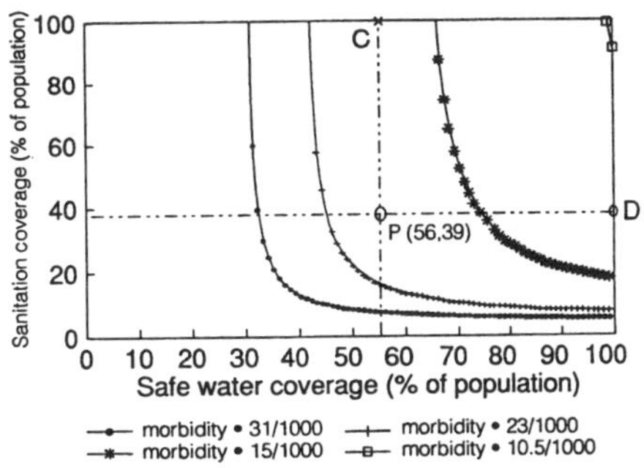

WHO 921088

To illustrate how morbidity declines if the levels of the inputs changes, we show below the expressions for the elasticity of production. For *MWB* the elasticity of production with respect to safe water supply ($\xi_{WTR\text{-}MWB}$) is given by:

$$\xi_{WTR\text{-}MWB} = 1346.6SAN/(1346.6SAN + 136.1WTR)$$

Table 4: **Minimum requirement for the coverage of safe water (*WTR*) and sanitation (*SAN*) at four morbidity levels**

Morbidity level	% coverage for: *WTR*	*SAN*
Waterborne diseases (MWB)		
41.7/1000 (mean + 0.5 SD)	33	5
31.0/1000 (mean)	45	8
20.2/1000 (mean − 0.5 SD)	71	20
15.0/1000 (best case)	99	89
Diarrhoea (MDR)		
31.0/1000 (mean + 0.5 SD)	31	5
23.1/1000 (mean)	42	7
15.2/1000 (mean − 0.5 SD)	66	17
10.5/1000 (best case)	99	91

while the elasticity of production with respect to sanitation ($\xi_{SAN-MWB}$) is given by:

$$\xi_{SAN-MWB} = 136.1WTR/(1346.6SAN + 136.1\ WTR)$$

For *MDR* the elasticity of production with respect to safe water is given by:

$$\xi_{WTR-MDR} = 938.5SAN/(938.5SAN + 101.5WTR)$$

and the elasticity with respect to sanitation by:

$$\xi_{SAN-MDR} = 101.5WTR/(938.5SAN + 101.5WTR)$$

From these expressions it can be seen that the values of ξ_{WTR} and ξ_{SAN} for both morbidity of waterborne diseases and diarrhoea are always <1. In other words, if the coverage of either *WTR* or *SAN* is multiplied by a positive constant, *m*, while the coverage of the other is held constant, the morbidity of waterborne diseases and diarrhoea decline by less than $1-1/m$. For example, doubling the sanitation coverage while holding *WTR* constant less than halves the morbidity.

The sum

$$\xi_{WTR-MWB} + \xi_{SAN-MWB}$$

is equal to the elasticity of production of *MWB* (ξ_{MWB}), and the sum

$$\xi_{WTR-MDR} + \xi_{SAN-MDR}$$

to the elasticity of production of MDR (ξ_{MDR}).

We can easily see that both ξ_{MWB} and ξ_{MDR} are always equal to one. Thus, the production functions for *MWB* and *MDR* exhibit constant returns to scale. Therefore if we multiply safe water and sanitation coverage by a positive constant, *m*, the morbidity of waterborne diseases or diarrhoea decreases by $1-1/m$. For example, if the coverage of both safe water and sanitation are simultaneously doubled, the morbidity of waterborne diseases and diarrhoea will be halved. Table 5 shows the potential morbidity reduction resulting from various levels of input.

Along an isoquant one input can be substituted for another to maintain the same morbidity level. The elasticities of substitution between safe water and sanitation (η) are constant (0.5) for both the *MWB* and the *MDR* production functions.[a] Hence at any level of morbidity, safe water and sanitation exhibit a low and constant substitutability.

[a] Mathematical proof available upon request.

Table 5: **Expected reduction in morbidity if the sanitation (*SAN*) and water (*WTR*) inputs are increased simultaneously or if one input is held constant while the other is changed**

Both inputs changed			*SAN* held constant			*WTR* held constant		
% inputs increase	% *MWB* reduction	% *MDR* reduction	% *WTR* increase	% *MWB* reduction	% *MDR* reduction	% *SAN* increase	% *MWB* reduction	% *MDR* reduction
1	1	1	1	1	1	1	0	0
50	33	33	50	29	29	50	4	5
75	43	43	75	37	37	75	5	6
100	50	50	100	44	43	100	6	7
200	67	67	200	58	58	200	9	9
300	75	75	300	65	65	300	10	10
400	80	80	400	70	69	400	10	11

Discussion

This study has provided additional evidence that safe water and sanitation are efficacious in improving health status (*5–7, 11*). The health production functions that fit the data best have a reciprocal form, and both safe water and sanitation are significant regressors for morbidity from both waterborne diseases, as a whole, and for diarrhoea in particular.

Some workers have suggested that provision of sanitation may be more efficacious than safe water in reducing morbidity from waterborne diseases (*2, 24*); our findings, however, indicate that a safe water supply is more important than sanitation (sanitary excreta disposal) in this respect. If there are budget constraints, investment in provision of safe water should therefore be given higher priority than investment in sanitation.

The above suggestion does not mean that investment in sanitation is unimportant. First, safe water and sanitation have a low substitutability, making it relatively difficult to replace one input with another while maintaining the same morbidity level. Second, a reduction in morbidity is unlikely to be maximized (in relation to increased investment) if an increase in safe water coverage is not accompanied by an increase in sanitation coverage. Finally, if the sanitation coverage falls below the minimum level required to achieve a particular targeted morbidity level, this target will not be achieved even if safe water coverage is increased to 100%. Consequently, if health policy aims at maximizing health status in relation to investment, i.e., minimizing morbidity levels, the coverage of safe water and sanitation facilities must both be increased simultaneously.

We estimated the reduction in morbidity resulting from a given increase in safe water and/or sanitation coverage. This differs from the case–control approach (*5–7*), which estimates the reduction in morbidity caused by a shift from "not being exposed to safe water/sanitation facilities" to "being exposed to such facilities". Thus, the case–control method implies an increase from zero to 100% coverage, which was not necessarily the situation in our study.

We calculated a larger reduction in morbidity than that reported by other workers (*5–7*). The 20% morbidity reduction reported in these studies requires an increase from zero to 100% coverage. In our study, the same reduction was produced by a 25% increase in safe water and sanitation coverage.

Fig. 1 and 2 show that if safe water and sanitation coverage are maximized (equal to or almost equal to 100% coverage), total eradication of waterborne diseases and diarrhoea is unlikely. Other parameters such as habitat and socioeconomic factors also influence their incidence.

The approach used in our study is not intended to be a substitute for the case–control method; rather both are complementary. The case–control method permits in-depth observation of an individual's health status with greater capability for controlling the confounding variables; however, the possibilities for model exploration are limited because of its binary-dependent variable. Our approach uses community observations and has a greater potential for model exploration (a quantitative dependent variable is used); however, its ability to control the confounding factors was lower because of data limitations.

The study demonstrates how proper medical records and/or surveillance data can be used to assess the relationship between health inputs and community health status. The quality of medical records and/or surveillance data, particularly morbidity records, plays an essential role in this case. As discussed above, the morbidity data collected may be an underestimate, even though strenuous efforts were made to obtain complete data. Thus, it is necessary to develop an improved medical or surveillance record system that incorporates data from all medical facilities, including health centres, clinics, hospitals, and private practitioners. This will not only be beneficial for research purposes, but also for health planning and policy-making.

Acknowledgements

The comments on this paper made by Dr D. Doessel (Department of Economics, University of Queensland) and by Dr J. Hunt (Development Policy Office, Asian Development Bank) are gratefully acknowledged. We also thank the two anonymous reviewers for their valuable comments. Special thanks are extended to Mr Soedardjo, Mr Soekamto, Mr. Soenarko, Mr I. Darmadji, Mr Y. Hardjono, Mrs R. Astuti, Mr Purwanto, Dr Koentoro, and Mr S. Kanthi (Ministry of Health, Central Java, Indonesia) for their cooperation during data collection.

Résumé

Santé, eau saine et assainissement: fonction de production transversale à Java Central, Indonésie

Cet article décrit l'application des méthodes économétriques et de la théorie de l'économie de production au calcul de fonctions de production en santé. Les fonctions obtenues ont été utilisées pour examiner l'impact de la fourniture d'eau saine et des investissements dans le domaine de l'assainissement sur l'état de santé. Les données ont été recueillies à partir des registres officiels de la province de Java Central, en Indonésie, qui couvre 194 sous-districts. L'étude a été réalisée entre janvier et décembre 1990. Les fonctions de production en santé qui s'adaptent le mieux aux données sont des fonctions inverses, et les résultats montrent que la fourniture d'eau saine et l'assainissement (évacuation des excreta) sont des facteurs de régression significatifs pour la morbidité due aux maladies transmises par l'eau et à la diarrhée. La fourniture d'eau saine est un facteur plus important que l'assainissement pour réduire la morbidité. Les fonctions de production que nous avons obtenues montrent des régressions constantes, c'est-à-dire que si la couverture de la fourniture d'eau saine et de l'assainissement est multipliée simultanément par une constante positivive *m*, la morbidité due aux maladies à transmission hydrique et à la diarrhée baissera d'un facteur de 1-1/*m*. Si la couverture de l'assainissement est constante, une augmentation d'un facteur *m* de la couverture de la fourniture d'eau saine réduit la morbidité d'un facteur inférieur à 1-1/*m*, et inversement. De plus, une faible valeur de l'élasticité entre les variables eau saine et assainissement a été trouvée. L'emploi de ces seules interventions pour réduire la morbidité a un impact limité, ce qui montre la nécessité d'utiliser d'autres programmes sanitaires. La connaissance des fonctions de production en santé est un préalable indispensable à la bonne exécution des analyses coût/avantages des investissements réalisés dans les domaines de la fourniture d'eau saine et de l'assainissement.

References

1. **Walsh, J. & Warren, K.** Selective primary health care: an interim strategy for disease control in developing countries. *New England journal of medicine*, **301**: 967–974 (1979).
2. **Esrey, S. et al.** Interventions for the control of diarrhoeal diseases among young children: improving water supplies and excreta disposal facilities. *Bulletin of the World Health Organization*, **63**: 757–772 (1985).
3. **Blum, D. & Feachem, R.** Measuring the impact of water supply and sanitation investments on diarrhoeal diseases: problems of methodology. *International journal of epidemiology*, **12**: 357–365 (1983).
4. **Okun, D.** The value of water supply and sanitation in development: an assessment. *American journal of public health*, **78**: 1463–1467 (1988).
5. **Young, B. & Briscoe, J.** A case–control study of the effect of environmental sanitation on diarrhoea morbidity in Malawi. *Journal of epidemiology and community health*, **42**: 83–88 (1988).
6. **Baltazar, J. et al.** Can the case–control method be used to assess the impact of water supply and sanitation on diarrhoea? A study in the Philippines. *Bulletin of the World Health Organization*, **66**: 627–635 (1988).
7. **Daniels, D. et al.** A case–control study of the impact of improved sanitation on diarrhoea morbidity in Lesotho. *Bulletin of the World Health Organization*, **68**: 455–463 (1990).
8. **Doll, J. & Orazem, F.** *Production economics, theory and applications*, 2nd ed. New York, Wiley, 1984.
9. **Beattie, B.R. & Taylor, C.R.** *The economics of production.* New York, Wiley, 1985.
10. **Warner, K.E. & Luce, B.R.** *Cost–benefit and cost–effectiveness analysis in health care: principles, practice and potential.* Ann Arbor, MI, Health Administration Press, 1982.
11. **Doessel, D. & Wibowo, D.** The role of public health and curative medical services in health status: an economic analysis. Paper presented at the *Twentieth Conference of Economists, Hobart, 30 September–3 October 1991.*
12. **Bersh, D. & Osorio, M.** Studies of diarrhoea in Quindio, Colombia: problems related to water treatment. *Social science and medicine*, **21**: 31–39 (1985).
13. **Feachem, R.** Interventions for the control of diarrhoeal diseases among young children: promotion of personal and domestic hygiene. *Bulletin of the World Health Organization*, **62**: 467–476 (1984).
14. **Ashworth, A. & Feachem, R.** Intervention for the control of diarrhoeal diseases among young children: prevention of low birth weight. *Bulletin of the World Health Organization*, **63**: 165–184 (1985).
15. **Feachem, R. & Koblinsky, M.** Intervention for the control of diarrhoeal diseases among young children: promotion of breast-feeding. *Bulletin of the World Health Organization*, **62**: 271–291 (1984).
16. **Feachem, R. et al.** Diarrhoeal diseases control: reviews of potential interventions. *Bulletin of the World Health Organization*, **61**: 637–640 (1983).
17. **De Zoysa, I. & Feachem, R.** Intervention for the control of diarrhoeal diseases among young children: rotavirus and cholera immunization. *Bulletin of the World Health Organization*, **63**: 569–583 (1985).
18. **Tisdell, C.** *Microeconomics of markets.* Brisbane, Wiley, 1982, pp. 145–181.
19. **Pineo, C. & Subrahmanyam, D.** *Community water supply and excreta disposal situation in the developing countries.* Geneva, World Health Organization, 1975, pp. 4–5.
20. *World health statistics annual, 1988.* Geneva, World Health Organization, 1988, p. viii.
21. **White, K. et al.** *SHAZAM econometrics computer program. User's reference manual, version 6.1.* New York, McGraw-Hill, 1988.
22. **Judge, G. et al.** *Introduction to the theory and practice of econometrics*, 2nd ed. New York, Wiley, 1988, pp. 325–378 and 844–850.
23. **Ramanathan, R.** *Introductory econometrics with applications.* San Diego, Harcourt Brace Jovanovich, 1989

24. **Esrey, S.A. & Habicht, J.** Epidemiologic evidence for health benefits from improved water and sanitation in developing countries. *Epidemiologic reviews*, **8**: 117–128 (1986).

Annex

Explanation of the production economics terms used in the text

- The *Production function* expresses the maximum output that can be produced as a mathematical function of a set of variable inputs, at a given technological level.
- *Marginal productivity* is the variation in total output if the quantity of an input is increased infinitesimally, holding the quantity of other inputs constant.
- *An isoquant curve* represents all combinations of inputs that yield the same level of output.
- *The elasticity of production* measures the proportionate change in output relative to the proportionate change in all inputs. The elasticity of production with respect to an input measures the proportionate change in output relative to the proportionate change in that input, holding other inputs constant.
- *Constant returns to scale* occur when the output increases m-fold if all inputs are multiplied by a positive constant, m, i.e., the value of the elasticity of production is equal to unity.
- *Elasticity of substitution* is a measure of how "easy" it is to substitute one input for another along an isoquant. Low substitutability between inputs occurs if the value of the elasticity of substitution is below unity.

Name index